D1195390

LETTERS OF ROBERT BROWNING
COLLECTED BY THOMAS J. WISE

ROBERT BROWNING

Letters of

ROBERT BROWNING

Collected by Thomas J. Wise

EDITED
WITH AN INTRODUCTION AND NOTES BY

THURMAN L. HOOD
Dean of Trinity College

New Haven: Yale University Press

1933

Contents

Illustrations

Introduction

WHAT Browning would have said to the publication of this volume is a matter of speculative interest to all who esteem his genius and respect his memory. He feared the triviality, goose-gossip, and pawing of vitals in unsanctioned treatments of his private life. Even his poetic history he wished to limit to the finished aspects of his art. He destroyed all his boyish poems that he could recover. *Pauline* he tried for a long time to suppress; and, finally, in self-protection, made a revision of it and included it in his collected works. His son, in a note prefixed to the published love letters, wrote that his father "destroyed all the rest of his correspondence," though he had preserved the love letters in a special box and "not long before his death said . . . 'There they are, do with them as you please when I am dead and gone!' "

In one of his letters to Isabella Blagden he reminded her of their agreement to burn each other's letters—hers written on the twelfth of each month, in memory of Browning's wedding date, and his replies of seven days thereafter—and he did burn hers. But what is the sequel? She saved most of his, or all. After her death they were returned to him—and he did not destroy them. Mrs. Sutherland Orr had access to these letters, and made much use of them in dealing with the poet's life between 1862 and 1872.* After the Browning sale of 1913, the more representative of the letters to Miss Blagden were selected by Mr. Thomas J. Wise for the collection here presented. The rest of them Mr. Wise declined, though he might have had the entire lot for but little more than the price he offered for those he thought worth keeping. Probably, Browning would have favored tossing the remainder into the fire—to keep them from Autolycus.

But the publication of the best of these letters to Miss Blagden as part of a large collection of his more representative letters is a very different matter. No lover of his poetry ever found him churlish; no sensible admiration of him ever met rebuke. No doubt, therefore, he would only have laughed good-naturedly and incredulously at the

---

* Mrs. Orr misdates some of these letters, so as to confuse the facts about where Browning spent his vacations in 1862, 1863, and 1864 and put the writing of *The Ring and the Book* two years earlier than the autumn of 1864, the correct date. Miss Blagden died at Florence on January 20, 1873; biographers have given 1872 as the year.

thought of fifty years of Boswellizing in the hope of gathering a sizable volume of his selected letters.

Together, they make a Browning monologue not wholly unlike one he might have put into the mouth of one of his own characters. In fact, Browning's hearty, deep, and variously modulated voice, and the thought that the words and the sound of it could never be preserved, first suggested to Mr. Wise the idea of gathering the letters, as the thing nearest to preserving his ebullient conversation. The work began in the early eighties, when Mr. Wise was a young worshiper at the great man's shrine. He soon became a friend, and, as a member of the Browning Society, then flourishing in London, often called on Sunday afternoons with questions from his colleagues for the poet to answer (that, at least, was the excuse). He is now the last man living to have broken bread at Robert Browning's table. Typical of the attitude of the young bibliographer toward the old poet is a little chain of incidents recounted in an article about Mr. Wise.*

In the year of 1884 Mr. Wise first met Robert Browning; and one of his visits to the poet was an exciting one. Dr. Furnivall, a friend of both, went along with him to 19, Warwick Crescent. Browning was in a front room on the ground floor destroying letters and papers. He had dragged from the top of the house an old leather trunk that had once belonged to his father, and was dipping into it. Mr. Wise, to his horror, saw letters of Carlyle go into the fire and a lot of Browning's own early verses. At one time Browning had intended these verses for a volume to be called *Incondita*.

Out from the old trunk came two precious copies of the original edition of *Pauline*.

"If I had asked Browning for one of them I am convinced he would have given it to me," Mr. Wise has declared. "But I let the chance go."

On leaving the Browning's house, he told Dr. Furnivall how keen he was to get the book. The good Furnivall was amused at the thrill his friend had got at a glimpse of such a prize in duplicate.

"Write to Browning," he said, "and ask him for one of the copies. Offer in return to give to a charity any sum he thinks just."

Delicacy held back Thomas J. Wise; but the story does not end here. A few days later, James Dykes Campbell invited him to dine at his flat in Albert Hall Mansions. Browning was the only other guest. After dinner

---

* Augustus Muir, "A Treasure-House of Books: Mr. Thomas J. Wise and the Ashley Library," *The Strand Magazine,* September, 1929.

Mr. Wise and his host sat and smoked, while Browning, who did not smoke, was making a leisurely tour of the bookshelves in the room.

"I see you have everything here of mine," he said to Campbell.

"No," replied Campbell, "I still lack *Pauline*."

"Oh, that gap can soon be filled!" exclaimed Browning. "The other morning I came across two copies of it. One of them will be sent to you tomorrow."

Here again was a god-sent chance for Mr. Wise to ask for the other. But again he let it slip.

Next day, after much wrestling of spirit, he took Dr. Furnivall's advice and wrote to Robert Browning. But he was too late. Browning had already decided to give the other copy to his son.

The copy of the original *Pauline* which Mr. Wise secured afterward, by hunt and purchase, now bears the following inscription, in the poet's hand.

I see with much interest this little book, the original publication of which can hardly have cost more than has been expended on a single copy by its munificent Proprietor and my friend—Mr. Wise.
Feb. 12.'88.

Robert Browning.

From that distant time, Mr. Wise has served as central treasurer of Browning lore, the untiring helper of Browning biographers and scholars. The factual resources of his growing store of letters from the poet to various correspondents have never been exhausted. And in its present range it provides a new approach, on the human side, to the understanding of Browning's personality. It thus becomes a tribute to the poet, in consummation of the longest, and in spite of unusual difficulties one of the most successful, bibliophile labors ever spent upon an English poet.

Browning would hardly have believed that such a collection could be brought together; but as a student of men's lives, he would have respected the collector's faith in the value of such materials. He might have recalled his own use of similar materials preserved in *The Old Yellow Book;* or perhaps his pains in collecting quaint old prints of Paracelsus and fitting them in proper sequence in his manuscript, to represent the alchemist as he developed, ever more Olympian yet ever more strongly marked with the stamp of his time.

The human side of Browning is the side from which these letters come. The Lives have sprung from the poems; and though they catch some color from them and certainly clear up facts about them, they somehow miss the full Boswellian quality. To trace the history of the poet and his poetry is to leave the man to find what place he may in his own biography. Johnson, as Boswell inevitably realized, was obviously greater than his works. With Browning and his biographers the case has been to some extent reversed: his poetry has overshadowed his flesh-and-blood existence.

His greatness as a man has been partly eclipsed, therefore—save only in the love affair. As for that, a certain little matter of Caponsacchi and Pompilia and other direct and indirect poetic dealings with it, as well as the complete collection of the love letters themselves, have conspired to give us, vivid as lightning, the full image of it. Sir Frederic G. Kenyon's chapter on it, written after the publication of the love letters, furnishes an interesting comparison with the chapter by Mrs. Orr which it replaced in his revision of her *Life and Letters of Robert Browning*. It was the only chapter he rewrote entire. The letters of the collection here produced, springing from the rest of the poet's life, should similarly widen our conception.

No Life of Browning uses for illustration the now time-darkened photographs done in the Roman days, showing the man full length, standing, hat in hand, sturdy, hale, good humored, and not so smoothly dressed as in the later days. Browning saved them in his own album. Mrs. Browning, sending Mrs. Martin a similar photograph of herself and the boy Pen, wrote:

You will like to have them, we fancy, but it is Robert's gift. I was half inclined last year to send you a photograph from Field Talfourd's picture of me, but I shrank back, knowing that dear Mr. Martin would cry out at the flattery of it, which he well might do. But this photograph from nature can't be flattered, so I hazard it. You see the locks are dark still, not white, and the sun, in spite, has blackened the face to complete the harmony. Pen is very like, and very sweet we think.

The famous and now thrice familiar Talfourd drawings of both poets, done in 1859, hang side by side in the National Portrait Gallery. Browning had them in his house but not in the place of honor in his dining-room at 19, Warwick Crescent; there, at his right as he sat at table, he hung the two far more realistic portraits done in the same year by Giordigiani. (Sometimes, we are told, he lost himself in contemplation of his wife's picture there.) The Talfourd drawings are obviously "idealized" likenesses of "poets," and that of Browning appears particularly saccharine. "My sister—a better authority than myself—has always liked it," he wrote, "as resembling its subject when his features had more resemblance to those of his mother than in after-time, when those of his father got the better—or perhaps the worse—of them." Most of the illustrated Lives include this portrait; in one, it serves as frontispiece—and here is a literal text for the statement that in the biographies of Browning the portrait of the artist tends to displace the likeness of the man.

The tendency to come to Browning's life through the poems is no doubt encouraged by the abundance of spiritual autobiography in them. *Pauline* is an example. A century ago, when that little work did not even bear its author's name, the autobiographical element in it was naturally overlooked; the poem was taken only literally, for instance, by no less discerning a person than John Stuart Mill. So taken, it is indeed the crabtree in a "fool's paradise" that Browning later called it; the hero is caddish beyond all nature, and inconsistent even for a madman or crazed adolescent lover. Mill's penciled scorn of its implausibilities remains in the Forster copy in the South Kensington Museum, in proof that he read it and even admired its beauties, without an inkling of the allegory it holds of the boy Browning's high adventures with the Spirit of Poetry, of which Pauline herself is but the symbol. Today we know that Browning's way was to bring such matters into many poems. One of the most striking works of recent years about the poet has been Professor William Clyde DeVane's exposition of the way in which the *Parleyings* are "the autobiography of a mind." Such fruitful sources of information about the poet's inner self—much of the self-revelation very thinly veiled, if veiled at all, and some of it as direct as in Wordsworth—have been ever present as a first resort for his biographers.

But the evidence furnished thus in the poems bears strictly upon the poet rather than upon the human being. The result is a shading, dimming, or ignoring in the Lives of matters essential to full understanding of the man who wrote the poems. A long list of questions vital enough, but unanswered or not clearly answered in the Lives, is fully answered in the letters. To begin at the marriage date—what, for example, were Browning's feelings toward the man who had made the marriage possible? Wherein, exactly, did he differ in opinions with his wife? How did he face the world in England with his son, after her death? How was he talked about? How did he look back on the life in Italy? What friendships did he cherish? What were his ways of working? What gave him rest in rough vacation spots in France? How did he write *The Ring and the Book*, and how did he take his fame? Were the Oxford undergraduates justified in their remark that "Browning was dining himself out"? What were his thoughts of actors, musicians, painters, statesmen, women? What did he see in other poets' work? His tones, beautiful or harsh, from the depth of his feeling in the last beautiful moment of Elizabeth Barrett's fading out of life to the stern disciplines and busy worldlinesses of later days, sound clearly in these letters.

And clearly from them appears his personality as a man among men in the Victorian age. Browning as a poet is of the ages more than many a lesser genius, but as a man he strikingly reflects his time. His strong insistence on the right to privacy, for instance—was it not a point of honor in that time—most often noted with laughter in our own? Contrast Browning's destruction of his letters with Bernard Shaw's pressing Mrs. Patrick Campbell to sell at the height of the market everything of his she could lay hands on, autographed copies, letters, postcards—everything! With Browning, this idea of "House" as a private thing, divorced from "Shop," was a dogma rather than a personal solicitude, for in that sterling age men prided themselves on rightness and dignity in private, as in public, conduct, and Browning more than most. Independence, loyalty, courage, restraint, the gracious boldness of security, all came to him perhaps by blood and by upbringing; they were, however, made prominent and developed by an environment which called them into play.

His opinions of men and affairs suggest these traits. He was not submerged by the Italian struggle, though deeply interested for the triumph of the right; he neither huzzah'd for Louis Napoleon nor cursed him—only saw him clearly from the start and recognized his place in politics. The silliness of spiritualism (the new fad) he attacked, while holding to the idea of personal immortality. He declined academic honors that might divert him from his poet's mission, but accepted those which promised merely to help him help his son. Though in a conventional prosaic sense he "loved" at least three women after his wife's death, there was no sign of flaw in his complete soul's devotion to her, no second love of that kind. When he felt bound by his son's imagined needs to try out the thought of marrying again, it was reluctantly, and on distinctly other grounds than those of love; his "heart was buried in Italy"—that, he took pains to make the lady fully understand, at once. These chosen courses any right man would have followed in his time.

As we observe his continuing intense interest in the most approved musicians, painters, actors, and men of letters, we find him maintaining firm standards of judgment, ever demanding and holding to conscious faith in the divinity of art. He might with cool, discerning eye point out privately to one most trusted intimate some weakness in the work of a dear friend—even Tennyson, or Swinburne—yet maintain the fullest friendship and most sincere esteem for those men whom he regarded as his peers.

Friendliness was of his essence, yet he could strike out like a savage against sheer prejudice and personality in criticism—as he did at Fitzgerald and at Alfred Austin. And his impulsive action could bring him grave concern. The rich vitality, the confidence, the decency, dignity, and settled security of mid-Victorian days are all apparent in his conduct. He was considerate of others to a fault; ever constructive, desiring to spoil none of this world's satisfactions. In all these ways his letters show him the exemplar of his time.

Mr. Wise's collection has been open always to biographers as to scholars. The late Professor W. Hall Griffin, for example, made extensive use of it in preparing his *Life of Browning,* which was completed by Mr. H. C. Minchin. But at no stage in the growth of the collection has its complete and unified effect been calculable. In its present state it has attained the proportions of a chronicle of Browning's mature life. Here may now be found the completion of the story, year by year, of the writing, revising, and publishing of *The Ring and the Book.* Here are the details of one outburst against Fitzgerald in the famous stanzas and of another against Alfred Austin in a poem not hitherto adduced. Here are the more significant of the letters to Isa Blagden, for the publication of which many students of Browning have been particularly eager. And here are previously unknown letters to the Storys, containing an account of the episode with Lady Ashburton.* The letters carefully saved by the Carlyles are among the more recent additions.

Many have been interested in the literary quality of Browning's letters. Their style is individual, forceful, rapid sometimes to the point of roughness, sometimes deft and graceful; they are simply and strongly phrased, highly personal and concrete. Browning's reputation as a letter writer has been bound up with the delicate intensities of the love letters. That widely known correspondence, with its continuous beauty, subtlety, and concentration, has eclipsed his other letters thus far published—the privately issued groups of letters from Mr. Wise's collection, and the letters or bits of letters scattered through the Lives and elsewhere. The ill-advised and unauthorized printing in Texas a few years ago of that larger portion of the letters to Miss Blagden which had been rejected by Mr. Wise has impaired the reputation of the poet as a letter writer, if only by adding nothing to it. Literally, hundreds of letters bearing Browning's signature have passed through Mr. Wise's hands, and been retained only when they clearly merited to be preserved. Since his first consideration has been representative quality rather than mere "style," the volume may tend to mar or to enhance the poet's uncertain reputation for prose, or serve merely to define him as a robustly direct correspondent, cognizant of the world about him; its main purpose, however, is to present him plainly in his own words. Neither the factual importance of the volume nor the style of the letters is of paramount concern. If the work is to deserve the name one Browning savant has applied to it, "the richest literary haul since the love letters," it must depend for that distinction mainly on the fact that it constitutes a full and a fresh presentment of Robert Browning as a man among his fellow men in the Victorian age.

For the initiate the vintage of Mr. Wise's collection (The Ashley Library) needs no bush. Mr. Wise once lived on Ashley Road, North London, and the name of that street was first attached to Mr. Wise's private treasures by his comrade-in-arms in gathering literary materials, the late Clement Shorter. Under that name it has become familiar to bibliographers and literary scholars. "Supreme among the libraries of the world" it has been called, and in its field it is no less

* See Appendix, "Browning and Lady Ashburton."

than that. Since 1922, when the first volume of *The Ashley Library* appeared, that "catalogue of the printed books, manuscripts, and autograph letters collected by T. J. Wise," amounting now to eleven large volumes, has been in constant requisition among students of the great writers whose names appear in it—Arnold, Borrow, the Brontës, the Brownings, Burns, Byron, Coleridge, Conrad, Dickens, Dryden, and the rest. Separate volumes devoted to single names—*A Landor Library, A Swinburne Library,* and so on—have appeared, always extending to new limits the known writings of their subjects. The Bonchurch Swinburne and The Shakespeare Head Brontë have come from the same source, consummate texts made possible only by labors of love similar to the toil expended on these Browning letters. In the Catalogue of the Library of the British Museum more than seventy entries appear under the name of Mr. Wise.

It is with an overwhelming sense of good fortune in having been the first to ask the favor, that the editor expresses his gratitude for the freely granted privilege of publishing this collection of Robert Browning's letters. He has made full use not only of Mr. Wise's letters but of the many notes which Mr. Wise and the late Professor W. Hall Griffin prepared. Such scholars have always been concerned solely to further knowledge of the great poet. The editor desires also to thank, perforce inadequately, Mrs. Fannie Barrett Browning, without whose inspiring interest the work would not have been undertaken, and without whose willing consent it could not have proceeded.

Many letters have been added in this volume to those in Mr. Wise's own collection, since opportunity has served. Some important letters to the Storys have been contributed by the Rev. Howard Chandler Robbins, D.D., and Mr. Harold M. Landon. To them and to others who have offered similar assistance the editor is deeply indebted. The Rev. Herbert Dunnico, J.P., C.C., in his capacity as Hon. Warden of The Robert Browning Settlement, has placed at the editor's disposal the resources of the Robert Browning Collection at the Settlement in Walworth; from it two letters have been taken for this volume. Two letters to Sir Frederic Leighton are reprinted by permission of Messrs. George Allen and Unwin, Ltd., publishers of *The Life, Letters, and Work of Frederic Leighton,* edited by Mrs. Russell Barrington.

To the Master and the Faculty of Balliol the editor owes thanks for cordial and early assistance and specifically for permission to reproduce some of the photographs in Browning's album, which is now in the Browning Collection in the Hall of the College.

Sir John Murray, K.C.V.O., D.S.O., has not only given the necessary privileges of copyright but has assisted the editor in other essential ways.

The authorities and the staff of the British Museum have assisted the editor at every opportunity. Some letters are printed by permission of the Museum. Likewise, the authorities of the Bodleian Library have been of all possible service, as have those of the Victoria and Albert Museum in South Kensington. The Yale University Library has kindly provided three letters.

For counsel and other coöperation the editor thanks the Hon. Wilbur L. Cross and Professor William C. DeVane of Yale University; Professor Leslie N. Boughton of Cornell University; and Professor Arthur Adams of Trinity College, Hartford.

To the John Simon Guggenheim Memorial Foundation the editor is indebted for the award of a Fellowship which materially assisted him in launching the project of this publication.

To the many other friends and fellow admirers of the poet both in England and in the United States who have offered encouragement and assistance, it is impossible to detail here the editor's obligation. He hopes for no better fortune than the continued interest of all lovers of the poet, and bespeaks their coöperation in the preservation and further collection of his correspondence.

T. L. H.

Trinity College, Hartford, Connecticut,
  February 23, 1933.

THOMAS JAMES WISE

Letters of Robert Browning

1830 : 1

To Christopher Dowson, Jr.[1]

[London, *ca.* 1830.]

Dear Sir,

You are probably by this time aware of the unfortunate state of our friend P[ritchard].[2] Mr. Walton[3] transmitted your pacquet to me, on the score of his being perfectly unable to attend to any communication whatever. I therefore forward the letters, &c.

For myself, I must feel highly honoured and obliged by an invitation which I cannot bring myself to decline, and which I can as little venture to accept. Cutting the pathetic, I must own that "I am not what I have been," and a good deal to do—very indifferent health and very uncertain spirits, must incline you to be "merciful to man of mould," *i.e.* the veriest dirt e'er licked into shape, but no less,

My dear Sir,

Very truly yours,

Robt. Browning.

Sunday Night.

Best respects to your brother.[4]

1838 : 1

To Miss Euphrasia Fanny Haworth

Tuesday Evening [July 24, 1838].

Dear Miss Haworth,

Do look at a Fuchsia in full bloom and notice the clear little honey-drop depending from every flower . . I have but just found it out, to my no small satisfaction,—a bee's breakfast. I only answer for the *long* blossomed sort, though,—indeed, for this plant in my room. Taste and be Titania,—you can, that is.—All this while, I forget that you will perhaps never guess the good of the discovery: I have, you are to know, such a love for flowers and leaves—some leaves—that I every now and then,—in an impatience at being unable to possess myself of them thoroughly, to see them quite, satiate myself with their scent,—bite them to bits . . so there will be some sense in that. How I remember the flowers—even grapes—of places I have seen!—some one flower or weed, I should say, that gets some strangehow connected with them. Snowdrops and Tilsit in Prussia go together; Cowslips and Windsor-park, for instance: flowering palm and some place or other in Holland. Now to answer what can be answered in the letter I was happy to receive last week. I am quite well. I did not expect you would write; for none of your written reasons, however. You will see Sordello in a trice, if the fagging-fit holds. I did not write six lines while absent (except a scene in a play,[1] jotted down as we sailed thro' the Straits of Gibraltar)—but I did hammer out some four, two of which are addressed to you, two to the Queen . . the whole to go in Book 3[2]—perhaps. I called you, "Eyebright"—meaning a simple and sad sort of translation of "Euphrasia" into my own language: folks would know who Euphrasia, or Fanny was,—and I should not know Ianthe or Clemanthe. Not that there is anything in them to care for, good or bad. Shall I say "Eyebright"? I was disappointed in one thing, Canova. What companions should I have? The story of the ship must have reached you "with a difference" as Ophelia says,—my sister told it to a Mr Dow, who delivered it, I suppose, to Forster, who furnished Macready with it, who made it over &c &c &c—As short as I can tell, this way it happened: the Captain woke me one bright Sunday morning to say there was a ship floating keel uppermost half a mile off; they lowered a boat, made ropes fast to some floating canvass, and towed her towards our vessel. Both met half-way, and the little air that had risen an hour or two before, sank at once. Our men made the wreck fast, and went to breakfast in high glee at the notion of having "new trousers out of the sails," and quite sure she was a French boat, broken from her moorings at Algiers, close by. Ropes were next hove (hang this sea-talk) round her stanchions, and after a quarter of an hour's pushing at the capstan, the vessel righted suddenly, one dead body floating out; five more were in the forecastle, and had probably been there a month—under a blazing African sun . . don't imagine the wretched state of things. They were, these six, the "watch below" —(I give you the results of the day's observation)—the rest, some eight or ten, had been washed overboard at first. One or two were Algerines, the rest Spaniards. The vessel was a smuggler bound for Gibraltar; there were two stupidly-disproportionate guns, taking up the whole deck, which was convex and—nay, look you, these are the gun-rings, and the black square the place where the bodies lay. Well, the sailors

(All the "bulwarks," or sides at the top, carried away by the waves)

covered up the hatchway, broke up the aft-deck, hauled up tobacco and cigars, good lord such heaps of them, and then bale after bale of prints and chintz, don't you call it, till the Captain was half frightened —he would get at the ship's papers, he said; so these poor fellows were pulled up, piecemeal, and pitched into the sea, the very sailors calling to each other "to cover the faces": no papers of importance were found, however, but fifteen swords, powder and ball enough for a dozen such boats, and bundles of cotton &c that would have taken a day to get out, but the Captain vowed that after five-o'clock she should be cut adrift: accordingly she was cast loose, not a third of her cargo having been touched; and you can hardly conceive the strange sight when the battered hulk turned round, actually, and looked at us, and then reeled off, like a mutilated creature from some scoundrel French surgeon's lecture-table, into the most gorgeous and lavish sun-set in the world: there,—only, thank me for not taking you at your word and giving you the whole "story." "What I did"? I went to Trieste, then Venice—then thro' Treviso and Bassano to the mountains, delicious Asolo, all my places and castles, you will see. Then to Vicenza, Padua and Venice again. Then to Verona, Trent, Inspruck (the Tyrol) Munich, "Wurzburg in Franconia"! Frankfort and Mayence,—down the Rhine to Cologne, thence to Aix-la-Chapelle, Liège, and Antwerp—then home. [*Four lines—about forty words—are here very carefully blotted out.*] Forgive this blurring, and believe it was only a foolish quotation:—Shall you come to town, anywhere near town, soon? I shall be off again as soon as my book is out—whenever that will be. This sort of thing gets intolerable and I had better have done. I never read that book of Miss Martineau's so can't understand what you mean. Macready is looking well; I just saw him for a minute yesterday after the play: his Kitely was Kitely—superb "from his flat cap down to his shining shoes." I saw very few Italians, "to know," that is. Those I did see I liked. Your friend Pepoli has been lecturing here, has he not?

I shall be vexed if you don't write soon,—a long Elstree-letter:—what are *you* doing—drawing—writing?

Ever yours truly
R BROWNING.

1840 : 1

To Miss Eliza Flower[1]

London.
March 9th [ca. 1840].

My dear Miss Flower,

I have this moment received your very kind note. Of course, I understand your objections—how else? But they are somewhat lightened already (confess—nay, "confess" is vile—you will be rejoiced to holla from the house-top)—will go on, or rather go off, lightening, and will be—oh, where *will* they be half a dozen years hence? Meantime praise what you can praise. Do me all the good you can, you and Mr. Fox[2] (as if you will not!), for I have a head-full of projects—mean to song-write, play-write forthwith.

And believe me, dear Miss Flower,

Yours, ever faithfully,
ROBERT BROWNING.

By the way, you speak of *Pippa*. Could we not make some arrangement about it? The Lyrics *want* your music—five or six in all—how say you? When these three plays are out I hope to "build" a huge Ode—but, "all goeth by God's will!"

1840 : 2

To William Macready

[ca. December, 1840.]

Dear Macready,

"My friends—do they now and then send"—and so on. Have you divined, arch-diviner as you are, that I have been sick, and doctored, and slowly convalescent, and enforcedly quiescent, and all and everything except indifferent to you and yours—new play included? I may go out on mornings already (loquitur Medicus)—on evenings, Haymarket-ward, next week—and have to get as far as Clarence Terrace through a few more bottles-full of Tonic: what motives are here for getting strong! (I ought to have said that something is, or was, wrong in my circulation, and that it nearly stopped of a sudden.) Will you do me the favour to remember me to Mrs. and Miss Macready?—But

I must call myself,—for we remove into a new house, the week after next,—a place really not impossible to be got at—and monstrously ambitious thoughts begin to rise like clouds within me! "By that sin fell the angels" . . . noun—no use!

Ever yours, and ambitious of that,

R. BROWNING

Tuesday night

1840 : 3

To John Macready

Hanover Cottage,

Southampton [St.]

Monday Morning [ca. 1840].

My dear Macready,

"The luck of the third adventure" is proverbial. I have written a spick and span new Tragedy[1] (a sort of compromise between my own notion[2] and yours—as I understand it, at least) and will send it to you if you care to be bothered so far. There is action in it, drabbing, stabbing, et autres gentillesses,—who knows but the Gods may make me good even yet? Only, make no scruple of saying flatly that you cannot spare the time, if engagements of which I know nothing, but fancy a great deal, should claim every couple of hours in the course of this week.

Yours ever truly,

ROBERT BROWNING.

1841 : 1

To Laman Blanchard[1]

'My dear Blanchard,—I have to beg the favour of your acceptance of the accompanying little poem, and to beg that you will forgive the tardiness of its arrival on the score of my having just got up from a very sick bed, indeed, where a fortnight's brain-and-liver fever has reduced me to the shade of a shade. I shall gather strength, I hope, this fine weather. Shame, shame, shame on you that the giving of rhymes is all on my side; or—not to talk of giving—what would I do to once again run (real running, for I was a boy), run to Bond Street from

Camberwell and come back with a small book brimful of the sweetest and truest things in the world: it is many years ago since I gave it away to a friend nothing I could give seemed too good for, but the noble and musical lines, that fine "sun-bronzed, like Triumph on a pedestal," that bridge "dark trees were dying round," that superdelicious "song of the wave," live within me yet, "being things immortal."

Will you please to notice that I have changed my address; if, in a week or two you will conquer the interminable Kent Road, and on passing the turnpike at New Cross, you will take the *first* lane with a quickset hedge to the right, you will "descry a house resembling a goose-pie"; only a crooked, hasty, and rash goose-pie. We have a garden and trees, and little green hills of a sort to go out on. Will you come? I say in a week or two, because at present I can hardly crawl, and could barely shake your hand.

Yours very truly,

ROBERT BROWNING.

'Craven Cottage, Saturday.' [April, 1841]

1841 : 2

To MISS EUPHRASIA FANNY HAWORTH

Thursday M^g [*ca.* December 30, 1841.][1]

Dear Miss Haworth,

You are kindest of the kind, now and always.—I just remember having said something about wanting to know Etty—but some owl-faced people perched opposite my desk and looked at me—. I don't know what I said—"that I worshipped Etty"?—Well, and why not—as well as Polidoro da Caravaggio?[2] But then "my worship is not like other mens' "——to quote Mr Poole's friend's play—Who is Mr P's friend?—One who, quoth P., made somebody thus soliloquize—

> I love her so—
> That when I see that beauteous cheek of hers
> I long to bite it as ye would a peach—
> Nay, there's no part in all my mistress' frame
> But I could cut it off, devour it up . .
> —To show my love is not like other men's.

(Very possibly I quote ill—I remember thro' a mist of claret)—However, thank you, dear friend of mine—if I can I'll call at this week's end—(do I understand you that the note should precede me by Post?) I am getting to love painting as I did once—do you know I was a young wonder (as are eleven out of the dozen of us) at drawing? My father had faith in me—and over yonder in a drawer of mine lies, I well know, a certain cottage and rocks in lead pencil and black currant jam-juice (paint being rank poison, as they said when I sucked my brushes)—with his (my father's) note in one corner "RB aetat. 2 years 3 months—"How fast, alas, our days we spend—How vain they be, how soon they end!"—I am going to print "Victor,"[3] however, by Feb^y—and there is one thing not so badly painted there—— Oh, let me tell you—I chanced to call on Forster the other day—and he pressed me into committing verse on the instant, not the minute, in Maclise's behalf—who has wrought a divine Venetian work,[4] it seems, for the British Institution—Forster described it well—but I could do nothing better than this wooden ware (All the "properties," as we say, were given—and the problem was how to cataloguize them in rhyme and unreason) ————

> I send my heart up to thee—all my heart
>   In this my singing!
> For the stars help me, and the sea bears part,
>   —The very night is clinging
> Closer to Venice'-streets to leave one space
>   Above me whence thy face
> May light my joyous heart to thee—its dwelling place.

Singing and stars and night and Venice streets in depths of shade and space are "properties," do you please to see. And now tell me, is this below the average of Catalogue original poetry? Tell me—for to that end, of being told, I write it. (It is, I suppose in print now and past help) I dined with dear Carlyle and his wife (catch me calling people "dear," in a hurry, except in letter-beginnings!) yesterday—I don't know any people like them—there was a son of Burns' there, Major Burns whom Macready knows—he sung "Of all the airts"—"John Anderson"—and another song of his father's.

I am forced to go and dress. I shall be very glad to see you when you return to Town—tho' sure to do something or other snub-worthy— witness what you say about my absent thoughts—but I will do my endeavours.

                                        Truly yours,
                                          R BROWNING.

1842 : 1

To Mrs. Jane Welsh Carlyle

New Cross, Wednesday [*ca.* 1842].

Dear Mrs. Carlyle,

I will breakfast with you gladly indeed, and sit on the proper side of the Countess.[1] She is very much as you say; and Mr Carlyle knows a great deal more about true beauty than anybody else, "Comme de droit." How good you were to me that day!

Ever yours and his faithfully,

R. Bg.

1842 : 2

To Richard Henry Horne

New Cross, Hatcham,
Friday Mg [*ca.* December, 1842].

My dear Horne,

More of your generosity, and, alas, more of my inability to thank you for it!—And you, who write thus to me, and about me,[1] wrote that "Orgy" I have just seen in a Magazine,—to your glory!

When do you redeem your promise and delight us all by coming here? The sun will surely enjoy his own again ere very long, and our hills be traversable.

Ever yours,

R Browning.

Moxon has probably sent by this time "Paracelsus," "Sordello," and the "Bs and P.s" to the Office of the P. T. I saw him yesterday.

N B. (A picturesque bit of ghastliness: in this little writing-room of mine are two sculls, each on its bracket by the window; few brooms trouble walls and ceiling, you may be sure—so here has a huge field-spider woven his platform-web from the under-jaw of one of these sculls to the window-sill—and, (the two sole remaining teeth keeping the jaws just enough apart) the spider's self is on the watch, with each great *arm* wide out in a tooth-socket—thus.

[*Here follows a rough drawing of the spider, the jawbone, and the web.*]

1844 : 1

To Christopher Dowson, Jr.

(*Private.*)

New Cross, March 10 [1844].

My dear Dowson,

You may remember I told you my appointment with C. Kean *had* been for *that* morning (Monday)—and *then* stood over for the next Saturday (yesterday)—but that, having made an effort and ended work the evening I saw you, I meant to call on Kean the following morning:—I did so; but in consequence of my letter, received the day before, his arrangments were made for the week—so that till Saturday the business had to wait. Yesterday I read my play[1] to him and his charming wife (who is to take the principal part)—and all went off *au mieux*—*but*—he wants to keep it till "Easter next year"—and unpublished all the time!—His engagement at the Haymarket next May, is merely for twelve nights, he says:—he leaves London for Scotland to-morrow, or next day—and will be occupied for ten hours a day till he returns—my play will take him two months at least to study, he being a 'special slow-head, and after the Haymarket engagement nothing is to be done till this time next year.—Of all which notable pieces of information I was apprised for the first time *after* the play was read and approved of . . for, it certainly never entered into my mind that anybody, even an actor, could need a couple of months to study a part, only, in a piece, which I could match with such another in less time by a good deal.

But, though I *could* do such a thing, I have a head,—that aches oftener now than of old,—to take care of; and, therefore, *will* do no such thing as let this new work lie stifled for a year and odd,—and work double-tides to bring out something as likely to be popular this present season—for something I *must* print, or risk the hold, such as it is, I have at present on *my* public: and, on consideration of the two other productions I have by me in a state of forwardness, neither seems nearly so proper for the requirements of the moment, as this play— and two or three hundred pounds will pay me but indifferently for hasarding the good fortune which appears slowly but not mistakeably setting in upon me, just now. You will not wonder, therefore, that— tho' I was so far taken by surprise as to promise Kean a copy for Scotland and a fortnight's grace, to come to terms in, before I either published the play or accepted any other party's offer—I say, you will not wonder if I have determined to print it directly (acting on the best advise, I sent it to press yesterday) and merely put the right of *the acting* at his disposal—if he will purchase it with such a drawback as Macready would.: for I fear the only other alternative I shall allow— that of his getting up the part for *next* May, is quite beyond his power. The poorest Man of letters (if *really* of letters) I ever knew is of far higher talent than the best actor I ever expect to know: nor is there one spangle too many, one rouge-smutch too much, on their outside- man—for the *inward* . . can't study a speech in a month! God help them, and bless you, my dear Dowson, says and prays,

Yours,

R. BROWNING.

1844 : 2

To F. O. WARD[1]

July, 1844.

My dear Ward,

Many thanks for your very kind note.

So far from "boring me" with corrections, you helped me essen- tially. But here was the blunder. Your last note with the "gossamer" emendation came *after* the proof[2] had been received and corrected according to the *last but that* (in which you said: "Hood thinks 'that not too much' is better than 'never a,' and he would omit 'whole,' mak- ing a long line of it," etc. etc.).

When the proof had been duly returned your note reached me, after more inexplicable delay, and I thought it no use to countermand what I had written. Another time we will manage better.

I have only had time to read your *Old Man's*[3] lyrical praise of Six- teen, very happy it is. Your other piece presently, I was in town all the morning.

Thank God, my poor uncle,[4] to whom you allude, is happily set free from a most sorrowful life, or death in life. There was no such deplorable event as that frightful visitation which you mention.

The increasing darkness (nine o'clock, nearly) only lets me say I will do my best for you next month.[5]

Once more thank you very heartily.

Yours, my dear Friend,

Very faithfully,

R. B.

1845 : 1

To Henry Fothergill Chorley[1]

Friday morning [1845].

Now, dear Chorley, take the very hearty thanks of one gratified much, very much, by your "Pomfret";[2] it is full of beauty and truth, and the power that is in both—and I do think that when I bend the "quiet of a loving eye" on the whole of it now clearly in my mind, I do not lose in my general admiration one point of good artistry and happy contrivance; for it is all well, from the charming *framing round* of those quaint, kind Grays, to the quiet, indefinite, but no less assured comfort of the end; and I would write about it all, *l'ami* Rose and Cousin Harriet, had I not the memory of last week's letter from *you*—and that stops me, as I would not "set off" *my* encouragement against yours if I could. Besides it is now an old story—my reading your letters and criticisms, verses and prose stories, and enjoying everything and saying nothing. But I let none of your kindness fall to the ground, nor much of your cleverness even; and this "Pomfret" is more than clever every way. Thank you once more, and always, too.

Believe me yours faithfully,

R. Browning.

1846 : 1

To Richard Henry Horne[1]

London,
January 8th, 1846.

My dear Horne,

I very sincerely congratulate you on the fine things in this new volume.[2] The *Swinestead Monk* is admirable, and the Camelott adventure, sylvan "to the height"—perfect! Bedd Gelert is most beautiful too. These I only particularize because the Reviews will be sure to compliment you especially on the Bohemian Story,[3] though its greatest value to me, by the side of the others, is in the proof it gives to those same Reviews that, as Carlyle has it, Pegasus can furl wing and ride post if it please him, at an approved pace, in an accepted and allowed path. There is good sailor-logic and sailor-language in Ben's adventure[4] and a funny tingling pelt of ferns, woodruff, lichens, and such like forest-wrack in the Elf legend[5]—and if I rather wish the children away, Grandmamma Grey and all, it is because all good stories, fairy or otherwise, are *meant* for grown-up men, and children only like them in their childish degree. Children should know their place, and look between our knees at such work—not make us look over their heads through the half opened door, as if stealing a fearful joy! Delora remains Delora!

For the whole, thanks and admiration, now and ever, my dear Horne, from

Faithfully yours,

R. B.

Shall I never be satisfied and see reprinted that capital *Merrie Devil of Edmonton*—which first gave me a taste of your quality? It would have gone well between any two in this collection. And remember that the suppression of the notes to Delora is only the printer's affair.[6]

Shall I be so ungrateful as to leave out the famous Bear History?[7] it is furry, warm, and genial.

1846 : 2

TO THE REV. ARCHER THOMPSON GURNEY

March 10th [1846].[1]

My dear Gurney,

When I received the Review I could not so far deny myself as only write back my extreme gratification at both articles, without putting into immediate exercise the right you had given me a week before of mentioning the day you were to give us the great pleasure of your company; and all kinds of hindrances were in the way, old engagements and fresh ones—so at last March finds *you* unthanked (that is audibly and visibly), and *me* no nearer my promised pleasure than a month ago. But your kind note now only *prevents* one of mine by a day or two.

So first, I return your number, with the truest acknowledgment. Both pieces are admirably written, and the one which more immediately concerns me is amends for a great deal of the ordinary measure dealt out to the book[2] since its appearance ten years back, whether of praise or blame. As I have, I think, said before—or, certainly, often thought—you have been my very kindest of critics, and I hope and trust your kindliness may be returned to you on occasion.

And now may I simply say that *next* week all my days are open except Monday and Saturday? Because of the delight your visit would—let me say *will*—give us, I need not speak. Will you fix your own hour, too, an early one?

All here unite in best regards with,

Yours ever,
R. B.

May I ask for an early note to tell me, and keep off the appointments?

1846 : 3

To Richard Henry Horne[1]

Pisa, Dec. 4 [1846].

Dear Horne,—Your good, kind, loyal letter gave me all the pleasure you meant it should. I mean to 'answer' it ere long, but as my wife wants to send a letter by an enclosure I am now getting ready for this evening. I could not help shaking your hand, through the long interval of Italian air, and saying, if only in a line, that I know your friendliness and honour your genius as much as ever. One of these days we shall meet again, never fear—and then you shall see my wife, your old friend, and hear from her what I have often heard from her, and what, perhaps, the note tells you. She has long been wanting to send it. She is getting better every day,—stronger, better wonderfully, and beyond all our hopes. It is pleasant living here. Why do you not come and try? This street we live in terminates with the Palace in which your Cosmo killed his son.

Ever yours faithfully, as of old,
R. Browning.

1847 : 1

To Edward Moxon

Pisa, Collegio Ferdinando.
February 24th, 1847.

My dear Moxon,

Many thanks for your note with its good news. I delayed answering it in the expectation of a note from Procter, whom I had asked (as I told you) to lend me his eyes, for I don't trust mine implicitly when they look on home interests through this lazy Italian air. He does not write, however, so I must.

I and my wife think your account a very satisfactory one, and we have commissioned Mr. Kenyon to receive what you promise us; that is to say, so much of the £75 and odd, as shall remain when you have deducted the proper sum for those advertisements you advise. I suppose £15 will be quite enough for them, so that we take £60 with the best will in the world. All your advertisements are in such good taste, that one needs say nothing about dropping "Esqs." and "Mr's." and "Mrs's." and putting simply R. Bs. and E. B. Bs.

With respect to what you recommend to me in the matter of a new edition, nothing can be more sensible—only, observe, I use the words people put into my mouth when they begin to advise me. They will have it that the form, the cheap way of publication, the double columns, &c., do me harm, keep reviewers from noticing what I write— retard the sale—and so on. For myself, I always liked the packed-up completeness and succinctness, and am not much disposed to care for the criticism that is refused because my books are not thick as well as heavy. But the point which decided me to wish to get printed over again was the real good I thought I could do to *Paracelsus, Pippa,* and some others; good, not obtained by cutting them up and reconstructing them, but by affording just the proper revision they ought to have had before they were printed at all. This, and no more, I fancy, is due to them. But you know infinitely best what our policy is; "ours," for if we keep together, there is not such a thing as your losing while I gain. When you speak of postponing this till my return to England you may be thinking of a speedier return than is probable. I shall certainly stay another year, if not longer, in Italy; but by Christmas, Providence helping, my wife and I want to print a book as well as our betters, after what we think a new and good plan—all which it would be premature to allude to at present. To return to the matter in hand, therefore, thank you heartily for your kind wishes, and prompt attention to my note. Surely, after all, the account is not unfavourable. If all these "devices" can sell, without a single notice except from the *Examiner,* things will mend some day, we may hope.

I say nothing of my wife's poems and their sale. She is, there as in all else, as high above me as I would have her. She sends her best respects and regards to you—for I must leave off.

And do you, dear Moxon, believe me,

Ever with great sincerity,

Yours,

R. BROWNING.

I look out in the *Times* for your notices, and hope this novel of Knowles' will profit you.

1847 : 2

To Mrs. Anna Brownell Jameson[1]

Pisa, April 1, 47

Dearest friend: let me lose no time in replying to your note, just received. Ba is next to quite well—dressed at this minute and lying on the sofa—and only affected by the weariness that is inevitable. No cold, no feverishness,—all one steady progress to perfect health, thank God, as I am sure I hope I do. This good, moreover, has been nature's doing, without strengthening-medicine of any kind. The fine Spring weather is very favorable.

And now for our travelling-projects—which go easily together, you shall see—for ours was only changed in order to meet what we took to be your convenience. We leave here on the 17th inst. for Florence—as we always meant to do—the way to Florence was the uncertain point. Had the weather permitted, we might have made the circle of Sienna, Colle and Volterra, and returned here, to leave again, by Prato and Pistoja, for Florence. In that case, we should have seen enough of Tuscany for the present, and be ready for Bologna and the north. But Ba's illness changes the ulterior plans altogether—we cannot venture to do so much, I fear—and we now mean to return from Florence, when the heats oblige us, to the Baths of Lucca, as a *safe* place,—and as our road will be via Pistoja, *then* will be the time for that visit, and *now* (on thought) for Volterra and Sienna, as we go to Florence: we also thought this made no kind of difference to you, as, since you had arranged to see Bologna *before* Ravenna, thro' Florence you could not but pass,—and we intended to order our journey, as I said, so as to coincide with your arrival, making a three days affair of it, or prolonging our stay at each city, just as that event should prescribe. But when your last letter mentioned your objection to even crossing Florence if it could be avoided,—I merely spoke of our being *able* to meet at Sienna or Volterra—for, of course, if you could reconcile yourself to Florence, we should prefer it. Now, you *decide* for Florence on the 22", do you not? If Ba had been well, and the original journey determined on, the interval of six days would have satisfied all our curiosity and punctually on the 22d, should we meet: but yet another variation (the last, I do hope) fits our projects to your most perfectly: it is this—to run no risk, and escape the possibility of the cold lingering on these high nests of Etruscan cities, we shall not see them till *after* our stay at Florence: it will evidently be better to go *at once there,* on the 17th—get Ba well rested for a month or six weeks, —then return by the aforesaid Sienna and Volterra, to Lucca and the B[aths] and thence in early Autumn, go by the picturesque way you mention, to Bologna and Venice. So we shall be arrived six days before you,—and the good *seventh,* blessed in all ways, will bring you to us. There! And now a dear kiss by anticipation, if you please! Do you think we would let you leave Italy without seeing us?—And as for seeing anybody else, you *cannot.* for our current of talk will hold out two mortal days and then be unexhausted, be sure! Meantime, I will make all enquiry about the books you ask for, and get them, if possible—with whatever else you may want. And you,—will you not write a word to say this last of all arrangements is also the best— write soon—for who knows but we may coax yet another final letter out of you? Ba's love and thanks,—the extreme of both,—to you and Geddie,—mine go with them too. Can you get us any precise information about those Recoaro Baths? We would have gone there, could we have ventured, *and about the capabilities of Venice as a winter residence,*

Ever yours,
R. B.

1847 : 3

To Thomas Carlyle[1]

Florence, May 14, '47.

My dear Mr. Carlyle,—Mr. Kenyon writes to me, that, in a letter which ought to have arrived a month ago, he mentioned your kindness in keeping me in mind and wishing to hear news of me! When I read this second letter with my wife yesterday morning, we took it as the best of omens in favour of one of our greatest schemes, which had been discussed by us in its length and breadth only the evening before, and then, not for the first time. We determined that whenever I wrote to you, as I meant to do for the last six or seven months, it would be wiser to leave unsaid, unattempted to be said, my feelings of love and gratitude for the intercourse you permitted since a good many years now—but go on and tell you what an easy thing it would be for you to come to Italy—now, at this time of times, for its own sake and the world's—and let us have the happiness—the entire happiness of remembering that we got ready the Prophet's-Chamber in the wall, with bed and candlestick, according to Scripture precedent. In this country, the wheels of one's life run smoothly—a very simple calculation finds what kind of a carriage, with more or less commodious fitting up, is within your means—and once fairly started in it, you may look out of the windows or ponder the journey's end without further cares about lynch-pins or grease-money (in Germany you must know you are taxed every post for "Schmiergelt," etc.), one man finds you house and furniture for so long—another contrives you dinner—for so many—you pay what you mean or can, and there is an end of it. Then in this land of solid vast honest houses, built to last—a few rooms cost more than many—or not less—seven or five, nine or seven, it is little matter. You see all I mean, I am sure; and it would not become me to speak more. Only, if ever you are disposed to pass a winter here, we will go to any part you decide for, and be ready for you at any time. I hope it is not wholly for ourselves (for my wife and myself) that I say this—I heard you once allude to Jesuitism—to an intention you had of writing about it: and when I look over the extracts from books on that and similar subjects, as I find them in Newspapers here, I ejaculate (like I don't know what virtuoso, in some great gallery of pretentious painting), *"Raphael, ubi es?"*—

But in Italy, or in England, I shall ever keep it my first of affectionate prides—something beyond affection and far better than pride—that you have been and are what you are to me—not a "friend," neither. I dare believe, on the whole, that there is no better nor sincerer relation than that in which you stand to me. One might fancy I did not profit as I might have done by the facilities you gave me for seeing and communicating with you in England; but I always hoped to be better qualified to profit one day. I don't apologize for writing in this way, and of these things. Here in Italy, it seems useless and foolish to put into a little note any other matter than what comes uppermost (and yet lies undermost).

When I was about to leave England I should have been glad to talk over my intentions with you, respecting my marriage, and all the strange and involved circumstances that led to it. I did not do so, however, not from any fear of your waiving the responsibility of giving counsel, but because, in this affair which so intimately concerned me, I had been forced to ascertain and see a hundred determining points, as nobody else could see them, in the nature of things. And I was nearly as convinced then, as by all that has happened subsequently, that I had the plainest of duties to perform; and there was no use in asking for an opinion which I might know as certainly as I know anything—without giving us both much pain and many words. Through God's providence, all has gone with us better than my best hopes. My wife, in all probability, will become quite well and strong. She only feels weakness, indeed, and may be considered well, except for that. I believe—from the accounts from England, and from the nature of the place in the country to which she was to have been removed a day or two after that on which we determined to leave England—that this winter would have ended the seven years' confinement without my intervention. You will let me say that it could be nobody's true interest that this should be, with an entirely good, unselfish, affectionate creature, in whom during these eight months that I have been by her always, I have never seen an indication of anything but goodness and unselfishness. When I first knew her more than two years ago, we soon found out a common point of sympathy in her love and reverence for you—she told me how you had written to her, given her advice. So that there was one way left for me to love you the more. She is sitting opposite now, and answers (when I ask her, this minute, what I am to say for her), "But you *know* my feelings"! And I do know them.

Much of what I have written will go to Mrs. Carlyle likewise—I never can dissociate you in my thoughts: if we, or *when* we go to England again, I shall try and live near you—as much nearer you as I can. Will you give my truest regards to her? I trust you are both well. You would not suffer by the cold weather I think. It is very hot here just now, but has been cold beyond example.

I see Lely's picture of your Cromwell, in the Pitti Palace here. I make no doubt you do not want any news now about the reported *cast* of the head; but I will inquire and let you know, on the chance of your wishing it.

Mr. Kenyon mentions a note you have given Miss Fuller—and which she will probably bring when she comes here; it is a delight to expect. Let me say, that should you want a *person* to find me, the address is *Via delle Belle Donne*, 4222—but for a *letter* the best direction is to R.B., *Poste Restante, Firenze, Toscana*, simply, as I get such a note duly when I go to the Post Office, and not when it pleases the man to call.—All my space is covered, except to reassure you

I am ever yours,

R. Browning.

1848 : 1

To Richard Henry Horne

Florence, Dec. 3. '48.

Dear Horne,

Nobody puts into every scrap they write, so much of their own self (pure, "drawn from the wood") as you, to my thinking. Your note was, and is, a true delight to lay to heart: I don't much care about your straitnesses for the passing moment,—you seem so strong and fit to bear them, and of course be all the happier after. Does not the old wise book say "Better is a dinner of herbs where love is, than the stalled ox" . . with the devil to carve it, or something to that effect? The main vexation is when, wanting money, you have to break up your mind's Cellini plate into dollars, as our poor Duke is said to have done—but you touch and spoil none of it while you dig in the garden—rather you keep it the safer—(if you don't, rather, add to its value . . but here the figure breaks down woefully.) By this, however, times must be mending,—the cholera having barked at the door, not really bitten,—is it not so? Yes, I saw your "Judas" advertised, and reviewed in the Athenæum,—one of the best subjects, it strikes me, possible for poet—the one extract I read was admirable, and the plot and purpose admirable. I shall have a great read of it, whenever the lucky day comes. I wish I could have referred you to a pamphlet of the last century called something like "Remarks on the life or character? of Judas,"—with striking things, as I seem to remember them—an anonymous letter to Lord Lyttelton who had printed remarks on the life of St. Paul,—I remember for certain that one tradition concerning the end of the traitor is that he settled in Portugal and founded a family still flourishing there!—and sure enough there are the D'Ajudas,—'wish 'em joy of it! Now of me and mine: you spoke (and very kindly) about an advertisement—it chronicled only the decease of my father's mother-in-law—thank God! Indeed, Florence is only some ten days and nights' journey from London, and were there a real need like the very hint of that, I should leave here at a day's notice. I only heard of Mrs Adams' death[1] by the papers—what you seem to tell me,—of which I was altogether ignorant, knowing none of her friends now,—is sad indeed. I will mention a matter to you—knowing your delicacy, and trusting in your discretion, to do a thing for me, or not to do it—as you see or know best—simply here is the matter. I knew the Flowers when I was five or six years old,—earlier

I do think—when I got older, perhaps at twelve or thirteen, I wrote a book of verses which Eliza read and wrote to me about,—I wrote back, —then came the acquaintance with Fox, if meeting him one evening be worth that name,—but she gave me his opinions at second hand, and more letters came of it: then in a few months (for one grows fast at that age) I saw the proper way, and put my blessed "poems" in the fire. I lost (soon after) sight of Eliza,—but when, years after I began again, and printed a little thing, "Pauline,"—I could not but send it to Fox, my old praiser—thence fresh generosity from him, and reacquaintance with the Flowers, and one day Eliza told me to my amazement and discomfort that she had "still by her somewhere, safe," all the letters I had written to her—"never being used to destroy a scrap of any such thing"—moreover producing on some occasion or other, a sort of album-book in which were entered "poem" this and "poem" the other, duly transcribed from my delectable collection aforesaid. "I grinned and bore it"—promising myself to speak about it some day, so as not to offend; alas, a few more years have gone by, and poor E. F. has left us only her strange beautiful memory! I heard it at Pisa, and, three or four months after, wrote a note to Mrs Adams —a few lines, but they must have shown how I felt, I think. I added, (thinking it would be best to say and get done with it) that I should be glad to have my letters back—just mentioning what Eliza had told me, as an excuse for the seeming absurdity of not being sure all such boyish rubbish had not been at once properly disposed of—(and it is on that account, that I tell *you* the matter in detail). No answer ever came to this—and I don't think I had written a week before a letter arrived from you, describing a horrible raking up of the correspond-ence in general—then I was glad I had written, and, in due time, angry at the silence,—since there was no overdelicacy to respect in the undertaker*ers* of all that dead mournful ware—so I meant to wait till I returned to England and then see to it.* But here comes this second end of poor Mrs A.—and who is the person to deal with now? So I write all this, that in any possible conjuncture that *may* happen, you may know my exact mind on the matter, just at the time when one word would be worth a hundred *after,*—and act for me—since in your goodness you offer to do so at need. I should have been vexed and uncertain what to do, perhaps, had Mrs A. been projecting one of those hateful memoirs &c—but nobody is left now to occasion that feeling, and make one hesitate at availing oneself of the law, which overhauls these ungodly appropriations, I believe. There,—this to your secrecy, dear Horne, unless you see good reason—for the letters &c are purely nonsensical, as could not but be, at the age of the inditer,—and it *does* seem so ludicrous to suppose they were not pitched into the fire at the time they came to hand,—but that, unluckily, I know they were *not:* then the verses, which nobody had ever a right to copy, they being lent her by a friend to whom I confided the volume,—who has not heard of these things being raked up, a long day off, when one dies &c?—Well, another tack—by this you will have seen Phelps' fortune with my play:[2] he surprised me some weeks ago by asking to play it, and I just hear that it *was* to be done last Wednesday. As nothing worse can well come than *did* come, I care very little about the event,—always wishing Phelps well, of course, and the play, too, for one or two friends' sake moreover, yours preeminently, staunch supporter of mine that you always were. My new edition[3] . . but you will see—I have done my best at correcting enough and not too much. Now I will turn you over to my wife—bidding her tell you something of our summer ramble to Ravenna and Loreto. She is quite well, and we sit here over the log-fire hearing the wild news go in and out,—don't expect me to write about that! Of Powell,[4] poor wretch, I [have] heard nothing since the Athenæum noted his handsome sale of manuscripts and letters, mine among others. Well, he is a finished creature of the kind, that you and I and one or two more have been privileged to see, with his head carried erect in impudence four feet above the water, and sixty feet of a floating body on the water's top, with no propelling power visible, and the whole wonder going past us as with some determined purpose, straight to the father of the family, the devil "that old serpent." I find poor Sherman, one of the witnesses, is rather like to be invited to "the Fleet" than to the Admiralty, and Gurney is another victim, but "que diable allaient-ils faire à bord de cette galère?" Goodbye, dear Horne! My true regards to Mrs Horne, whom we shall see face to face some day, I trust. Don't be long in writing. I would tell you more about our ways (sure of your sympathy always) but that my wife has the readier pen. We have been obliged with quantities of Father Prout, these last two months—and one or two American visitors—otherwise we know no English-speaking people—and so much the better—for one could not make them exquisitely happy by one's best gifts of speech or writing as I made a friend of ours yesterday, a Vallombrosan monk, by giving him a silver threepence and twopence I had providentially by me. "O certainly I shall not refuse, so beautiful they are, so beautiful!" He did the honors to us at the Convent last year, but is now come down to the city-monastery, because of the toothache the cold gave him.

Ever yours

R B.

* Understand that I never fancied that any use would be made of my stupid scrawlings in *that* business—or any other, by Mrs A.—but simply was nervous at the possibility of some packet's being lost, given away, let lie in unknown hands for a time, and then turning up to bother one's survivors and make them ashamed of one—and all for what?—for having played at verses and letters, instead of cricket and trapball!

1849 : 1

To Miss Mary Russell Mitford[1]

March 9., '49.

Dear Miss Mitford,

Ba desires me to tell you that she gave birth, at 2¼ this morning, to a fine, strong boy, like Harry Gill with the voice of three,—a fact we learned when he was about half born—Ba bore the 21 hours,—a long 21 hours' pain, without one cry or tear, as I know, who held her hand whenever they would let me. Now all is over; the babe seems happy in his cradle, and Ba *is,* I suppose, the very thing you call happy—this is God's reward for her entire perfectness to me and everybody but herself. You know something,—perhaps a great deal of her—but *I* know, if not all, quite as much as my knowledge can hold. So, be joyful with her, and so kind to me as to allow me to consider myself, dear Miss Mitford,

Yours very faithfully ever,

Robert Browning.

Here is Flush.[2] "How is Miss Barrett, Flush?" (a screwing of the eyes together answers)—"Did not she give you her hand to kiss just now?" (wag, wag goes the tail) "And her babe,—you that like all babes, won't you love *him?*" (Both ears drop) "And what shall I say for you to Miss Mitford?"—Here Flush, having licked his lips and made a sham swallow down his throat, says "Don't ask such folly—send my love and have done,—I could speak if I liked, but you see I

FLUSH

THE PET OWL

These pictures of Flush and of the Owl are here reproduced from photographs in Browning's album, now at Balliol College. The Owl was kept in Browning's study at 19, Warwick Crescent, in the 80's. The poet each day had a bowl of chopped beef brought to his desk, and fed this bird bit by bit as it stood perched on his left arm.

am swallowing something and otherwise engaged." So, goodbye to Flush, who goes to the fireside, and to his friends who must go to the bedside.

1849 : 2

To Sarianna Browning

Bagni di Lucca,
Monday July 2. '49

Dearest,

I wrote from Florence on the 23rd and may as well begin now to tell you that we arrived here on Saturday night, or evening; babe bearing the journey very well. I fancied him of a worse temper than he turns out to be, for he is always merry and laughing and never cries without reason: he is very fat and well and cannot fail to profit, one would think, by the delightful change from the burning heat at Florence to the delightful cool of this place,—which exceeds our expectations: to be sure, we are up at the very top of the mountain, and out of the way of the company at the bottom—we chose the house on that account, and a very pretty one it is, nor dear—we took it just in time, as the granduke (?) is expected, and other arrivals threaten— the scenery is delightful, hills covered with vines, olives, chestnuts, and corn—with the river thro' the valley beneath. Ba walked with me some hours yesterday (resting included). Our babe was baptised on the 26th at the French Evangelical Protestant Church, being the chapel at the Prussian Legation at Florence. I enclose the certificate, which is of the birth as well as baptism; please take care that it is properly registered, with the whole of the above description, as difficulties sometimes arise from omissions or negligent entries; you will see, nothing can be more exact than this, and Ba and I particularly congratulate ourselves on having managed the matter as we did: the service was very simple and evangelical—just the same as at Mr. Clayton's,[1] except that there is a form of prayer and service. I saw the minister, a very simple, good and sincere man apparently. You will see what name we have given our child; and will not like him the less on that account: it was all Ba's doing—strange to say,—tho' I have been thinking over nothing else, these last three months, than Mama and all about her, and catching at any little fancy of finding something which it would have pleased her I should do,—yet I never was struck by the obvious opportunity I had of doing the honor in my power, little as it was, by keeping up the memory of that dearest of names²—the name, beside, of her own father and mother, whom she loved so much, and of dearest aunt, too—who must have had that feeling for it, or she would not have called one of her own children by it. When we had decided that the baptism should take place before our leaving Florence, Ba told me I should greatly oblige *her* by not only giving our child that name but by always calling him by it, when he is old enough: she thinks the name very pretty in itself, and sees many advantages in distinguishing between the two Roberts, avoiding nicknames for either of us, etc. all which she ought to have seen as clearly when the name Barrett was decided on.—and so it shall be. It is, of course, a very insignificant instance of Ba's sympathy with me, —still I mention it, because it gratified me more as coming from her, than from anybody else. I only account for my own stupidity by the fact that we have a boy, not a girl—and that one associates the naming girls with women, not men. I believe the spelling is right—should it not be, register the true name, and let me know (The minister's name, illegible in the certificate, is *Droin.*)

Tuesday / We continue to be pleased with this place,—and as the beauty and novelty of the walks tempt Wilson and the nurse to be out all day in the open air, the babe has the benefit of it—he likes being out of doors so much, that they cannot so well keep him amused in the house as before. Everybody admires his size and appearance. Flush benefits, too by the air and exercise, not to speak of the hot bath he gets—the springs of hot water gush out of the rock close by us. The fertility of the soil comes from the volcanic nature of it. I wish you were here with all my heart: We have seen nobody yet, except the Ogilvys, we went down to call on yesterday evening. I see no newspapers, the establishment to which the news room is attached consists of assembly rooms, billiards, etc., and the subscription is for *all* these together, no one singly—and, in my case, I should pay for my 'family' beside! So, how the world goes on, I am not likely to know for these two or three months. You must tell me if anything happens. Pray write good long letters, remembering what a comfort they will be. But we get the thing we came for—coolness—and I should think, no where else can it [be] got near Florence—the mountains are so situated here as to cause the sun to rise above them (and shine into the valley where we are, as regards *them,* tho' on a hill when you look from the valley itself) two hours later, *and* to set two hours earlier, than anywhere else,—ensuring cool mornings and evenings. This evening I climbed to the top of a mountain, over loose stones in the dry bed of a torrent, and under vines and chestnuts, till I reached an old deserted village, with perhaps a half dozen inhabitants—one of whom, an old woman, told me I was "too curious" by far, and should lose myself up there. Now you see I do a plain duty in taking exercise and trying to amuse myself and recover my spirits,—and I tell you all this in order that you may do what lies in your power to produce the same effect: you have not such a place as this to take exercise in, I know— but this place, or any other, would do me no good of itself, any more than Florence—for, apart from the folly and wickedness of the feeling, I am wholly tired of opening my eyes on the world now—and if I have advantages and comforts of various kinds that you have not, yet—it seems to me, at least,—your comforts and memories are infinitely beyond mine, those of the best kind. The end of it all is, that you must try as I do, to be thankful for them. Good night, and God bless you.

Thursday. July 5. We go on as usual in this pretty place: friends, arrived from Florence yesterday, tell that the heat there is intense, so we are well out of it—not to mention other helpfulnesses. I never go down to the village below, and am quite alone here—we occupy the highest rooms in the place (not *house* . . . but our 2^d story is on a level with the top of the house figuring as the highest) and all about us are mountain paths amid woods and rocks, and complete loneliness. Ba is writing a little note to you—and will give you a better account of the babe than I can, no doubt. Sophia Cottrell came up here with her child yesterday,—12 months old,—and with nothing like the size of our baby. Everybody seems to think him remarkably flourishing. All which ought to be unmixed pleasure to me, but is very far from it. Well, dearest, I have nothing to add but that we shall count on your coming: you had best begin thinking steadily on it as a certain thing, so it will lose its formidableness very soon. It will do you all the good in the world. Good bye, dearest Papa and Sis—best love to Aunt and James. Tell me how Capt. Pritchard goes on, and give him my love also. Do you see anything of the Arnoulds? I must write to them, next time. Remember I see no newspapers, and write soon and at length. I had a bilious fit, these two days, but it is over this morning.

Ever yours most affectionately,

R BROWNING.

1849 : 3

To William Etty, R.A.[1]

Bagni di Lucca, Sept. 21st, 1849.

My dear Mr. Etty—I was duly informed, by my Sister, of your very kind call of inquiry, at Hatcham. Yet, surely, you must have divined I could not be in England these three years past, or I should not have been so neglectful of my privilege, as to leave you unvisited so long. It was always too great a delight to me, when near your quarters, to knock at your door and convince myself that a great Painter and Poet could realize his conceptions, as exquisitely in London, at this latter day, as in Venice, when the Doges were there. I see noble pictures often now. But a noble Painter I do not hope to see, again, before I return to England; as I shall probably do next year: when it will be indeed an honour and a pleasure to shake his hand, instead of being forced to content myself, as at the present, with saying simply, that
I am, dear Mr. Etty,
Yours very faithfully, as admiringly ever,
ROBERT BROWNING.

May I venture to send my wife's homage along with mine?—We have often remembered your grand *Sirens*.[2]

1850 : 1

To Thomas Carlyle

Florence, June 10, '50.

My dear Sir,
It must be three years since a letter from you[1] went straight to my heart—I could not trust myself to answer it at the time: and of late many changes have happened. You know very well how happy and proud (for want of a better word) your friendship has made me,—how happy and proud. It will always seem, as it does now, enough to have lived for. And now, putting aside your friendship, which is too precious to be lightly appealed to,—may I ask a kindness of your good nature? A year ago, I had great pleasure in making the acquaintance

of a very cultivated and interesting person,—Mr. Story, an American; and I could find no better method of repaying him, than by engaging to make him know you, should he ever go to England. He is there for a very short while, and writes to remind me of my engagement. May I venture to hope that a very loveable and talented person may not fare the worse with you on account of this recommendation from

> Dear Sir, Yours ever faithfully
>   and gratefully,
>   ROBERT BROWNING.

I shall take the occasion of offering my wife's truest respects to you, and to Mrs. Carlyle—whom she only knows thro' me, yet seems to know well. Mr. Story, I should not omit to say, has a very delightful wife. You understand that this little hurried scrap is no attempt (even) at a reply to your letter—but just meant for the specific purpose I mention. I will take heart and write ere very long.

1850 : 2

To John Kenyon

Monday night,
July 29., '50

I must tell you, dear Mr. Kenyon, exactly how your letter finds us, else you will not quite understand how it affects us. Yesterday morning Ba had another unfortunate miscarriage, she was, it is thought, two months advanced toward confinement, and had seemed particularly well, not that we have any sort of rashness to reproach ourselves with on that account, every sort of risk was avoided, and she kept the house, indeed the sofa, for the last six weeks. Spite of all precautions, however, she became unwell some days ago, and the result has been more serious than on former occasions. But we had good, prompt medical assistance, and though a painful, dubious day was followed by a worse night, yet morning brought decided relief, by noon the distressing symptoms had greatly abated, and now (10 o'clock) my own eyes assure me that the Doctor's entire satisfaction, on his last visit just now, may be safely shared in by us all. She is wonderfully better indeed, has slept at intervals, and taken a little nourishment, and may be expected to pass a good night. To let you know what she rallies from—ought I to subjoin that Harding assured me this morning she had lost above a hundred ounces of blood within the twentyfour hours? Not one in five thousand women would suffer to the same extent, he says. I pain you, I am sure, but how otherwise can I put you into my place and make you fancy that, after sitting all night by the little patient white face, that could smile so much more easily than speak, your letter and its proposal for her good reach me? You surely feel that whatever I say presently, the real business is over and indeed, in the truest sense I have, as you express it, "already accepted" this last of your kindnesses and laid it away with its fellows in my heart forever: also you will feel that there can be no room in me for any silly affectation of pride, or playing at independence or the like folly. You have a noble princeliness of spirit to which such generosities come readily, and would be glad if I took your money—hear why I cannot. I should be vexed, of course, to leave Italy without Ba seeing the south of it; such a pleasure has always been dreamed of and schemed for every year, little attempts, indeed, were made and broken off; and this present year, when we formed the Paris plan, there was no avoiding the fact that unless we put our project into execution this winter, the hope must be given up. Then came Ba's situation to render the journey all but impossible. As the event proves, that difficulty is gone. Our finances are straitened certainly, nor will this new doctor's bill improve them, but we have economised of late, and I do not see so imperative a bar to our getting to Rome (at least) and staying there a month or two, as to justify me looking beyond for help which on every principle ought to be reserved for extremities. All my life I have elected to be poor, and perhaps the reason, or one among other reasons, may be that I have a very particular capacity for being rich, like Chaucer's monk "to ben an Abbot able," so that there is no poor spiritedness in my choosing to bound my wishes by my means, seeing that fortune could not easily supply me with means which I could not, if I pleased, outgo, at one stride, by my wishes, and were R. B. the R. P. of the divers thousands a year, noticeable just now in the newspapers, be assured I could so effectually turn those moneys to account that not one unprofitable penny should cumber my pocket at the year's end. But it was decreed otherwise. Now, in all likelihood, I am wronging myself in your thought by writing lightly, a very outside lightness! Set it down at worst to an awkward attempt at ridding myself of any symptom of the sour ungracious air of one who should say in his self-conceit "Let you delight me so much? No, indeed"; and so, shouldering arms, as it were, mount guard more stiffly than ever over the

Wordsworthian allotment to "mighty poets in their misery dead" I might blamelessly say "For me, I want nothing of Rome and Naples, knowing each nook of one and corner of the other. But since Ba will not see them unless by your help, why, you shall, like yourself, help her, for you know whether kindness might not be worse bestowed." But it would be a vile habit, to say no worse, that of looking wistfully up at the clouds, on all occasions, to see what facilities may drop down to carry into effect any pleasant wish that one might be tempted to frame in her behalf. Observe we have £100 less shipmoney this year than last, and are likely to fare no better for the future. So let nothing be of this offer, beyond the memory and gratitude which I shall often enough enjoy, both in company with Ba, and "by myself walking, to myself talking" as Charles Lamb hath it. See what I have tried to say in two letters, which I tore for saying it so ill—this must go. Well, the doctor orders Ba into the country, as soon as she recovers sufficiently to bear the transporting. I had heard before of a little comfortable and cheap villa, just our affair, at some four hours' drive from Florence, on high ground, four miles from Vallombrosa, and shall hope to take her there for six weeks or two months, and our child will share in the benefit. On our return, who knows how things may look? There is Ba's new edition (full of beautiful new things)[1] there may be reviews &c., Perhaps we may see an opportunity of letting these rooms to proper people (because there are things easy to spoil); in that case we may manage the journey, and with such a house as Miss Bayley[2] describes (with such kindness, but Ba will thank her when she can) in that best of situations for us, as I well remember, would suit us exactly, if we can compass the expense, for it seems a little beyond us, just now. To be sure our requirements are not unlike the boy's memorable pennyworth of cheese which he wished to be "very long and very thick." So we want situation, spaciousness, and as many other advantages as possible, and all for an old song, or rather, a new one! Still, if Miss Bayley does really mean to go to Rome, and particularly, *to our very house there,* why, we may be "dazzled with the Forum and pleased with ruin." Will she follow up her good offices by sending "the plan" she speaks of? And any other information in her power. Briefly, if we can, we will go and be happy. If not, we will stay, and not be unhappy neither, when we think how we might have gone. Let me leave off lest I grow indignant at this letter also.

Tuesday eg. Ba has passed an excellent night, and day, and is much better, could not well be better. The doctor's opinion confirms mine, he has been twice. Did I say that I read your letter and Miss Bayley's to her yesterday? Spite of the wrongness of exciting her at all, but there was no helping it and I did properly by instinct. Yet she is a little vexed, she says, at having perhaps, unconsciously, given an impression which was the last in the world she wished to give. I never see her letters, nor she mine, lest we should lose freedom in writing of each other. But I can fancy something of the spirit of her letters to Miss Bayley and how it might be misunderstood. We get the habit of telling our two or three intimates how we housekeep, to interest ourselves in what else is dull enough, but as I might tell you about my picking up pictures without being arrogant, so, if I said that "having had losses" like Dogberry, we yet were not put to selling one of our "two good suits to ourselves," there would be not an atom of querulousness in it. Bless you, we are rich and excellenza'd and signoria'd all Florence over, and I patronise art in a way. Come to Italy and see, for after all, I have a presentiment that it will be less difficult to meet *so* than by any contrivances of our own, we who are here and likely to be. And now a word on other matters. The Storys were very kind and attentive at Florence—all Americans are. I had a half-thought, when sending them the letters desired, of giving them one for you, but I remembered your crowded way of life and how emphatically you conceive hospitality and that it would be better to give you the chance, sure to follow, of meeting them elsewhere and taking your own course. The lady is charming, is she not? I find Forster has been very kind to them, as to another friend I sent him, indeed he is always most kind, and just now, among his multifarious occupations, is caring for Ba's new Edition. Chorley,[3] too, is ever friendly to us both. The Ward[4] you mention is a capital fellow, full of talent and congeniality. And now I will leave off—All thanks and gratitude to you, dear Mr. Kenyon, from yours ever most affectionately,

ROBERT BROWNING.

1850 : 3

TO JOHN KENYON

Florence
Aug. 16., '50.

My dear Mr. Kenyon,

Ba sends a letter home to-day, written at easy stages, and I will take the opportunity of telling you that she continues to recover strength, though slowly, she cannot stand yet without help, but sits up for several hours every day. As soon as she can bear it, we shall take a few drives and then try to get into the country for a month or six weeks, as the doctor enjoins on us, promising that the change of air will repair all the mischief, though *four* of these mishaps, beside the advent of our babe, amount to a serious drain on such a constitution as hers. Our babe, too, has been very unwell, it is thought from exposure to the sun, and made us duly uneasy for the first time, but the feverishness ended in a simple cold and cough, and all is right now. The worst has been this dreadful loss of dear, brave, noble Margaret Fuller, with her husband and child; you must have heard of the calamitous wreck of the "Elizabeth" in which she embarked, "taking the name for a good omen," she said, but it could have been the only one, so visible a presentiment of evil had she, or so we seem to see it now. We loved her, and she loved Ba, coming here oftener as the time for departure approached. She would too gladly have staid here, but was dependent for comfort on the arrangements with booksellers, newspapers, etc, which friends had engaged to make, and taken their time in making, which was not her time, unfortunately. When she had engaged a passage (and indeed gone on board the vessel, tho' a delay in its sailing suffered her to return to Florence for a few days) she received the letter she had been waiting for, bidding her set her mind at ease, as the requisite negotiations had been completed. "Had it arrived a fortnight ago!" she said; so she left us, giving our babe a little bible from her own, *"in memory* of him." She wrote to us from Gibraltar, a sad strange letter, but most affectionate, telling us how disastrously the voyage had proceeded thus far, the captain had died of small-pox, they *supposed,* for at Gibraltar they were neither allowed the visit of a surgeon, nor the burial of the body, she had tended the dying man, whose sufferings had been horrible, and now they were about to continue their adventure uncertain if some fatal disease were not waiting to break out among them when once more out of help's reach. The letter began, "Dear precious friends"—and ended by bidding us write what should be the first thing to meet her at home. You see what *did* meet her, and the more particular accounts that have reached us are simply heart-rending—for our best *hope* is that after she had lashed her child to the Italian woman, and launched them from the ship on the desperate chance of their reaching the shore alive, she fainted and felt no more, since she was drowned in the forecastle, easily by comparison, while her husband remained on the ship till it broke up, nearly eleven hours of that agony. All the sailors, mates included, seem to have saved themselves and left the passengers to their fate—those of the crew who perished were *foreigners,* too,— our English way is for the officers to quit the ship *last,* not first, as would appear to have been the case here. Forgive me for all this pain I cause you by telling what will not out of my thoughts. Ba sends her truest love, with that of yours ever most affectionately,

                                                    R. BROWNING.

Poor Ossoli, the husband, was a quiet, kind, melancholy-looking creature—deeply attached to her and to his child, and believing in her superiority with a simple and affecting faith. The child looked lymphatic and short-lived to our apprehension; yet was doing well when she wrote, the better for the voyage indeed. She told us, in Ossoli's presence, "that he had been warned never to make a voyage, as the sea would be fatal to him." I remarked to him *"that* does not much discompose you?" and he smiled and shook his head. She said once, all things went ill with her, and *would,* yet she was always cheerful.

1851 : 1

To Thomas Carlyle

                                        26 Devonshire Street,
                                        [28 July, 1851.]

My dear Mr Carlyle,
    Mr. Kenyon had promised me your presence at his house to-morrow, or you would have seen me ere this; but he brings me, this minute, the news that you go into the country the next day and cannot dine with him. What am I to do,—with my five-years' hunger for the sight of you and Mrs. Carlyle?—unless you let me call tomorrow,—as I do-think you *will* let me. Just a word by post to say at what hour in the day I may call,—or may *not.* For instance, I will venture to call at 1. *unless you write.* In any case, my whole greeting and duty to you! My wife is with me in all this, and will accompany me of course—we being ever yours
                                        faithfully, she as well as
                                                    R. BROWNING

1851 : 2

To Thomas Carlyle

26 Devonshire St.
Aug. 22. '51.

My dear Mr Carlyle,

What will you say to my stupidity when I tell you that it had entirely passed out of my head, until this moment that my wife reminds me,—that she has already, some three or four months ago, contributed the whole sum of both our recollections of the two Ossoli to Mr. Emerson's work.[1] We were applied to, in the first instance, last year,—as I told you—by a lady—and after a rather vague fashion—at least we could not see how we could materially help such a scheme: and it was to *this* application that I referred. But just before we left Florence, our friend Mrs. Story wrote more precisely in the interest of the memoir now in question; and of course my wife and I gathered our memories together, or rather put them into words, subject to each other's correction, and the whole was comprised in a letter to Mrs. Story which she was made at liberty to use as might seem best. I had wholly forgotten this!

I fear I have given you too great a notion of the amount of our intimacy with the Ossoli, and perhaps the nature of it, even. We saw but a few hours and half hours of her,—and much less of him—but they were compensating times when they came—and her own feeling to us,—if words gave it aright, justified our quick love and respect for her. While I write this, I get to remember my wife's letter, and am sure that it contains *all* we know,—and, indeed, most of what we guessed. I was vexed (when I thought over what you enquired about at Chelsea) that I had not remembered that a tolerably accurate likeness of the husband was made by Mr. Latilla—(either in London now, or on his way to New York; I will enquire which)—would not that be of interest and value to friends?

The first application was not refused nor disregarded by us: the maker of it was at Rome, "expected to see us on her return to Florence" &c; and said simply that a scheme for a book was on foot. We meant, I believe, to tell her, whenever she saw us, exactly what there was to say, and then ascertain if so much would be acceptable: but Mrs. Story's request was definite, and we were bound to attend to it directly—as we did. (Surely it must have reached Mr. Emerson by this time? It was sent from Florence before the end of April last.)

I am happy to hear of your amended health, from whatever cause —as I was most happy to see you—and am most happy, most proud to see your handwriting again when I do. My wife desires me to offer her best regards to Mrs. Carlyle and yourself with those of yours ever faithfully,

R. B.

1851 : 3

To Thomas Carlyle

26 Devonshire St. Tuesday.
[Sept. 23, 1851.]

Dear Mr. Carlyle,

I find to my great vexation that I have missed you—and I am unfortunately engaged this evening. Can I write anything that will serve?[1]

We leave London on Thursday: the L. Brighton and South Coast Railway's *Express* train (I suppose) leaves the L. Bridge terminus at 10 a.m. and arrives at Newhaven by 12. 10^m. A steamer leaves Newhaven, *on that day* at 1.30^m p.m. for Dieppe. (Next day, an hour later, —and so following.) From Dieppe the trains go through Rouen to Paris at 7.15^m 11.35^m A.M. and 4.30./ 9.45. P.M. to arrive by 2.15m./ 4./ 11.5m/ 5 P.M. We purpose staying all night at Dieppe, and leaving in the morning,—for our child's sake. At Paris we go to the *Armes de la Ville de Paris, Rue de la Michodière, Boulevard des Italiens*—a very small place that we know. What our delight would be if by any combination you could accompany us, I shall not need, I hope, to say. The objection to this route is the length of the sea-passage, but the day passage is in our favour. We were, I think, some eight hours on board, *with bad weather,* and hope better things now. This route is the cheapest, however—and having return tickets we can hardly change our plans. I write in utmost haste—can I do anything, beyond earnestly wishing?

With truest regard to Mrs. Carlyle,

Pray believe me, as ever,
Yours faithfully
R. Browning.

1851 : 4

To Dr. W. C. Bennett[1]

London,
September 23rd, 1851.

Dear Mr. Bennett,

How good you have been this many a day and year in sending me and mine your poems,[2] with not a few kind words in the fly-leaf of this last volume! We have spent a few hurried weeks in London, and leave it to-morrow for Paris, but I would—that is, I and my wife would—not go without thanking you very heartily for your remembrance of, and kind feeling towards, us.

Your poems have abundant evidence of the right spirit, and some of the child-pictures go to our very hearts in their truth and beauty, now that we have a child of our own. I hope we shall see you one day, for I hardly count the one evening when I met you years ago, as giving me a sight of you. Meantime, take this hearty expression of our good-will for more than it seems worth, and know us for

Yours, very faithfully ever,
R. and E. B. Browning.

1851 : 5

To Thomas Carlyle

Paris, Avenue des Champs Elysees, 138,
[October, 1851.]

My dear Mr. Carlyle,—Certainly I enjoy and am grateful for any letter of yours, after an original fashion: I seem to think that when once *I* write, *you* will begin to perceive how little you have got by writing—so I keep silence, like the man spoken to by mistake and over simply in the dark—that is the good policy. This time, however, I have waited till the trouble of getting lodgings was well over—as it now is, fortunately. We have found pretty much what we looked for —a place somewhat more out of the way than was desirable—but sunny, cheerful, airy and quiet. I observe you say nothing about returning in the Spring; but when that horrible "Eleven hours" have done their worst and been forgotten, won't you reconsider the matter? And if Mrs. Carlyle will so far trust me, and tell me point by point what you both require, it shall go hard but I content you in some sort. Do "try the luck of the third adventure"—as Falstaff did—an ominous co-incidence![1] As it is, we here have had all the good fortune, in your journey with us, and visits to us; the weather is admirable— what I should fancy you would pronounce the perfection of fresh warm clearness; and we get all that to ourselves too! Well—for Mazzini, I and my wife thank him very heartily: such a letter as you promise, will oblige us greatly, and I shall no doubt be able to find out, from people here, the best way of bringing it to bear with effect on the great person.[2] We heard quantities about her the other night— from what may possibly be an authentic source—how she has grown visibly aged of a sudden (like Mephistopheles at the Brocken when he says he finds people ripe for the last day), and is getting more resigned to it than she had expected, seeing that with youth go "a Hell of Passions"—(which is all she knows about it). Meanwhile, the next best thing to youth, and the Hell and so on, is found to be strenuous play-writing. She writes in the country and her friends rehearse, test effects, prophesy of hits or misses of the Paris auditory; whereat she takes heart and writes again, points this, blunts that: one might as well or better, try and make articles for Chapman's Review, certainly! I saw him in London by his desire, and he told me all about it;—how he had got in some measure rid of his *Lombago,* under which he must have been stiffened past even writhing. I conceive your kindness in pointing out a way to him, had I wanted it. I have just done the little thing I told you of—a mere Preface to some new letters of Shelley;[3] not admitting of much workmanship of any kind, if I had it to give. But I have put down a few thoughts that presented themselves—one or two, in respect of opinions of your own (I mean, that I was thinking of those opinions while I wrote). However it be done, it is what I was "up to," just now, and will soon be off my mind. I shall always hope—for a great incentive—to write my best *directly to you* some day. Will you remember me as kindly as you can to Mrs. Carlyle— whom, rather than any other woman in the world, I have always wished my wife to know—as she could tell you. She is grateful for your good words, and now can understand how I am, dear Mr. Carlyle,

Yours very faithfully,
R. BROWNING.

1851 : 6

To Sir Thomas Noon Talfourd

My dear Talfourd.

I received from London, I dare say a fortnight ago, an extract from the "Household Words"—a sonnet—with an intimation that *you* had written it. You will believe, that but for that intimation,—(which, indeed, amounted to an assurance) no amount of beauty and feeling in the verse would have justified me in attributing the authorship to such a source. It has been always the truest and deepest pride to me that you have given me, and kept me, a place in your kind esteem—this public appreciation is too much for me—but perhaps not for you, with whose character, so far as I have been privileged to know it, every kind of generosity finds itself in place. For my poor poetry—it has been the best I could do—it should have been far better to deserve your sympathy and recognition: what it may be, hereafter,—in whatever I may be able to effect yet—there is no saying: but it *has been* good for one of the best events of my life—it procured me the knowledge of you, the friendship with you—which would have well rewarded it if it had been infinitely better. Take my best thanks for all—and believe me ever,

> My dear Talfourd,
> Yours very gratefully and affectionately,
> ROBERT BROWNING.

Paris, Avenue des Champs Elysèes, 138.
Dec. 17. 1851.

1853 : 1

To John Kenyon

> Florence,
> Jan. 16. '53.

My dear Mr. Kenyon,

A courier leaves for London to-morrow or next day and I have leave to send a letter by him. What can I do better than write to you? I fear we must not hope for you at Florence now, with that mild winter in London which would seem to be phenomenal with its fruits, almonds in blossom, and the like, as the papers tell us duly. Here there has been *no* winter, instead of a mild one. I have just come in from an afternoon walk round the garden-walls from S. Miniato to Poggio Imp^le and felt as if May were set in. A letter from Rome (from Miss Blagden, you remember her?) speaks of the ruin of the wood-sellers, nobody having as yet needed a fire. Yet you might reach us, after all, might you not? Having other objects in travelling than simply to escape the bad weather only, be where you are best and happiest, now and ever. Well, I must tell you our news, where Ba left off. We thought it best to rest here for the cold months and go to Rome, say in March, and so we hope and mean to do. This dear old place made itself more agreeable to us than ever, and Ba, who had suffered from the journey, is got quite well,—well, to hearts' content, the cough entirely gone. *Thank you!* The letting our house was a good specula-tion, for though, through various blunders of our agent, it was not turned to the greatest advantage, yet on the whole we gain decidedly. Another time we should manage better. We found most of our old friends here, Kirkup[1] wonderfully well, and Powers[2] moving into a larger house, which he has earned, like the brave fellow he is. He is finishing a fine simple and heroic "Washington," and a charming *conceit* of a thing "California"—with an arch dubiety of mouth, sig-nificant of the trick she will play you if she can, having a rod of thorns which you don't see, as well as the golden one she tempts you with. You know poor Greenough's end, no doubt—most melancholy. I did not know that he had been actually deranged once before, and re-stored by the sea voyage, for they had sent him home. And here is his "Group" (which he left Florence to see placed properly) here at Leg-horn, two years after his departure, just where he saw it last.

We have made an interesting acquaintance in Tennyson's elder brother, Frederic, settled here with an Italian (Contadina) wife and family: He is very shy, and very full of qualities which make that all the greater shame. He seems to like us, too. We have also seen a little, and liked it too, of Mr. Lytton-Bulwer's son. We don't go out, how-ever, but live our old life. The boy gets the best little fellow in the world, he draws, reads and so on, but his loving little heart is worth all that and much more. He was a little unwell some time ago—caught the chicken-pox—but is quite well now.

I ought to tell you something of my Father's news, you bade me do so indeed. Everything has gone on without a hitch since we left Eng-land. Those people applied—*She,* to the Principal of the office, the Attorneys to the governor of the Bank, and more than once. They were answered briefly that the Bank knew nothing of my father's private business. Seeing the failure there, they have actually written to our own lawyer, who sends the letter to me, and here it is, to say that if we will pay *their costs* we need not pay the plaintiff's damages, she never having had any intention of claiming them! They have her in their power, of course. They add, that my father may return to his home forthwith, they having no intention whatever to molest him. "Springes to catch woodcocks!" My London informant who sends this precious letter (which begins with "It is our pleasing duty to become the medium of conveying a proposal") adds "I do not consider you are bound to make any sacrifice in favour of what really appears to me a shameful speculation, so it is useless to dwell upon the different points of the letter." I think so too, and shall not even answer it. They will just take their last revenge in an outlawry, which we must put up with, as with much worse. And meantime, to guard against any ill chance, I shall advise my father to send in his resignation, which, it has been communicated to him, the Bank will accept, and allow him to retain two thirds of his salary "with which they hope he may live comfortably abroad—very kind and handsome of them, certainly. And thus far ends, if God please, this strange and calamitous visitation which has grieved me as few things could. Sarianna writes cheerfully enough, however, of the Paris life. Ba and I had made some dear friends of Mr. and Mrs. Corkran;[3] they were lovers of Ba's verses and admirably kind people, and now all their kindness and comfort have gone where it is most needed—to my Father and Sarianna. Nothing could be desired better. In a month or two we shall all see our way clearer, and the worst is past now. I should add that my Father is well as ever,—of all his old spirits—strange, in one sense, not in another. He reads at the Library and draws at the Louvre, having got leave for both, goes book-hunting as of old, "shaping his old course in a country new," like Lear's Kent. My child sends him real letters, all his own, conception and execution alike, which gladden his heart and so, "*This, all!*" as the last letter sensibly ended. Mine ought to end, too. I know of no London news. I was fearing Forster might be ill again, but his name opportunely re-appears in the papers at Dickens' dinner, so all's well. Will you give my kindest remembrances to him? With forgiveness for not noticing a bit of a goodbye letter I wrote at going away. Miss Bayley does not write to Ba, I shall observe, our most affectionate regards to her. We had a not very comfortable letter from Mrs. Jameson,[4] after the one you forwarded; she seemed annoyed and overworked as usual. The Procters,[5] too, you will kindly take care that they don't forget us. I felt all those spark-like hours in London struck out of the black element I was beset with, all the brighter for it! But I need not say that, or more. I have tired you, dear Mr. Kenyon, but you will put up with it for the love's sake. Ba's truest love to you (with some impertinence muttered to effect, "ask if he calls that last, a letter," and about your sending her the "very parings of your nails" —which, in Chinese, would not be so unpoetical a thought. I, on the contrary, had rather you did not write, so long as you walk instead. I shall not let you off from taking that Bust, remember, which you will not like, Ba says. But she cannot know. I shall find some way of sending it, or Powers will help me. God bless you, dear Mr. Kenyon,

Yours wholly,
R. B.

1853 : 2

To Mrs. William Burnet Kinney[1]

Casa Tolomei, Bagni di Lucca
July 25. '53

My dear Mrs. Kinney,

We have been some little time in subsiding into our old lazy life in this new place—but a week is got thro', and I shall take a pleasant re-payment of sundry nothings in the way of work and business,—which seemed somethings at the time,—in writing as you bade me and, more-over, in hoping that something may come of it—for I can testify that this beautiful and joyous little place is looking its best,—very green, very cool, very picturesque or even more. There are the old magnifi-cent mountains and chestnut-woods, and great moonlights—won't you come and see?

If Mr. Kinney continues to recover health (as you shall make us very happy by assuring us) he shall direct me,—and "The Pelican," here, shall put you both in the coziest corner of his pouch. (Have you got to such touches of poetry in America, by the way, as to have an Inn style itself the "Pelican"? Here the thing is common-place. The landlord, it is taken for granted, tears up his very breast to feed his young,[2] his visitors—and, besides, has a good long *bill* at their service!)

I have read your verses with great interest and satisfaction that as "many waters cannot quench love," so, much Diplomacy and Court-practice need in no wise extinguish a firm and generous nature's feelings and impulses. As for your criticism, I take it thankfully from your hands—the "good nature" you appeal to, won't answer, because the business is not with *it*—What? Shall I be graced by not a few kind pats of encouragement on the cheek, and refuse to profit by the occasional lift of an admonitory finger? No, I shall mend my ways, I assure you, get as smooth as I can, and as plain as I can, and you shall re-criticise, if you will be so good, and take due credit to yourself for my improvement—which Ba (my wife) declares is manifest already. But what a pleasure it will be to talk over these matters under the chestnuts— will you not try to give it us? There are many Americans here—the best chances having befallen us, too, in the apparition of the Storys the day after our arrival. I shall leave my wife to speak for herself and only repeat very heartily and sincerely that we remember you too pleasantly not to hope for as much more of you as we *ought* to have had at Florence but for the untoward departure. With all kind regards to Mr. Kinney, pray believe me

Yours very faithfully,
ROBERT BROWNING.

1855 : 1

To DANTE G. ROSSETTI

102, Rue de Grenelle,
Paris,
October 29th, 1855.

My dear Rossetti,

I have taken you at your word—you will receive my portrait forthwith. You must put it in the sun, for I seem to fear it will come but blackly out of its three months' case-hardening. So it fares with Page's pictures for the most part; but they are like Flatman the Poet's famous "Kings" in a great line he wrote—"Kings do not die—they only disappear!" You must tell me your whole mind on its merits—I am anxious to have it—and more, to know what you think of Bailey's Poem,[1] and anybody else's Poem, and other delights—as promised— and as I hungrily expect.

We are in little, inconvenient rooms here, and I have been in continual hot water, the landlady, a "Baronne," profiting by the blunder of an overzealous friend, who took the apartments against my direct orders. But the water is getting tepid now, and we shall do well

enough in time, it is to be hoped. I supposed I should find myself in a
blessed quietude here after the London worry, but it's much such an
improvement as one specified in the case of a Beato my servant was
telling me, yesterday, he heard a sermon about, in Naples. The Beato
went into a swoon from sheer misery to begin with, and then "Riavu-
tosi un poco il saint' uomo—'Che ho visto tutt' intorno, fratelli miei?
Figuratevi! Otto cento mila Demoni!' "—That's nearly my case. The
first comfort came in the shape of a dear, too dear, and good letter
from Mr. Ruskin. He spoke befittingly of you in it, too. I have lain
perdu and seen nobody.

By way, let me tell you something. I perceive some blunders in my
poems,[2] which I shall not, I think, draw attention to, but quietly correct hereafter. But it happens unluckily that the worst of them occur
just in a thing I would have you like if it might be—so, please alter
the following in your copy, before you begin it, won't you?[3]

Vol. II.

Page 34, line 3, all their work is—their work is.
                 7, That a—*dele* That.
      35   4, here's its transit—then *sic tran.*
      36   3, Change the line to ("Earth here, rebuked by Olympus
                    there)"
      36, line 4, You grew—And grew.
      39   6, His face—Man's face.
                13, the Hopes—new hopes.
      40   6, Which if on the earth—dele *the.*
                 1, Change the line to: "Give these, I exhort you, their guer-
                    don and glory."
      44   11, For "Rot or are left to the mercies still," read "Their pic-
                    tures are left to the mercies still."
      46   11, For "But a kind of Witanagemot," read "But a kind of
                    sober Witanagemot."
                13, For "To ponder Freedom restored to Florence," read
                    "Shall ponder, once Freedom restored to Florence."
      47   12, For "Turning the Bell-tower's altaltissimo," read "And
                    turn the bell-tower's *alt* to *altissimo.*"
     188   18, one called—him called.
     189   3, one circumcised—and circumcised.
     231   4, with it—cried too.

I have left myself no room but to wish myself cordially kind remembrances to your Brother.

R. BROWNING.

1856 : 1

To Thomas Carlyle[1]

Paris, 3 Rue du Colisée. Jan. 23. '56.

My dear Mr Carlyle,

I know well, and too well, how nearly I am at the end of your allowance of six weeks for the verifications. I will try and say a word in excuse presently.

1st. The Marquis du Châtelet mentioned in D'Espagnui's Histoire du Maréchal de Saxe, under date 17th May, 1743, was Florent-Claude, M. du Châtelet, chevalier, and Seigneur de Cirey. Born at Namur, Apr. 7. 1695. Entered the 1st comp[y] des Mousquetaires du Roi 1712; made the campaigns of Landau and Fribourg; made Lieutenant dans le Régiment du Roi, 1714—Colonel dans celui de Hainaut, (infanterie) 1718—at the head of this he made the campaign of 1733—served the next year as Brigadier, and at the siege of Philipsburg. In 1738, was made Maréchal de Camp; and having served with much distinction in the auxiliary army sent to Bavaria, was made (in 1743) Grand-Cross, Commander of the Ordre de St. Louis: and Lieutenant General des armées du roi in 1744. After his return from Bavaria, he was employed in the army on the Rhine; and having succeeded his father in the employments of Grand-Bailli d'Auxois et de Sar-Louis and in the government of Sémur, he married, June 20th 1725, Gabrielle-Emilie de Breteuil, daughter of Nicolas, Baron de Preuilly, "Introducteur des ambassadeurs et Princes étrangers auprès du Roi"—and of Anne de Froulay, (all this on many authorities, but here extracted from the Dictionnaire de la Noblesse. Vol. 4. Paris, 1772). And she, of course, was the Marquise of Voltaire as you surmised, and as I verified in the books about him and her.

2nd. The "official Marquis de Breteuil" of the "Fastes" was—Francois Victor le Tonnelier de Breteuil, conseiller au parlement et commissaire aux Requêtes du Palais (in 1705)—Maitre des Requêtes, intendant de Limoges (1718)—prévot et maitre des cérémonies des ordres du roi (1712) and secretaire d'état ayant le department de la guerre (1723). He died 7th Jan. (not 1st) 1743, aged 57. He was only collaterally related to the House of Breteuil-Preuilly aforesaid. (Dictionnaire Généalogique, Héraldique, Chronologique, et Historique. Vol. 3. Paris, 1757.)

3rd. Daniel-Marie-Anne de Talleyrand-Périgord, Marquis de Talleyrand, comte de Grignoles, et de Mauriac, was born 1706. Blown up by an accident in the trenches at the siege of Tournay, May 9th, 1745. (The last Marquis de Biron had passed the night by his side on a bearskin and left him for a few minutes to give orders, when a common soldier, en nettoyant l'amorce de son fusil, blew up a barrel of powder, our Marquis, and eighty others. Maréchal Saxe *wept* at his fate, for a wonder, says the chronicler. He was father, by his second marriage, of Charles-Daniel, born 1734, whose second son was Charles-Maurice, born 1754, *our* Talleyrand. This is from the "Histoire généalogique et héraldique de Paris de France," &c. Vol. 8. Paris, 1827.

And now how I shall be punished for delaying to send this, if you get it too late or have (what is more likely) got it yourself with any trouble! When your letter arrived, we were in miserable lodgings through the blunder of a friend, really to my wife's danger: that is over now—my friend Milsand helped me to the Library of the Chamber of Peers—where the librarian Miller has been very kind—will you never try me again?

There was a precious word in your letter about one of my own things that went to my heart.[2] Now, have you understood me in another point? I was without the courage to send you the book—fearing the fate of Talleyrand's grandfather. I hold so to what kind feeling for me you express, and which I cannot have a right to doubt, therefore,—that it seemed foolish to hazard this by sending you poems to read you might like me none the better or somewhat the less for. But that fear seems stupid on reflection—for you have written, beside the word now, many words once on a time—the best I ever got for my poems. If you do really care to give me so much honor and pleasure, you will ask Chapman for the book and take it with many fears (more than hopes) but much gratitude. So that is said to your understanding.

We are well now, in a warm and snug little place, just turning out of the Champs-Elysées: my wife, who had been grievously affected by the abominable quarters our poor friend had insisted on our bearing with (only, we could not)—she is better again. Many interesting people are here and a few old acquaintances. Dickens, for one. We were rejoicing the other evening over Forster's good fortune,—from him, I have not heard. Shall I really hear from you, a sincere word such as you helped me with fifteen years ago and more? There are one or two misprints—easy to rectify, however. As I believe no man a real poet or genius of any sort who does not go on improving till eighty and over, I shall begin again and again as often as you set me right. Kindest remembrances to Mrs. Carlyle from us both—will you please give them? My wife's affectionate duty going to you, as it does, with that of

Yours ever faithfully,
ROBERT BROWNING.

1856 : 2

To Leigh Hunt[1]

39 Devonshire Place.
Oct. 3. '56.

My dear Mr. Hunt,

You see how unfortunate we have been; our stay in the country was prolonged till two days since by circumstances beyond our control. Are we necessarily to lose the delight of your visit? I know the weather is uncertain, the autumn advancing,—still I will not be so far wanting to ourselves as not just to say—[*would*] *could* you still give us that great and good evening that was to have been ours, we should be happy to your kind heart's content, I really believe, and moreover believe that you *will* give it us if you can. So my say is said.

I hope you received the new edition of my wife's Poems which I directed the Publishers to send you. "I" means always "we" in a letter of mine, my wife's most affectionate regards accompanying, in this instance, those of

Yours ever gratefully
ROBERT BROWNING.

Our stay here, I ought to mention, can hardly exceed a fortnight.

1857 : 1

To Sarianna Browning

[La Villa, Bagni di Lucca],
Thursday, October 1st, 1857

Dearest,

I feel quite uneasy at not hearing from you, having written three weeks ago. Can you have received that letter? I know I was long in arrear, but I always find you kinder and more considerate. I directed the letter to the Rue de Grenelle, though when you last wrote you were still at Dieppe. Perhaps *my* letter was lost, yet I think you would have written. Lytton went, as I said, a fortnight ago.

Dear little Peni became unwell this day fortnight, and has been ill in bed till half an hour ago ever since last Monday week, of gastric fever—very mild, never dangerous, but teazing. He is fast recovering and allowed to sit up to-day for two hours and eat some dinner—little enough—for the first time. He has been perfect, poor little dear, in all to be done or left undone. Ba is pretty well considering the worry. Wilson became ill—premature confinement was expected, but after lying a week in bed she got better, and left last Saturday for Florence. We got another, and very good maid, and alas! she too is laid up with cold and fever, but better, we believe.

We shall go to Florence the moment it is possible, in a week I hope, direct *there*. I do trust dear papa is not unwell, nor yourself. I write in a great hurry. Ba would write, but I won't lose another post, being sorry I waited till now.

All love to you. God bless you. Mrs. Jameson is here.

Ever yours affectionately,
R. BROWNING.

Peni is wonderfully well, and unreduced.

[Continued by Elizabeth Barrett Browning]

Dearest Sarianna,

Mrs. Jameson is here, but I must write a word lest you should think worse of our precious darling than the case is. God has been very merciful to us, and the fever was light—only you may understand what terrible apprehensions and anxiety we have suffered under. Think, too! Wilson forced to go!—all in tears, poor thing. The new maid is happily taken a fancy to at once by Peni, and proves most devoted. Then, by exposure at night, she too is struck down by fever. We have moved her upstairs, and the doctor says it is very slight. Still, we have another stranger. See what a complication. Peni's came on from over-fatigue one day. During the rains, after the heat of the summer, there are tendencies to such things, but Peni was so strong (my darling) we were foolhardy with him. *I* was that day, and let him play by the river after over-heating himself.

Oh, such a joy it is to see him up, looking quite himself. He complains of famine ravenously, poor child, yet he has been kept low. A little, little bit of bread, and a little, little bit of turkey he is to have to-day.

The English physician had gone to Florence—we had a strange Italian. But he has dealt well with the case. Poor Peni called him a "cruel man" for not letting him eat. Such a darling the child looks! Rather paler and thinner, but able to run even as he joyfully points out. We are anxious to get back to Florence, very. Do write. Why have you waited so? Give my love to the Corkrans. Oh, I am so sorry for them! Write. Robert stands behind, urging me to have done. Observe, this gastric fever is not contagious. But there have been more cases than usual this year, from the heat of the summer.

1857 : 2

To Leigh Hunt

Bagni di Lucca, Oct. 6.'57.

Dear Leigh Hunt—(It is hard to write, but you bade me do so: yet I had better say "Master Hunt," as they used to call Webster or Ford) a nine-months' silence after such a letter as yours—seems too strange even to you perhaps.—Do understand that you gave us more delight at once than we could bear,—that was the beginning of the waiting to recover spirit and try and do one's feeling a little less injustice: but soon followed unexpected sorrows, to us and to you,—and the expression of even gratitude grew hard again. Certainly all this while your letter has been laid before our very eyes, and we have waited for a brighter day than ever came till we left Florence, two months ago and more: then we brought it here to "answer" among the chestnut-trees: but immediately on our arrival, a friend[1] was attacked by fever, and we were kept in anxiety about him for six weeks; at last he recovered sufficiently to leave for Florence, and (just think) our little boy became ill, for the first time in his life, and gave us solicitude enough for a fortnight: it is nothing now that it is over,—he is going about now, almost as well as before; and we go away tomorrow, as I said— but I will try and get one, at least, of the joys I came to find here, and really write to you from this place, as I meant to do—"I"—you know it is my wife that I write for,—though you entangle and distract either of us by the reverberations (so to speak) of pleasures over and above the main pleasure you give us—I intend to say, that you praise that poem,[2] and mix it up with praise of her very self, and then give it to me, directly, and then give it to *her* with the pride you have just given me, and then it somehow comes back to me again increased so far,— till the effect is—just as you probably intended. I wish my wife may know you more—I wish you may see and know her more—but you cannot live by her eleven years, as I have done: or, yes, what cannot you do, being the man, the poet you are?—This last word, I dare think I have a right to say; I *have* always venerated you as a poet; I believe your poetry to be sure of its eventual reward: other people, not unlikely, may feel like me that there has been no need of getting into feverish haste to cry out on what it is: yet you, who write it, can leave it and look at other poetry, and speak so of it: how well of you!

I am still too near the production of "Aurora Leigh" to be quite able to see it all: my wife used to write it, and lay it down to hear our child spell, or when a visitor came—it was thrust under the cushion then. At Paris, a year ago last March, she gave me the first six books to read— I having never seen a line before,—she then wrote the rest, and transcribed them in London, where I read them also. I wish, in one sense, that I had written, and she had read it, so: I should like also to tell you that I never suspected the existence of those "Sonnets from the Portuguese" till three years after they were written: they were shown to me at this very place eight years ago, in consequence of some word of mine, just as they had been suppressed thro' some mistaken word: it was I who would not bear that sacrifice, and thought of the subterfuge of a name. I shall commend myself to you by telling you this— Indeed the proper acknowledgment of your letter seems to be that one should do something, not say something: if you were here, I might quite naturally begin repeating "Giaffar" or "Solomon" and the rest —You would see whether I was not capable of getting all the good out of your praise.

While I write, there is a strange thing that happened last night, impossible to get out of my thoughts. It may give you pain to tell you of it—yet, if with the pain, come triumphant memories and hopes, as I expect there will, you may choose the pain with them: what decides me to tell it, is that I heard you, years ago, allude to the circumstances of the destruction of a volume of "Lamia, Isabella" etc—*"to be restored to you yet"*—now you remember: also, I think of your putting my name near Shelley's in the end of your letter, where you say "since I lost Shelley." Is it not strange that I should have transcribed for the first time, last night, the "Indian Serenade" that, together with some verses of Metastasio accompanied *that Book?*—That I should have been reserved to tell the present possessor[3] of them—to whom they were given by Capt. Roberts—*what* the poem *was* and *that it had been* published!—It is preserved religiously—but the characters are all but illegible—and I needed a good magnifying-glass to be quite sure of such of them as remain—the end is that I have rescued three or four variations in the reading of that divine little poem, as one reads it, at least, in the "Posthumous Poems"—It is headed "The Indian Sere-nade"—(not "Lines to an Indian Air"). In the first stanza the seventh line is "Hath led me": in the second, the third line is "And the cham-pak's odours fail"—and the eighth, "Oh! Beloved as thou art!"—In the last stanza, the seventh line runs "Oh, press it to thine own again." Are not all these better readings? (even to the "Hath" for "Has") Then, I give them you as you gave us Milton's hair.[4] If I have mis-taken in telling you, you will understand and forgive.

I think I will ask my wife to say a word or two: so I shall be sure that you forgive. First I will speak about what she will be little likely to allude to—that act of Mr Kenyon to which you refer.[5] The notice in the newspapers was altogether a misconception of his intentions— which had nothing to do with literature: probably you may have heard a truer account since then. Your appreciation of him is just and right. I wish he had known you, face to face, as he knew others—but the mention of any name in the will executed a few days before his death gives very little indication of the degree of his feeling for its owner, do believe. Now let my wife say the remainder. All I have wished to do,—know how little likely it was that I should succeed in that,—was to assure you of my pride and affectionate gratitude.

God bless you ever.
R B.

[*Continued by Elizabeth Barrett Browning*]

Dear friend I will say—for I feel it must be something as good as friendship that can forgive and understand this silence, so much like the veriest human kind of ingratitude. When I look back and think— all this time after that letter, . . and not a sign made, . . I wonder. Yet if you knew!—First of all we were silent because we waited for information which you seemed to desire—about that will: and we waited long for that. Then there were sadder reasons—Poor 'Aurora' that you were so more than kind to (oh, how can I thank you?) has been steeped in tears, and some of them of a very bitter sort. Your letter was addressed to my husband, . . you knowing by your delicate true instinct, . . where your praise would give most pleasure—but I believe Robert had not the heart to write when he felt that I should not have the spirits to add a word in the proper key. When we came here from Florence a few months ago to get repose and cheerfulness from a sight of the mountains, we said to ourselves that we would speak to you at ease—instead of which the word was taken from our mouth, and we have done little but sit by sick beds and meditate on gastric fevers. So disturbed we have been—so sad! Our darling precious child the last victim. To see him lying still on his golden curls, with cheeks too scarlet to suit the poor patient eyes:—looking so frightfully like an angel! It was very hard. But this is over, I do thank God,—and we are on the point of carrying back our treasure with us to Florence tomorrow, quite recovered, if a little thinner and weaker, and the young voice as merry as ever. You are aware that that child I am more proud of than twenty "Auroras," even after Leigh Hunt has praised them. He is eight years old—has never been *"crammed,"* —but reads English, Italian, French, German . . and plays the piano —then, is the sweetest child! sweeter than he looks. When he was ill he said to me . . "You pet! don't be unhappy about *me*—Think it's a boy in the street, and be a little sorry, but not unhappy!" Who could not be unhappy, I wonder.

I never saw your book called the "Religion of the heart"—it's the only book of yours I never saw; and I mean to wipe out that reproach on the soonest day possible. I receive more dogmas perhaps (my 'perhaps' being in the dark rather) than you do. I believe in the divinity of Jesus Christ in the intensest sense—that he was God absolutely. But for the rest, I am very unorthodox—about the spirit, the flesh, and the devil—and if you would not let me sit by you, a great many churchmen wouldn't. In fact the churches do all of them, as at present constituted, seem too narrow and low to hold true Christianity in its proximate developments. I, at least, cannot help believing them so.

My dear friend, can we dare, after our sins against you, . . can we dare . . *wish* for a letter from you sometimes? Ask, we dare not. May God bless you. Even if you had not praised me and made me so grateful, I should be grateful to you for three things . . for your poetry (that first!) then for Milton's hair, and then for the memory I have of our visit to you when you sate in that chair and spoke so mildly and deeply at once.

Let me be ever
affectionately yours
ELIZABETH BARRETT BROWNING.

1858 : 1

To Miss Isabella Blagden

Le Hâvre, Sept. 4. '58.

Dearest Isa,

So many thanks for your kind and dear letters—two,—indeed three, —for the packet addressed to us "poste restante" was delayed some time. Ba will tell you how busy we have been in doing the hospitable to her brothers and sisters—and then Milsand came from Dijon and spent ten days with us—he could stay no longer being forced to return to his sick mother—but they were very precious days. What is to say about such a dull life as this daily one of ours? I go mechanically out and in and get a day through—whereof not ten minutes have been my own—so much for your "quantities of writing" (in expectation) —I began pretty zealously—but it's of no use now: nor will the world very greatly care. Your letters are the most striking events that befall us, I really believe: why have you been so unwell?—you said nothing about it till this last letter came: are you at Leghorn indeed? I hope so,—the sea being an approved remedy for your illnesses, I remember: pray, of all things, be well and cheerful when we return—and that will be early in October, I hope and pray. We stay here till the 20ᵗʰ but the strange weather,—now cold, now hot, never pleasant,—renders it impossible to calculate on going sooner or later.

You seem to have been passing your time pleasantly,—at least with amusing people: I wonder, did you see Landor that evening? What a bombardment of indignant articles and fusillade of scandalized paragraphs he is enduring just now! I feel more grieved about it all than I choose to tell you. Such writing is wholly indefensible on his part, no doubt: and he is no more in his dotage than you or I—but it pricks the nerve of one to feel that in some quite inexplicable way, the great old man was foolish enough to believe he did God service in so writing: I can't imagine how he fails to see the cowardice in the act of publication: if he thinks these abominations of anybody, why not be content to stand alone in his belief—why call on us all to help him with our opinion and sympathy?—and yet, as a coward he certainly is *not*—one ends as one begins—by repeating . . inexplicable. However, I—for one—am profoundly grateful to the author of the "Conversations" and would not abuse him as all these wretched catch-penny "Presses" "John Bulls," and the like, do just now—if he had libelled *me*.[1] Have you heard anything more of Hatty?[2] Do the Story's give

sign of life? Any more news of Frederic Tennyson? How is Major
Gregorie? Do you still sit round a table and see who will turn it least
apparently? And you have patience still to hear the French Spirits
speak thro' a young Lady, while the Flemish spirits stick in her
throat? How mournful and old-fashioned it all sounds to me here at
this living and veracious Hâvre! I have only left myself room to thank
you again, dearest Isa, and bid you once again take all care of yourself.

Yours aff^y
R B.

1859 : 1

To Miss Isabella Blagden

Siena, Aug. 11. '59.

Dearest Isa,

Both your letters, the thick no earlier than the thin one, reached me
this morning: I make haste to send you Lytton's letters:[1] they were
written nearly two months ago in consequence of our notice of his
Poems. I never could make out why he did not forthwith despatch
epistles to all three of us—and, you see, he really did, whatever has
been the reason of the delay in getting them. There is nothing to answer in our share of his labours, but you will satisfy him as your good
heart prompts you. You will, I hope, have just received Ba's little note
sent this morning the first thing.[2] She continues better,—the cough
does almost cease to torment her, but she remains very weak: the intense heat does not help the case. I may say, however, that she im-
proves quite as much as could be expected in the time. We get plenty
of fresh wind, spite of the heat, and are no doubt well off here: Ba has
seen no one, as yet. Mr Landor is established close at hand. I see him
every now and then. I receive satisfactory letters from Forster and L's
niece[3] in England. I believe I am to have the poor dear old man per-
manently "added to my portion" as the Methodists phrase it. *You* do
the sister-of-charity business generally—and I am bound to act my
best on "Mr Browning's First and Only Appearance in that Character, at Particular Request,"—I hope I may add, "The Performance
being exclusively for the Benefit of a distinguished Member of the
Company"—. His son has sent in the *"account"*—Oh! Kirkup who
transmits it to me uses sundry flowers of language about it, whereof
the one that best suits your *bouquet* is that "Such a beastly mess he

never saw!"—I had also a letter this morning from Annette[4]—she is at "Stone House, Broadstairs"—which I mention because she says you do not write: yet you *did*, I feel sure. She says nothing about her health, but is going to Scotland and Ireland. Mrs Bracken is in London and Mrs Mackenzie still in Rome. Give my kindest regard to Dr Grisanowski—I mean to write in reply to his note—only to-day I have been uninterruptedly busy for I don't know how many hours: Ba's true thanks accompany mine: and her love goes to you also with that of yours ever affectionately

R BROWNING.

Ba's love and mine to Miss Field: as she collects autographs give her the note of L. to me.

1859 : 2

To Miss Isabella Blagden

Foligno, Nov. 30. '59.

Dearest Isa,

Here we are, at the end of our third days' journey, in capital condition—all having gone unexceptionably with us hitherto—indeed, beyond my best hopes. The weather has been just what we desired, rather than expected—we keep the carriage windows open, and Ba never coughs nor appears to suffer. The stages have been easy and yet we get along quite as fast as we wish—having reached this place a day earlier than we did last year. On Monday we rested at Incisa and slept at Poggiobagnoli: on Tuesday, at Camuscia and Passignano: to-day, at Perugia and this Foligno. To-morrow night, we shall reach Terni, I suppose. I enjoy the journey much—so evident is the advantage to Ba, were it merely these long doses of fresh open air which she would have made no effort to swallow in Florence. Pen. is quite well—and the poney's performances are really admirable—he keeps the pace of the other horses perfectly, and comes in fresh as at starting and without having turned a hair. Of course Ba is tired enough on her arrival at the Inns after a day's jolting: she takes tea and goes to bed at once—but one expects *that,* and is happy it is no worse.

Now, dearest Isa, why did you behave so foolishly and Isa-like as to sacrifice yourself to that extent with giving us (or Ba) those expensive books, those poems of Victor Hugo?—I have no heart, nor energy, however, to blame you as you deserve: let Ba do justice on you when she writes from Rome—for my part, I read one volume on Monday and the next on Tuesday and have satisfied my appetite. A few of the poems are very fine; many, indeed all, are thickly spiced with good things; but, except in two or three transcendent instances, he gives you a *pan-forte* for the sacramental wafer—(to do a bit of Hugo myself!) The first volume is by far the better: the latter half of the second being bad, indeed—sometimes outrageously so. The most absurd thing, however, is the magniloquent preface—all the vast plan that was in the poet's mind, and all his humility about the little of it he has been able to accomplish, and all his modest confidence in the efficaciousness of that little—and the whole, one big bubble of mere breath which a touch breaks—in turning over the leaves of the book itself: for any of his former collections of miscellaneous poetry would just as exactly answer to this particular plan as the present. But he can't let truth be truth, or a number of remarkable poetical pieces speak for themselves, without assuring you that he meant them to join Man to God, with the like pleasant practicabilities.

Dear Isa—I had no time to get the cigars: but it is little matter—I will find somebody to bring them. Ba has been asleep, I hope, this long while: but I know, as you know, that her truest love and thanks go with mine to you. Take care of yourself, get ready to follow us, write meanwhile, keep an eye on Mr Landor, and shut the other on all but the real affection of

Yours ever
R Browning.

1860 : 1

To Thomas Woolner

Florence, June 15, '60

Dear Woolner,

I happen to have an occasion of sending to England. I was your debtor for a long, kind—most welcome letter, introducing Mr. Wilson to us. I don't write often, and may easily do myself great injustice—but not, I really think, in your mind—so fresh is its kindness in my memory. I follow your career with true delight, as I see one work succeed another in the registry of the newspapers—but I need no assurance of your genius.

PEN AND THE PONY

Will you like to have, for our sakes, these photographs, just done in Rome? The horseman is Pen on his pony, from a capital little painting by Hamilton Wild, an American artist of achievement and promise besides.

We have just returned from Rome—and go presently to Siena for the hot months. Anything directed *here* will reach us—who knows but you may good naturedly incline to write? There is no England for us this year—but next year, if all goes as we hope, you will see us again. Meantime be sure of the true regard of my wife and of

Yours most sincerely ever
ROBERT BROWNING

You will find the photographs left for you at Chapman's, 193 Piccadilly.

1860 : 2

To HENRY FOTHERGILL CHORLEY[1]

[1860]

You will have read my wife's letter, dear Chorley. I know she feels gratified and honoured, as she tried to say—and you must understand that I take that feeling of hers, and add others of my own to it —"thank you most truly." I agree, too, in the main, with her estimate of the book,[2] though I should be inclined to dwell more on the artistic merits (great they are) of the characters, and agree to take more for granted in the pre-supposing a sufficient cause for action of some sort, of which you, in the present case, only choose to consider the irregular and blamable examples. Still, I wish you had given satisfaction on this point to everybody by a paragraph, no longer, of necessity, than a pregnant one I admired in "Pomfret," which disposed of the previous question of the right or wrong doctrine, and then explained that the story would only deal with conscientiousness and its results, upon any conviction whatever, so long as it was honest. After that admission in this case of the existence of a great cause requiring great sacrifices, I should go on to enjoy the portraiture of the false, cowardly, or foolish instruments, self-elected or ill-selected, just as one enjoys the castigation of Sir Samuel Luke, 'that Mameluke,' and does not cry out against the outrage to Milton or Vane. I don't think it would be hard to prove this, by accepting for a moment all your characters as samples

of the whole body of professing patriotism; abolishing them accordingly with hearty good will, and then *'beginning over again,'* by dropping you into the middle of an Italian province, suffering, as you
would see; and bidding you, supposed an Italian born, set about
remedying what you saw, as your conscience should instigate, and
with the best means your intelligence could suggest. Here is on the
table, for instance, an extract from the documents now publishing at
Bologna in exemplification of the Pope's rule in Romagna; the first
three letters, declaring the simple state of things, written by those who,
having caused it, are not interested in understanding it, say—that of
Cardinal Massimo, the legate of Ravenna, that *"tolti i vecchi, le donne,
e i fanciulli, il resto della popolazione dai 18 anni in sopra, meno po-
chissimi spauriti legittimisti, è tutto per massima ostile al Governo"*;
for which state of things he simply recommends *"polizia vigile,
giustizia esecutiva rapida, armata, sicura."* The letter of the Governor
of Rome, Marini (now Cardinal) replies to this that *"il quadro nero
di quella provincia è pur troppo naturale, per le precedenti cospiranti
notizie e per la perspicaccia del descrittore"*; and the last letter is from
Antonelli himself, complaining bitterly that, after a month's quiet
occupation of Bologna by the Austrians, only one citizen had as yet
"fatto atto di ossequio a Sua Santità" by a letter to the Pope at Portici.
Here you have the universal grievance: protest against it in any degree, take the poorest means to make your protest effective, and help
the whole population to a voice, if not a blow, and you begin Roccabellaism; better than he, because you *are* better in head and heart; but
when he, or the like of him, begins to imitate you *badly,* and the rest
to simulate you both for worse purposes, all I ask is, don't let *yourself*
be blamed; don't condemn all heroes because they breed *faquins!*
Even these last do call attention to the corrupt carcass, though they
feed on the same; and because of all the last ten years' Roccabellaism,
comes this day of the Congress's judgment, at worst, or a continuance
and extension of the present state of things, which would be best of all.
Archbishop Cullen gets up and declares that the Pope's subjects love
him of all loves, and that nobody but Sir Eardley Wilmot says otherwise; and what would disprove this had the Roccabellas been silent
some ten years? Even loud talking pulls down a snow-mountain on
people's heads, in default of more active measures; and somehow or
other, it does seem rolling down at last. God speed it!

I hope you will write another novel, and manage it more dexter-
ously than the booksellers seem to have done in this case. I never see
you advertised, nor, consequently (I suppose), noticed; and your

book just wants that only to succeed. What a notice was that in the "Athenaeum"! Your self-abnegation is wrong in the very interests of the journal; for if a writer, doing deliberately his best, deserves such a comment and no more, what would his weekly thoughts and fancies deserve in the way of paragraph-room? I expect you will analyse a brace of novels at adequate length, for many a week to come, before you stop the way with somebody else's "Roccabella." These are poorer considerations to *you,* however, than to your friends. And we two here, are, as of old, your fast friends, dear Chorley. I have got stiff at a distance with daily nothings to do and chronicle (in head at least), and my words do not fly out as promptly as I could wish and as once may have been the case; but I know what I know, and remember all your kindness to us both. You are often in our mouths, generally in our thoughts, always in our hearts. God bless you!

Yours affectionately ever,
R. BROWNING.

1861 : 1

To the Storys

Florence, June 13, '61

Dear Friends,—are you really at Leghorn? I had such a fancy that you would be detained longer than you hoped, as to feel it useless writing; but I hear you must be really arrived now,—and how glad we are—Our own journey was prosperous enough, with favorable weather. We rested a day at Siena and got in tolerable plight to Florence on the Wednesday evening—before the saddest of all mornings! My wife was thoroughly tired, of course,—has not attempted to leave the house since,—but is regaining strength now. Our journey to France would be absurd and is given up—I have no notion where we shall choose to spend the warm months. I saw Alberti at Florence and Mencini also—as surmised, both the Villas are perfectly at our disposal and are likely to continue so—I can hear of nobody intending to molest us—what do you say? Florence is empty of stranger-folk, we are absolutely quiet from morning to night.

Did I overwhelm you with commissions that day of our departure? Whatever you found intolerable, I do trust you threw over, in pure kindness to us.

And the apartment? Have you heard anything more from agent or principal? No word has reached me, you may be sure; we are both of us anxious to know.

We found Mr. Landor very well and rationally disposed,—looking, as you may imagine, without a lock of hair or tuft of beard! He wished to look "younger," say some—"cleaner" suggest others. He was glad to hear what news I could give him about you all. And now, —what news do you give us? How is Mrs. Story,—relieved from those vile headaches which seemed as if they would never go, those last days of our stay in Rome? And how are you, dear Story, who were wanting change, we fancied, after all the great doings of the year? And Edie and the Boys,—tell us they are well as soon as you can. Only to be at Leghorn! But for how long,—and what is to be done next? Can we help you in any poor way here in Florence? Ba will put in a word for herself—and I shall then begin calculating post arrivals and looking—so eagerly—for more than a word from you. All love to you all from

Yours affectionately ever,
ROBERT BROWNING.

[Continued by Elizabeth Barrett Browning]

Ba can only write a word—She has not the heart—in the face of this great calamity[1]—what a return to Florence!—I have felt beaten and bruised ever since—though the banners are all out this morning for the as-good-as-official "recognition of Italy"—but there's a crepe on the flag, and the joy is as flowers on graves—May God save Italy without his angels.

I sent about the corset, dear Evelyn, but the business takes time and is not finished—

When shall we see you?—Peni talks much of writing to Edie—

Your affectionate E B B

1861 : 2

TO SARIANNA BROWNING

Sunday, June 30, '61

Dearest, I know I have shocked you deeply, and perhaps more than was need—but you must forgive me and consider the need of doing something at once, as the news might have reached you even more

ELIZABETH BARRETT BROWNING
AND HER SON

ROME, 1860

abruptly,—and my own stupid state of mind yesterday. I can't even yet say of myself whether I was surprised or not, by this calamity; there is such a balance of reasons for fear, reasons for reassurance as they seemed then) that I don't know what I feel nor felt. She had been gravely affected by a series of misfortunes moral and physical,—or united, as they always were. The Villafranca Peace and the illness with it thro' the summer at Siena the year before last,—last year's still worse trial for six month's together, the daily waiting for news from Henrietta and the end—(stopping as it did all chance of good and reparation from the summer) rendered her weaker—weaker—she did *nothing* at Rome, took some three or four little drives, never walked two paces out of the room so, could not but be in a worse state to meet an illness: yet, on the other hand, her cheerfulness, and the quick succeeding of good and quiet looks to the suffering, and the quiet of the last six months, made everyone say "how wonderfully she recovers,—she will soon be strong again, another *quiet* summer and *then,"* &c., &c. Also her own impressions were in furtherance of this hope— and when I determined to forego the journey to Paris, in opposition to her expressed wishes, I not only knew but got her to confess candidly that for *herself* the reprieve from going and the trials it would entail on her would be an inestimable advantage—only, "still," "for my sake," &c., she would run the risk—*I* would not, however. We travelled, as I have told you, easily and with as little fatigue as possible, and on reaching here I let her repose at will, not asking her to go out, but take the air and exercise of the large rooms to begin with. She saw no one, two or three friends at most, had no one to tea (except when intimates looked in once or twice) and began to look well, everybody said. But the weather was suffocatingly hot, and she said to me—"My cough has got well at once, as is always the way in such weather, but, curiously, it begins to affect me, as usual"—I said—"Let us *go* at once"—we talked of places, the choice being with respect to her different requirements—when last Thursday week it seems that, while I was away at the newsroom, Miss Blagden came—say at six or seven in the evening: the windows which had been closely shut all day (as the only way of excluding the burning external air, were opened to the ground to admit the breeze which usually springs up after such days, and she placed her chair, I am told, in the doorway, between cross-draughts of many windows—all the rooms opening into each other,—whereupon Isa B. remonstrated—but Ba said "Oh, the cushion at the back of the chair prevents my suffering." It was her constant way, besides. I came in and we had tea—and then she remarked "I think I have a sore throat." Next day was past just as usual, only she told me she had a cold: at night she coughed much and sate up, restlessly, a good deal—and next morning took two Cooper's pills, I afterwards heard, with a view to staving off the attack she felt imminent—still, nothing happened unusual in the day—but toward night she felt so oppressed that she said, "I think you shall go and get me a blister and a little Ipecacuanha wine, to relieve the oppression: I find the medicine has acted inordinately,—she rarely had recourse to it, but had taken this dose before with benefit—this time, the effects were beyond her expectation. I ran (at 10 p.m.) to the Chemist's, got and applied the blister, and administered the wine —but she seemed little relieved till at 1 o'clock about or later she began to suffer distressingly from the accumulation of phlegm, which she had no power to cough up: I left her with Annunziata, dressed and knocked up (with difficulty) Dr. Wilson, a physician of great repute here, and specially conversant in maladies of the chest: he followed with me—and we found her worse, laboring most distressingly and ineffectually: Wilson prescribed promptly—got two prescriptions made up by two chymists (our porter and I got them) put a sinapism to breast and back, and hot water with mustard to the feet. For a long while she continued unrelieved—he remained till nearly *five*.—at last she recovered and we hoped all was over—but this was the second night she had passed in violent exertion without a minute's sleep. From this time things went on thus,—the symptoms were said to be always "a little better"—but Wilson examined carefully and reported, with a very serious face, that one lung was condensed (the right) and that he suspected an abscess in it—but he was aware of her long previous experience of the possibility of making shift with damaged lungs, and could not say how it might be—"it would require a long time to get well." I told part of this to Ba who repeatedly answered "It is the old story—they don't know my case—I have been tapped and sounded so, and condemned so, repeatedly: this time it is said the right is the affected lung while the left is free—Dr. Chambers said just the contrary. This is only one of my old attacks. I know all about it and I shall get better"—"It was not so bad an attack as that of two years ago," and so she continued: every day I carried her into the drawing-room where she sate only in her nightgown in her own chair, for the airiness of the room. She read the newspapers, a little—saw nobody of course—going to bed about seven; I sate up most nights,—lay down by her only once, I think, or twice at most, when I was up so often that I discontinued it, which she seemed not to notice

—for we brought a small bed into the drawingroom and placed her in it—and she began to doze very much, restlessly, and seemed unaware I was not in bed on a sopha behind: from the first the prescription was "Nourishment, even wine, a little, often if in small quantities." But Ba never could or would try to take solid nourishment: she had strong brodo (clear soup) but would take nothing else. So we went on, "rather better—but still with the unfavourable symptoms"—was I told twice a day. She was cheerful as ever, with voice all but extinct—still, "it would be nothing" she repeated. On Thursday night we tried asses' milk, with success—"had a better night decidedly"—always much expectoration however, and her feet swelled a little. I let Isa Blagden come and kiss her—she whispered "I am decidedly better"—and gave that impression to Isa. On Friday she had asses milk, broth twice, some bread and butter: we talked about our plans—about the house, Casa Guidi, which had suddenly grown distasteful to both of us, noisy, hot, close—poor place we had liked so for fourteen years! I said "it would be best to take a Villa—you decide on Rome for the winter, and properly,—what good of coming in the summer to a town house you cannot stay in?" She said "Ah, but I can't leave Florence, I like Florence,—you would like to establish ourselves in Rome." I said—no, there's Villa Niccolini, for instance—that would just suit." She said "that would suit—try, enquire"—and after seemed so interested about it, that I said "There's no hurry,—we can get in there at once if you like—and it will be just as cool as Siena, with the convenience of being near the city." "Oh" she said—"that's not it"— we must change the air now, that is my one chance,—I meant, that if you take it for three years you can send up our furniture and we can enter at once in it when we return next Spring." I observed a tendency to light headedness in all this—as she did—complaining of it to the doctor, and telling me how she had strange thoughts, about the windows, which "seemed to be hung in the Hungarian colours"—And she smiled to Isa Blagden at eight on Friday, as she took the glass, "Oh, I not only have asses' milk but asses' thoughts—I am so troubled with silly politics and nonsense." Isa told her something she had heard about the politics of Ricasoli which interested her so much that I interposed—"No talking, come, go Isa"—and I pushed her out—but Isa says that while my back was turned for a moment to pour out some medicine she whispered "Did you say Ricasoli said his politics were identical with those of Cavour, only they took different views of the best way of carrying them out?"—Yes—"Ah, so I thought." Isa left convinced she was better,—the doctor came—"perhaps a little better."

We talked over her aversion to food. I caused to be made a very strong fowl-jelly—placed in ice in readiness—and then asked if she would not try it during the night—"no"—I did not know how little good it would do—the weakness came from other causes, and *these* were important—the other could be easily got rid of. I sat by her at night—she coughed little, took the emulgent duly, and another medicine, but dozed constantly: if I spoke she looked, knew me—smiled, said she was better, and relapsed. I continued this till past three in the morning, when the dozing made me very uneasy. She said "You did right not to wait—what a fine steamer—how comfortable! I called Annunziata, bade her get hot water, as the Doctor had done, and sent the porter for himself. I bade her sit up for the water—she did with little help—smiling letting us act, and repeating "Well, you do make an exaggerated case of it!"—"My hands too" she said and put them in another basin. I said you know me? "My Robert—my heavens, my beloved—kissing me (but I can't tell you) she said "Our lives are held by God." I asked, "will you take jelly for my sake?" "Yes." I brought a saucerful and fed it by spoonfuls into her mouth. I then brought a second, and poured some into a glass—she took all. She put her arms round me "God bless you" repeatedly—kissing me with such vehemence that when I laid her down she continued to kiss the air with her lips, and several times raised her own hand and kissed them; I said "Are you comfortable?" "Beautiful." I only put in a thing or two out of the many in my heart of hearts. Then she motioned to have her hands *sponged*—some of the jelly annoying her—this was done, and she began to sleep again—the *last*, . . I saw. I felt she must be raised, took her in my arms—I felt the struggle to cough begin, and end unavailingly—no pain, no sigh,—only a quiet *sight*—her head fell on me. I thought she might have fainted—but presently there was the least knitting of the brows—and A. cried *"Quest' anima benedetta é passata!"* It was so. She is with God, who takes from me the life of my life in one sense,—not so, in the truest. My life is fixed and sure now. I shall live out the remainder in her direct influence, endeavoring to complete mine, miserably imperfect now, but so as to take the good she was meant to give me. I go away from Italy at once, having no longer any business there. I have our child about whom I shall exclusively employ myself, doing her part by him. I shall live in the presence of her, in every sense, I hope and believe—so that so far my loss is not *irreparable*—but the future is nothing to me now, except inasmuch as it confirms and realizes the past. I cannot plan now, or at least talk about plans—but I shall leave Italy at once, only staying to take away the necessity of a return, for years at least. Pen has been perfect to me: he sate all yesterday with his arms round me; said things like her to me. I shall try and work hard, educate him, and live worthy of my past fifteen years' happiness. I do not feel paroxysms of grief—but as if the very blessing, she died giving me, insensible to all beside, had begun to work already. She will be buried tomorrow. Several times in writing this I have for a moment referred in my mind to her—"I will ask Ba about that." The grief of everybody is sincere, I am told. Everybody is kind in offers of help—all is done for me that can be; and it is not a little just now. Isa came at the early morning and stayed till night, taking away Pen. I shall now go in and sit with herself—my Ba, forever. The service will be that of the Ch. of En., that I may hear those only words at the beginning. Bless you both, dearest papa and sis. I will write after tomorrow. Don't be in any concern for me, I have some of her strength, really, added to mine. Love to dear Milsand.

Ever your own
R BROWNING.

How she looks now—how perfectly beautiful!

1861 : 3

To W. C. MACREADY

Florence, July 18, '61.

Why should I *not* have expected a letter from you, my very dear friend, or any kindness it might be in your power to render me? I thank you from my heart for your goodness and I lay there what you say—with many a precious memory of you and yours. Do not imagine that I am prostrated by this calamity—I have much or everything to do as directly in my wife's interest as if she were enjoining it on me when we talked over our plans the last evening of all. The greatest comfort I have, and that which in its degree I try to give those who loved her, is that she had so little physical pain as to [be] confident up to the end that there was nothing to distinguish this from so many previous attacks and that she should presently recover and go away with me for the summer—and absolutely no touch of what would have been anguish indeed to her, the knowledge of parting from us. She was smiling at my "exaggerating the case" a few minutes before the end. I dare believe (from much I cannot write) that God did really take her to himself without even the momentary awe of a warning—while, by some inexplicable way, I was permitted to lose nothing through her ignorance that she was about to leave me.

I shall go to Paris now, to England eventually—Italy is done with for many a year. I shall certainly see you one day—shall I not? Wherever you may be, God bless you! I had always intended to write a friend's word to you on your marriage,[1]—only to say what you can well imagine, to be sure—will you help me with Mrs Macready and assure her of my best congratulations and wishes? My boy, you will like to know, is not suffering in health, and is behaving to me in something like his mother's old spirit.

Ever yours affectionately and gratefully,

ROBERT BROWNING.

1861 : 4

To Miss Euphrasia Fanny Haworth

Florence, July 20. '61.

My dear friend, I well know you feel as you say, for her once and for me now. Isa Blagden, perfect in all kindness to me, will have told you something perhaps—and one day I shall see you and be able to tell you myself as much as I can. The main comfort is that she suffered very little pain, none beside that ordinarily attending the simple attacks of cold and cough she was subject to, had no presentiment of the result whatever, and was consequently spared the misery of knowing she was about to leave us: she was smilingly assuring me she was "better," "quite comfortable—if I would but come to bed—" to within a few minutes of the last. I think I foreboded evil even at Rome, certainly from the beginning of the week's illness—but when I reasoned about it, there was no justifying fear: she said on the last evening "It is merely the old attack, nor so severe a one as that of two years ago—there is no doubt I shall soon recover"—And we talked over plans for the summer and next year. I sent the servants away and her maid to bed—so little reason for disquietude did there seem. Thro' the night she slept heavily, and brokenly—that was the bad sign. But then she would sit up, take her medicine, say unrepeatable things to me and sleep again. At four o'clock there were symptoms that alarmed me,—I called the maid and sent for the Doctor.—She smiled as I proposed to bathe her feet "Well, you *are* making an exaggerated case of it!" Then came what my heart will keep till I see her and longer—the most perfect expression of her love to me within my whole knowledge of her—always smilingly, happily, and with a face like a girl's—and in a few minutes she died in my arms, her head on my cheek. These incidents so sustain me that I tell them to her beloved ones as their right: there was no lingering, nor acute pain, nor consciousness of separation, but God took her to himself as you would lift a sleeping child from a dark, uneasy bed into your arms and the light. Thank God. Annunziata thought by her earnest ways with me, happy and smiling as they were, that she must have been aware of our parting's approach—but she was quite conscious, had words at command, and yet did not even speak of Peni who was in the next room. Her last word was—when I asked "How do you feel?"—*"Beautiful."*

You know I have her dearest interest to attend to *at once*—her child to care for, educate, establish properly—and my own life to fulfil as properly,—all, just as she would require were she here. I shall leave Italy altogether for years—go to London for a few days talk with Arabel[1]—then go to my father, and begin to try leisurely what will be the best for Peni—but no more "housekeeping" for me, even with my family. I shall grow, still, I hope—but my root is taken, remains.

I know you always loved her, and me too in my degree. Forgive my old peevish ways, which came from being too rich,—I shall trouble nobody with them now—but always be grateful to those who loved her—and that, I repeat, *you* did.

She was, is, lamented with extraordinary demonstrations if one consider it: the Italians seem to have understood her by an instinct. I have received strange kindness from everybody. Pen is very well, very dear and good, anxious to "comfort me" as he calls it. He can't know his loss yet. After years, his will be more than mine, he will want what he never had—that is, for the time when he could be helped by her wisdom, and genius and piety: I *have* had everything, and shall not forget.

God bless you, dear friend: I believe I set out in a week: Isa goes with me,—dear, true heart. You, too, would do what you could for us were you here and your assistance needful. A letter from you came a day or two before the end—she made me enquire about the "Frescobaldi Palace" for you,—Isa wrote to you in consequence. I shall be heard of at 151. Rue de Grenelle, Faubourg St Germ^{n}.

Faithfully and affectionately yours
ROBERT BROWNING.

1862 : 1

To Miss Isabella Blagden

19. Warwick Crescent, Harrow Road,
June 19. '62.

Dearest Isa,

It is the greatest of comforts that I have thus secured to myself, by a word to your kindness, a certainty to the end of one of our lives of knowing something about you every month, wherever you are, however you are.[1] I shall never try to even amuse you,—on the other hand, writing the little note or long letter will be so pleasant to me that you may possibly sometimes get some of my pleasure thro' the poor words. If you were here and I could see you alone for a few minutes every now and then, I suppose there would be always a little to interest you in what I saw or heard the day or night before: but there's too much, and the various sorts of noticeable matter kill each other: I keep going out and forgetting all about it next morning: when I can save a thing that I think would interest you on your own account, (not as a thing happening to me merely) you shall have it. Let's see: I dined two days ago with Mrs Fitz-Patrick: I sate by my old friend Mrs Cust—who confirmed what I had heard six months before of Gertrude having refused Mr Beaumont and 80,000 a-year. At the same place I found Mad^e B. de Burg, of whom I have a fear, besides an unanswered letter praying me to go and see her she having been daily with Lytton at Vienna, consumed with the study of my things, and all that. Kingslake sat next her—sucking in authentic news about new cessions of territory and so on. Yesterday I met the Storys at a dinner, and afterward went with them to the Athenæum, where I saw nothing worth the trouble of going but the Parsee girls,—prettier to my corrupt and rotten cheese loving taste than any of the English fineness and loveliness (aquiline nose between two pudding cheeks with lightish hair and eyes, and "fine" complexion—give me these coal black little bitter-almonds!) To day I dine at the Martin's—as I did last week—charming people they are,—Thackeray and his girls to be there. I was at a House four days ago, where an English young bride of a year's standing began the dinner by getting hold of her husband's hands, with other significancies before us all,—me, an entire stranger; by the evening she was resting her head on his shoulder, and *I* did not stay for the little more that could well happen, and which probably *did,* for the edification of boys and girls: Thackeray was there too, and I mean to ask him what he thought of it—expecting to hear great plainness of speech: she was very pretty, too. I saw Rossetti on Monday,—mean to go and see him soon, and meet his sister and mother. Hatty and Gibson² arrive in a week. Story's success continues: he refuses £1500 for the Sibyl (I know) and there is a talk about his getting £2000 for the Cleopatra: such prices mean nothing, properly understood—but I like his being able to give just the answer most folks require when they ask "what are the works worth?"

Mrs Story would gladly give you the Photograph were a single copy obtainable—there has not been such a chance this long while, as I feared. She will give you, if you please, the last done of the boys— good but not so good. She got your letter and thanks you cordially. I see very little of the party,—just a little at somebody else's house every other evening or two.

My sister went away last Friday—is safe in Paris and found my Father in great force. I am heartily glad you like her, you dear Isa, and can assure you that she feels warmly for *you*. Miss Haworth is here, but I have not yet seen her. I want particularly to mention a circumstance to you, that I feel sorry about: Forster expressed, when I saw him last, about the day after you left, the greatest astonishment and regret at your having been here and his missing you: he maintains it was my fault, which it certainly was not,—says he fancied you had stayed at Paris, &c. I suppose that when you were here, he was always or mostly away—it *was* so at the beginning: anyhow, he evidently is very sorry to have missed you, and I promised to acquaint you with the fact. Just think of little *Alessandro,* the red-headed boy Peni liked so to play with, coming here on a visit,—to his grandmother who lives at Highgate! He walked over a fortnight ago, and I was amazed at hearing a chatter of Tuscan and seeing emerge his unmistakable locks! Lady Lyell's mother is dead in Florence, and poor Annunziata must be in want of a place again! Do always what you can for her, won't you? Pen is quite well—tho' he caught cold on Saturday at a picnic in the vile weather at Sᵗ George's Hill, Weybridge: I've stopped the rowing till it's remedied. He's at his German, but shall confirm the love I send you. For you,—I don't wonder at your friends being anxious to get what they can out of you during your stay: next time, *I* may be three-parts "the aged snake"³ and have house-room for you! Heart-room, meanwhile! Sarianna will come every year, I dare say. Now, Good Bye, dearest Isa, my truest and best of friends,—I may get queer, I shall get white, I shall not get one whit farther from you than where you now stay with

Your affectionate
R Browning.

[At the top of the first sheet]

*) To begin and to end,—these notes are *always private,* you know, and I trust—No setting me right, please, if I'm ever so wrong—as in Mrs Baker's affair about the letter of praise,—I'll knock under at once —but no more referring to the best sources of information and so on: I tell you what I think true, but may be wrong, and don't in the least care about being thought so—but let an end be *there!*

1862 : 2

To Miss Isabella Blagden

19. Warwick Crescent, Harrow Rd.
July 26. '62

Dearest Isa,

There can be no doubt that your letter from Florence is *much* later than my bad news, given by Chapman nearly a fortnight ago. I know nothing else: poor people, the end is in sight, be it delayed or acceler-ated. Of course Chapman only hears when business letters have to be written—you certainly will be better informed than he—but should I ever hear of anything you shall receive it immediately.

I have got my poor old things from Florence and write this with the Bookcase beside me—it is a sad business and I hardly know—or care to think—whether I like the things best here, or there, or at the bottom of the sea. When you return to Florence, please see if there be not at least one case, containing pictures and *specchi,* left with your property—with which, in all likelihood, it has been confounded.

I have just heard from Landor—first that *he* could never go to Rome, *he* with only *three lire* in the world &c &c and, in a postscript, these words "The Letter *is* mine. It was sent to Walker for the "Times"—but the signature was not for the *"Times"* but for *him."* Anything more disgraceful to him or to Walker I cannot easily fancy: as he confesses the letter was one lie, I shall not scruple to set down the "signature for Walker and not for the "Times" "—as another.[1] Poor old man, this is a break-down far beyond the infirmities which he brings forward in the same letter as his stock in trade. And Walker, to receive this and print this, knowing there was not a word of truth in it! A friend and a (Plymouth) brother! I have at least kept him out of such friendly and brotherly hands, but he really deserves little better. He writes about his book (another service of Hookey's[2]) and grieves (or grunts rather) over its delay—I shall not put out a finger to help any of them, depend on it. I have not seen Fraser—but will try and get it. My engagements are just as wearisome as ever—but in a fortnight at farthest I shall escape from it all.

Pen is quite well: here is a second summer's-day, yesterday being the first. Mrs Forster was better, decidedly, last week—I have not called since. I know nothing, not having cared to enquire about T's marriage.[3] I heard from Annette again yesterday—she talks about being in Paris in October. I could see that Mrs M. wanted to begin talking to me about the P. Mall, but I turned a deaf ear. Goodbye and God bless you—

Ever affy yours, R B.

1862 : 3

To the Storys

Chez M. le Maire de Ste. Marie
près Pornic, Loire Inférieure
Sept. 13 [1862]

Dearest Friends:

I have no more than a word to say, but you will take that of me with your old goodness. The letter of Aug. 28th arrived safely—you must let me hear once more of you before we leave this place, which will be very soon now, unless the fine weather should be prolonged extraordinarily. Our arrangements are for going on the 24th. Pen seems to enjoy himself so much and the daily swimming must be so good for him, that I should decide for another week, but we must stop a few days in Paris. At any rate we hope (*I* hope, at least) to be in London a few days after the beginning of October, and shall we not find you there? Indeed it cannot well be otherwise, and what a comfort to look forward to—never mind the pain after it all! I never much expected you would be able to do as you wished (I know) and pass a few days with us here. It was too hard, indeed impossible. Our early time was made sad enough by the sudden illness and death of our hostess, the Mayor's wife—a young woman leaving four little children and the husband who feels her loss. But things go on as usual now—three weeks since then. I did not mean to give you the notion that this place at all resembled Dieppe; the country is solitary and bare enough, but the sea is everywhere and the land harmonises entirely with it. I like the rocky walks by the sea and complete loneliness. At Pornic, gaiety enough, but it does not reach us. Mrs. Bracken strolls with us of an evening—the boys fish and divert themselves. I brought some old books with me, and read odd things in Latin and antique French. Let me remember that I made a note for William of a passage about the Evil Eye[1] in Cap: IV. Lib. IX Auli Gellii Noctium Atticarum in which quoting from Plinius secundus, he says that those in Africa who have such an eye possess a double pupil to it—a ghastly circumstance! In another crazy old Latin joke book, I came upon the "Piper of Hamelin" done into verse, by one Lucas Lossius who has simply left out the whole story of the rats and only mentions the spiriting away of the children as a singular instance of the devil's power. He makes him a bag-piper moreover.

Now, *how about the purchaser of the statues?* Do tell me. I am very glad the book is in hand. If you write at once, I shall get your letter, and a great delight here, but if you cannot manage it, direct to 151 Rue de Grenelle, Faubourg St. Germain. I am really anxious to know and hear. Pen's true love with mine to you all. My Father and Sister's kind regards and my complete stupidity all go together.

from your ever affectionately,

R. B.

1862 : 4

To W. W. Story

Ste. Marie, near Pornic
Oct. 1, '62
Address (Paris) 151 Rue de Grenelle
Faubourg St. Germain

Dearest Friend,

We leave this place tomorrow, hope to be in Paris by Friday night, and in London, say, a week after that. If we could meet once or twice more before you go away, it would be pleasant indeed. I rather fancy we may, supposing that friends will continue to snatch at you, and that Chapman and his printers will not be more miraculously expeditious than usual. Anyhow, I rejoice heartily in the sale of the statues

—a good comfortable fact, freeing you from any *back-thoughts* and bother. William has a clear way before him and may do what he pleases. I see from here the complacent curl in my friend the Tuscan's fat cheek and mouth, he of the studio, and that nice sympathetic helper (I forget both their names for the moment)—it will delight him also. All of which I shall not see, but it will do William good, and I expect the fruits in many a fine and true thing to come.

These last news from the North are admirable and consolatory, and I think, by such poor glimmer of light as comes to me, that the Italian news is far from discouraging. I go away with a sort of beginning of joy chimes in my ears. At all events, I go away with Pen in prodigious force—he has taken his fifty-first good swim in the sea, is brick-coloured and broad-shouldered—he wants to see you all, as you may suppose—you and Edie.

If I get a word before I leave Paris—on your receiving this—I shall know what I am to expect on arriving in London. I might lose some days by waiting to enquire about you till I arrive, and, according to the promise of your letter, I may extend or curtail my stay in Paris, by a day or two. Remember that the "season," for publishing is terribly early in October. Forster writes to me that he will not let the little collection of my things,[1] which has been printed and ready more than two months ago, appear before "the middle of November at very earliest." Of course you can't wait till then, and I understand little about the ways of such successes.

We are glad indeed to hear that the Boys are so flourishing. Pen's love to them and to you goes with mine, you know, and the best regards of my father and sister.

Ever yours affectionately,
ROBERT BROWNING.

1863 : 1

To the Storys

19 Warwick Crescent,
Harrow Road,
Jan. 18, '63

Dearest Friends:

Long as the time is since I have written, the fault cannot have been mine, *that* I know. When you left, the run of ill-luck in letters, appointments and so on, was extraordinary. Mrs. Sturgis' invitation,

which I had made up my mind to accept, came too late—a quarter of
an hour before the last starting of the train, which it would have taken
an hour to reach: your own letter apprising us of the going away next
morning came also too late: but I hardly regret this last, as such part-
ings are no good. Well, I could tell *you* nothing, you know, and you
would not tell us whether you were alive or dead, for ever so long, till
one day a dear letter from Edie was sent from Walton, nearly a month
after date: this was followed by a second letter (because longer) than
the first, and it reached me as swiftly as surely: but, lo, the courier on
whom I counted for the carriage of the little book[1] she was good
enough to want, set off in a hurry for some reason, at a few hours'
notice, and I had nothing to do but wait for the next. Here is the book
for her, and with more love than should go with so little a thing, and
true thanks for what I was allowed to see in her letter when Pen had
done with it—which was not at once. Now let me go to another matter: a month ago, at least, I received one evening the proofs, five or six,
of the "Evil Eye"[2] with a note from the printer to Chapman, saying
that there were duplicate passages, and other difficulties, and that they
could not proceed—and another from Chapman to myself adding
that he had just got a telegram from you urging the immediate publication of the book, and asking me to help—I supposed that for some
reason, probably connected with republishing in America, you were
in some sort of Author's fix—so did the business at a sitting,—that is,
I corrected English, Latin and Greek, suppressed two repetitions of
passages, and otherwise did the needful, and carried the proofs to
Chapman first thing next morning—but had I known that *after all*
there would be the delay of another month or more, I should have
taken my time, and made sure that no error escaped me—which at
present I can only hope. Another thing—of the Greek quotations,
some few were partially accented, the rest not—and, under the pres-
sure of time (or the lack of it) I thought it safest to remove all accents,
as the regulation of them is a ticklish business: as to the references, I
could not of course attempt to verify them, though I changed one or
two (the wrong Idyll of Theocritus, etc.). Chapman tells me, you have
been good enough to destine a copy to me,—thank you heartily for it,
—but as it is not yet here, I cannot see what is done or undone,—but
the sum of it all is, that I fancied you were in an emergency, and that
the thing must be got out of hand at *once:* with a single day's leisure
I should have done better work, though not with a better will.

I go every now and then to Lady A's, and hear if there is anything to
hear: she seems to me tolerably well, though she complains greatly of

EDITH MARION STORY

ROME, MAY, 1863

pain, and makes no effort to walk—there can hardly be any great improvement expected; but her good spirits and great cleverness are remarkable as ever. I met at her house a Mrs. Grey who had seen you, and spent a pleasant evening with you. But I can't chronicle all these people that come and go before me, and whose very names I forget next day. Why do I like so much to hear gossip from you and fancy that London news can no more interest you than it does me? You throw bits of porphyry and marble pavement from Rome, and I have only London mud, that's the fact. Give my true love to all Roman friends—the Perkins, Bruens—the Lockers, Hatty, Miss Cushman. I cannot say I am dull here—I work, or at least, am employed all day long. Pen is growing a great fellow and a dear good boy besides. I am much satisfied with him. He rows every day almost, and capitally,—rides, too, though the pony is getting little indeed. I believe I have done the best for him—now I shall leave off—do you Mrs. Story, you William, and you Edie, remember me whenever half an hour is disposable, and set it down with charities and alms giving. Story is of course getting on with his Saul—if it isn't the grand thing we expect, shan't he catch it! Tell all about the Boys, and yourselves and your neighbors and be sure of the affectionate gratitude of

Yours ever,
R. BROWNING

1863 : 2

TO MISS ISABELLA BLAGDEN

Athenaeum Club
Jan 19. '63.

Dearest Isa, I shall not be able to write much even now—after wanting and meaning to say so much to you: here is my day, and here must be my scrap of a letter: I am plagued with work and calls on my time of various sorts—let me however begin and write fast. How I know, dearest, that you mean what you say—and don't you know that *I* know it, am the better for your wishes, and wish you, not in return, but always wish you every good? I am very well and Pen is quite well: there are many things that vex me—I'll tell you if I have time—but on the whole I see progress for him, work for me, the passing of time,—and other helps,—well,—for your request, and all your urging, coaxing and eloquence—take my laugh at you for a goose! You ought to be sure that only at a word I will go, and be happy to go, not simply to Mrs Alexander but to her housemaid's cousin,—I will go the first day I can—to-day if I find I am in time,—if not,—next to certainly, to-morrow; and not merely call and return, if she is out, but repeat the call till I see her—and take Pen whenever she likes. For the photographs, being *here* at the Club,[1] I can't get at them—but I shall be writing to you in a few days, as soon as I get the information about your Sanscrit Professor which you want, for which I shall write presently,—and Mad[e] Tonearsa shall receive one with all my heart: the whole lengths of Pen are gone, but I have ordered more from Paris— and will send you one as soon as they arrive—it was very kind and considerate to give it to Wilson. Now of your book,[2]—I have read two volumes only, thro' Mudie's stupidity *twice* sending the second, i. e two second vols: I can only say that so far I think you write with visible improvement and limpidity: the subjective matter is very good indeed,—the letters from Siena, for instance, which are truth itself, and very dear: you don't treat us to very new or striking types—but you manage the ordinary people very well, and are certainly improving: there are a few slipshod phrases,—but a few,—(such as "cauterizing a *pain*"—for, "a wound" &c) and one *name* is unhappy to me— Bifrons, because impossible, and tale-telling: when I read the whole, —as I am glad to see is necessary, since you have a decided plot and work up to a crisis,—I will say what occurs: meantime I am happy to say that those who have read it, like it much—make my heart glad by praising it: Mrs Procter was most laudatory, for instance. Chapman tells me the sale is very good: you will get better and better prices for your books. He said it was wholly thro' a mistake of yours that *he* did not publish it and pay you that price—he waited for some reason or other, and *you would* not wait: but then, he tells more than I vouch for. I saw Mrs Lewis[3] again the other evening—and continue to like her exceedingly: I am going even to dine with her on Thursday to meet A. Trollope: the change in *L:* is astounding! She spoke very kindly of you,—had not read the book yet, however.

Now, dear, let me say a word to you, strictly to you only, about the Monument,[4] about which I think you are in a misconception. Leighton made that design, with all love and effort. So far from despising the criticism of an Architect, he had all along the superintendence and advice of Cockerell, son of the Architect, and said to be of great ability: his aim was, to make something new, and not *dozzinale,* something beautiful, and something *safe*—a difficult matter: indeed, Mr Kirkup had previously written to me twice or thrice to warn me

that such erections (pillars supporting an arca) were ruinous—
thro' the arca's being always too heavy: snow lies on it, one pillar
breaks, then all falls. Leighton studied this difficulty, and, in the opinion of the competent, removed it—I don't hear a word of objection as
from an Architect, i. e, with respect to the *building*-part, which is just
where fault, as in a painter's work, might be most easily found. Cottrell saw leisurely this design, talked over it with Leighton, might
have found any objection he pleased, but found *none*. After several
weeks, he called on me for the drawings—I begged him to state
frankly any objection that had subsequently struck him, anything he
had not liked to mention to Leighton,—still,—*none*. He then returns
to Florence, and writes to me that "Mathas" says the styles are mixed,
the arca should be altered, the pillars changed for cariatides, and that
he will make a design and send it. This is merely one artist bidding
you accept a work from *him* rather than what you have ordered from
another. And *who* is "Mathas?" "Very clever" and so on: I daresay,
but I never heard his name before: would you really recommend that
at first mention of it, I should throw up Leighton, renounce what I
had entirely admired and gratefully accepted,—all for a design still in
the air, promised as a better thing, by a man wholly unknown to me?
If Mathas had *sent* a design, by which I could judge of the superiority
of his taste to Leighton's,—well and good: Leighton would have been
the first to entreat me to accept it if I so willed—as he *has* entreated
me to give up his design if I have the *least* inclination to do so—but
indeed I have *not:* you say, "Rafael would have consulted Michel
Angelo"—now, I don't say L. is Rafael—but does anybody call the
other Michel Angelo? I really want to know—is it meant that
"Mathas" is an arbiter and judge as the other would have been? Recol-
lect, I have only M's word and C's opinion that something better will
be done by this great man, and I am to throw up what, at least, I have
seen and do like. Suppose when we had all accepted the Inscription on
the Tablet,[5] somebody had said, "A or B, a very clever writer, now
employed in cutting the letters on such a public monument, finds the
metaphors mixed, the style unclassic, he's for altering the first line,
changing the second, and removing the third, and I'm sure that Tommaseo if on the spot would applaud his performance, for would not
Horace have consulted Virgil on such a matter?"—So I see the matter, at least: and the vexatious circumstance is, that Cottrell who is
kindness itself, who means all for the best, probably misunderstands
me, thinks my disinclination to adopt his view pure obstinacy and,
perhaps, ingratitude—such are the misfortunes of friendship! He has

never answered my letter, sent a month ago: nor, by the bye, will he do the simple favor of making some enquiry about that missing *cassa* with many precious things of mine in it—it don't help me to have been all this time in Florence without asking de Faublan or the Packer a word about *that*. I lose pictures and papers, beside the other things—but never mind. *Don't mention it*. There are worse miseries, —those I referred to. Ever since I set foot in England I have been pestered with applications for leave to write the Life of my wife: I have refused—and there an end. I have last week received two communications from friends—enclosing the letters of a certain Geo: Stampe of Great Grimsby, asking them for details of life and letters, for a biography he is engaged in—adding that he has "secured the correspondence with her old friend Hugh Stuart Boyd." Think of this beast working away at this, not deeming my feelings, or those of her family, worthy of notice—and meaning to print letters written years and years ago, on the most intimate and personal subjects, to an "old friend"—which, at the poor, old blind, forsaken man's death fell into the hands of a complete stranger, who, at once wanted to print them—but desisted thro' Ba's earnest expostulation enforced by my own threat to take law proceedings—as fortunately letters are copyright: I find this woman died last year, and her son writes to me this morning that Stampe got them from him as autographs merely: he will try and get them back: Stampe, evidently a blackguard, got my letter, which gave him his deserts, on Saturday—no answer yet; if none comes, I shall be forced to advertise in the Times, and obtain an injunction. But what I suffer in feeling the hands of these blackguards (for I forgot to say, *another* man has been making similar applications to friends)—what I undergo with their paws in my very bowels, you can guess and God knows! No friend, of course, would ever give up the letters: if anybody ever is forced to do that which *she* would have so utterly writhed under—if it ever *were* necessary, why, I should be forced to do it, and, with any good to her memory and fame, my own pain in the attempt would be turned into joy—I should *do* it at whatever cost: but it is not only unnecessary but absurdly useless—and, indeed, it shall not be done if I can stop the scamp's knavery —along with his breath.

I am going to reprint the Greek Christian Poets and another Essay: nothing that ought to be published, shall be kept back—and this she certainly intended to correct, augment and reproduce—but *I* open the doubled-up paper! Warn anyone you may think needs the warning of the utter distress in which I should be placed were this scoundrel or any other of the sort, to baffle me and bring out the letters. I can't prevent fools from uttering their folly upon her life, as they do on every other subject, but the law protects *property*—as these letters are. Only last week or so, the Bishop of Exeter stopped the publication of an announced "Life"—containing extracts from his correspondence. And so I shall do.

Dearest Isa, I will end now—as soon as I get the information from Paris, you shall have it. I have not gone out much lately, having suffered from bile and cold—both are subdued plagues just now. Arabel B. is returned: I shall probably go to Paris for a week at the end of next month—as a change to Pen and a pleasure to my Father. Give my love to all old and dear friends: I am so happy, Isa, to think that you prosper, as you manifestly do, in your house and society: that is right! I am glad you went to those Balls,—you will find the good of them in your novels. Kind love specially to the Cottrells—Trollopes —Mignatys: you don't see Kirkup, I suppose? I will write you, if I can, a supplementary letter of gossip, to take the taste of this bitter sheetfull out of your mouth. Thank my kind understander, Mr Brett,[6] for his goodness to me: I shall be glad to know him whenever he comes to England. Now, good bye and God bless you, my dearest friend: I comfort myself in the thought of you in dear, dear Florence: I wait for your letters,—they come and I wait again,—nothing delights me so much.

Ever yours affectionately
R BROWNING.

1863 : 3

TO FREDERICK LEIGHTON

Chez M. Laraison,
Ste. Marie, Près Pornic, Loire Inférieure,
August 20, 1863.

My dear Leighton,—Don't fret; you will do everything like yourself in the end, I know; wait till the end of October, as you propose. I cannot return before the beginning of it, though I would do so were it necessary, but it is not, for I have only this morning received the notification of which I told you, that "the marble is in the sculptor's studio." We shall therefore be in full time.

The portrait you saw was the autotype which I lent to Mr. Richmond, and concerning which I wrote to him before leaving London, directing that it should be sent to you. He engaged to let you have it whenever you desired. I therefore enclose (oh, fresh attack on your envelopes and postage stamps!) a note which I presume he will attend to, and which you will of course burn should he have sent the portraits meanwhile. I have also two others nearly like that portrait, taken the same day with it, which I was unable to find, but which shall be found on my return.

Dear Leighton, I can only repeat, with entire truth, that you will satisfy me wholly. I don't think, however, you can make me more than I am now—Yours gratefully and lovingly,

ROBERT BROWNING.

1863 : 4

TO MISS ISABELLA BLAGDEN

19th Dec. '63

Dearest Isa, I am bilious to day and only able to write a word or two —but you know what I feel: I believe you wish me all the good in the world and out of it—and I wish you,—*that* I know,—whatever happiness life can bring. Yes—the years go—we are in the *third*: at first, when you were here, the business was of the hardest, for nothing seemed *doing,* nothing *growing,*—only the emptiness and weariness of it all: now, there seems really *use* in the process, and fruit. Pen is evidently the better for my being here, so it is all easier to go on with: if I live, I suppose I shall get done in five or six years more: but enough of me. I have various pieces of gossip to give you, could I find them in my head to-day: Sir E.[1] has taken a house in Park lane,— hopes L. will live with him. He is at Bath and very well—with the Ernsts: it must have been H. B. (now here) who passed thro' Florence and was taken for L. You see Hatty's character as given by Story in the Ath.:[2] I don't think I should have troubled my head about such a charge in such a quarter, had I been she. Hume[3] went to Rome with a letter from Mr Mitchel to Story, asking to become his pupil: Story refused, but got him a studio, conceiving himself bound to do so much by the letter: Mrs S. wrote me this: of course Hume immediately wrote to England (to Dr Gully a Gull indeed) that S *had* taken him as a pupil—it is Story's own business,—he chooses to take this dung-ball into his hand for a minute, and he will get more and more smeared.

I mean to write to Kirkup, whom I really love—only the incessant press on me has delayed my replying to his letter: Landor is teazing various friends about his book and what has come of it—he and Walker are at daggers-drawn—he accusing Walker of various delinquencies, quite forgetting his own stupidity,—if these be truly charged,—in getting into a passion of wonder over the perfection of the man: but life, even L's, is not long enough for this repeated imbecility—of which I suppose old age is the excuse, poor man.

I have a mind to tell you something that happened the other day in illustration of what I said was the Barrett character: a stupid family lawyer told Henry Barrett that an estate in England now belonging to Charles John B. *ought* to have been divided between him and a cousin, in their grandfather's time—adding that of course it was not to be mentioned: H. at once wrote to tell C. J—who by return of post wrote to the cousin—bidding him take the half, and all arrears of profit. The cousin replied that he knew better the state of the case, that the right had been settled long ago, and there was not a pretence for a claim on his part: so far good—but C. J. really meant to make an immense sacrifice and would gladly have done so.

This poor letter is only made worth receiving by the love in it, my dearest friend: next time I will be in better condition, I hope, and make amends; always I am yours—till death and after. All goes well: Willy[4] and Pen take fencing lessons together. W. is very often with Pen—he is a very nice boy. Pen learns boxing also. Goodbye, dearest Isa—I am

yours affectionately,
ROBERT BROWNING.

Can you have the goodness to send the enclosed to Cottrell?

1864 : 1

To Robert Barrett Browning

April 22. '64

My dearest Pen,

I shall only be able to write a word or two for I have just come in from meeting Garibaldi (at last) at the American Consul's: I was very glad to shake his hand and say a few words to him in Italian: he leaves London to-day—not England yet.

I am very happy that you are enjoying yourself and that your cough is so much better: I care more about that than the Hand. I had a kind note from Surtees[1] yesterday saying how glad he was at the prospect of seeing you, and asking you to go there some Friday and stay till Monday—because Altham passes Saturdays and Sundays at home: so you can do that, and I will tell him so. *Next* Friday—till Monday or Tuesday, will end the complete fortnight nicely. I shall be anxious to know how you get on in riding a horse of the ordinary size. I must tell you that Mrs Story writes a very long letter—so that our missives have crossed each other. They are all very well, and full of enquiries about you—they seem to have given up the notion of going to England, and will be at Leghorn. I had also some Italian newspapers from George, with accounts of Garibaldi's reception, which has delighted the Italians. I saw Willy this morning: he says he had a letter from you which he will answer to-morrow, as the boys get a holiday on account of its being Shakespeare's birthday. I dine with Dickens, Wilkie Collins, and Forster at Greenwich. My best love and truest thanks to your Uncle and Aunt.

Yours most affectionately
Robt Browning.

1864 : 2

To Miss Isabella Blagden

19. Warwick Crescent,
Upper Westbourne Terrace W
Oct. 19. '64

Dearest Isa,

I returned on the 11th—We stayed three weeks at Biarritz; in the loveliest weather possible—just spent a day in Spain, to get a taste of its quality (a very pleasant one)—going to Fontarabia, Irun and St Sebastian. We returned easily by Bayonne, Bordeaux, Tours and Paris: I only stayed one day there, though the Storys, arriving the same evening, caught sight of us and pressed us to stay—but I was wanted at home: and here I hope to be for many a month. I doubt whether the warm sea and air have "braced" us all as the Breton place used to do—but the return to the South was attractive indeed. Pen enjoyed himself besides, and is very well.

It was fortunate indeed that I was saved from the addition to my annoyances which I should have had to bear had my journey been to Florence. Leighton writes to me that nothing can be more *impudently* bad than the execution of his designs[1]—there has been no pretence at imitating some of them—and the four capitals of the columns will have to be sawn off and carved afresh,—also two of the medallions

THE PAS DE ROLAND

From a pencil sketch by Sarianna Browning, August 27, 1864.

have to be cut out and replaced—as infamous: while the third "though indeed detestable is not quite irremediable." The Profile is "less slovenly than the rest," though open to many objections—"the hair, with the designing of which I took great pains, is entirely different: the fellow had the coolness to say that he thought I had probably done the thing hastily without nature, and that he had put up a plait, and done the thing afresh himself (if you could see it!)—also, in the ear, "*ho cercato di migliorare!*"—he added that he had obtained from Cavalier Mathas and Count Cottrell the sanction to improve these parts of the work—let us hope there is no truth in this. Cottrell says he saw all the criticisms I make, *himself*—but that he thought it better to leave them to me to make, as the mischief was irremediable."—On the contrary, Cottrell wrote to me that it was "extremely well executed,"—and as he paid up the last instalment, though not due till the work was really erected, I have no sort of remedy. Don't say one word about this—I won't have any wrangling over—literally—the grave. Cottrell has done his best, I daresay—but *my* best in such a case would have been to tell the sculptor "You will please to reproduce exactly what you have given you in the Designs, good, bad, or indifferent— if you want to practise drawing of your own, do it elsewhere; and be particular in bidding the Cavalier Mathas mind his own business."

I am glad that poor Landor is out of the weakness and sorrow of his old age, and that nobody went to his funeral. By his will, he has left me certain pictures &c   I notified at the time to his relatives that I only let that clause stand because unable to prevent it, but that I would never hear of taking a scrap of the old man's—excepting any papers he might wish me to examine, preserve or destroy. I have again—although unnecessarily—repeated my determination: which I mention to you, in case the amiable people at the Villa should declare that the Rafaels and Correggios are intended to grace my rooms here. I have been more than rewarded for my poor pains by being of use for five years to the grand old ruin of a genius, such as I don't expect to see again.[2]

Your letter about Annette and her husband was graphic indeed: I quite understand all about it. After such a blunder as hers, she cried "Anywhere, anywhere, out of the world"—i. e of Grosvenor Place, and her old friends' reach: and she is safe from them all effectually.[3] After all, when folks *fail* I like them to *fail*—not patch up, make shift, keep going wretchedly.

I can't tell you how little I care about Lytton[4]—he is utterly uninteresting to me,—I seem to know all about him. His cleverness surprised me a little, when I saw him,—he can extend *that* to almost any extent   As to his being "kind" to any woman wholly in his power, I wonder what makes you hope that?

I have not seen Miss Cobbe's book,[5]—spite of finding that there is something about "the Brownings" in it. I was ungracious to her, I remember, in those days when I did as seemed right in my own eyes.

I saw Geo: Smith yesterday;—don't know his wife, who seems a very nice person; I like him, however,—his generous ways and unpretentiousness. He told me about you, and was delighted with his visit to Florence.

Tell Jessie White[6] that I beg her pardon and trust to her kindness. I got her letter, at a time when every moment of mine was taken up; she never told me when she would certainly be at home, and I delayed calling: when I was about to do so, I heard she had left Town to return—at last my time was up, I was very unwell, I hesitated at writing, I could not ask her to come to me—at last the wrong was irreparable. I tell her the plain truth, in belief of its efficacity. Another time, it shall go hard but I will see her for old days' and enduring love's sake. ·

No book yet! Well, you lose little: but you shall have it soon, somehow. I hope to have a long poem ready by the summer, my Italian murder thing.[7] Do you see the "Edinburg" that says all my poetry is summed up in "Bang whang, whang, goes the Drum?"[8] I have not got to see your article in the Cornhill,[9] though I went yesterday to the club in order to get it: I shall read it with great interest. Miss Smith says she is much disappointed at getting no letter from you—but this is two days ago.

Good bye, dearest Isa—Pen's love always

Yours affectionately ever
R B.

1865 : 1

ROBERT BARRETT BROWNING AND ROBERT BROWNING TO MISS EDITH STORY

Saty. Jan. 14. 1865.

My dearest Edie,

Many many thanks for your kindness, or rather your naughtiness in wasting so much of your time in making such a beautiful pair of slippers for a stupid fellow like myself. Why they are more fitted for a prince than for me! However there is one thing which is that you may be assured that I shall wear them out (although they ought rather to be put under a glass case) and that in doing so they will cause me to remember you still oftener, (although I don't think that there is much danger of my forgetting you). I must ask for your forgiveness for my not having written to you before but really this is the first moment that I have had since Xmas to write in.

. . . The weather here is anything but wintery—today it is almost temperate outside and as yet we have had no skating. You must answer this stupid epistle—for I want to hear about you all. How are Mr. and Mrs. Story, and the two young prize-fighters, whom I had the honour of meeting in Paris? I wonder if there is any chance of our seeing each other soon. I hope you will come over here next summer, and that if you do come, I shall see a little more of you than last time. Give my love to Mr. and Mrs. Story, and to the above-mentioned members of the "P.R." and of the Society for the encouragement of the "Noble Art of Self-Defence." As I have nothing else to write that could possibly be interesting to you, I think that I had better shut up.

Do write to your aff^{te}

OLD BOB

[*Continued by Robert Browning*]

My dear Edie—or rather, dear friends all three—I have kept this letter of Pen's far too long, meaning to do myself something like justice in another of my own—but as the week gets on, I see the best way will be to be content with a word or two. I am literally engaged all day long. I heard, after some time on my arrival in London, that your Papa had been seriously ill,—was that true?—and, after a rather shorter interval, that he was quite recovered. I hope whatever was wrong is right again: take care that he spends his energy with regard to the many years wherein it is intended to last—not all at once,— he knows that, well as I,—but you must make him mind his knowledge. I hear very little from, that is, about you—a word from Ly. W. now and then: it is all my own fault, I ought to take care and satisfy myself. But why does [not] a good, great budgetful of news arrive now and then to me the unworthy from Mrs. Story, who engaged to find me in food of the kind? How I should enjoy it now! Well, the days and weeks and even years go by, and, by my reckoning a couple of years more and Pen will be full-fledged: in two months he will be sixteen. I can't think of what I may do in my own idleness then—for thinking of all the care that will begin again, about him. It's for the best, of course. How are the boys,[1] big fellows now—have they a master, or what do they do, and what is meant to be done with them? And you, how do you like Rome, all of you, after the London gaieties? What is brooding in the Studio? I don't care much to know who is at Rome, Lord This and Mrs the Other. So, you see, though somewhat tardy, acknowledgement has been made copiously enough for the good office about the statues: I have not seen them,—to my shame, —can't find the clear morning to bestow, however worthily,—they can wait, moreover.

I shan't give you gossip now—nor make this into anything but a long-drawn sigh to have wings and flee to the blue country. Florence will not be itself much longer, by all accounts,—Poggio to be built over, and all up, far as Fiesole, they say. I don't care, it's all gone anyhow. Good bye, dear Edie—and goodbye, the dear others! If you have already any plans for the Summer, you may as well tell me: can it be possible you will come here? No! Yes! No—Yes.

Ever yours aff[y],
R Browning.

1865 : 2

To J. Bertrand Payne[1]

19, Warwick Crescent
Upper Westbourne Terr.
Feb. 15. '65.

Dear Mr. Payne,

Certainly you may do whatever you think best with the Book,[2] and I shall be glad indeed if it suit you in the numbers as well as otherwise.

I purposely made the selection numerous, so as to bear thinning ("thinning" this blot is meant to be) and thin it we will to any extent. The few words of preface shall be ready, of course.

As for the Shelleys,[3]—which I receive likewise, thank you,—it shall go hard but I give you a wonderful little book: I should like however to hear anything you may incline to, concerning the way of work.

Very faithfully yours
Robert Browning

1865 : 3

To W. C. CARTWRIGHT

19 Warwick Crescent,
Upper Westbourne Terrace W.
May 18. '65

My dear Cartwright,

Should the M. S. notice, which you mention, be one beginning thus
—"Dimorando da qualche tempo in Roma Guido Franceschini, no-
bile di Arezzo in Toscana, ed al servizio di personaggio eminente, si
decise a prender moglie" &c¹—it will be unnecessary to trouble Mr
Craven. Should it be another account, the loan of it would oblige me
exceedingly.

Ever yours most truly
ROBERT BROWNING.

1865 : 4

To MISS EDITH STORY

19 Warwick Crescent,
Upper Westbourne Terrace, W.
July 8. '65.

Dearest Edie,

What will you have thought of this week's silence, after sending
me and Pen that kind note and request? I thought I should be able
to go to-day, and waited to become sure before sending word,—but,
after all, you know very well how we both of us long to see as much
of you as we can. I want to get to Mount Felix as early in the morning
or afternoon as may conveniently be, and walk about the beautiful
grounds. Shall it be next Saturday?—unless there should be visitors,
for we want to have you to ourselves, for the little time there is left us.

I want you, too, to tell Mr. and Mrs. Sturgis how glad I shall be to
see them again: I have no time,—can never call, much less leave town
for a day, but I neither am forgetful nor ungrateful, I hope: It is now
the end of the season, (and *my* working season, besides—for I have
written *8400* lines of my new poem¹ since the autumn,—there's for
you!)—and there is a little breathing-space before going away. Pen's
love is especially sent to you with that of

Yours affectionately ever,
R B.

1865 : 5

To Miss Edith Story

July 20, '65

Dearest Edie:

If we go to Mount Felix[1] on Saturday shall we find you alone, and will Mrs. Sturgis bear with all this stupid fuss that I seem to make, and let us come early, and give us some luncheon, and let us go—not late?

If visitors are expected, we will take another Saturday: that Goose-Pen would not go without me, finding that I really meant to go some time or other!

Kindest regards to Mr. and Mrs. Sturgis,

from yours affectionately ever,

ROBERT BROWNING

May I have a word in answer?

1865 : 6

To Miss Edith Story

19 Warwick Crescent,
Upper Westbourne Terrace, W
July 26, '65

Dearest Edie:

If I was "perverse," I am now paid for my perversity—since I find that I shall have to leave London without seeing you, after all the pleasant things that were to have been. Letters from Paris induce me to hasten our departure, and next Saturday,—the day I meant to ask leave to pass at Mount Felix,—will break on us in London and set on us in Paris (poetically expressed). Pen's vexation is what it should be: he went to the Academy last Saturday hoping to meet you there—but to no purpose. Perhaps you will still be at Mount Felix in October, when we return—in the very beginning of it,—if so—but where is the use of proposing pleasant things, they never come to good now—with me, at least.

Thank Mrs. Sturgis exceedingly for me; "perverse," indeed, because, being only able to excuse myself from other people's invitations by saying—"I never accept such,"—and finding life bearable in consequence,—I don't give way to the temptation the first time that it would be delightful so to do! Then, Regattas—what has a grey owl like me to do with Regattas and the lovers of the same? No, No! the dark for me—

I want to tell you that the Bust[1] arrived yesterday: I have hardly looked steadily enough at it yet: there are some things admirably produced there—more, by far than I thought possible—nobody else could have saved them, or made so beautiful a thing—Tell your Papa so when you write.

Ever affectionately yours,
ROBERT BROWNING

We go to St. Marie near Pornic, as we did two years ago and the year before—Willie Bracken and his mother go also,—though we don't travel together.

1865 : 7

To Miss EDITH STORY

Dearest Edie;

Indeed it was impossible for either of us, Pen or myself, to get to you to-day—the kindness of your invitation remains with us both. We go off early to-morrow—and whether we meet or no, shall always keep you in mind and be, as now,

Affectionately yours,
PEN AND R. B.

Kind regards and thanks once again to Mrs. Sturgis. Love to your Papa and Mama when you write.

July 28, '65.

1865 : 8

To W. W. STORY

19 Warwick Crescent,
Upper Westbourne Terr; W.
Sunday M^g [July 30 (?), 1865.]

Dear Story, You will have found my letter, if you had not seen it when you wrote—not that it is needful to tell you that I should greatly enjoy one more word with you all. The letter reached me at eight o'clock last evening—Had I imagined you were at Chapman's yesterday,—why, I passed the shop!

To-day I have engagements I can't put off. All I can say is—if you find it possible to say "We shall be at such a place, at such a time,"—any day—I will certainly be there.

Whatever happens, and whether we are to see each other sooner or later—I am always yours as ever. I begin to see a pin-point of light out at the end of this London life,—Italy at the end of a few years more, you know!

I wrote to Edie as soon as the Bust came—as I had been frank in confessing my fears, you may depend on the honesty of my wonder and delight. Would you like me to take it for a portrait, when I publish a "Selection" that is projected?

Ever affectionately yours
R Browning

1865 : 9

To Miss Isabella Blagden

Ste. Marie près Pornic,
Loire Inferieure,
France
Aug. 19. '65.

Dearest Isa, Your letter came safely enough from St. Marcello: I am glad you have been there, little satisfactory as circumstances may have made your stay, for I feel affectionately about that little place which I never saw, nor probably shall see: when I first went to Italy, *that* was the place we rather wanted to go to—having heard about its seclusion and attractiveness from an English family that tried it: San Benedetto is another retreat akin, I think. I wish the poor Cottrells well out of all their troubles, especially this—I know: *he* means well, I believe. Let him make amends now, and I won't mind the past. I want to hear all is over, and be able to think of seeing Florence, if so minded, some day, without having to face that particular pain. What *you* can do, you will—I know also. You see I am here again—as two years ago. Mind the address, and write to me *here next time*—I shall have the delight of your letter a day sooner. We are the same party, in the same house—and all but the same *other* house—for Mrs. Bracken and Willy could not get the old one, and are a few yards nearer. Nothing is changed—Pornic itself, two miles off, is full of company, but our little village is its dirty, unimproved self—a trifle wilder than before, if possible. The weather is not good: rain every day, with intervals of sun, but a contrast to the wonderful Biarritz and Cambo blaze of last year: at the same time, it suits me, and I think the others, better by far: the sea is the great resource. I used not to care about it inordinately till of late years—now, it seems to be the *obbligato* accompaniment to my last home but one. I bathe daily—and feel much the better for it. Pen and Willy swim capitally—far better than any other person out of the many who exhibit daily—(not at my little retired creek, which is close by.) My sister seems particularly well,—and my Father also. Mrs. Bracken does well enough, I believe. She is a woman of a mild mournful voice over minute grievances, chiefly culinary, but really devoted to Willy—I don't see much more to say about the place except that since our arrival a fortnight ago, they have pulled—or are busy pulling down Pornic Church, mentioned in a poem of mine: on arriving, I went inside and found all as I had left it—last evening I looked through great gaps in the walls and saw the inside a mere shell: it was very old, and built on a natural pedestal of living rock—and there's the whole bare country round about to build on: also at this Ste. Marie church opposite they have taken away old pillar-ornaments, column-heads with quaint figures,—made all smooth and white-washed where they were,—and flung them where they now lie, on a heap of stones by the road-side—where my father goes to draw them in his sketch-book—groaningly.

As to those nonsensical reports, I never supposed you believed any of them, but then, after all, people change their minds, and I have no right to pass for something above changes even of that sort: only observe that these reports were more impertinent and intentionally false than merely nonsensical: my sister told me that Mrs. Carmichael Smith, Annie's grandmother, regularly came to condole with her (S) about Pen's approaching change of circumstances under another mother-in-law,—whose name, as you don't mention, I shall not: this was my first acquaintance with *that* report, just as stupid or spiteful as the rest. If there were *not* an intention of being spiteful, there are other names of people in houses where I visit, which are those at least of ladies I *do* occasionally see and converse with, and like well enough,—but you'll never hear of *them,* I think. I suppose that what you call "my fame within these four years" comes from a little of this gossiping and going out, and showing myself to be alive: and so indeed some folks say—but I hardly think it: for remember I was uninterruptedly (almost) in London from the time I published Paracelsus—till I ended that string of plays with Luria: and I used to go out then, and see far more of merely literary people, critics &c—than I do now,—but what came of it? There were always a few people who had a certain opinion of my poems, but nobody cared to speak what he thought, or the things printed twenty five years ago would not have waited so long for a good word—but at last a new set of men arrive who don't mind the conventionalities of ignoring one and seeing everything in another: Chapman says, "The orders come from Oxford and Cambridge," and all my new cultivators are young men: more than that, I observe that some of my old friends don't like at all the irruption of *outsiders* who rescue me from their sober and private approval and take those words out of their mouths "which they always meant to say," and never *did*. When there gets to be a general feeling of this kind, that there must be *something* in the works of an author, the reviewers are obliged to notice him, such notice as it is: but what poor work, even when doing its best!—I mean, poor in the failure to give a general notion of the whole works,—not a particular one of such and such points therein. As I began, so I shall end, taking my own course, pleasing myself or aiming at doing so, and thereby, I hope, pleasing God. As I never did otherwise, I never had any fear as to what I did going ultimately to the bad,—hence in collected editions I always reprinted everything, smallest and greatest. Do you ever see, by the way, the Numbers of the Selection which Moxons publish? They are exclusively poems omitted in that other selection by Forster: it seems little use sending them to you, but when they are completed, if they give me a few copies, you shall have one if you like. Just before I left London, McMillan was anxious to print a *third* Selection, for his Golden Treasury, which should of course be different from either: but *three* seem too absurd. There, enough of me. I certainly will do my utmost to make the most of my poor self before I die—for one reason, that I may help old Pen the better: I was much struck by the kind ways, and interest in me shown by the Oxford undergraduates,—those that were introduced to me by Jowett: I am sure they would be the more helpful to my son. So, good luck to my great venture, the murder-poem,[1] which I do hope will strike you and all good lovers of mine.

Now, good bye, dearest Isa, I shall be glad to know what you decide on for your "pied-a-terre"—how is the plan for the Cottage with Trollope? And how is he, pray? Do you read the "Fortnightly," with the "Belton Estate" in it? I like that much: it is the only novel of Anthony's that I have read of late years: very unpretending, but surely *real,* and so far a gain. Miss Braddon's I stop my ears to. I conjure you to be careful, to digest and re-digest what you write, and to do yourself justice. Don't trouble yourself about "keeping your name before the public," or anything but the main thing—to produce a real book. I wonder whether if I were by your side, snake-fashion,[2] a-snubbing you in my ogre-fashion (as you used to say) I should be of any use: or *can* anybody be of use to any other body? How I wish you success in all things, you must know well enough.

That Bust arrived. There are reminiscences in it, certainly, and on the whole, it is much to my mind: I wish it were mine: nobody but Story could have brought so much together.

At Paris, I saw a friend of my sister's, Miss Church, an American young lady,—who desired to be kindly remembered to you. I like her extremely: she is just going home. I have only time to add that Pen sends his best love—so do my Father and Sister. You hear from Miss Smith—and probably know that she is going to live with some friends, finding the solitary life irksome after her sister's death.

Ever affectionately yours,
ROBERT BROWNING.

1866 : 1

To Professor Edward Dowden

19, Warwick Crescent,
Upper Westbourne Terrace,
W.
March 5th, 1866.

My dear Sir,

Pray forgive the delay in replying to your very kind letter. I was much engaged at the time I got it, and wanted to look a little deeper into the matters you enquire about. But I keep you waiting far too long, so will try and answer off-hand, premising that I have a facility at forgetting my own things once *done,* and that, in this case, I have put this particular poem away and behind me long ago—not at all meaning to undervalue it thereby, but because it is good husbandry

an artist to forget what is behind and press onward to
e. "Elys,"[1] then, is merely the ideal subject, with such a
amor's poem—and referred to in the other places as his
tion, realised according to his faculty (El lys—the Lily).
ite right about the classification of *Sordello's*—neither
nor the second of those moods of mind:[2] it is the second
' and modified by the impulse to "thrust in time eter-
'—*that,* or nothing. This is just indicated in the passage
ords occur, and the rest of the poem is an example of the

o make a companion to *Paracelsus,* and remember while
it, telling Leigh Hunt so. Let me say that, I heartily
such sympathy and such expression of it. I hope you
poem on which I am now at work.[3]

Pray remember me ever as
Yours most truly,
ROBERT BROWNING.

1866 : 2

To Miss Isabella Blagden

May 19. '66.

arly glad to get your letter, as I had received one a
ore from Miss Smith inquiring about you,—she had
l communication, it seems, and fancied you might be
nd trust, from the absence of allusion to it in this
right. I am glad you like Pen's photograph,—by no
ng one, however,—too dark,—still very like un-
ght to be somebody above nobody by virtue of the
eive, which gets stronger and stronger: but his de-
en very gradual indeed, I think: his moral qualities
ll I could wish,—his truthfulness, and deepness of
ness of mind,—I hope the other good things will
fortnight to Oxford, on a second visit to Jowett at
t my heart just beat! I don't know whether Pen
or after the next,[1]—what shall I do, pray, when
begin conjuring horrors up,—in this world where
by surprise rather than by what one has foreseen

and feared. My father has been very ill,—he is better and will go into the country the moment the East winds allow,—for in Paris,—as here, —there is a razor wrapped in the flannel of sunshine. I hope to hear presently from my sister, and will tell you, if a letter comes: he is eighty-five almost,—you see! Otherwise his wonderful constitution would keep me from inordinate apprehension. His mind is absolutely as I always remember it,—and the other day when I wanted some information about a point of mediaeval history, he wrote a regular bookful of notes and extracts thereabout. Well,—I forget whether I answered a question about Lytton,—if I did not, I can say, from having seen Drummond Wolf two days ago, that he is quite well, going to get extra pay as *Chargé d' affs* in the absence of his *chef*, which Uncle Clarendon will considerately prolong, and then will get leave to return to Eng^d for the winter: his eyes are all right, and his happiness with his wife entire. I wish, by the way, you would give me one word, toward satisfying my natural curiosity, and tell me if the following personages are alive and *how?* Made Tassinari, Mrs Baker, Dr Trotman. Not that I care three straws about the three,—but that I would like to know where they are, as Florentine stocks and stones. I agree with you, and always did, as to the uninterestingness of the Italians individually, as thinking, originating souls: I never read a line in a modern Italian book that was of use to me,—never saw a flash of poetry come out of an Italian *word:* in art, in action, *yes,*—not in the region of ideas: I always said, they *are* poetry, don't and can't *make* poetry,—and you know what I mean by *that,*—nothing relating to rhymes and melody and *lo stile:* but as a nation, politically, they are most interesting to me,—I think they have more than justified every expectation their best friends formed of them,—and their rights are indubitable: my liking for Italy was always a selfish one,—I felt alone with my own soul there: here, there are fifties and hundreds, even of my acquaintance, who do habitually walk up and down in the lands of thought I live in,—never mind whether they go up to the ends of it, or even look over them,—*in* that territory they are,—and I never saw footprint of an Italian there yet. I shall not go to Florence again to stay—certainly not now—but I should like to have earned a few years of that sort of solitude somewhere else in the divine Land of Souls: perhaps Greece would suit me even better. Never mind about it now. As for Mario, I daresay he is a born baby and less of a politician than the first mechanic you meet in the street here.

My poem is nearly done—won't be out for a year or perhaps more. Suppose I am ruined by the loss of my Italian Rents,—how then? I shall go about and sell my books to the best bidder, and I want something, decidedly, for this performance:[2] 16,000 lines, or over,—done in less than two years, Isa!—I having done other work besides,—and giving the precious *earlier* hours of the morning to it, moreover, which take the strength out of one. Poor Mrs Carlyle's death was sad and strange,—but by no means "shook" me rudely;—after all, there are people to take care of her husband,—and she might be considered fairly as entitled to go: I have not seen C.,—he talks much about her, and *shows* more deep feeling than is usual with him: I dined with them both, and saw her for the last time, when he completed his seventieth year. God bless you, dearest—Pen was pleased with your "shake of the hand" and sends his best love. I am just going to write to Cottrell.

Ever affy yours
ROBERT BROWNING.

1866 : 3

To ROBERT BARRETT BROWNING

151. Rue de Grenelle, Faubg. St. Gn.
Wednesday 2½ p.m. [June 13, 1866.]

Dearest Pen, Indeed there was no use in sending a telegram, it could have told you nothing: Sarianna and Milsand both thought so. I can now give you the account, impossible before. I arrived at 8 a.m. and found Sarianna on the staircase waiting me—she and Mme. Louis had made certain that I could not arrive in time, and I thought at first Nonno[1] would pass away without knowing me, and in a few minutes, for he was in a kind of convulsion-fit, and insensible—however he recovered presently, and knew me and spoke like his old self. He is in all probability dying—from mere exhaustion caused by excessive loss of blood: there is an internal tumour, though of what nature the doctors differ,—for there was a consultation with the first surgeon of the Hôtel Dieu,—in any case there *is* the fatal thing. Yesterday both doctors said he might die any minute, or linger on some days, but the end would be the same. He told me, with just the usual air, that he was perfectly well—and seemed to wonder that we saw anything to grieve about: he is in the full possession of his senses, and every now and then asks Sarianna to read a chapter in the Bible to him—men-

ROBERT BROWNING, SENIOR

tioning the particular one, and what verses he wishes to hear. He is in the most complete peace of mind, and as unconcerned about death as if it were a mere walk into the next room. He told Sarianna yesterday that this was dying, and that he had no sort of doubt as to his future state, "having the promise of One who cannot lie." Consequently he never has even enquired what were the opinions of the doctors,—takes it all in his habitual entirely-confiding way. He says he does not suffer any pain, is quite comfortable. He wished Sarianna *not* to send for me,—could not see why she should: he said "You know I love him." Sarianna said, "And Pen, you love *him* too?"—"Oh, *don't I!* Give him my love." Now, I have told you nearly all that there is to tell,— and I think,—as does Sarianna, and Milsand too, that you are far better spared the sight of poor Nonno's prolonged passage into the other world: for tho' I do not think he suffers much, yet it is sad indeed to see him lying for hours, half-insensible and breathing heavily, while we can do nothing but look on. At the same time, so extraordinary is his constitution that Dr. Frébaut told me he still had hopes, —there might be a recovery yet: I think it impossible,—nor wish to witness this lingering pain and weakness. Sarianna has been sitting up these last two nights, as has Mde. L.—now I shall take my turn. Dear Milsand stays here, too, all the day. I shall stay till the end, which cannot be very distant. Let me have the comfort of knowing, dearest, that you do your work well,—and act like a man in my absence. I will write to-morrow: you will write to me, I know. I beg you to take exercise, to row as usual, and to walk more than usual. Sarianna and Milsand send their true love to you,—you know what mine is, I think. Give my love to Arabel, and Ocky—I hope the boy is better,—you must tell me.

God bless you ever, Dearest
R B

1866 : 4

To Robert Barrett Browning

Thursday. June 14. '66

Dearest Pen,—This morning at 8.25. dearest Nonno died. You will have been expecting this from the letter I sent yesterday. I feared the worst, you know, but might have been led to hope from the opinion of Milsand as well as the Doctor,—who said there was no sign of approaching death,—on his afternoon visit. But the loss of blood was very great, and could not be stopped: it would have overcome a man of thirty in just the same way, I think: and Nonno was simply *overcome* by death, in that manner,—there was no sort of weakness in any of his vital parts,—I almost wish there had been, for he suffered sadly indeed: he was, you see, twenty-four hours exactly in passing out of the world,—the beginning being that attack under which I found him labouring when I arrived at a little past eight yesterday. He was entirely conscious the whole time,—up to the very last, understanding and answering to whatever I said,—so that I was able to do little things for his relief, without fear of mistake. At night he asked to see Milsand, "just to shake hands with him"—and he said to Sarianna and me—"If we do not meet again, I hope we shall meet in Heaven." I made Sarianna go to bed—she was worn out with sitting up the last two nights, besides the previous anxiety—and I and Madᵉ Louis kept watch. He got worse and worse,—retaining his consciousness, as I have said and about 2½ began to breathe with difficulty: Sarianna got up then—and it all ended about six hours after—to my infinite joy, for the suffering was terrible to see. All the time he kept up that divine gentleness and care for others that made him by far *the Finest Gentleman* I have ever known:—"Shall I fan you?" I said—"If you please, dear—I'm only afraid of tiring you"—and so on: this, in the very agonies of death. It is over at last, and he is with God. I am most thankful that you were not here to be distressed by the useless sight of pain you could not relieve: I persuaded Sarianna, even, not to witness the last struggle: dear Madᵉ Louis did all that was possible. Milsand came this morning of course. We expect that the funeral will take place on Saturday, at Montmartre. I will write you to-morrow: and you must write to me. I can't tell you how pleased I am with your letter, and the learning that you have been so good and diligent. Sarianna bears her loss, as I expected of her goodness and sense: when anybody has been so perfect and dutiful as she always was to Nonno, —there is a comfort ever afterward. I hope to return early in the week, —and expect that I shall induce Sarianna to follow me at no great interval: but all this, when we can think of it: I will then talk about Wilson's note.

Now, will you take the paper I enclose to Whibley and bid him get it inserted in the next "Times"?—Tell him to charge it to my account. God bless you, my own Pen.

R B.

1866 : 5

To Robert Barrett Browning

151. Rue de Grenelle,
Friday [June 15, 1866].

Dearest Pen,—Thank you very much for your kind and satisfactory letter. I very well know you would have liked to see Nonno again,—but you would have been miserable to see that kind-hearted man who never hurt a fly in his life suffer for twelve hours, more or less, acute pain—knowing you could not lighten it in any way. I told you what he said about you the day before—"Oh, *don't* I love him! Give him my love!"—It was very unusual for him to talk in that way. If you loved him too,—as I am sure you did,—why, try and do as he wished, and be a distinguished, good man,—and an honour to his name, which is yours likewise. He will be buried to-morrow, Saturday, at 12 o'clock: I wish you, particularly, to row as usual,—it is good for your health and right: but if you please, in memory of what is going on here, read by yourself in the morning those last chapters which he had read to him a few hours before his death: first, St. John's Gospel, 1st Chap^tr. up to verse 34: then Daniel, 9th Chaptr. to verse 20: then, Ezra, Chapr. 9th beginning at Verse 5 to the end, and last—"what is more proper," he said, "to a person in my circumstances—John, Gospel, Chap. 14 and three next chapters." It can do you no harm to hear what an extraordinarily learned and able man like Nonno, who might have been a great man had he cared a bit about it, found a comfort to him in, I suppose, the greatest sufferings he ever underwent in his long life.

Sarianna will arrange matters here, and come and live with us as soon as she can: you will like that as much as I. I shall write to-morrow and tell you whether I return on Monday, as I hope. I believe you will have no time before then,—but, if it suits you, I should like you to go to Thompson's and order a mourning suit, to last the summer, for yourself—and another, of a like kind, for me (he has my measure too recently to want another—) : I want them as soon as possible, you know. Tell him why I was unable to go and pay his bill—and bid him include it in the new one: I shall get any letter you write to-morrow—not after, I think. God bless you,

Yours ever affy
R B

Milsand sends his kind love to you—Sarianna, of course: Milsand has been doing everything for us: but you know him. Love to Willy and Mrs. B.[1]

1866 : 6

To Robert Barrett Browning

Sunday M^g [June 17, 1866].

Dearest Pen,—I have two letters to thank you for, as there is no post to-day in London: I have no objection to your going to Henley, —but I shall be back long before Thursday,—on Tuesday, that is: either in the morning, if I leave to-morrow night; or the evening, if I take the tidal train: not later, I am sure. I have nothing more to do here: Sarianna will settle her affairs and join us very soon: she will bring her chairs, and Nonno's dear books, and pictures &c and establish herself in the little room which I will make comfortable: but she must take her own time to do this. Dear Nonno's funeral took place yesterday, with all possible respect: Milsand, Mr. Conolly, Mr. O'Meagher, Mr. Digweed,—and others,—poor old Tellier and Servan, Madame Louis' nephew included,—in three coaches. To-day there was a very kind and good Funeral sermon preached at the Chapelle Marboeuf by Mr. Gardiner, the Chaplain,—who also read the service yesterday: he knew Nonno,—and loved him of course,—but had been always struck with his humility and goodness, as well as his acquirements,—he spoke of him in a way honorable to both, and very grateful to me and Sarianna and Milsand who was present. Tellier came this morning, and cried while he praised him. I don't think I have said enough about Madame Louis—who was perfect from first to last.

You did quite right about ordering the clothes for yourself, and I daresay what you say about colours is true. I shall wait till I go to London, as it will make little difference, and I may have what I want, already.

Understand therefore, that I shall either arrive *early* on Tuesday— or late,—in all likelihood: if anything happens to keep me another day, don't wonder nor be alarmed—I will write, and come next day, Wednesday, in that case. Send or take the tickets for Ella's to the Storys at once, if you have not done so.

Good bye, dearest—all love from Sarianna, and Milsand, who is here while I write.

Ever affectionately yours
ROBERT BROWNING

Thank dearest Arabel for her kind letter to me.

1866 : 7

TO MISS ISABELLA BLAGDEN

June 20th '66.

My dearest Isa,

I was telegraphed for to Paris last week, and arrived time enough to pass twenty four hours more with my Father: he died on the 14th,—quite exhausted by internal haemorrage, which would have overcome a man of thirty. He retained all his faculties to the last—was utterly indifferent to death,—asking with surprise what it was we were affected about, since he was perfectly happy?,—and kept his old strange sweetness of soul to the end—nearly his last words to me, as I was fanning him, were "I am so afraid that I fatigue you, dear!"—this, while his sufferings were great,—for the strength of his constitution seemed impossible to be subdued. He wanted three weeks exactly to complete his 85th year. So passed away this good, unworldly, kind hearted, religious man, whose powers natural and acquired would have so easily made him a notable man, had he known what vanity or ambition or the love of money or social influence meant. As it is, he was known by half a dozen friends. He was worthy of being Ba's father—out of the whole world, only he, so far as my experience goes. She loved him,—and *he* said, very recently, while gazing at her portrait, that only that picture had put into his head that there might be such a thing as the worship of the images of saints. My sister will come and live with me henceforth. You see what she loses,—all her life has been spent in caring for my mother, and, seventeen years after that, my father: you may be sure she doesn't rave and rend her hair like people who have plenty to atone for in the past,—but she loses very much.

I returned to London last night—the 19th—I could not write then. I have at once gone on with business this morning, and begun by writing to Chapman. I am profoundly discontented with him, and shall dissolve our connection,—on my own account, not yours only. I think you are too desponding: the rejection of Mazzini proves that the Reds do *not* carry all before them; and the necessities of a war may be repaid by the advantages of a triumph, in which I believe. To be sure, I have not had the misfortune to hear a Red (perhaps Jessie) lay down the law. Depend on it, the fire can be kept within the stove, and not burn the whole house it warms. I will do what you want about Ferdinando. God bless you—expect a better letter next time and forgive this, and

> Yours ever affectionately
> R Browning.

1866 : 8

To Miss Isabella Blagden

Le Croisic, Loire Inférieure.[1] Aug. 7. [1866]

Dearest Isa,

This time let my letter precede yours—otherwise you will not know whither to send one: we all found Dinard unsuitable and, after staying a few days at St Malo, resolved to try this place—and well for us, since it serves our purpose capitally: usually it is fashionable and full, but this season reports of the cholera and other causes have kept people away, and we have it nearly to ourselves: we are in the most delicious and peculiar old house I ever occupied, the oldest in the town,—plenty of great rooms,—nearly as much space as at the Villa Alberti: Mrs Bracken is well-lodged too, close by: the little town, and surrounding country are wild and primitive, even a trifle beyond Pornic perhaps: close by is Batz, a village where the men dress in white from head to foot, with baggy breeches, and great black flap hats,—opposite is Guerande, the old capital of Bretagne,—you have read about it in Balzac's Beatrix,—and other interesting places are near: the sea is all round our peninsula, and on the whole I expect we shall like it very much. But I want to tell you that, on arriving at Jersey, I at once found out and called on F. Tennyson: he was not indoors, but his wife welcomed me most warmly—said they had been talking of me that day before, and so on. She showed me over the garden and house—which contents them greatly—has quite obliterated Florence from their thoughts: so it would not from mine,—nice enough as it is, but quite another thing from the Garden Palace they were used to: she spoke very eagerly of your coming to see and stay with them,—as if you had promised to do so: it would be a good visit—for the island seems beautiful, and the delight of seeing Tennyson again would affect you as it did me when I returned in the evening to take tea with them: I brought Pen and Willy with me: he was just as of old, pleasant and genial to the last degree,—I told him about you,—how you gave me his address (—which I had preserved, and gave *him*) and how I had seen you the day before: I saw also his three daughters,—two very pretty—and a young Alfred Tennyson: in short I enjoyed it all greatly, and, but for the arranged plan, would have passed our holiday there. Mrs T. told me he is wholly addicted to spirit-rapping and writing—in which she also believes—moreover he is "quite changed" (from what?) and "is of the faith of the New Jerusalem"—i. e Swedenborgian: she said a word or two on both subjects, but no more—and the fewer the better. He seemed to hope you would come and see him. I groan over such a noble, accomplished man being as good as lost to us all. At St Malo we made excursions to Dinan, which I knew, and the Mont St Michel, which I didn't,—a very wonderful sight. I shall try and see the great things in this region which, for one cause or another I have hitherto missed,—Carnac &c.

It was very vexing to see so little of *you*—still that little may help me over a few more stages of the journey: I shall not hope to return to Florence,—but somewhither in the Land of the Souls I will go to, if I can. Poor Italy,—whosever the fault, how ill she has come off,—in the sea-fight, strangely so: and to get Venetia in this way! I don't envy you if you are to be dosed with Jessie's comments and explanations of it all,—helped by the "Vice-Admiral's" experience.

Tell me about your book,[2] your arrangements with the Publisher, —and whether you have heard anything from Chapman: I told you I had written a letter to him that morning—which I had in my pocket, on the chance that you might say something admitting of an excuse for him,—for I hate quarreling with the poor fellow,—but I could not make matters better, so the letter was posted in the evening,—a decisive one. I don't believe he meant worse than delay—but that is a vile thing, and the carelessness also that he cannot deny. I see by the Athenæum that Swinburne's Poems[3] are out. Have you seen them? Tell me: I am not badly off for news however,—receiving the "Times," "Ath^n" and "Illustrated News."

I will now follow the others to the bathing-place: I wanted to write and apprize you whither to direct the letter I shall be so glad to receive. Direct the *next* hither also,—I stay till the end of September. The weather is not warm, rather chilly, but sunshiny and pleasant. Tell me all about yourself—and where I am next to think of you. Of course I found out much I had forgotten to enquire about,—and written words profit little, in my case. My sister is quite well, and sends her best love, as does Pen: the Brackens are quite well. Goodbye, dearest Isa. Give me a good full letter, not eked out by *M* because I value every dear word you write. God bless you.

Ever affectionately yours
ROBERT BROWNING.

1866 : 9

To Miss Isabella Blagden

Le Croisic, Loire Inférieure.
Sept. 24. '66—and not the 19th

dearest Isa, this time, because I have been waiting fruitlessly for above a week the letter which I am sure is written—and I wanted so much to know about you and let *you* know that I did know it. You said in your last "I may not be in Florence by the 12th but will write from wherever I am." Perhaps the letter waits me at London: anyhow, for the future I will keep to my day—and this time it was the very day[1]— how many years ago! At all events, you got my last month's answer at Stone House. The time here is drawing fast to a close: I feel a real attachment to the place—tested attachment, too, for the weather has been abominable these three full weeks,—rain and rain again. This, and the earlier report of cholera kept all visitors away, and the little peninsula was wholly our own. Miss Egerton Smith arrived a month ago,— I liked her always, and as much now. She is lodged at the Bathing Establishment, where they have sometimes a hundred and fifty inmates,—and, this season, a dozen or two: these also are all but gone; and, out of the pale, ourselves and Mrs Bracken are the famous "last roses." Pen and Willy have bathed regularly and led long days in the open air—shooting, alas! But the health is helped, if somewhat at the expense of the "morale." We go to Guérande to-gether,—the delicious little town,—dine there at an inn "Les Guérandaises" (where two pretty sisters do the waiting, and return early—generally catching a wedding-dance at some one of the intermediate villages—Saillié or Batz. Had the weather resembled that of last year at Pornic—when we had two months of golden days—the leaving all this, as we shall early next week, would have been difficult. I see Guérande—from this room —hardly farther, if at all, than Fiesole from Bellosguardo: but the sea

SARIANNA BROWNING

is between, and the road goes round it, doubling the distance. I should suppose this is the last of our holidays of the kind: if Pen goes to Oxford next Michaelmas, it must be,—and he is summoned there, by the official letter: we should go somewhere and somehow, but not exactly after this careless way: so end good things! I was resolute not to return to Pornic, full of my poor dear Papa—as I never broke the habit of calling him: I wonder whether Pen will long come and kiss me, morning and night, as he now does. I don't in the least know how he will turn out *eventually:* he is still, to all intents, growing,— a boy: he seems to me able to do many things for which at present he has little or no inclination,—and that inclination may arrive at any moment: but the bases of a strong and good character, on the other hand, are more than indicated,—they are laid: he is good, kind, cautious, self-respecting, and true: I ought to be satisfied with these qualities which are valuable enough. I want him to be what I think he may be: next year or two will decide perhaps if I shall be disappointed or no. Well, Isa—write to me next time—tho' you have not forgotten me now, I well know. I wish I had seen more of you,—that rushing way of yours,—unavoidable under the circumstances of a short stay,— drives the thoughts *in* instead of out: I have said nothing. How did your bargain conclude? Did you get the sum you asked? It will not come out (the book)² till the winter, of course. Goodbye and God bless you. Sarianna and Pen send their true love with mine—ever affectionately yours

Rob^T Browning.

1866 : 10

To Professor Edward Dowden

19, Warwick Crescent,
Upper Westbourne Terrace,
London, W.
October 13th, 1866.

My dear Sir,

I was out of reach when your very kind and welcome letter arrived here,—you guessed this, I will believe, hence these very tardy thanks for it.

The first blunder you point out is enormous—only explicable to myself—and hardly that—from the circumstances under which I well remember having written the poem, *Transcendentalism.* I was three

parts thro' it, when called to assist a servant to whom a strange accident, partly serious, partly ludicrous, had suddenly happened; and
after a quarter of an hour's agitation, of a varied kind, I went back to
my room and finished what I had begun. I have never touched the
piece since, and really suppose that the putting "Swedish" for "German," or "Goerlitzist," is attributable just to that—for I knew something of Boehme, and his autobiography, and how he lived mainly,
and died in the Goerlitz where he was born. But the thought in my
head was of that revelation he describes, not of his nationality;[1] hence,
I hope, my blunder—and such excuse as it may admit of. Depend on
it, I will alter the word in the next edition, ay, and look more warily
after what may be other slips of the kind.

But, here I get up from my knee and assure you there is no slip in
the other case; at least, I was wide awake when I made Fra Lippo the
elder practitioner of Art, if not, as I believe, the earlier born. I looked
into the matter carefully long ago, and long before I thought of my
own poem, from my interest in the Brancacci frescos, indeed in all
early Florentine Art. I believe the strange confusions and mistakes of
Vasari are set tolerably right now: you may know, he took Lippino
the son for Lippo the father. I suppose Lippo to have been born, as
Baldinucci says, about 1400. He entered the Carmine aged eight years
and immediately "in cambio di studiare, non faceva altro che im-
brattare con fantocci i libri."[2] Let us assume even, with the last Edi-
tors of Vasari, that he was born in 1412, and that this entrance took
place in 1420; still, since it is certain that Masaccio did not begin the
paintings in the Brancacci before 1440, you see there was a good score
of years wherein Lippo might well work and Masaccio watch him
working. The Editor sums up "Se le pitture del Chiostro e della
Chiesa del Carmine furono fatte da Lippo quando vestiva l'abito
Carmelitano, bisognerebbe conghietturare con ragione che le pitture
sue furono poi e studiate e imitate da Masaccio,"[3]—which is my own
reasonable conjecture. Masaccio was born in 1402, and, as Vasari
writes in his life, "lavorava nel Carmine seguitando sempre le vestigie
di Filippo."[4] But all that "Life" is a tissue of errors. I could never have
had *these* facts shaken out of my head, even by the crying and laughing of poor W. my servant afore mentioned.

But—thank you just as heartily in this case as in the former. I don't
deserve such kind care about my works, but am very grateful for it,
all the same; and shall ever be, my dear Sir,

Yours most truly,
ROBERT BROWNING.

1866 : 11

To George Henry Lewes

My dear Lewes,

I am unlucky, as usual,—having a particular engagement for Tuesday evening, to my sorrow.

With all regards to Mrs Lewes,

Yours most truly ever
ROBERT BROWNING.

19. Warwick Crescent,
Upper Westbourne Terrace, W.
Nov. 18. '66.

1867 : 1

To Baron Seymour Kirkup[1]

19. Warwick Crescent, Upper Westbourne Terrace.
Feb: 19. '67.

My dear Friend,

You will almost think I have forgotten you,—not so, at all. I had a long letter from you in the Spring last year, and a packet of Landor's letters also,—these I gave to Forster, who wished himself to thank you and, no doubt, did so. Just as I [had] in mind to write, my poor Father died; he had been ailing—rather than absolutely ill—for some few years, with an internal complaint, I hardly know what, except that a sort of varicose vein in the bladder used to burst at intervals and heal itself, without any treatment beyond a little taking "tisanes," and a little cooling medicine: the doctor said it was hardly to be regretted, as being in some degree a natural prevention of worse evils attending old age in florid health, and that the occasional loss of blood was of no great consequence: nor was it, at first—but afterward it grew considerable, occurred oftener, and interfered with the walking exercise which was necessary to him: yet the autumn before (in '65) he made the usual journey with me to Brittany, a good three days' business, and enjoyed his daily walks pretty much as usual: but on the following Easter, I found a great change in him,—that the continual loss of blood was making an undue demand on his strength. The intellect, always very extraordinarily active, was quite unaffected: he continued his studies to the very last—and, on my requesting him to investigate the history of one of the Popes—(I did it to interest him, mainly) he sent me, a few weeks before the end, a regular book of researches, and a narrative of his own, exhausting the subject. His sight, hearing, memory,—all were absolutely as I remember them thirty years ago—even his appearance was singularly unchanged. I was summoned by telegram, reached Paris on the 13 June, and found him dying—in full possession of his faculties. He had no more fear about death than I have in penning this paragraph: he assured me so, most emphatically. He had been violently seized by a fresh attack of his malady and, two days before, compelled to keep his bed for the first time in his life. Vigla, the head-surgeon of the Hôtel-Dieu was called in, and pronounced the case hopeless,—my father never took the trouble to ask what he said—wondering what was the use of "consulting" about so clear a case. When my sister proposed to send for me, he asked "Why trouble him? He knows what I feel for him." But I was sent for and came, and was by him till he died, twenty four hours after. He suffered most painfully—his great strength having to be subdued by main force, as it were. But he was sensible to the last, and utterly kind and considerate of others, as he had always been. He wanted a fortnight of completing his eighty-fourth year. He was a perfectly unworldly, good man,—not so much disinterested as without the notion of self-interest. With a touch of ambition, even a spice of vanity, he would assuredly have won a reputation in more ways than one,—but he loved whatever he loved for its own sake only, and, had he discovered the longitude, would have given his discovery to the first stranger, quite content to let *him* get all the credit, and profit too. He was an unhesitating believer in Christianity: and I tell you all about a man who would have stared to hear himself mentioned as remarkable, knowing your sympathy with me and mine. My sister (my only one, I never had a brother) is come to live with me here. She has always been perfect in her relation to everyone she was naturally a help to. I returned to London—we then went to France for the autumn,—not to Pornic, as before, but to a delicious place in Brittany, Le Croisic—glorified to me long ago by the Beatrix of Balzac, which I used to devour as it came out in feuilletons in the "Siècle" of those days. Croisic is the old head-seat of Druidism in France, probably mentioned by Strabo: the people were still Pagan a couple of hundred years ago, despite the priests' teaching and preaching, and the women used to dance round a phallic stone still upright there with obscene circumstances enough,—till the general civilization got too strong for this. Close by, is the strange, solitary Bourg de Batz—a Saxon colony of stalwart men who retain exactly the dress of their forefathers, three hundred years ago—white tunic, baggy breeches, stockings, even shoes, all white, but a great black flap-hat with red fringes. These are the *paludiers* who collect the salt from the *salines,* which forms the staple produce of the place. Still farther on, is the delicious old city of Guerande, intact with its moat, wall, towers and gates: it is the old seat of all the genuine Bretagne noblesse, who live on in the old way and with the old ideas. The whole district is wild, strange and romantic, with a fine fierce sea, and driving sands. I lived at Croisic in a fine old house, fit to contain a dozen families, bathed daily (except when the sea was too fierce) and made excursions in the neighbourhood. On my return I found myself with plenty of work to do,—Robert has to go to Oxford next Michaelmas, and is reading hard for his matriculation at Balliol,—they exact terribly at that college.[2] I want him to be under Jowett, Tutor there, who manages young men admirably. Robert is a fine little fellow in his way—wanting a month of being eighteen. He is strong, healthy, inordinately given to boating, quite a boy still, but good, truthful, *loyal*—I may safely say: all depends on the turn he may take just now. I shall enclose you the last photograph of him,—you will hardly recognize the curly little creature that was. I have heard much of *you* lately, from various people who passed thro' Florence,—Arthur Russell &c. And Lady Westmorland showed me parts of a letter, two days ago, you had much gratified her by writing. She often talks about you,—so does Lady William Russell, Layard—indeed, all friends. Shall I see you soon for myself, I wonder? Now that Robert will go to the University, there will be no longer an imperative reason for my presence here. I should find Florence much changed, I am told,—but there must be much left, and the rest I can supply from my heart. Yet, by an odd chance, there was a possibility, a few days ago, of my choosing to hamper myself for the next five years, by taking the Professorship of Poetry at Oxford, now vacant! A body of the young men actually came and declared they wanted me in that capacity,—whereon, no less than forty-five of the Congregation (Resident Body) signed a paper requesting the Council to propose to Convocation that I should be qualified to compete by receiving a M. A. Degree: the Council however refused to do this, on the ground that it would be unfair to the candidates long ago in the field,—Ruskin (withdrawn, however) and others of less note: now, *I* thought, and think, just the same,—but *that* was for them to consider, not me. I could only take the proposal as a compliment to a complete *outsider* like myself. I would have accepted the office—because it would have brought me into close relation with the University just now when Robert goes there,—and, for his sake, I would, if it might comport with a gentleman's behaviour, black the boots, much more brighten the brains, of Oxford aforesaid. However, it is best as it is—I have acknowledged the kindness and honor, and keep my liberty all the same. But you, by the way—you are a Baron, I find! Capitally thought and done of the chivalrous King, for which, and much beside, I thank him heartily. Thus comes, occasionally, honor to desert! I can easily imagine it surprised you— who would not have turned your head for it,—so it came to you— which is right and just, and reconciles one to the pomps and vanities in this kind, which have got their ill-name thro' their habit of going after the wrong man: I congratulate them, this time.

Forster's Life of Landor will very much interest us all: Henry Landor died a few weeks ago—having long been blind and incapable of enjoying life: Robert still lives,—quite his old self, they say. He has furnished Forster with ample materials—I hope poor Landor's unwise career won't come out too startlingly in relief: he wasted the finest powers and abused the happiest position in the world, there is no denying. But I love his memory, poor dear grand misguided good and foolish man! His wretched sons, at least numbers one and two, are getting their deserts—Julia, too, got hers in a way she little suspects, and would be so sensible of, that I hope she will never know: Henry Landor had left her a legacy of £2000—and revoked it in consequence of her behaviour to her father. Her father was unjust to her in some respects—but *was* her father. Here is a long letter, I shall not venture to re-read: can you *once* read the same? I did not observe the vileness of the paper till past remedy. Do write me a word, my dear friend— tell me all your news: how is Bibi?[3] Remember me to her and assure her of my love. Robert is away—but I may dispose of his love too— knowing what he would say and send.

Ever affectionately yours,
ROBERT BROWNING.

1867 : 2

To Miss Isabella Blagden

19, Warwick Crescent, Upper Westbourne
Terrace, W.
Feb: 19, '67.

Dearest Isa,

I am glad you are back again: you are glad too, I dare say, after the change and inevitable fatigue. The next three or four months are the pleasant time in Florence. Afterward,—where do you go? But it is foolish to ask, or even think, in this world of changes and warpings of plans.

Pen will soon know his fate now: he goes on a visit of a week to Jowett on the 25th March,—Jowett most kindly meaning to look into his case at his ease in that way. Nothing can exceed his kindness. By the bye I ought to tell you what you are likely to hear of in some distorted way, that a number of young men at Oxford made a request that *I* might be their Poetry Professor, on Arnold's vacating the chair next June,—that, in compliance with this, a formal application was made, of which I have the printed copy, signed by forty-five of the most eminent people composing the "Congregation," or resident body, at Oxford,—to the effect that the Council would qualify me to compete, should I please, by conferring on me the degree of M. A. required by the Statute,—and that the Council declined to do this, as unfair to the Candidates already in the field. I think this declining on their part very fair and just. I should not have liked, had I been one of the members of the University, to be ousted of my chance by an outsider called in and made eligible just for the purpose: but I thought it was entirely for the University itself to decide on *that*,—just as, if you proposed to dedicate a book to me it would be impertinent to object, "But is that fair to this man or the other?" Had it been offered me, I should have accepted it—simply on account of the wish I have to stand well with,—and, above all, near to—the University where Pen will spend the next three or four years: I should have had a legitimate reason for going down there, and a greater likelihood of hearing the truth of things,—how he got on in every way,—than I should otherwise have: besides I really feel the compliment of being pulled *inside* the body from its extreme outside. But of course there would have been drawbacks in the shape of the curtailment of liberty for the next five years, when I should perhaps want to dispose of my time otherwise. Moreover the three Lectures in the year would take as much trouble to write as three tragedies,—for I try to do things thoroughly. As it is, I have gained my point, by having taken the opportunity of showing the University my sense of their kindness—for I was applied to to say *if* I would take what they meant to try and offer me. Had they wished me to blacken their boots instead of polish their heads, I should not have demurred, you understand, in the prospect of possible advantage to Pen. So much for me. I see your book advertised—and will of course read it, and tell you my exact feeling about it,—why not? You know me by this time, and know that, whatever my opinion may be worth, my wishes for your good are deep as deep can be. I have not seen Chapman since he saw you—can't help it, but distrust the man, without dislike of the poor, goodnatured fellow otherwise. I suppose he won't send me the book,[1] but I can get to read it.

I am very sorry about Locker—the case is hopeless, as I told George Barrett and Arthur Locker,—Payne[2] insulted Forster abominably—and must have *known* that Forster would never have allowed him to print pieces belonging to him,—the wonder is, he felt inclined to do so,—for Landor's poetry hardly makes such a book attractive. The thing is going to get to a regular trial, I fear, and the costs will be pro-portionate: it is inconceivable that Payne should not at once put up with his actual loss, call in the copies, and have done with the matter. Locker was wrong in not applying to Forster, and getting a plain answer: who is Chapman, to give leave or refuse it? I am very sorry, but nothing can be done: Payne has even added to his offences by writing a letter so insolent that it will be brought forward in the pro-ceedings, as an aggravation of the wrong.

Yes,—poor George is simple enough with his "warmth of char-acter"! Hatty[3] is just the old Hatty—less interesting, as is the way with all such pretty things after a time: the "not-niceness" of her conduct is the old story,—I observe that it is an unfailing characteristic of *talent* as distinguished from *genius*—that it cleverly uses all sorts of helps and as carelessly shakes them off: Genius sees the possible help quite as clearly, but, having besides a strong preference for the *best* and truest, *cannot* pretend to take all sorts of counters for good coin, merely because of the convenience,—it *prefers* saying "this is no coin but a counter"—even to its own loss. Hatty used to take up and be "dearest friend" with any and everybody, dropping them at a minute's notice or without it,—of course, for some defect or fault: but then genius would have foreseen and refused the thing, while talent either could not see or—likelier *did* see and only said to itself—"We shall break off the easilier." Hatty has seen into the characteristic points of the Storys long ago, and exposed them liberally enough. Now, there is another thing genius does occasionally—see a faulty thing, never suf-fer it to be taken for anything but a faulty thing, yet—all the same, with *that* admitted, get good of a kind out of it too. Just so I feel for Hatty's little self—not mistaking her, but liking her considerably in her way: so the Storys are likeable in their way.

Well, here is the season again, dinners again, parties again and more than ever. Sometimes, you know, I am in a mood to tell you gossip,—not to day, however. I promised to say, though, that I met Mr and Mrs

Bowen at John Coleridge's two or three days ago—and talked about you. She is a nice gentle creature,—how do people get in love with that thing, though? Lewis[4] and Mrs L: are in Spain, I believe: his health is deplorable. I wrote a long letter to Kirkup yesterday—do you ever see him? He likes you much, poor old man,—besotted, I hear, with his spirits. Tell me—you *won't* however—about the Tassinaris—is she dead or alive! Mrs Baker and her sister and mother, and the others. Is the Philipson family still thriving? Trollope I hear of sometimes. No,—Florence is done with, for me—I shall *serpentize*[5] elsewhere, Isa! Did you read a book called "Florence as it is" or something of the kind, by Weld, Brother-in Law to Tennyson? I looked over the pages, no more: but noticed that Casa Guidi was to be let furnished, and that it was extravagantly dear. How is Jessie White,—near you? Give her my love, if you see her. I hear nothing of Annette, even from Mrs Bracken. Willy grows an immense fellow, very gentlemanly and pleasant.

Good bye, dearest Isa—I have been busied these seven hours and feel stupid and weary. Your letters are always a bright spot in my month. I can't bring myself to make mine so, as I might, by merely putting in little notes of people you would be interested about: thus, I met Macready the other day,—so old and changed, so uninterested in his old life! His wife is a Plymouth Sister,—never entered a theatre in her life.[6] This seems to abolish the whole past existence of such a man. This is vile paper—*runs*—and probably renders what I write of very little consequence: I will beware another time. Sarianna's best love to you—Pen's also: both are very well: Pen *boats*—cares more for that than aught else,—unless perhaps for shooting and breechloaders: but he is a good fellow all the same, and may wake up ambitious one day.

Ever yours affectionately,
ROBERT BROWNING.

1867 : 3

TO MISS ISABELLA BLAGDEN

Athenaeum Club
Pall Mall S. W.
19th March (by rights!) really, March 21, '67.

Dearest Isa,

I waited thus long in the hope I should be able to get your book[1] before I wrote: I *cannot,*—get whoever may the novel,—I cannot get

it, though, thro' Arabel Barrett, my name is long since down on a
library-list for it. Will you wait till next time? By when, depend on
my reading and criticizing to heart's content. I never see Chapman,
and there is no wonder he don't send it or lend it. I have seen no review as yet, even a line in length: I hope they will come in thick and
threefold, all the better considered for not being done in a hurry as
usual.

I shall interest you by telling you that Lytton and his wife are here,
—I met them at Forster's the day of their arrival. She is very nice and
distinguished,—not, to my mind, with a trace of prettiness—but that
may be owing to her health (she is to be confined in June). He is
just the same as ever,—was very affectionate and demonstrative,—
seems very fond of his wife, too,—and she, I hear, gives him a wonderful character,—let it all be as it looks. He wants much to know Mat
Arnould,[2] and I will bring it about, if I can: but he called on Lady
Strangford, at whose house A. was to be, and when I could have done
it, and got no invitation—to his surprise—the fact being, I *suspect,*
this—Strangford is the man who wrote that memorable review of
"Serbsky Pesme" in the Saturday,—and may have his own likings or
dislikings in the matter: I don't think Lytton guesses this,—and what
is the use of telling him? They may arrange it among themselves.
Lytton looks older, very bearded, seems occupied with his child,—in
short is in good case, which you will be glad to hear.

All you say about the inadequate test of superiority in a young man
which college honours indicate I know very well; I don't want them,
in fact,—only the ordinary proficiency as a step to something else,—
tho' I value learning too. I certainly shall feel it much if he can't get
into Balliol,[3]—that difficulty tided over, I shall only exact the ordinary
application and gaining of a degree. I shall not be long kept waiting
now. I told you, I think, that Pen goes on a visit to Jowett next Monday—for a week: and that the matriculation takes place—or should—
on the 2^d of May. Pen is not nervous at all—is in excellent health and
strength, and has worked really hard this *month*—not before then: in
fact, he is immature, and could not realize the nearness of the trial
and necessity of preparing for it. I should not allow him to study long
at this rate—and his progress has been great for the time.

This is the season of dinners: I dined last eg. with *Bright,* and other
notables,—I liked him much, we talked about poetry of which he is
very fond. It was funny to see him sitting by a Duke and bating no
syllable of his radicalism. But I was at a still better entertainment last
week—dining with Ld Russell and Gladstone and only one other
guest: the two talked unreservedly, and very interesting it was. I saw

Gladstone at another party afterwards, looking radiant: also saw your friend Miss Elliot—and perhaps three hundred other people.

I told you I had not the least wish to be made Professor—I should just think not!—only wished to propitiate the Dons, and repay the young men for their partiality—which I am flattered with in a mild way. Three lectures would cost me as much pains to deliver as three tragedies to write. I do believe I forgot to tell you that I had seen Bowen and his wife lately at John Coleridge's—(that admirable person)—and that we talked pleasantly together about you.

Indeed I don't think you told me those particulars about those Tassinaris and so on—tho' you may have done so: at all events, I decidedly read and reread your letters always—as you very well know. I don't care one brass farthing about the Tassinaris or Mrs Baker—yet —they are of Florence, and I never even see the name without a stir of heart. I am most sorry for the poor Cottrells—the annoyance to Cottrell is probably in the *change* in his fortunes—he began somewhat showily, flourishingly at all events,—and feels the altered figure he cuts in the eyes of foolish people more than those would who never had cared about their opinion: his wife's ill health may depress her: after all, "five or six hundred pounds" contribute materially to oil the wheels of life, in the case of folks of moderate means. Kirkup wrote a long affectionate letter to me a few days before yours arrived—containing most of the matter that is in your note. Poor man! Provided they don't stifle him or poison him, and afterward rob the house!

Good bye, dearest Isa: Sarianna and Pen send their kindest love— both are quite well moreover. The weather here is vile to an extraordinary degree. Garibaldi is just what I always took him for, once out of a mountain pass! Give a kind of modified love, if you like, to Jessie. I have not seen Mrs Sartoris story—nor any new English story this long while—so yours will find me fresh.

Ever affectionately yours
R B.

1867 : 4

To FIELDS, OSGOOD, AND Co.[1]

London, 19 Warwick Crescent,
Upper Westbourne Terrace, W.
July 19, '67.

Gentlemen,—I beg to thank you for the two letters which contained your handsome acceptance of my proposal,[2] and directions as to the way of forwarding the sheets. I shall do my best to satisfy you, depend upon it, and will manage all about the packets, duplicates, etc., scrupulously. But the people, with a right to advise me in this matter—in which they will be quite as interested as yourselves—demur to my sending anything *seven* weeks before publication; they insist on my avoiding all possibility of even extracts getting here before their own proceedings; especially they want to announce the name of the poem themselves. I must beg for your indulgence and sympathy in these matters, and that you will believe my honest determination is to make you as secure as you would wish.

Meantime I give you what particulars I can, for your guidance. The poem is *new* in subject, treatment and form. It is in Twelve Parts, averaging, say, 1600 lines each. The whole somewhat exceeding 20,000. (It is the shortest poem, for the stuff in it, I ever wrote.) This will be printed here in two volumes of six parts each. The name is that of the collection of law-papers on which, or out of which, rather, the poem is developed. I hope to be able to begin to print in October. I go in a week to a quiet place for two months, where I shall finally dispose of at least three quarters of this thing. Should you want to communicate with me, write to me "Au Croisic, Loire Inférieure, France," where I am to be from August to the end of September.

I hope I do not dissatisfy you in any respect, and, repeating my own satisfaction at your kindness, am, gentlemen,

Very faithfully yours,

ROBERT BROWNING.

1867 : 5

To Miss Isabella Blagden

19 W. C. July 19. '67.

Dearest Isa,

First, as foolishest, will you be good enough to put no M. A. at the end of my name,[1]—unless as a joke, which I don't mind. I have been very pleased, in a way, with the occurrence, because it was purely the Dons' own doing, under the gentle spur of a requisition very plentifully signed,—and is no sort of honorary nonsense but a real advantage (to whoever is disposed to use it, which I don't tell you that I am) and an out of the way proceeding—since, except a few royal people, nobody has had the distinction these hundred years and more, except the Duke of Wellington in 1814. Dr. Johnson don't count, as he had previously belonged to the University and was only prevented taking the degree by circumstances. The D. C. L. (which it was originally proposed to give me) is a mere honor, conferring no privilege whatever: whereas I am now member of the Congregation and Convocation, with a vote for the University, and eligible to any good thing in the same, tenable by a Layman: for instance, any college may elect me a fellow next Term. Well, the good of this to Pen is, that it gives me a natural right to come down to Oxford every now and then, nominally to vote against Dr. Pusey, really to see what the said Pen is about,—and renders it easy that I should know more than would be otherwise possible for the next three or four years. That's all, but that's enough. I got my Diploma last week, wherein I am prettily complimented on the "remarkable sweetness of my verses," among other things—and have duly answered it in as pretty a Latin letter, I'll have you to know.

Next, I wrote to Lytton and am answered that "the name of the Paris aurist is Turnbull, Dr. Turnbull, an Englishman, tho' he lives in Paris,—I don't know his precise address, but will send it to you the next time I see my father." Tell this to Mr Trollope, and it will be quite sufficient indication,—he may make inquiries, if you write in time, before he gets to London: if he wants it, I will send the address when I get it to Ampthill Square. The said Lytton is suffering, or was, last week, from the results of an operation, which was successful, but left him in a feverish state, preventing him from going to his post, and so on: you know probably by the papers that his wife gave birth to a daughter a few weeks ago. I saw her the other day—very pleasing, and perhaps pretty to some eyes. Her sister, Mrs Locke, is prettier, I think, but very like. I was sitting opposite him (and by Mrs Locke) at dinner when my neighbour began "Did not you know poor Marguerite Power? She is dead at last, out of her pain." I said "Speak low, if you please." He is going to publish two volumes of new poetry, after his "works"—next year, I suppose. He is prodigiously discontented with Chapman,—which I can't explain, if the loan, or gift, which Chapman boasted about to you, was made to him, as you fancied. I need not say, it is a matter in which I have not the remotest interest. I have not seen Chapman since that Finis on business:[2] I am sorry for him, but my mind is made up.

Do you hear anything about the trial of Mr Hume which is coming on? I dined this day week at Stanley's and met the Dean of Christchurch who is a near relation of Mrs Lyon,—I think he said, her brother in law,—and interested greatly in the result. He told me all the rascality of Hume, and how his own incredible stupidity as well as greediness wrought his downfall in the foolish old soul's estimation. Next day I saw James, the Counsel in the case,—who told me that, by some oversight, they were unable to get at once the warrant to arrest Hume,—had to prepare a fresh affidavit—and could only act on it two or three days after the application to the Judge which, if it had reached Hume's knowledge, would have let him escape: but "the spirits" said James "told him nothing and the sheriff's officer arrested him at a snug evening party—threw him into prison,—and only let him out on condition of his giving up all the deeds, papers &c to be used in the case. He will be tried "for getting money under false pretences,"—pretending he was inspired by a spirit when there was none. He says—the transaction took place before spiritualism was mentioned at all!—but it so happens, that an old servant, with commendable sagacity, thinking he and his respectable associates S. C. Hall and Wilkinson (who have both got pretty pickings out of the plunder) could be after no good with her mistress, listened at the keyhole, and heard all the proceedings. Hume wanted in the first place to marry Mrs Lyon, James says. There's a misfortune for dear Miss Hayes, Mrs Milner Gibson, and such like vermin! Yet I am going to dine to-night at the house of a lady of rank who believes implicitly in a medium-girl who "darkens the room, and then brings a shower of bouquets down from heaven all over the table,"—(heaven, probably, being underneath her own petticoats, which, I imagine, they don't search previous to the performance.) How much more picturesque and honest was the exhibition of Mrs Clara Hoyt, as described to me by an eye-witness,—did I ever tell you that? Yes, I think.

Well, Isa, I go away in a few days to that wild attractive place where we were last year: I want to start next Monday, stay a few days at Paris for the Exhibition, then go and be salted and solitary for two months. Mrs Bracken and Willy go by the sea to St. Malo—and Miss Smith follows in a little time—each of us going to the same house as before,—we have taken the old Maison du Bochet we liked so much. Direct next time, therefore, to RB. "Au Croisic, Loire Inférieure, France": pray take care, and don't disappoint me, where I should feel such a disappointment particularly. I shall take my poem with me, and get it ready, I hope, to go to press next Oct. or November. I am glad you like the Bagni so well. If you have Annette, as you expect, give her my best love and tell her I never forget our old rides and walks and talks: I have plenty of new lady-acquaintances, some of them attractive enough, but I don't get intimate with any of them. A fortnight ago, I was talking about Rubinstein (he is a marvelous player, beyond what I remember of Liszt, and immeasurably superior to everybody else)—a lady said "And now it is too late to hear him." I said, "No—I know he will be playing at Erard's, quite alone, this afternoon."—"Will you take me?" "And me" said one sister, "and me" said a third. So we all started: and I think Rubinstein was a little surprised as they sailed in,—the three loveliest women in London, perhaps—one being incomparable. He played divinely. Now, they all pet me, you must know, and yet, when I handed them into their carriage again, I made an excuse about wanting to go elsewhere, rather than accompany them farther. Yet I would gladly ride with Annette once more up to the little old ruined chapel, by the bridge,—she may remember,—where we took shelter in a thunderstorm. This is because she is part of the Past, while Ladies This, That and the Other are of this present time which wearies me—yet you think I shall never leave London. Wait and see, my beloved snake!³ By the way, in the new poems of Mat. Arnold just coming out, he has re-placed "Empedocles," he tells me, with a note saying it is all through my desire it should not be withdrawn: I am really flattered by that.

Good bye, dearest Isa,—I must go—having plenty to do this morning. Write me a good long letter. Do you make excursions,—climb to the villages on the top of the hills? I thought Professor Campbell would miss you,—I daresay my letters never reached him, or rather were sent after him. It was to oblige Jowett that I stirred in the matter. How is poor Cottrell? I can't sell his picture, do what I will.

Ever affectionately yours

ROBERT BROWNING.

1867 : 6

To Miss Isabella Blagden

Au Croisic, Loire Inférieure, France.
Aug: 19. '67.

Dearest Isa,

Here we all are, just as last year: the weather is delightful, the sea air delicious, of course,—there can hardly be anything better in summer heats than this little promontory with abundance of Atlantic all round. We arrived on the 1ˢᵗ Miss Smith followed about a week ago. I swam, this morning before breakfast, for half an hour and over without touching ground or even turning on my back, and came out not a bit more tired than when I went in: nothing agrees with me better. This house is the most delightful old place I ever *wholly* occupied:— therefore,—I wish you were here, Isa.

Tell me something,—(mind, this,—and all, except the plainly otherwise intended,—is, according to our compact, *private:*) the day before I left London, I met T. Trollope in the street—I was delighted to be able to give him the Aurist's address, which I had sent you: he had heard of the man as *a quack*—but will reconsider the matter. I was hurried, but said a few words about my pleasure at seeing him, displeasure at seeing no more of him, and . . not seeing his wife,—for politeness sake: he smiled and said nothing: I thought him looking out of sorts and worn,—but attributed it to the journey. A few minutes after, I met at the "Athenæum" a common friend who began "Have you heard this about T.?"—seemed surprised that I had not,—then said there had been a great quarrel, revelation of the past misfortunes of which T. had been ignorant altogether, and a separation." He said, "pray don't quote me, however"—and mentioned a house where I am intimate where they would tell me all about it. As I was leaving the club, I met one of the members of that family, and asked him,—he said it was all true,—he had heard it from Anthony T.—I think, in Paris. Now, *per regolarmi,* I should wish to know the facts —sparing you any comment on them of the many which occur. If things have gone *so*—if the wife *did* enlighten poor T. for the first time on the paternity of the child and so on,—I hardly ever knew so deplorable a case. I take it, that peoples' tongues, never very tight, were absolutely loosened by Theo's death,[1]—as if it didn't matter holding them any longer. It cannot be that *you* don't know the facts.

When I left London, I heard that Lytton had been very ill—erysipelas had followed the operation: however he was better,—I wrote begging him,—as he always had the pen of a ready writer, to give me a word of his news here, nothing however has come yet. It is a great pity for him, in the way of his profession, that he can't be at his post, —as his *Chef* is away, and the Chargé d'Affaires, which he *would* be, must be the Second Secretary in the absence of *him,* the First,—and so till the Chef's return, as it is etiquette that the *Chef* only should introduce his substitute—in person—which can't be in this case. T told you he had new volumes coming out, which I shall be interested to see. Unluckily, thro' some blunder, no Athenæum nor literary journal has reached me this fortnight, and I know nothing of the doings of our penmen. I should like to know something about Arnold's new volume: he told me he had reprinted therein "Enceladus[2] on Etna" —"with a pretty note saying that it was done thro' my request." I am really flattered at *that*—I like the man as much as his poems. Miss Ingelow sent me her poems just before I came away,—the new ones,

—with a too modest note to the effect that her first volume had been so overpraised that she was ashamed of it, but this second seeming to be generally found fault with, she should give it me—I got the note and not the book. Did you see Emerson's new poems? with very fine and true things,—but not in any new key,—the old voice and tone. We are all well,—my sister bathes &c. We have not yet been to Guerande, but go to-morrow, all of us. The two boys went yesterday to see some races,—not to my taste. I am glad you understand the Bagni this time, —get the cool side of the state of things. Do you make excursions? "The Trelawneys" are problematical to me,—he has so many wives and daughters,—the last he married, I fancied had been the Baronet's wife, whose divorce he caused: he was living last month in his house at Brompton,—I called there. I met him at dinner at the Sartoris's. He lives with a niece,—I suppose she is *that,* but won't swear,—a light-haired girl. He told me he had been three times *drowned*—and resuscitated,—after being hours in the water. I am going to write to Kirkup, of whose illness I had not heard. Write to this address next time, of course.

Ever yours affectionately
R. B.

I happen to have a photograph with me—and send it, wisely, to save you from a shock the next time you see me.—I think it pretty good. Love of course from Pen and Sarianna always.

1867 : 7

To Miss Isabella Blagden

Le Croisic, Sept. 19. '67.

Dearest Isa,

I was truly glad to get your letter and to find that the statement (*not* report) is in all probability an immense mistake and untruth. Observe, I never believed it—that is, that if such a separation had taken place it could be on the ground alleged (—for it would be too absurd for a man's second wife to quarrel with him because his first had used him ill; such a reason could only be a pretence covering something deeper—) and I at once applied to *you* for corroboration of it—partly through real concern should it be true,—partly from fear at having ignorantly given pain to a person I much like. But you cannot class with "reports" like that cackle about my marriage, the deliberate statement of as veracious a man as I know that he had been told what I told you by Anthony T. himself: if instead of the goose your informant, you had been assured by Milsand that Sarianna had told him such a piece of news,—why, I should expect a question to myself of the kind I have put to you. I believe there has been some most extraordinary mistake, caused—the devil knows how or why,—and I do not at all care how,—only am very glad it should be so, thinking that our friend has had quite his share of being dragged thro' the dirt already. I should be delighted also to think, if I possibly could, that the falsity of this report is "good ground for disbelieving in all those old stories," as you suggest: that seems to me not unlike the lady who would not credit the execution of Maximilian, seeing that John Brown was not married to the Queen after all. Better let us "Gently raise so weak a fame, Or softly drop so poor a shame." As to the "principal calumny,"—if that be, as I suppose, the paternity,—why, some part of it should be called "self-calumniation": a person told me only a few weeks before I left London,—one who never saw the mother nor, I believe, heard a word about the scandal,—that the demeanour of Mrs So and So with the child was improper and unintelligible except as coming from a near relation. What is the amount of evidence people *do* expect in such cases? The seventy-two eyewitnesses which, it is said, are required to prove the adultery of a Cardinal? Let's drop it all, Dearest Isa: above all, don't fancy me "hearing news about it from London"—I should never have mentioned it to anybody but you, and only you, under the circumstances I mentioned: wait till we two get to be "bright and aged snakes by the Adriatic,"[1] and then I may begin disbosoming a little. I need not repeat that I depend absolutely on your silence as to all of this,—indeed, the nature of the story shows it could hardly be a deliberate lie,—for the first letter that comes, like those you received, mentioning that the parties are together, disposes of the "separation," which either *was* or was *not:* no goose tells you I *am* married,—only, that I *shall* be,—and six years hence, the same goose can cackle "So it *was* to be,—only, it was broken off"!—(I never saw Miss Ingelow but once, at least four years ago, at a musical morning party, where I said half a dozen words to her: only heard of her, as I told you, by her writing a note to accompany her new book, a day or two before I left London. It is funny people think I am likely to do nothing naughty in the world, neither rob nor kill, seduce nor ravish,—only honestly *marry*—which I should consider the two last, —and perhaps two first,—naughtinesses united, together with the grace of perjury. Enough of it all.

Our time for departure is approaching, and you must write next

time to 19. Warwick Crescent. The weather broke up, partially, yesterday: we have had fifty consecutive fine days here,—with rain and
sometimes thunder storms in the night only,—all washed away, and
brightness restored by the early morning,—delicious weather: I bathed
this morning for the fiftieth time,—the water was cold, but I swam
for a quarter of an hour,—the shortest swim I have had: last week
but one, I swam for very nearly three quarters of an hour, without
stopping. I am rather proud of my doings this way, inasmuch it is a
new acquisition: I could only swim a few strokes in my youth,—only
took to the sea at Pornic five years ago, and then used to bear only a
few minutes' dipping: now, it seems to suit me better than any other
exercise, at any hour and for any time. All that hampers my performance is a nervous spasm of the throat, to which I am,—or rather
used to be subject some time ago,—which once or twice came on me
while swimming, and was dangerous enough *there:* but, this year,
there has been no return of it. I dearly like this wild place: Guerande,
where I was two days ago, is delightful—and a wilder place still,
Piriac, where we all went, for the sake of the coast and caves. There
was a great enterprise begun there and abandoned fourteen years ago,
—the working a tin and silver mine: an English company built houses,
sank wells, brought machinery, spent "trois millions," then abandoned everything: there lie the boilers, pumps &c. exposed like rocks
and sand. An old fellow, who had been to England, and was always
in the employment of the head man, Capt Peters, (if he pronounced
aright) pointed to one and another "That, now, is still worth 25.000
fcs—and that as much." He said all the money had been wasted in
unnecessary expense,—house-building &c. and that when the mines
began to be worked, and give good metal,—in rushed the sea,—their
funds were at an end,—there was no more to be done but go and leave
all this ruin, "these fourteen years now"! Depend on it, the imaginative men are not exclusively the poets and painters, as Balzac knew
well enough. And you too will return to Florence, I suppose. I am particularly glad you have got the right sense of the Bagni: those villages,
—the hill-roads through the woods,—how I remember them. And the
Lima, where I used to bathe, or duck rather. Is old Mrs Stisted still
alive and stationed there? It can't well be, yet I have never heard of
her death. I think you said the place was little changed. I was there
three times. α.β.γ.δ.ε.ς.ι. There! Those letters indicate seven distinct
issues to which I came with Ba, in our profoundly different estimates
of thing and person: I go over them one by one, and must deliberately
inevitably say, on each of these points I was, am proved to be, right

and she wrong. And I am glad I maintained the truth on each of these points, did not say, "what matter whether they be true or no?—Let us only care to love each other." If I could ever have such things out of my thoughts, it would not be to-day—the day, twenty years ago, that we left England to-gether. If I ever seem too authoritative or disputative to you, dearest Isa, you must remember this, and that only to those I love very much do I feel at all inclined to lay down what I think to be the law, and speak the truth,—but no good comes of anything else, in the long run,—while, as for *seeing* the truth, it seems to me such angelic natures don't—and such devilish ones *do:* it is no sign of the highest nature: on the contrary, I do believe the very highness blinds, and the lowness helps to see.

Yes, I assuredly remember "the fiery earwig"—it was an expression pointed out by Leigh Hunt, from the "Tales of the Fairies"—some fairy-king went to war "mounted on a fiery earwig,"—my little spirited horse got the name that way. So you are getting on with another "novel,"[2]—that's right: if I were at your ear's reach, would not I be a "fiery earwig," and make you show your horsemanship. I like your saying of Mrs T. "you know she has written another novel": I do *not,* I assure you: as for "All the Year Round," I never have seen the outside of it, that I remember, since my stay in England.

Goodbye, dearest Isa: I shall go back presently to bother enough, —I predict,—and your letter will be pleasant to look forward to,— like the lighthouse-spark here, over the sea of dark evenings. Sarianna and Pen are quite well, and send their best love. Pen and Willy swim and shoot and enjoy themselves. Mrs Bracken and Miss Smith are always here, and enjoy the place. Good bye,—see my long letter, equal to any three of yours! God bless you ever yours affectionately

ROBERT BROWNING.

1867 : 8

TO PROFESSOR EDWARD DOWDEN

19 Warwick Crescent,
Upper Westbourne Terrace,
London, W.
October 16th, 1867.

My dear Mr. Dowden,

I have been away, and only got your note and the Magazine[1] on coming back. I had heard there was to appear some article, and when, by the advertisement, I found the Author was no other than you, I became interested indeed. How could I be otherwise than delighted with such a criticism? I am hampered in saying more, and shall not try, from what you will understand—the repugnance to seem paying your opinions with thanks and compliment, which would harass you likewise. But very grateful in the best sense I certainly am, be it said or unsaid.

I hardly dare be sure you describe me, as the writer, properly, and not too generously. Anyway, I cannot but wholly sympathise with such an one as you describe; will *that* seem too Jesuitic? And there is a passage in my new poem[2] that comes curiously in proof of it, as I hope you will not be long in seeing for yourself. I am finishing the exceedingly lengthy business, and hope to be rid of it in a few months more. May I send it to your present address?

I wish you could rather come and take it *here*. If you visit London at any time, I think you will remember how much I should enjoy seeing you.

Every yours most truly,
ROBERT BROWNING.

1867 : 9

TO PROFESSOR EDWARD DOWDEN

19, Warwick Crescent,
Upper Westbourne Terrace,
W.
December 13th, 1867.

My dear Mr. Dowden,

I can't in the least see into the mystery of the rejection of the article.[1] I believe the fault of it must be that you have so disinterestedly stuck to the business of making my poem speak for itself, and not, as most critics do, diverged and flourished with your own tendrils over my brickwork. One of the reasons you give, or re-deliver, is too impossible —that I should consider the appreciation inadequate! "Inadequate" it certainly is in some respects—the greater your goodness and for-bearance! Of course such a demonstration that, after all, there *was* a wondrous understander of the poem, would be valuable. I wish with all my heart I may yet see that phenomenon registered beyond the reach of incredulity, and that I may be honoured by the publication, as you seem to think possible.[2]

By a coincidence there is just going to appear a volume of Essays,[3] published by Macmillan, containing one on *Sordello,* which was sent to me in MS. perhaps a year ago by a person no more personally known to me at that time than yourself. I do know him now. I hope you will one day help me to extend the parallel so far also, and am sure he would be glad of such a concurrence.

As for me, I feel very deeply and gratefully your care for my works and kindness to me, and shall always remember that what I write is more than likely to reach *you.*

I happen again to have the opportunity of correcting my "works."[4] I fear there are more blunders than those you so kindly pointed out. Somebody told me a week ago there was an expression "blooming carroch"[5] which he felt difficulty in understanding! Such printer's-perversity as this I shall rectify by myself, but, should any slip of my very own seem discovered in the course of your reading, I shall regard the mention of it as one more favour from one who has so much favoured his, or rather.

> Yours ever truly,
> ROBERT BROWNING.

I send the article by the post with the present letter.—R. B.

1868 : 1

To LADY WILLIAM RUSSELL

> 19. Warwick Crescent,
> Upper Westbourne Terr:
> March 27. '68.

Dear Lady Russell,

I am very sorry indeed to hear you are unwell, and very grateful for your goodness in taking so much trouble to let me know. I shall be delighted to dine with you next Friday, provided you are quite well again, as I hope will be the case. With all respect to Lord Russell pray believe me, Dear Lady Russell,

> Yours ever faithfully
> ROBERT BROWNING.

1868 : 2

TO MISS ISABELLA BLAGDEN

19th. June, 1868.

Dearest Isa,

On the first day after your return (Thursday) that I find myself able to call, I will, writing a word before hand to apprise you.

Yes, I could have seen you on that Wednesday, because, ill as Arabel[1] was, the Doctor saw no danger. I made him call in a second wise man, who saw with the eyes of the first, and a third was to come and help on Thursday at 3 o'clock; there was superabundance of female attendance, and though I had my own convictions (rather than fears) from the beginning, I was not warranted in breaking the usual engagements. I heard therefore Rubinstein play at a party whence I returned late, and was summoned to Arabel's by the servants at six next morning, when I found her in a deplorable state: I stayed till the Doctor came, who repeated that there was no immediate danger, and that he was anxious she should not look worse than she really was when the other Physician arrived at 3 o'clock. So he went, and, five minutes after, I raised her in my arms where she died presently. When the doctor returned he began on "the miracle it was she had lived so long" &c.

George, the useful brother, was away touring it in Ireland, nobody knew where. Only last night could we hear from him, he is in perfect ignorance of her being other than quite well. He is to arrive to-morrow (prepared by telegrams) at 4½ a. m., and I and a brother will have to meet him at the station and break the news to him—that she is buried. He is alarmingly susceptible, and may find the blow too much.

And this is the 19th. once again, and in ten days will be the 29th.[2] "The years, they come and go, the races drop in the grave, but never the love doth so!"

You know I am not superstitious—here is a note I made in a book, "Tuesday July 21. 1863. Arabel told me yesterday that she had been much agitated by a dream which happened the night before, Sunday, July 19: she saw Her,[3] and asked "When shall I be with you?" The reply was "Dearest, in five years," whereupon Arabel woke. She knew in her dream it was not to the living she spoke, and her question referred to her own death." In five years, within a month of their completion. I had forgotten the date of the dream, and supposed it was only three years ago, and that two had still to run. Only a coincidence, but noticeable.

God bless you, dearest,

R. B.

1868 : 3

To Miss Isabella Blagden

[1868]
Audierne, Finistère, France.

Aug: 28—for 19—and this is why, dearest Isa,—I had a notion I might receive your letter, along with others sent for from England. I never get anything by waiting after this fashion, and shall not be so foolish again. You never heard of this place, I daresay: after staying a few days at Paris we started for Rennes,—reached Vannes and halted a little, thence made for Auray—where we made excursions to Carnac, Marienloker, and St. Anne d'Auray,—all very interesting of their kind,—then saw Brest, Morlaix, St. Pol de Léon, and the little seaport Roscoff,—our intended bathing-place: it was full of folk, however, and otherwise imprac- ticable, so we had nothing for it but to "rebrousser chemin" and get to the south-west again. At Quimper we heard (for a second time) that Audierne would suit us exactly, and to it we came—happily, for "suit" it certainly does. Look on the map for the most westerly point of Bretágne—and of the Mainland of Europe: there is niched Au- dierne, a delightful quite unspoiled little fishing town, with the open ocean in front, and beautiful woods, hills and dales, meadows and lanes behind and around,—sprinkled here and there with villages each with its fine old church: Sarianna and I have just returned from a four hours' walk in the course of which we visited a town, Pont- Croix, with a beautiful cathedral-like building amid the cluster of clean bright Breton houses—and a little farther is another church, "Notre Dame de Confort," with only a hovel or two round it, worth the journey from England to see: we are therefore very well off—at an Inn, I should say, with singularly good kind and liberal people, so have no cares, for the moment. May you be doing as well! The weather has been most propitious,—and today is perfect to a wish. We bathe, but somewhat ingloriously in a smooth creek of mill pond quietude (there being no cabins on the bay itself) unlike the great rushing waves of Croisic: the water also is much colder: but the gen- eral effect is admirable.

Pen is perhaps still in Oxford,—but in a day or two will go to Scotland, and join Mr. Jowett: he writes constantly and seems in good health and spirits. You know I must be back in London, for many reasons, at the beginning of October: shall I find you, by good chance? It might be, I seem to think, from something you said: I hope so!

Direct your letter of the 12th to this address,—(be *exact*, pray, in the addressing, as I am really out of the way now) Sarianna sends her best love with mine,

who am yours, dearest Isa, ever affectionately

R B.

1868 : 4

To Messrs. Fields, Osgood, and Co.[1]

19, Warwick Crescent,
London, W.
September 2nd, 1868.

Gentlemen,

I have just received your letter of the 8th ult.—any delay in replying to it must be attributed to my absence from England.

I am very sorry that you find the arrangements of my publishers inconsistent with such as you wished to make, and that you break our bargain in consequence; so, let it be broken by all means! No doubt my first notion was to print the poem[2] in two volumes! but the publisher, on reading the MS.,[3] thought so well of the thing as to believe it would bear, indeed be advantaged by, printing in four volumes, one a month. I rather thought of proposing, with his leave, to send you *two* volumes at once (they are here in type), but I like just as well making no further appeal to a liberality which has been munificent indeed, and would make my acceptance of your new offer of £50 for my twenty thousand lines altogether inexcusable.

If I may express a hope, in parting company, it will be that, suppose I find another American publisher disposed to take what you refuse, you will remember all the drawbacks and difficulties, and not determine upon printing my poem after all—and in spite of them. But that would give too ugly a look to the rupture of our bargain, and I only mention it because pen is in hand and paper to spare, and I may not so soon have an opportunity of assuring you that I am, gentlemen,

Yours very faithfully,

Robert Browning.

1868 : 5

To E. S. Dallas[1]

> 19, Warwick Crescent,
> Upper Westbourne Terrace, W.
> October 10th, 1868.

My dear Mr. Dallas,

I have only just returned to London after a few weeks' absence abroad, hence, you will have guessed, I hope, the delay in replying to your note. And, upon my word, I could in some sort wish the delay might continue indefinitely, since it has to end with an unlucky—not "yes"—to everything you ask of me.

The simple fact is, I have not a scrap available for such a purpose as you mention. The business of getting done with some twenty thousand lines[2] very effectually suppressed any impulse to whistle betweenwhiles; and out of the long twenty aforesaid I honestly don't think, and cannot but hope, as an artist, that not a paragraph is extractable as an episode or piece complete in itself. It is gone to press, moreover. Will you please believe that I wish I could do what you want, and ask for so kindly?

> Ever truly yours,
> ROBERT BROWNING.

1868 : 6

To W. G. Kingsland[1]

> 19, Warwick Crescent,
> London, W.
> November 27th, 1868.

My dear Sir,

Will the kindness that induced you to write your very gratifying letter forgive the delay that has taken place in answering it?—an unavoidable delay, for I have been far from well, and oppressed by work.

I am heartily glad I have your sympathy for what I write. Intelligence, by itself, is scarcely the thing with respect to a new book—as Wordsworth says (a little altered), "you must like it before it be worthy of your liking." In spite of your intelligence and sympathy, I can have but little doubt but that my writing has been, in the main,

ROBERT WIEDEMANN BARRETT BROWNING
"PEN"

too hard for many I should have been pleased to communicate with; but I never designedly tried to puzzle people, as some of my critics have supposed. On the other hand, I never pretended to offer such literature as should be a substitute for a cigar, or a game of dominoes, to an idle man. So perhaps, on the whole, I get my desserts and something over,—not a crowd, but a few I value more. Let me remember gratefully that I may class you among these; while you, in turn, must remember me as

Yours very faithfully,

ROBERT BROWNING.

Mr. W. G. Kingsland.

1869 : 1

To ROBERT BUCHANAN

19, Warwick Crescent,
Upper Westbourne Terrace,
London, W.
January, 1869.

My dear Buchanan,

I was hindered by real stress of work from writing even a word to you yesterday. I don't know what other thing and better may come of your "Readings"[1]—this first has greatly delighted me—you might well have written the poems[2] without being able to recite them so dramatically and finely, and the capital management of the dialects was surely a success one could not be prepared for.

I changed the ticket (you kindly sent me), finding I could not else be accompanied by a friend. I was not so near you, but lost nothing, I think; your voice serves you indeed!

Ever yours truly,

ROBERT BROWNING.

1869 : 2

To MR. GILLESPIE

19, Warwick Cresc[t].
Feb. 14 '69

My dear Mr. Gillespie,

I supposed there was some cause for the strange delay in binding the remaining volumes:[1] I have just received a note to inform me that a fire has consumed vols: 2 and 3. and nearly all the poor man's substance, including the *pattern* of the 1st volume. If you will therefore kindly return that volume, your completed copy shall reach you speedily. Please be at the trouble of taking it and leaving it with Mrs. Bracken, who will convey it to me: meantime, I shall provisionally furnish you with the fourth volume at the month's end. I shall feel much interest in seeing your criticism, and will bear with proper patience whatever animadversions may be interspersed with the kindness I am sure to experience at your hands. I find, by the bye, that in part 8th there is an odd blunder or misprint[2] of *Maro* for *Naso*,—to whom, of course, should be attributed the passage referred to at page 166

"Effodiuntur opes, irritamenta malorum"

In your kind note, you regret that Robert was not examined in Virgil: this was duly mentioned to Robert, who replied yesterday— "Please tell Mr. Gillespie that I have already had means of showing my knowledge of Virgil, as I have had to write out many passages in the 4th Book for one of the Dons: he put *"Bene"* at the bottom: it is not usual to set any remarks down."—This will gratify you quite as much as

Yours ever most truly
ROBERT BROWNING

1869 : 3

To FRANCIS TURNER PALGRAVE.[1]

19, Warwick Crescent,
Upper Westbourne Terrace,
London, W.
April 1st, 1869.

Dear Palgrave,

Yes, . . . metamorphōsis, the right way when we can,—but when can we,—without even more of clumsiness than is attributed usually to me by those nicely-eared, my critics,—in serious heroic measure? Is it not naturalised, a long while ago, like "encyclopedia," and a heap of other words of which the corruption has use enough to reconcile one to it? Taking the word by itself I would treat it as you wish,— but if it needs an article or short monosyllable prefixed, you get, to my sense, four short syllables in succession,—the fourth being inevitably pulled up with the others—as

Thĕ mĕtămŏr | phōsĭs | sūng bў | Ŏvĭd | ōnce—

though

> *"Ovid who once metamorphosis sang,"*

would be passable; and in a burlesque with metre to match, you might preferably write,

> *'Twas Goethe taught us all*
> *By diagnosis,*
> *That change in plants we call*
> *Metamorphosis!*

But I bear this brotherly blow the better that, only the other day, a Balliol man looked unutterable things as I said something about Mrs. Sartoris, and assisted me by enquiring "If Mrs. Sartōris was not once Fanny Kemble's sister?" "Acted at the same theātre," I was minded to reply.

But my time is up, so, enough of the verba "quae versu dicere non est," and never enough of good will to you from

Yours unirritatedly,

R. B.

1869 : 4

To Mr. and Mrs. W. W. Story

> 19. Warwick Crescent,
> Upper Westbourne Terrace, W.
> Sept. 28, '69

Dear Friends,—it is a real comfort to fancy one can do anything for you, however minute,—anything akin to the handing a rug or carrying a hat-box: it is too horrible to be quite cut off, as I am now, after two months absolute indivisibility![1] Tilton's[2] speedy removal is more than ever necessary to me,—keep it in mind when you are able to give him a push! But about the poor little commission: I enclose you the Ticket,—all is safe and waiting your arrival.

This morning I called, in company of my sister, on Mr. and Mrs. Eldridge,—they arrived last evening only; they leave London, on the

3ᵈ—or perhaps the 4ᵗʰ—for Liverpool, whence they depart on the 5ᵗʰ. Mr. Shaw is expected to arrive tonight or tomorrow: he sails with them: not so Miss Williams who remains in Paris, at the Hôtel d'Orient, Rue Neuve des Augustins, intending to pass the winter at Cannes or Pau or Arles. She is not quite so well as before, though far from an invalid. We did not see your Brother, who was busy somewhere somehow. There,—I wish I had something more to tell, as an excuse for continuing this effort at intercourse!

I found all well at home, but was weary, myself,—today, however, I feel well enough. The day is exceedingly warm and fine,—unseasonable, I suppose. You really should be in no hurry to return—that is, when once you have reached London,—it is still Summer-time with us,—what then at Rome?

Good bye, dear Friends,—I get a little of the light of your faces, as I bid you remember

Yours affectionately ever
R B.

1869 : 5

To Miss Edith Story

19 Warwick Crescent,
Upper Westbourne Terrace, W.
[ca. September, 1869.]

Dearest Edie, it is good indeed of you to care about a special word for yourself, when I have told Mr. and Mrs. Story all the little there is to tell. Since you exact it, know then that I was tired and out of sorts on my arrival at 10 o'clock; and, having somehow got out of my good old habit of soundly and expeditiously sleeping, I continued to weary myself in bed,—but in the end the sleep came, and I woke aware of the accustomed curtains and furniture, and none the worse for a little tossing and tumbling. I sincerely hope your ailments,—far more important than mine,—have been disposed of as easily. You seemed nervous and fatigued,—take care of yourself, will you?

I found some letters of no particular interest. One from Leighton's sister mentions that she has no idea where he can be,—such licences can some people permit themselves! You will hear from the other letter how I went to see your Aunt and found her.

ROBERT BROWNING, READING *THE RING AND
THE BOOK* AT NAWORTH CASTLE,
SEPTEMBER 19, 1869

*From a drawing by the Earl of Carlisle. Browning's nearsightedness in
reading is evident in this drawing.*

How stupid one feels at this vile writing after two months' live real talk! I shall get more used to it, I dare say, after a little practice; but at first,—why, I begin as you see—and end as you expect—for what news will there be in my telling you that

I am ever affectionately yours?

R B.

I saw Trevilian (so they pronounce, but probably don't spell it) just now,—he is going to be married to-morrow, and struck me as not exuberantly joyful.

If you get news of any interest, you will be kind in writing, you know; also "whether or no," as the Negro said.

1870 : 1

To Miss Isabella Blagden

19, Warwick Crescent, W.
Jan: 19. '70.

Dearest Isa,

You rather indispose me to expect rest and comfort in Italy,—which, as they used to be my portion while there of old, I should have expected to secure on my return—if that may ever be: but you talk now so constantly of "a quantity of things to do," "writing against time, being already two days late," as to give me the suspicion that you must be busied, at the very least, with Sella in his projected measures of finance: but even then, I don't know why you should send such a scrawly scrap while Gladstone can write a leisurely calligraph like yonder note on the mantlepiece. However, I was always thankful for small mercies, and am delighted to see your handwriting even if I can't quite read it. I gather that Wilson, to whom you have been kind indeed, will soon be a burthen to somebody again,—anybody but her selfish sisters who sent her adrift after helping her to throw away her savings: she is fit for little but the workhouse: though, to be sure, English residents of Florence do seem to have a faculty of screwing and flint-skinning which one don't look for or find here—making their maid-of-all-work the dame-de-compagnie! It is funnyish, though melancholy, to remember the profound contempt Wilson always had for Italians in general and Annunziata in particular—who yet holds

her own in first-rate families, and has supported *her* family all along.
It is a good thing that Ferdinando gets on to some degree.

Miss Mitford's letters are not exactly "sad twaddle"—the fashion of
these things passes away, and what looked fresh enough in its time
gets yellow with a few years' keeping: she has the usual woman's
characteristic of interpreting all according to the personal liking or
disliking of the moment,—the new acquaintance is a god,—paints,
writes, acts, talks, as none ever attained to before: then he treads on
her toe, or somebody else pushes in between them, and he is a devil
or, at best, remarkably poor creature. Witness Talfourd,—who is first
of all a miracle of genius and presently a poor envious not to say
malignant coxcomb: you see what she says of him while profiting
by the hospitality of his house. Her letters to Ba used to be stuffed
with such—worse than nonsense; but when they were required again,
Ba resolutely destroyed at least five out of six letters, and mutilated
the rest wherever they needed it,—else dear friends, such as Harness
himself and Chorley would have been treated to an odd sensation or
two. The editor[1] applied to me for some of Ba's letters,—which were
returned to her in exchange for what she gave; I refused, as you may
guess. But you are hardly right in despising so much the "Sketches"—
which were and are *original*—and quite able to compete with the performances I see from time to time. The fact is, contemporaries see but
little and amiss: wait thirty years, and examine your old idols and
abominations,—they will have hardly kept their original place in your
love or hate. I have just been reading Shelley's life, as Rossetti tells it,
—and when I think how utterly different was the fancy I had of him
forty years ago from the facts as they front one to-day, I can only avoid
despising myself by remembering that I judged in pure ignorance and
according to the testimony of untruthful friends. Well, I go with you
a good way in the feeling about Tennyson's new book:[2] it is all out
of my head already. We look at the object of art in poetry so differently! Here is an Idyll about a knight being untrue to his friend and
yielding to the temptation of that friend's mistress after having engaged to assist him in his suit. I should judge the conflict in the
knight's soul the proper subject to describe: Tennyson thinks he should
describe the castle, and effect of the moon on its towers, and anything
but the soul. The monotony, however, you must expect—if the new is
to be of a piece with the old. Morris is sweet, pictorial, clever always—
but a weariness to me by this time. The lyrics were the "first sprightly
runnings"—this that follows[3] is a laboured brew with the old flavour
but not *body*. So with Tennyson—the old "Galahad" is to me incom-

parably better than a dozen centuries of the "Grail," "Coming of Arthur," and so on. I ought to be somewhat surprised to find myself thinking so, since it seems also the opinion of everybody: even the reviews hardly keep on the old chime of laudation. I read, for a wonder, Miss Thackeray's "To Esther"—the praises of her having been long buzzing round me,—surely that is poorer than the poorest of Miss Mitford's sketches! I cannot conceive of anybody, acknowledged intelligent, writing worse. *That* sort of thing will not last very long, depend on it! Come, I will release you,—if your multifarious occupations have allowed you, during the month, to snap up here a little and there a little. Sarianna is pretty well: Pen goes back to college next week—both send their kindest love to you. I am bilious and out of sorts—but shall be quiet and collect my scattered forces. Is not Mrs Mackenzie with you—at Florence, I mean? Give her my kindest regards, if she be.

> Ever affectionately yours,
> ROBERT BROWNING.

1870 : 2

To MISS ISABELLA BLAGDEN

> 19. Warwick Crescent, W.
> March 22. '70. for the 19th.

Dearest Isa,

Another gap in our talk: I foolishly delayed writing on Saturday, because of a press of calls on my time,—and things hardly mend as the season grows exacting. If I spend my old age my own way, quietly alone,—how odd and dreamlike will all the people come and go in my memory! I suppose it is, on the whole, a gain in some respects to the soul to have seen so many people: I mainly care about human beings, yet I feel weary of the crowd I chose to fancy it would do me good to see: and only get an ignoble touch of satisfaction when I think that, after all, it "riles" such a filthy little snob as Mr Alfred Austin[1] to read in the Morning Post how many dinners I eat in good company. I heard a good story, the other day, about this literary "cad" and Thackeray,—at all events, a story which is true to my knowledge. The little fool sent Thackeray, when Editor of the *Cornhill*, an article for insertion, accompanied by a letter about his own genius, his wrongs, the result of a conspiracy, and so forth,—sent them up stairs and waited below for an answer: Thackeray understood nothing but that there was a petition in the case from some poor broken-down devil, and,—as best remedy for his sorrows, and way to an immediate riddance of a bore,—benevolently sent him down half-a crown! Off went the "blighted being" in such a rage as never entered into a flea on a dog's back at the first sprinkle of Scotch snuff bestowed upon him as a notice to quit,—and the result was blood and thunder in a letter, to which my informant had seen Thackeray's reply. As to Swinburne's verses, I agree with you—they are "florid impotence," to my taste—the *minimum* of thought and idea in the *maximum* of words and phraseology. Nothing said and done with, left to stand alone and trust for its effect in its own worth. What a way of writing is that wherein, wanting to say that "a man is sad," you express it as, "he looketh like to one, as one might say, who hath a sadness and is sad indeed, so that beholders think "How sad is he!" I saw Miss Smith yesterday: she is in the business of moving to Shepherd's Bush—now only thirteen minutes' journey hence by rail: She says you owe her a letter since some time. Yes, I have known Mad^e Schwabe this many a day: good, impulsive, not wise at all but generous abundantly. I dined with her last year and heard Rubinstein. I don't remember ever having seen L^y Mordaunt: there is going to enlighten you another scandalous trial,—a Lady So and so—with 14 co-respondents! I heard a story at dinner last week,—which as a handsome lady-friend whispered it into my ear, I shall venture to breathe into yours. A husband returns from the country, and begins to his wife "Dear, to be frank,—I have failed in my duty to you: forgive me,—as I would forgive *you,* were it possible you could forget yourself so!"—She replies "But, since you put it so,—I forgive you—for I *do* need forgiveness likewise!—"Indeed! Well,—with whom was the fault we will agree to forget?"— "With Mr —— the parson"—"And how many times did you err?"— "Impossible to say,—yet . . there may be a method of knowing: he used to come to read the Holy Book to me,—and, whenever he began to be naughty, he, first of all, doubled down the page he left off at." The Bible was produced, and found to be dogs' eared from Genesis to Revelations! Come, now, dearest, have I helped your liver at all? Good bye,—is there any chance of seeing you this year?

Ever affectionately yours,
ROBERT BROWNING.

Sarianna's best love—she is just going to Paris for a week or two. Milsand was here for a month, to my joy.

1870 : 3

To Miss Isabella Blagden

19, Warwick Crescent,
London, W.
June 19. '70

Dearest Isa, I have a headache and shall not be able to write much, but something I must write,—so glad was I to hear of your recovery, and so hopeful am I that it is confirmed by the change of air,—though I should have thought "bracing" air, rather than the sickly softness of Venice just now, was to your taste. Our weather here was abominable beyond precedent: Sarianna escaped it by going to Paris for a month, —she returned last week: and I had a drench of wholesome quiet for a longer time than I remember. The bustle is in full tide just now, and, as you see, my head feels none the better for it. O Italy,—how I should just like to be in some brigands' hole minus the murder-and-ransom inconvenience! But, patience and shuffle the cards! I daresay you, as often, yearn to be in London, "for the facilities of literary work." I never get to see Geo: Smith now: he is printing an edition of my poems, and I don't [see] a proof *for weeks:* I believe that whenever I connect myself with a person, that favoured one shows some unsuspected imbecility of a sudden: and nothing else could have kept Smith constant to his crotchet about the morning Pall Mall.

I suppose you will have heard of the ignoble, brutish outrage at Christ Church,[1]—the destruction of those statues and busts: remember that Pen was not at Oxford this term,—and so is not answerable for any of the disgrace: I heard a lady at dinner last night so earnest in declaring that a relative of hers, an undergraduate, was sick in bed, that it seems proper to mention Pen's absence also. He is quite recovered, and will return to Oxford early next month: I and Sarianna go there in a fortnight for a visit: but I have given up my rooms in pure shame,—finding that I kept them,—to the inconvenience of the College which is crowded,—for a whole year unoccupied even for a night: so I renounced *for the present,*—and am not a little relieved thereby. Yes,—I have read Rossetti's poems—and poetical they are,— *scented* with poetry, as it were—like trifles of various sorts you take out of a cedar or sandal-wood box: you know I hate the effeminacy of his school,—the men that dress up like women,—that use obsolete forms, too, and archaic accentuations to seem soft—fancy a man calling it a lil*ý*,—lil*iés* and so on: Swinburne started this, with other like Belialisms,—witness his harp-play*ér*, &c. It is quite different when the object is to *imitate* old ballad-writing, when the thing might be; then, how I hate "Love," as a lubberly naked young man putting his arms here and his wings there, about a pair of lovers,—a fellow they would kick away, in the reality. Good bye, for I am getting ill-natured: write duly on the 19th and tell me all is right again.

Ever affectionately yours
R B

1870 : 4

To Miss Isabella Blagden

19, Warwick Crescent, W.
19th. July '70.

Dearest Isa, I won't keep you waiting this time: I only got your letter last night—for I was in the country when it arrived. Last Wednesday, I travelled to Scotland, to attend the funeral of poor Ld Lothian,—a thirteen hours' Journey—five hours' stay—then thirteen more hours on Thursday night: however, I had a real affection for him, and, being telegraphed for, could not well refuse to go. On returning from another place last evening I found poor Pen in all the misery of the measles—for the *second* time in his life! He exposed himself too much to the sun, and perhaps this is the best form in which the fever consequent on the exposure could visit him,—not on the *brain,* that is. He is red and, yesterday, swollen in the face,—the doctor, (his old friend, who well knows his constitution) "never saw such an eruption in his life," nor did I. However, all is going on well,—the thing being only dangerous when *in* and not *out* of a man; and I will not send this till a second visit of the Doctor have helped me to the last account of the poor boy. Well, Isa, here is the horrible war,—after all the professions of peace! I don't doubt but Prussia is just as bent on it, and has been scheming for it as much as France—and that the precipitation of France was simply caused by the wish to be beforehand with Prussia: still, the way of the declaration has been cynical and revolts everybody: all I trust is that Italy will get Rome easily and naturally. I never, when liking Napoleon most, sympathized a bit with his dynastic ambition for his son,—who has no sort of right to be anybody in France,—and the truckling to Rome and the Empress has been stupid and suicidal: I think, in the interest of humanity, he wants a sound beating this time and probably may get it: though he is clearly good enough and to spare for all these frenzied fools who are shouting for the Rhine. Oh, oh, Isa—put not your trust in princes neither in the sons of men,—Emperors, Popes, Garibaldis, or Mazzinis,—the *plating* wears through, and out comes the copperhead of human nature and weakness and falseness too! I daresay Fraschesi is clever enough *in his art,* but it was not his cleverness *there,* that attracted poor A: Well, dearest, here ends my shabby letter: I know *nothing* of what will be my summer movements. My sister is immensely kind to Pen, as you may suppose. I will write to you if there be any need. Good bye, dearest Isa: God bless you.

R B.

1870 : 5

To Miss Edith Story

19 Warwick Crescent,
Upper Westb: Ter:
July 28, '70

Dear Edie, I write at Pen's desire—the poor fellow being unable himself to do so. I had to leave London last Wednesday, and on returning two days after, I found him very ill from exposure to the sun on the day he crossed the Park to call on you: there seemed nothing, however, to hinder my keeping another engagement on Saturday—but on Monday I found him in an outrageous eruption of the measles: the violence of the attack may have helped to end the ugly thing all the sooner,—for to-day he is plainly convalescent, beyond any expectation of the doctor, who saw him four times yesterday: this is the second time he has been visited by this pleasant intruder (the measles, not the Doctor!). He is anxious that you should not dream of enquiring about him,—a formality altogether unnecessary, for—red and hardly recognizable as he was on Monday, he is at this moment studying the newspaper and digesting a good breakfast—in bed, of course. (Since writing the last word, the doctor confirms me in all I conjectured, and promises that the cure shall be complete in a week or so.)

I suppose I ought also to notice that passage of your letter in which you speak of "the strange misunderstanding between us all—in the existence of which you cannot even believe, though one lives to learn many things." I am quite ready and glad to accept Mrs. Story's kind assurance that I *did* misunderstand the omission of the customary notice,—to which I have got used for the last eight or nine years,—that you had arrived in London. Pray let there be an end of all thinking or talking about it, and let our next meeting, whenever it happen, make amends for the mistakes of this year. Give my kindest regards to your Father and Mother, and remember me as

ever affectionately your
R B.

1870 : 6

To Miss Annie Egerton Smith

[St. Aubin, August 4, 1870.]

Dearest Annie,

We are here—how we travelled and to what purpose, Sarianna will have told you. There never was a more delicious day than this, in all my experience,—the heat is tempered by a fresh wind; and the sea so bright and inviting. I bathed yesterday and to-day, and feel absolutely well again. The wildness, savageness of the place, its quiet and remoteness, suit me exactly. I wish one could add a delight to these: but the ugly London wants all it can get of attraction, and one ought to reserve something to go back for. I could well have stayed in London, you know, but perhaps the week or two of fine weather we are told to expect here may be of more importance to me than merely enjoying peace and quiet in London. Write at once, and tell us what you are going to do. I will write at greater length another time and when there is more to say. Dear Milsand is his old self—can be no better than he ever was, though I seem to enjoy him more. May you enjoy yourself as I do, dearest Annie!—wishing for my company as I for yours!

Ever affectionately
R. B.

1870 : 7

To Miss Isabella Blagden

St. Aubin-sur-mer, Aug: 19. '70.

Dearest Isa,

Your letter came prosperously to this little wild place, where we have been, Sarianna and myself, just a week: Milsand lives in a cottage with a nice bit of garden, two steps off, and we occupy another of the most primitive kind on the sea-shore—which shore is a good sandy stretch for miles and miles on either side,—I don't think we were ever quite so thoroughly washed by the sea air from all quarters as here: the weather is fine, and we do well enough. The sadness of the war and its consequences go far to paralyse all our pleasure, however. I sympathise with you in a great degree: but the French have been wrong as well as foolish, and wanted the lesson they have so effectually got. There seems every likelihood that Napoleon is far from his old self, and these indecisions succeeded by rashnesses have tried the world's temper too long,—it is his own fault that Italy is not altogether on his side,—his own deference to the priests has brought him just the fruits he deserved, and wiped out the gratitude he might otherwise expect from the people: I don't think he has a chance of re-entering Paris as Emperor. You may imagine the disgust and contempt of the people—who don't deny the good they got from the civil talent of the man, but accept no excuse for his military ineptitude: *morally,* everybody from the highest to the lowest is as blamable as he,—and it is curious to read how they denounce "the *invaders*" . . who didn't wait to be invaded!

Well, you are at Siena—one of the places I love best to remember. You are returned—or I would ask you to tell me how the Villa Alberti wears, and if the fig-tree behind the house is green and strong yet: I have a pen and ink drawing of it, dated and signed the last day Ba was ever there—"My fig-tree." She used to sit under it, reading and writing. Nine years—or ten years, rather, since then! Poor old Landor's *"oak,"* too, and his cottage, ought not to be forgotten. Exactly opposite this house,—just over the way of the water,—shines every night the lighthouse of *Havre*—a place I know well and love very moderately: but, it always gives me a thrill as I see, afar, *exactly* a particular spot which I was at, along with her. At this moment, I see the white streak of the phare in the sun from the window where I write and I *think*.

Pen is better and at Ollerton with his tutor. We stay here three weeks more, then go elsewhere for another month,—(he will come to us)—*where,* is somewhat uncertain—perhaps at Tréport, where Miss Smith is. I shall escape if I can all visits in England this year: people are very kind, but the country-life does not suit me, and I prefer the utter roughness of this hamlet to the finery of that and the other great place where I might be.

Aug 22 / I was obliged to break off, and have let all these days go by:

in the meantime comes misfortune huddling upon misfortune to poor France,—how thoroughly beaten she seems to be! The government here *can't* tell the whole news,—yet the very dreadfulness of it has stricken a quiet and silence into the people, and there are no stupid outcries against the Emperor,—as if the people had no share in his folly,—or, indeed, have, even yet, any conception that the mistake was in the injustice of making war at all, not merely making it rashly. There seems every likelihood of the Prussians being at Paris soon enough. I can't imagine what you mean about the Orleans having anything to do with the war or to gain by it: just before I left London I dined with Ld Stratford de R:[1] who said the Princes (in England) were all in a state of profound despondency: they have no party, to speak of, in France—no chance of coming in before the Republic: and Milsand,—*what* ever led you to fancy he ever was an Orleanist? Not one human being could venture to approve the conduct of the Emperor—for what was ever more palpably indefensible? One's sorrow that France should be so humiliated is quite independent of,—or rather, all the more increased by,—her folly and ignorance in this matter: oh, the caricatures which filled the shops at Rouen, of a Zouave kicking Bismark, King, Prussia and all, leagues away over the Rhine,—the soldier who, turning a mitrailleuse too quickly, cleared the field before any sport could be had,—and so on,—surely all this "brag," and immorality too,—wanted the treatment it is getting only too energetically. The effect will be, that we shall all be forced into the Prussian system, of turning a nation into a camp; nothing but soldiering to concern us for the next generation. Well, I suppose all or much will be settled by the next time you write to me. The spirit of sadness is over even this little out-of-the-way place,—every ablebodied man is gone,—there was never such a drain on the population in the old days, they say. Milsand went to Paris last week, just before we arrived, to transport his valuables to a safer place than his house which is near the fortifications: to-day he writes that his brother may hire a room *inside* Paris, wherein to deposit his books papers and pictures. He is filled with as much despondency as can be—while the old dear and perfect kindness remains,—I never knew or shall know his like among men. Write punctually, dearest Isa,—to London, unless I bid you do otherwise: I am glad to be in France rather than elsewhere just now. Sarianna's best love,—Milsand's kind regard—both charge me to give you.

Ever affy yours,
R Browning.

1870 : 8

To Miss Isabella Blagden

19. Warwick crescent, W.
Oct. 19. 70

Dearest Isa,

I am very sorry you are ill—I have no doubt you suffer from helping to nurse poor Cottrell who was represented as in a bad way (in the letter I found here on arriving) but concerning whom you are altogether silent: is he dead or recovered? There was a good deal of amiability—indeed, warm-heartedness about him, poor fellow,—and the going out of his gay candle has been dismal enough. I am astonished at having apparently vexed you by something I seem to have said about either Napoléon or the French so as to give you the impression "that we probably differ *in toto*": in that case one of us can hardly be sane,—for at any rate there is no difference of opinion among French, German, or English people (out of Bedlam) as to certain and not a few points *"in toto"*—such as that the war was unjustifiably determined on, imprudently begun, and foolishly carried on to its natural end at Sedan: after that consummation of incapacity of every kind, there do arise many sustainable opinions as to what should be the wisest procedure for both France and Germany—and I, for one, fancy the German policy, so far as it is guessed, bad in their own interest as well as the world's: but with respect to Napoleon,—he should simply be blotted out of the world as the greatest failure on record. The "benefits of his reign" are just the extravagant interest which a knavish banker pays you for some time till he, one fine day, decamps with the principal,—and then where are you? But there has been no knavery, only decline and fall of the faculties corporeal and mental: these came to their height ten years ago: since then he has been sinking into all the ordinary ways of the vulgar king, with "the dynasty" dangled before his nose by the verminous people about him. The last time Ld Clarendon saw him, the Empress asked brutally, after the interview, "Ne trouvez-vous pas qu'il baisse beaucoup?" C. said, with all the politeness proper, "physically, perhaps, but mentally —no"! To which she replied "Moi, je le trouve imbécile." And she gave him no rest till he puffed out his soul in this great bubble that has burst. "Basta!" as you discreetly say—but as poor France will hardly say for a long while. As for Rome,—had he kept his word to Italy, this occupation would now be an old affair, and he would have had an Italian army to help him two months ago: but "who can control his fate?"—and his was only to be nearly a great man. Are you in earnest, by the bye, about Rome,—the crime of letting 7-8^{ths} of the Romans choose their own government: was "time" to operate on the Pope and Cardinals, as it had already pretty well operated on the people? Or were these to be plagued and policed and all the rest of it, that "the Spiritual Head" might excogitate dogmas to all eternity? In what way is he a prisoner, poor old "infallibility"? Because he can't catch and christen any more "little Cohens" with impunity? Dearest Isa, let us rather congratulate ourselves on having seen the extinguishment of this inveterate nuisance, and instead of saying "Il tempo è galantuomo," rejoice that "Il (Re) Galantuomo è il tempo-(rale) da quindi innanzi."

I wish Lemonnier's Fund all success, but we have Subscriptions opened in almost every street—whoso gives, gives more expeditiously than by sending to Florence, you know.

As to the lady of your postscript—all I want to say is a little word about myself. You propounded as a knotty problem to me some time since "How it came to pass that D. paid such sums for such novels as Mrs T's": whereto I could but answer "That I had no notion—but supposed there must be some reason beside the worth of the composition, if it were as poor as you assured me." Now, for the sake of my character, pray let me tell you that the relationship between Mrs T. and "Miss T." never crossed my mind: I must have heard it—very likely from yourself—but it took no hold of me: had it done so,—I should have been "green" indeed, to give no better a guess at the solution of the riddle.

Good bye, dearest Isa: all are well,—Pen is away: I keep the house and refuse invitations this autumn.

Ever aff^y yours

ROBERT BROWNING.

1871 : 1

To ROBERT BUCHANAN

19, Warwick Crescent,
London, W.
January 25th, 1871

My dear Buchanan,

I am very glad to know you are still within hand-shaking reach: from the impression left by Mrs. Buchanan on my sister, I somehow fancied you were just about to return to Scotland. If you can and she can take lunch with us on Saturday at one o'clock, we shall then be happy to see you.

Why speak at all disparagingly of your poem,[1] which I am sure is very admirable in every way, full of power and music, besides, I see my fancies or fears that you might treat in your undoubted right the main actor after a fashion repugnant to my feeling were vain enough. I think more savagely *now* of the man, and should say so if needed. I wrote, myself, a monologue in his name twelve years ago, and never could bring the printing to my mind as yet. One day perhaps.[2]

Ever yours, in hope of a word to certify your coming,

R. BROWNING.

1871 : 2

TO THE EDITOR OF THE *Daily News*[1]

Sir,—I am sorry that a mention I thought it right to make of the method which enabled me to contribute to the French Relief Fund— a mention simply due to the liberality of my publishers—should turn to their disadvantage. I wish I could transfer to the committee the munificent, and more than adequate, remuneration which was proposed to, and cheerfully accepted by, me for a very limited interest in "The Ring and the Book" before a page of it was printed. The payment now in question was made three days ago for the mere right of publishing in the *Cornhill Magazine* a poem in that lyrical form which you desiderate and, I hope, will be satisfied with in (I believe) the next number.[2]—I am, sir, obediently yours,

ROBERT BROWNING

19, Warwick-crescent, W., Feb. 9. [1871]

1871 : 3

To RUDOLF LEHMANN

19. Warwick Crescent, W.
Feb: 24. '71.

My dear Lehmann,

I wish I could fairly promise to oblige you by voting for Mr. Grove, as your friend,—but it happens that I simply oblige myself in so doing, and that I have already signed his certificate in the rooms, as earnest of my purpose to do all in my power on Monday next. You must,—

in justice to the extreme desire I cannot help feeling to make you some slight attempt at return for the manifold kindness you have shown myself,—you must tax your ingenuity to pick out, among your acquaintances, some really unpleasant and ineligible person; you will have difficulty enough, I know,—but find him, and, for your sake, be assured he shall have the vote of,

Yours ever truly,
Robert Browning.

1871 : 4

To Dante Gabriel Rossetti

19, Warwick Crescent, W.
Apr. 9. '71.

Dear Rossetti,

Any day, or hour, that may suit Mr Wallis to call here, will find the Bust ready for his inspection, if I am unluckily out of the way and prevented showing it: my sister, however, will effectually supply my place, would Mr Wallis be good enough to ask for her in the event of my absence. I never heard of a photograph being taken.

I must go and see you: meanwhile and ever know me for

Yours affectionately
Robert Browning

I don't know if I explained properly where the Shelley incident is to be met with. I found it in Leigh Hunt's "Byron and his Contemporaries," a book I think never reprinted, but I have no doubt that what relates to Shelley must have been transferred to some other work of Hunt's,—probably his Autobiography. I remember I made some rough sketches myself for a picture of it, which I projected calling—"Percy Bysshe Shelley—Cor Cordium," followed by the quoted incident.

[Endorsed as follows by Dante Gabriel Rossetti]

Monday

Dear Wallis,

I send you Browning's answer.

Ever yours
D G Rossetti

Miss Browning you will find very pleasant and friendly, should

Browning be out. I fancy, if you want to borrow the bust this might probably be managed, but I thought it better to leave you to make this proposal or not on seeing it. Turn to inside of this leaf.

1871 : 5

To Miss Isabella Blagden

19. Warwick Crescent, W.
July 19. '71

For so it shall be, dearest Isa: I was stupidly induced to postpone writing when I found my letter would be delayed or "forwarded" which means, often enough, lost. You will probably get it on your return,—which will be a propitious one, I hope and expect: nothing can promise better for health and amusement than such a "circular voyage" as you describe. I never took to the Ammergau Play, myself, but many people find it interesting to the last degree. A lady was telling me the other day as a most impressive thing that *no* actor but one of perfectly unblemished character was allowed to show his abilities: qy: in an artistic point of view, does this help the correct representation of Judas, Mary Magdalen and some others? Especially do the Americans sympathize with the exhibition,—loving as they all do to play at believing what they boast that they don't believe. By the bye, I have seen next to nothing of Kate Field; she was plunged into all sorts of sight seeing—and I, on the other hand, want heart to go and find her in the middle of Mrs P. Taylor and Co., Women's Rights, Anti-Contagious-Disease agitation and so forth. I shall be set down as a heartless mere man, with that true English love for the aristocracy &c. &c.: and I regret it, this time, for I really like Kate Field and remember her kindness of old, though she has turned it to some account undoubtedly.

I know *nothing* about Willy and his proceedings,—Miss Smith, whom I constantly see, never alludes to the business,—and as I have enquired about Mrs B. and their whereabout,—and have received information except on that point, it must be a thoroughly Brackenish injunction of silence that has been laid on her: Pen never heard a word about it: on all which points, I deeply congratulate myself. I suppose the suggestion that I should interfere came from Annette: it is curious as showing how little she knows any of the parties, for I am sure that if Mrs B. thought that by any particular obstinacy she could vex her sister, she would hug it to her heart the more. Pen, with plenty of faults, is altogether of another sort than Willy—is not cold bloodedly selfish,—far from that. He wants the power of working, and I give it up in despair: but his natural abilities are considerable,—and he may turn out a success, after all, though not in the way which lay most naturally before him. He is here—not very well; I mean to accompany him on a longish visit to Scotland; at the earnest request of a great friend of mine, Benzon,[1] who has just bought an estate there, with shooting &c. We shall inhabit a little lodge by ourselves, two miles distant, my sister will go to France: We had Milsand here for five weeks: he left last week only. It will be strange to be away from her, but I want the air and exercise for Pen, and know that my friend rather wants me. The neighbourhood of Glasgow would have been convenient had I accepted a proposition made me (which I have just refused) to become Lord Rector there. I mean to go nowhere else in Scotland: start in a week—stay two months, if the style of life suits.

Poor Lytton, I see by to-day's paper, has lost his only son, almost six years old: I have no doubt, about as dreadful calamity to him as any-one could imagine.

You say I am "out of the groove" for returning to Italy: dont be too certain! Not that I should ever attempt to get into the Florence groove. But Rome or Naples I could well live and die in.

I shall send you my little new Poem,[2]—done in a month,—and I think a pretty thing in its way.

Good bye, dearest Isa,—tell me how you have enjoyed yourself—and, above all, that you feel better for your excursion: only, don't you return into rather the worst of the heat? I thought Trollope had sold Villa Trollope,—how has he got it so as to entertain Kate Field there? My sister and Pen both send their best love—

Ever affectionately yours
ROBERT BROWNING.

1871 : 6

To Miss E. Dickinson West[1]

19, Warwick Crescent,
London, W.
July 27th, 1871.

Dear Miss West,

Will you permit me to say what a deep gratification it has been to me to find that you have cared so much about my poetry, and under-stood, at all events, the intentions of the writer so indulgently? It will always be a great comfort, far better than any pride I might be tempted to feel, that I have interested a person capable of so expressing that interest. I only regret that I cannot profit, as I assuredly should have done, by the continuation of the article. I received the book by the kindness of my friend Professor Dowden; but it had reached a familiar of mine through the intervention of another person, to whom I am indebted for the knowledge of the authorship.

I trust I have not presumed too much on your kindness either in making the enquiry or thus acting upon it. I will only say that should circumstances ever allow me the honour of your acquaintance, and such good fortune may not be altogether impossible, in this world of accidents, it will indeed delight me.

In any case, you will consider me ever, I hope, as gratefully yours,

ROBERT BROWNING.

1871 : 7

TO ROBERT BARRETT BROWNING

19 Warwick Crescent W.
October 17, 1871

Dearest Pen:

I was very glad to hear from you. I expected you would have written sooner, but you were better occupied, no doubt. I am alone here—Sarianna will arrive to-night, however. The weather is fine, and unpleasantly hot—there is no bearing a fire. Mrs. Cockran called yesterday, and said you had written to her. She is in great anxiety about her son who resides at Chicago.

I am surprised and grieved at the sudden death of poor Loftus Egerton, after two days' illness. I am going to write a word to his mother. I told you how much improved I found him, and how pleasant generally, at Dr. Russell's just before we left town,—nobody could have expected it was all to come to an end so soon. I fancy such an attack must have been Cholera—a fever does not end so expeditiously.

Give my kindest love to Mr. and Mrs. Story, Edith and Waldo. I might just as well be enjoying their company as staying here, now that I have despatched the business that required my presence. Write at all events and let me know when you mean to arrive here.

Ever affec. yours,

ROBERT BROWNING

Give Edie my love, and tell her how it was I could not send her a copy of the little poem when it came out: when I see her, I will give her one, if she cares about such a trifle.

1871 : 8

To Miss Edith Story

19, Warwick Crescent, W.
Oct. 20, '71

Dear Edie,

Thank you exceedingly for your letter alongside Pen's writing; fortunate he is to be enjoying himself with you while I endure the steaming unhealthy heat surrounded by everything that is ugly. Pray don't talk about "Rome," unless you wish to throw this place into even stronger shade than naturally belongs to it! No chance of Rome for me this year, if any year!

It was no word nor half-word of Pen's that induced me to send the message thro' him—natural enough, I hope—that I had been prevented sending copies of my little thing to anybody except three or four people whose addresses were known to the Publisher,—since I left town the day that he professed to publish the Poem.[1] On returning, I got a few copies for my friends,—and are not you a friend of mine still? All I wanted him to do was to explain why there was such an ado about next to nothing in the shape of a book.

I shall look forward with great pleasure to the promised sight of you this next week—if you are destined to increase the comforts of London,—at some cost to yourself, I fear. I am glad Pen has seen those beautiful places, and in your company. Give him my love,—he will excuse my not writing, or writing through your tongue if it will kindly charge itself with the no-news that I and Sarianna are very well.

Ever affectionately yours
ROBERT BROWNING

1871 : 9

To Miss E. Dickinson West

19, Warwick Crescent,
London, W.
November 14th, 1871.

Dear Miss West,

I did not wait for this last proof of your kindness, in sending me the two numbers of the Magazine,[1] to procure what was a matter of so much interest to me. You must feel what hampers me in the expression of a very real feeling, that I should misapply words if I "thanked" you for what only your conscientiousness permitted you to say or to be silent about; and I may take the occasion of adding that you are by no means—if you still do me the honour to examine what I do or hope to do—by no means are you to constitute yourself "my disciple," which suggests something like an unquestioning believer, but go along with me, side by side, and be the more ready to observe and tell me when I seem to tread amiss.

I think I assured you—in any case I may repeat what the reading of the second part of your essay has served to confirm me in—that I never read a criticism concerning my poetry which I so much wished to be true. Be certain, however, that, by the help of what has preceded, I shall never mistake the purpose of any utterance of yours, by writing or otherwise. You are free of all, but my sincere wish is that I keep that esteem that I value at least sufficiently, whether I deserve it or no. This is in some degree meant to prepare you for the announcement that I have just sent a rather important poem[2] to press, which will go to you, with your leave, in a few weeks, hoping and fearing a little: but, as I have said, one fear I hereby put from me—that you may feel bound to like it, though I hope you may.

Believe me, Dear Miss West,

Ever truly yours,

ROBERT BROWNING

1871 : 10

To MISS EDITH STORY

19 Warwick Crescent, W.

Dec. 20. '71.

Dearest Edie,

You bade me, in the kind little note you sent from Paris, write to you at Rome and say that I was coming. I am always "coming" in one sense, so far as wishing and even hoping go; but this winter is to be the usual dismal affair for me in London, too certainly. Mr. Benzon tried his best to get me to adventure in his company: but, after all, the difficulty will be for me rather to leave Rome, when I once get there, than to *go*: his visit will be a very short one. So, he takes you my new little book,[1] and I write to warn you that I expect you not to care three straws for what, in the nature of things, is uninteresting enough, even compared with other poems of mine which you have been only too good to. What poetry can be in a sort of political satire, made the milder because of the present fortunes of the subject? So, all you are to understand by the gift of the thing is that, for want of better, it is my best at present. Give my kindest love to your Father and Mother. Neither I nor Pen have been abundantly well, of late, but I am well now and he is better.

Ever affectionately yours
ROBERT BROWNING.

1872 : 1

TO MISS EDITH STORY

19. Warwick Crescent, Jan. 1. '72

Private

Dearest Edie,

First and last of all,—truest good wishes to you and everybody yours, for this year and whatever years are to follow after! Then, thank you very much for your letter, and the kind things you say about me and the little book;[1] only, I don't think, when you have read more, you will find I have "taken the man for any Hero"—I rather made him confess he was the opposite, though I put forward what excuses I thought he was likely to make for himself, if inclined to try. I never at any time thought much better of him than now; and I don't think so much worse of the character as shown us in the last few years, because I suppose there to be a physical and intellectual decline of faculty, brought about by the man's own faults, no doubt—but I think he struggles against these; and when that is the case, depend on it, in a soliloquy, a man makes the most of his good intentions and sees great excuse in them—far beyond what our optics discover! I really wrote—that is, conceived the poem, twelve years ago in the Via del Tritone—in a little handbreadth of prose,—now yellow with age and Italian ink,—which I breathed out into this full-blown bubble in a couple of months this autumn that is gone—thinking it fair so to do. What is the poem you allude to, which "I talked about at L—L." I have absolutely forgotten—if you tell me, and I still am of the same mind about it, I will try and keep alive what you will have helped me to recover—when this thing I am now engaged upon² (half-done, now) is out of hand.

And now, with respect to the "question quite between ourselves." I only know of one person in London, not "whom I would call my enemy," but who openly professes herself such,—Mrs. Sartoris. Three years ago, I found she was complaining to people that I had quarreled with her, she didn't imagine why—while, all I knew was that she had discontinued inviting me to her house. *I* didn't imagine why. I met her a year after at Wrest, passed some days in her company, thought all was right again. She accused me of "dropping her," I replied that she had "dropped me"—for the kindness was all of one side, in the nature of things, I had no home to invite her to, and could only accept her invitations—which ceased to come. To be sure, I might have "called"—but I never was one of the intimates she kept aware of her movements,—as to when she would be in town for a day or two, and as suddenly away again,—and, moreover, I never feel inclined to take much trouble to pick up a friendship anybody lets fall for so little reason, to dirty my hands by so doing. Last season, just before May's marriage, I met the whole family at dinner,—sat by Mrs. S. and found her friendly as of old,—and I took the occasion, from something she inquired about, to write a friendly little note next day. But then happened this that I shall tell you. Two years ago, *just* before we went to Scotland, Miss Gabriel gave me an account of her grievances against Mrs. S.—which account I received, never forgetting 1st that it was a one-sided account, and 2ly that if the conduct she complained of were truly described, there was nothing in it, which, *a la rigueur,* could not be excused after a fashion into a fault of judgment and temper,— nothing therefore which prevented the friendly feeling I showed, and, in turn, wished to get again at Wrest as I have mentioned—but this last year, Lady A.³ began upon me one day about the "utter falseness of Miss G."—"having just heard the whole story from Mrs. S." We got no further in the story than the first sentence "Miss G. wrote to Mr. Greville, with whom she had little or no previous acquaintance"— because I interposed—"with whom she had an intimate acquaintance." That was a point necessary to be cleared up, because all Miss G's veracity would have disappeared, were the facts otherwise. Accordingly I called on Miss G.—picked out a couple of the shortest notes from a heap she had retained,—for a purpose,—and sent them to Lᵞ A. that she might see for herself whether the writer was "intimate" or not with Miss G. The letters were returned to me with an expression of convenient wonder how—but I will transcribe from the letter itself—"The world is out of joint"—and "I can't imagine how two tales so entirely different can both be true." Both could not, indeed, "be true," but, with that evidence, it was pretty clear which was false. I make no doubt this was at once reported to Mrs. S. who is consequently, I have as little doubt, from many circumstances that are come to my knowledge, "an enemy of mine"—for which, be assured, I care not three straws, nor do I trouble myself to inquire what she said, written, or done in return for my "making the two tales look so very different." If poor Hatty heard some third tale, and at once threw up her old friend, I am sorry for her. The whole business has turned out too blessedly for me to much concern myself as to how it happened, and by means of whom.

Ever affectionately yours,

R BROWNING

1872 : 2

TO MISS EDITH STORY

Belton House,[1]
Grantham
April 4, 1872

Dearest Edith,—

Thank you very much for your letter and all its kindness. I have only a short quarter of an hour at my service, but I want to answer it with no more delay than I can help—and, to get done with the one unpleasantness[2] first,—what you tell me about Hatty and the "intimate friends" and their report of me which made her cut our old and long friendship short, is the one touch wanting to confirm my impression of her behaviour in that matter. I suggested that her authority *might possibly* be Mrs. Sartoris's, not at all because I saw reason to suspect her of anything worse than a little disliking, with or without reason, which she had, and still may have for aught I know, but from a remainder of respect to Hatty—who *might have* paid attention to any story reported by somebody who, at all events, was intimate with all three of the parties concerned,—myself, Hatty and Lady A.—she turns out, however, to have thought it quite just and proper to listen to people I never by any possibility can have mentioned Lady A's name to (for I *know* well to whom, and under what particular circumstances, I ever was induced to mention the name) and then, without giving me a hint of what the story was, how I might explain it or expose it, to take on herself to write that letter: that is,—to say she took it on herself,—for I don't believe any such nonsense, or that she was anything but the cat's paw of Lady A. in the business,—who, knowing she had only succeeded, after nine or ten months' teazing with her invitations, to get me to promise to visit her for one day, and so get handsomely done with it all,—wanted to have the air of shutting the door in my face with a final bang,—fancying that she could coax me round the back-way the very next day,—as she did by sending a servant and a letter of invitation to the house in Park Lane. I have told her my mind so thoroughly about *that,* and so effectually relieved myself from any further bother of the kind, that I need not bring up the nauseating remembrance. She and I have met once since, and I felt excused from even looking at—much less, speaking to her. But I should like to know,—whatever the story may have been,—what business Hatty had with my behaviour to Lady A. in Lady A's house? I suppose that Lady A. did not suppress what she considered the capital point of her quarrel with me when she foamed out into the couple of letters she bespattered me with,—yet the worst she charged me with was,—having said that my heart was buried in Florence, and the attractiveness of a marriage with her lay in its advantage to Pen—two simple facts,—as I told her,—which I had never left her in ignorance about, for a moment, though that I ever paraded this in a gross form to anybody is simply false; but had it been true,—does Hatty instantly practise impertinence on any friend of hers who intends to make an ambitious or mercenary marriage? As for her devotion to Lady A., begetting this chivalrous ardour in her, —Lady A has got plenty of friends quite as intimate, who never fancied for a moment that they were called on to fight her battles. For instance, I have been a week here with Lady Marian Alford, whom I was especially invited to meet,—she, I fancy, has received the utmost of Lady A's confidences, and heard whatever there was to hear; and nothing can exceed the friendliness with which we converse day after day; which is only to say, that she is a rational woman of the world, valuing her own independence, and understanding that there are two ways of telling a story. So, now, I have done with Hatty, for once and always. Had I believed stories about her, many a long year ago, and ordered her away from people's houses on the strength of them, I should have lost a friendship I used to value highly; but I have gained some pleasant memories by being less ready than she to believe slanderous gossip,—and, as she has elected to know me only through the reports of others, though I would have shown what they were worth in a minute, had she given me the opportunity,—so shall our relation be, and no otherwise, to the end of time. I scribble all this as fast as the pen can drive, but you will understand, and help with your sympathy and intelligence, I know.

Well, I am glad of all you tell me,—of the statue's news, of your approaching visit to London, of the enjoyments, in various ways, you tell me about so pleasantly. I have come here for a little change and relaxation, my six months' stay in town having begun to get the better of me. Pen is with his kind friends in Scotland, whence he writes in good spirits to-day. I shall return soon, having to go to "prep"—prepare, indeed! All my love to you all—don't let this very indignant letter hide the true feeling that is under it. This, I trust will be the last of my returning to that detestable subject.

Ever affectionately yours, dearest Edith,

R. B.

1872 : 3

To Miss Annie Egerton Smith

St. Aubin
Aug. 27 '72.

Dearest Annie,

I was very glad to get the news of you which, I began to fancy, would never arrive. Sarianna will tell you what little may be to tell: my pièce de resistance will follow the regular letter to myself—which you promise me and which I shall be grateful for. Thanks for the Spectators and Ev^g Post. Did you see little Austin's fresh piece of politeness in the "Standard," a few days before? Have you got your pictures,—the flowers,—and hung them to your satisfaction? We are very well—I bathe daily, Sarianna does not feel disposed to do so, but seems much the better for this short benefit of air, exercise, peace, quietness, and Milsand. Will you have the goodness to post the enclosed note to Miss Blagden? I don't remember her Town address. Write the moment you stop in your travels, and tell us what you can, as soon as you can. This bit of nothing must do for the present. We enjoy good weather, and it is a comfort to hear that London is less favoured. Good bye, dearest Annie!

Yours affy ever

R B.

1872 : 4

SARIANNA BROWNING AND ROBERT BROWNING TO MISS ANNIE EGERTON SMITH

19. Warwick Crescent.
Dec. 6th [1872]

My dear Miss Smith,

Your letter surprised and grieved me. I had believed you were comfortably installed at Florence, and expected to hear how much you were delighted with old beauties and new improvements, when the bad account comes that you have been kept sick at Biarritz,—a place I always remember as a very beautiful locality which made us all unwell. I do hope that you are now nearly recovered and will soon leave it—the suffering with your eyes seems to denote nervous weakness, and you have always complained of neuralgia, so come out of it as quickly as you can. I have received the Spectators regularly,—many thanks for them,—and I thought their arrival indicated that you were travelling southward. I forwarded them to Mr. Milsand when we had read them—was I right?—You don't say what it is you wish me to do for you, but I am sure you know my services are at your disposal. The other day we had a nicely written note from Phillips asking for the loan of two of my brother's small poems to be read aloud in an adult school for the poor, founded by the young ladies she is with,—we had much pleasure lending them to her. London is wet and foggy—we had one fine day—the first for weeks—on Wednesday, but it was followed by a speedy relapse. The gas-men having struck, the lamps are half of them extinguished, and the remainder give a grim, low light with a sepulchral appearance that does not make us look very cheerful. It is too bad that a whole city should be seriously inconvenienced for the sake of a private quarrel between two men and their employers. I have no news whatever to tell—my brother has had a bad cold, and has taken advantage of it to renounce provisionally all visits and dinners. Mrs. Orr is gone to Bath for a fortnight.

We shall be very glad indeed to have you back again at Greenbank—but I fear this delay does not promise us a speedy return. Let us hear soon from you. I shall look out anxiously for your next letter. Pray tell me what I can do for you. My brother will enclose a word. Pen is returned home, and sends his love. I think I told you that Sutton Corkran and his wife returned unexpectedly to London; he has a very pretty little baby.

Good bye. Take care of yourself and send us good accounts. With every good wish, I am

Very affectionately yours,
Sarianna Browning.

[On the inside of the flap of the envelope of this letter, Browning wrote the following note.]

Dearest A,

I have only a minute to say how glad I am that news of you arrived at last. I supposed you certainly at Florence, or on the road thither, as Miss Blagden wrote as if you would have left Biarritz long ago. I grieve that you have been ill: I myself have fared as badly: but I will write more next time

R B

1873 : 1

To Miss Annie Egerton Smith

St. Aubin, Aug. 3, '73

Dearest Annie,

Sarianna has written to you, and offers to slip into her envelope whatever I write,—it must needs be a shortish letter therefore. She will have told you, besides, all about our journey, and left me nothing to say but that, if the fates permitted, it would be exceedingly pleasant to have Greenbank pitched down in the neighbourhood, Annie and all. I should have some object to make me shut up my Greek books earlier and oftener, put on my hat, and go and see Miss Egerton-Smith. I am profoundly tired just now—for I have gone with my sister and the Milsands to hear a French Protestant service some five or six miles off, which is hard work under the sun—not that the heat is extravagant. I bathed yesterday, and found the water warm and pleasant. Repeating that process, seeing Milsand, and reading Aristophanes will be my portion for the next six weeks, I suppose and hope. What will you do? I went yesterday to review my old property—Tailleville; walked all round it, but found nothing material to alter in the poem.[1] It appears that the Cousins appealed, and tried their luck once again, and, only a week ago, were again signally beaten as they deserved. I am to see the newspaper report. I am tired with my walk and the weather as I said, but this line or two will tell you how much I want to hear from you, and how truly glad I should be, could one be here and there too—there, being where such friends are as Annie, whose I am, ever, in all affectionateness, so long as I am R B.

1873 : 2

TO MISS ANNIE EGERTON SMITH

St. Aubin, Saturday 16, '73

Dearest Annie,—I was thinking, and not for the first time, how unconscionably slow you were in replying to my letter, when the reply, in which I have a part, came—really to my great joy. I wish that Greenbank were, as you figure it, rolled alongside of our house here, —you should do more than look over the wall, I promise you. The feeling of the place you would like,—its quiet, simplicity, and the exceeding freshness of it,—such an open land and unobstructed sea; but you could walk nowhere, except on the sand after a monotonous fashion, or in the fields, which have not a bit more variety. We made one pleasant excursion, however, last Tuesday to Fontaine Henri, Creuilly, and St. Gabriel—thru delightful places, old, older, and oldest. This last, an old priory, with appendages in a ruinous state, I suppose one might buy for a trifle, and, for a moderate sum, repair and complete as a wonderful dwelling place. The Castle of Creuilly—a delicious relic—was sold a few years ago for £400. In England, such places to sell and prices to pay would be too absurd even to dream about. But here, they have quite other predilections. And who could comfortably build, live and die in the middle of aliens? All your papers arrive safely, and are properly valued. The prominence you gave Gillespie's article was not lost on me. I believe the dear old man is stiffish in the intellectual joints, but he *hops* his distance stoutly, and *I* am quite satisfied with his good intentions. In the Spectator which came yesterday, somebody repeated that foolish lie that I called Lord Byron "a flatfish." Those are the practices of your more lively articlemongers, who tell these lies, like Austin, for the malice rather than the fun of the thing. I never said nor wrote a word against or about Byron's poetry or power in my life; but I did say, that, if he were in earnest and preferred being with the sea to associating with mankind, he would do well to stay with the sea's population; thereby simply taking him at his word, had it been honest—whereas it was altogether dishonest, seeing that nobody cared so much about the opinions of mankind, and deferred to them, as he who was thus posturing and pretending to despise them. Well, I am glad to hear news from Italy.

Since poor Isa left off writing,[1] I have no means of getting informed about friends there. I wonder whether you will come to France; it is no use saying, what is simply true, that I should rejoice to meet you here—you know what obstacles are in the way. We have been just a fortnight here,—earlier than last time,—which may oblige us to spin out the week or two after the departure of Milsand—that is after we have left this place in his company, as we assuredly shall. He gives us uneasiness by a sort of rheumatic affection and lameness in the leg —it is better, and, I hope, about to leave him; but still it hinders his walking. Now, Annie, I must go and take advantage of the tide and bathe. The weather is brilliant, the sea warm as new milk. It agrees with me altogether. I think I did well to get away early from London and not run down so absolutely low. There is less to recover, you see. I am sitting writing this, in my bathing-dress, one step removed from the cool costumes of the Pistoja Villa. Do write at once, and a good long letter. Do you ever look in at our house, Warwick C? I have no news from Pen since he was with the Benzons. I suppose he has no wonderful feats to tell of—judging by the reports in the papers. Bathed, returned, and ever affectionately Annie's R BROWNING.

1873 : 3

To W. W. STORY

St. Aubin-sur-mer, par Luc, Calvados
Aug. 24, '73

My dear Story,

I ought not to think any proceeding of yours "singularly kind"— but I can't help doing so in the case of this long, particularizing letter, written amid so much to distract your attention—most full of interest it is, of course, at whatever trouble to yourself it may have been produced. Pen kept me sufficiently informed about the main result of every one of these sad days—but attempted no more, and I understand for the first time the nature of poor B's attack. What can I add but that I am deeply interested in the news I wait for each morning? How sorry I am, there is no need to say. It struck me as exceedingly fortunate for our friend that you were at hand—your services must have been valuable indeed. What an extinction of the light of that pleasant party,—even if there be an escape from the worst we have to fear. This will have done no good,—to say the least of it,—to Mrs. Story who was benefiting by the stay at North Berwick, according to Pen. His note,

—a day later than your letter,—mentions her being expected at Pitlochrie on Monday.

I am sure Mrs. Benzon understands how much I feel for her on this terrible occasion—if it could be otherwise, I would write every day. Give her my most affectionate regards. My presence at Allean would be a pure incumbrance, I very well know. Indeed, I fancy you oppressed with such a multitude of counsellors. Well,—at all events, I am not so circumstanced here as to be in unnatural contrast, thro' the gaiety of St. Aubin, with the misfortune at Allean. I and my sister walk, bathe, breathe fresh air enough, have our friend Milsand's company, and thereupon send another day to its account. I have out a little reading between whiles. The weather is not so constantly fine as last year,—seems to have broken up already. We have made just one expedition in a jolting cart-carriage; and yet three weeks of our term have been somehow got rid of. While I write, it is raining heavily. I know that you always take just this opportunity,—of country quiet,—to write, and otherwise turn your short holiday to account. You must stay the longer in England, and catch, if possible, whatever you lose just now. I write, as I cannot but feel, lumberingly—and with a weight of foreboding and dispiritedness—but my object may have been gained—for all I want is to thank you deeply, and associate myself, despite of the distance, with your anxieties and friendly feelings. My sister is not very well,—has a bad cold,—but feels as gratefully as I do your kindness in this matter—and all others, indeed.

Ever affectionately yours
ROBERT BROWNING

This is pricked on a bare deal table with an iron pen.

1873 : 4

To W. C. CARTWRIGHT

19 Warwick Crescent, W.
Oct. 3. '73

My dear Cartwright,

I have just returned to London, and find your letter. I was in Normandy at the time of poor Benzon's[1] first attack of illness in Scotland: Pen was with him, however, and kept me in constant information. B. would seem to have been suffering from a complication of disorders in head, heart, lungs and elsewhere: the action of these being precipitated and combined by something wrong in exercise, or exposure, or diet: the resources summoned to his aid were *enormous*—Jenner, Quain, Begbie of Edinburgh, Sir H. Thompson, and others did their utmost for a month: it was hoped that convalescence had set in, but a return of bronchitis ended all somewhat suddenly. The suffering was extreme; but our friend's sweet temper and patient goodness never failed him for a moment, and, though anxious to live for the accomplishment of various objects, his calmness and resolution were admirable. I can only give you the somewhat vague account of the malady which I myself am as yet able to collect from conflicting accounts: my own conviction is that we have one more victim to overwork and under-rest: I apprehended some ill consequence of the never ceasing activity of brain, and told him so more than once. You know my estimate of my own loss by this event: I cannot venture to calculate its effect on his family.

He was buried at Kensal Green a fortnight ago. I heard of his death the day I arrived in Paris, by the papers which came by the evening post. My plan had been to establish myself and my sister somewhere in the neighbourhood of Paris for perhaps a month longer: but I really lost inclination for protracting the holiday, and left for London as soon as was possible. Mrs Benzon came up three days ago,—I saw her at once. The extensive alterations begun in the house were countermanded, but the work had advanced and the place is not yet ready to receive her. She had been much gratified by your letter, she told me. It is hardly necessary to say that I would have gone to Scotland could there have appeared any conceivable good to B. in the visit: the house was full to overflowing, and Pen removed to Pitlochry, the nearest place, miles off. He is at present with Millais at Birnam. My sister's kindest regard to you.

Ever most affectionately yours

ROBERT BROWNING.

1874 : 1

To W. W. STORY

19 Warwick Crescent, W.
June 9, '74

Dear Friend, I write at once on the impulse of having seen Mr. Lowell last night at a party—to my great pleasure—and *then,* having heard from him the impossible news that you were not coming to London this year!—which was a most unpleasant thing to hear. Can it be? Here is Story a regular member of the "Athenaeum," and all for nothing! At all events, reconsider the matter, and if there be no very good reason for such a step, pray don't take it. I believe, you see, in what you tell me of your completely reestablished health,—otherwise, *that* would overbear all other considerations. At all events, the most likely way to *know* instead of conjecture merely what you intend doing will be to write—so I write. And if you are really purposed to stay away altogether, I think you will be disposed to answer me *nearly* at once. However, I ought to have told you earlier that I duly waited on the Semiramis and had every impression you could desire or expect of her grandeur and voluptuousness. I don't know what they intend to do with it—there is a sale of pictures, next week, but nothing else. The books seem all in their places. I know exactly as much as I wish,—i. e. nothing at all,—about the arrangements under poor Benzon's will. The bust, which I am anxious to see, is sure to be a great success—of course, the mere cast would have helped nobody by itself. Story knows how to keep faces in the gallery under his hat. Mrs. B. is very well,— doesn't go out, but sees old friends of an afternoon. Lily[1] is quite well, and the boy gets a big fellow; but you may hear of all this and more from herself, perhaps. My best report is to be of Pen. It is now four months and a half since he has been at steady work, and there must be immense good in that. His master, Heyermans,[2] evidently *is* the master, and, from Pen's letters, which are unremitting, I can see that he is happier than he ever was in his life. What a load this lightens me of. Who can judge better than you? He has never once budged from his butcher's-shop-lodging, and it is *I,* this time, who begin to be anxious that he should change the air and otherwise relax a little. If no other scheme presents itself, I and my sister will join him in an excursion somewhither in the autumn. We don't go to France, at any rate. Neither I nor my sister have been very well—our abominable weather may be to blame. I caught cold three weeks ago, and got otherwise out of order, but feel better at last. Lady W. is very fluctuating in health,—sometimes apparently at death's door,—then, a step backwards, and she is almost her old self again. The V de R's are here and will do much for her. I see every now and then that contemptible Lady Ashburton, and mind her no more than any other black beetle —so long as it don't crawl up my sleeve. The town is very full and busy, just now, but the season will be a short one. Do tell me, by a word or two, what you are likely to do. Your two young men are quite well, apparently, and Edith was about to visit Florence, when you wrote. Did she go? What a wonderful affair this American band of believing ones—as a product of your common-sensical country, seems to us here! I dined in company with Gen. Schenk last evening, and wish I had remembered to ask him about it. Lowell (but that was at another house) looked very well. He stays here for a fortnight only. His wife was with him. B Trollope[3] is notable also for her singing. She was present, and it only seemed yesterday when Pen and the little lady cantered about on ponies side by side like two butterflies. Well. some good things remain. My true love for you all—take it!

R B.

1874 : 2

To Richard Henry Horne

19, Warwick Crescent,
London, W.
June 25th, 1874

Dear Horne,

I am indeed glad at your success, tardy as it may be. Nobody can doubt your right to recognition and reward, far beyond what you are likely to get. Gladstone ought not have let slip this piece of graceful justice, but the Gods are against him just now.[1]

Ever truly yours,
R. Browning.

1874 : 3

To the Editor of the *Daily News*[1]

Sir,—In a clever article this morning you speak of "the doctrine of the enclitic De"—"which, with all deference to Mr. Browning, in point of fact does not exist." No, not to Mr. Browning: but pray defer to Herr Buttmann, whose fifth list of "enclitics" ends "with the inseparable De"—or to Curtius, whose fifth list ends also with "De (meaning *towards* and as a demonstrative appendage)." That this is not to be confounded with the accentuated "De, meaning *but*" was the "Doctrine" which the Grammarian bequeathed to those capable of receiving it,—I am, Sir, yours obediently

R. B.

Nov. 20. [1874]

1875 : 1

To Mr. George Barnett Smith

19, Warwick Crescent,
London, W.
January 11th, 1875.

Dear Mr. Barnett Smith,

I do hope—and, indeed, feel almost sure—that your kindness and sympathy, to say nothing of certain other qualities, will have prevented you from attributing the delay in acknowledging the receipt of your letter to any but the right cause—such a press of matters calling for immediate attention has put all thoughts of merely pleasurable pen-management quite out of my head for the time. And a pleasure it truly is, the thanking a friend for his good wishes and genial expressions. I reciprocate them with all my heart; and the foremost of the file is that earnest wish that the illness of your daughter, which you informed me of, may be a thing of the past altogether.

My son, who has paid me a short visit, leaves to-morrow. I get done with a book,[1] it is to be printed in a few weeks. The good weather may be expected, and nothing will hinder, I hope, the visit of Mrs. Barnett Smith and yourself which you promise—a promise of which I shall remind you.

As for the literary articles you mention, my prolonged absence in the autumn has made me lose a good deal; but I can recover something, and the more valuable part, at the Club. I am happy to know that your ability is properly recognised. *Scribner* I have just glanced at, and may more completely examine, one day. The notice had (to my apprehension) the usual fault of beginning at the very beginning of my somewhat lengthy series of works, and criticising those on a scale which, presently, the writer finds is impossible to sustain, and so he finds it convenient to dismiss the product of half my life with a summary sentence or two—which, in the nature of things, must needs be a condemnatory one, for there is no calling a thing simply "good" without advancing some proof of its goodness; whereas, if you call it indifferent or bad, readers will gladly dispense with a further sample. I myself have always liked to read a man's *collected* works, of any kind, *backwards;* and what I once thought a fancy I incline now to consider an eminently rational procedure.

But we will talk over such points some evening; and meanwhile you must remember me, with all regards to Mrs. Barnett Smith, as

Every truly yours,

Robert Browning

1875 : 2

To Algernon Charles Swinburne

19. Warwick Crescent, W.
Feb. 23. '75.

My dear Swinburne,

I feel much embarrassed in what I want to say. Your generosity has been, all along, so conspicuous, that one may doubt whether you any more expect grateful recognition of it than of justice or any other quality that a good man is bound to possess. But I cannot help thinking that you have,—in the case of this criticism upon me in your last performance,[1]—gone beyond the ordinary requirement and quite up to the Christian point of "compelling the needy to come in" and be most generously dealt with. For, with your mastery of matter and manner in literature, you could easily have said whatever was wanted, without reference to me and my poems: *that,* you know well enough. I wish you all success, and that the admiration of whomever it be you would acknowledge as competent to bestow admiration, may express itself as cordially, and far more eloquently than that entertained for you, Dear Swinburne, by yours

ever truly

ROBERT BROWNING.

1875 : 3

To the Rev. Alexander B. Grosart[1]

19, Warwick Crescent,
London, W.
February 24th, 1875.

Dear Mr. Grosart,

I have been asked the question you now address me with, and as duly answered it, I can't remember how many times: there is no sort of objection to one more assurance, or rather confession, on my part that I *did* in my hasty youth presume to use the great and venerable personality of Wordsworth as a sort of painter's model; one from which this or the other particular feature may be selected and turned to account: had I intended more, above all, such a boldness as portraying the entire man, I should not have talked about "handfuls of silver and bits of ribbon." These never influenced the change of politics in the great poet; whose defection, nevertheless, accompanied as it was by a regular face-about of his special party, was to my juvenile apprehension, and even mature consideration, an event to deplore. But just as in the tapestry on my wall I can recognise figures which have *struck out* a fancy, on occasion, that though truly enough thus derived, yet would be preposterous as a copy, so, though I dare not deny the original of my little poem,[2] I altogether refuse to have it considered as the "very effigies" of such a moral and intellectual superiority.

Faithfully yours,

ROBERT BROWNING.

1875 : 4

TO EDMUND GOSSE

Dinant, Belgique,
August 16th, 1875.

My dear Mr. Gosse,

I get your pleasant announcement[1] here, and make haste to wish you and your wife all possible happiness. I seem as if I knew the lady, —so lately have I been admiring a picture by her. Now, the great thing will be for both of you to work hard and show the power of the double twist, the silver in the gold thread,—the painter's power along with the poet's.

Ever truly yours,

ROBERT BROWNING.

1876 : 1

TO MISS E. DICKINSON WEST

19, Warwick Crescent,
London, W.
January 4th, 1876.

Dear Miss Dickinson West,

Your letter has no right to give me such deep pleasure as it did last evening. Did you really think "I was not likely to remember your name," and that I should read your poetry with I don't know what of humility and effort and sense of duty and so forth? Certainly one's feelings want reviving sometimes, yet, by my own experience, "four years ago" if they were alive at all, alive they remain. And why do you "forbear to trouble my courtesy," and bid me believe you "mine respectfully"? If I did not surmise the warm hand under the damp glove, I should be very sorry and ashamed of myself. You ought to remember how all the kindness came from you, all the gratitude should come from me.

Yet there was an odd circumstance attending the receipt of your book,[1] which I will tell you. It arrived on Monday evening, and about three weeks ago a letter was addressed to me by a lady complaining that "some verses" she had sent for my inspection had never been reported upon. They never reached me, or have been mislaid in my absence, as I told the stranger-lady: and, having surmised their quality, it was with a slight shudder that I put the book aside, unopened, even to the envelope. Last night, with something of your imputed "sense of duty and courtesy" it was that I tore off the covering and opened the little volume at hazard: when the first line that caught my eye made me call out to my sister (to whom I had made known my apprehensions), "But, they are by no means nonsense!" Whereupon, as reward to my acuteness of perception, out dropped the letter and all the mystery was at an end. So, after a thankful ejaculation, I began and ended *Verses*—"ended" for that time, only. They are very sincere, deeply earnest and—I dare declare—beautiful. It would have been a falling off from your earlier goodness had you denied me the privilege which no one of your friends can trulier value. It is not for me—in such an ignorance as mine of your aims in life—to urge you to write more: but if you do not—you *will* not: no other reason is admissible.

I ought to remark on your allusion to my own poem: you will have done your best to like it, I am sure. I do not fear your inapprehension will be that of my reviewers whom you had the first notion from. There would seem to be no sort of perception extant as to what dramatic writing means: my silly friend of *The Spectator* sees myself speaking out my own speech in this and the other character, and blames accordingly.

But never mind: let me end with you full in face. I shall be always cheered and encouraged by such a word from afar as you have now gratified me with. I wish you all happiness—dear friend, dare I say? —being,

Ever yours truly,
ROBERT BROWNING.

1876 : 2

To Edmund Gosse

19, Warwick Crescent,
W.
January 18th, 1876.

Dear Mr. Gosse,

I really have waited a little before writing to acknowledge your gift,[1] from an apprehension that the delight I must express at its poetry might seem influenced by the pride I needs must feel at its preface. Of *that*—the preface—I shall even now be silent, if you permit,—for you ought to guess my feeling: but I will say that the dramatic power and understanding management of character were somewhat of a surprise even to me—whose recognition of your faculty was from the first complete and immediate. I hope you will continue these surprises—though they will now be increasingly difficult.

Truly yours ever,

Robert Browning.

1876 : 3

To John H. Ingram

19, Warwick Crescent,
London, W.
February 10th, 1876.

Dear Sir,

I hope I need not assure you that the letter you mention having written two years ago never reached me: an answer would certainly have acknowledged it.

I am quite unable to give you the least information on the various points you specify. I never heard anything whatever from my wife on the subject of Poe, or her contributions (if any there were) to his magazine.

I remember, however, Mr. Buchanan Reid (*sic*), who was well acquainted with Poe, telling me as characteristic of the latter that he had described to him—Mr. Reid—the whole process of the construction of his poem of *The Raven*—and declared that the suggestion of it lay wholly in a line from *Geraldine's Courtship*—"with a murmurous stir uncertain, in the air the purple curtain,"¹ &c. I am bound to add what he added, "and yet, long afterward, just to answer another purpose, he printed an elaborate account of his selecting a long word, then looking out for another" and with much more of the kind,— "and all a lie." The consequence has been that a charge of imitation, if not plagiarism, has been brought against the wrong person.²

I am, dear Sir,

Yours obediently,

ROBERT BROWNING.

1876 : 4

To JOHN H. INGRAM

19, Warwick Crescent,
London, W.
February 11th, 1876.

Dear Sir,

I am quite sure that all is exactly as you say. I hope I told you distinctly that I was ignorant altogether on those points you mentioned. I do not remember the Mr. Thompson you quote from, but am quite sure that the "strong desire to see Poe's memory vindicated from moral aspersion" must have been simply an echo of a desire of his own. We neither of us had heard, at that time, any aspersion at all; and my wife could have known nothing one way or the other so as to do more than express a naturally "strong desire" that if a man of genius had been "aspersed," the aspersion should be removed by all means.

Mr. Bayard Taylor was, and is, my friend. As to our great admiration for Poe's power, that anybody who cared to question my wife or myself on the subject would be certain to hear. The notion that *The Raven* was derived from *Lady Geraldine's Courtship* is truly absurd; and I considered the statement of Poe himself, that he had really so derived any particle of it (except perhaps the measure, which belongs to whoever can manage it) as equally absurd. I believe he *did* make such a statement to Read, whose veracity I see no reason to doubt; and certainly my impression is that in Poe's *Philosophy of Composition* he undertook to show, not merely "how a poem might be written," but, by way of example, how *The Raven* actually *was* written.

There is no need to tell me how greedily the little men will catch up and carry about a little lie in the shape of a charge of plagiarism. Last year I wrote, and published, a poem about Aristophanes, and somebody, wholly a stranger to me, reviewing it in *The Athenaeum,* observed (for fun's sake, I suppose) that it was "probably written after one of Mr. Browning's Oxford Symposia with Jowett." Whereupon half a dozen other critics reported the poem to be "the transcript of the talk of the Master of Balliol"—whom I have not set eyes on these four years, and with whom I never had a conversation about Aristophanes in my life. Such a love of a lie have the verminous tribe!

Pray believe me, Dear Sir,

Yours very sincerely,
ROBERT BROWNING.

1876 : 5

To a Correspondent[1]

19, Warwick Crescent,
London, W.
May 11th, 1876.

Dear Friend,

It would ill become me to waste a word on my own feelings except inasmuch as they can be common to us both, in such a situation as you describe yours to be, and which, by sympathy, I can make mine by the anticipation of a few years at most. It is a great thing, the greatest, that a human being should have passed the probation of life, and sum up its experience in a witness to the power and love of God. I dare congratulate you. All the help I can offer, in my poor degree, is the assurance that I see ever *more* reason to hold by the same hope— and that by no means in ignorance of what has been advanced to the contrary; and for your sake I would wish it to be true that I had so much of 'genius' as to permit the testimony of an especially privileged insight to come in aid of the ordinary argument. For I know I, myself, have been aware of the communication of something more subtle than a ratiocinative process, when the convictions of 'genius' have thrilled my soul to its depths, as when Napoleon, shutting up the New Testament, said of Christ: "Do you know that I am an understander of men? Well, He was no man!" ("Savez-vous que je me connais en hommes? Eh bien, celui-là ne fut pas un homme.") Or as when Charles Lamb, in a gay fancy with some friends as to how he and they would feel if the greatest of the dead were to appear suddenly in flesh and blood once more, on the final suggestion, "And if Christ entered this room?" changed his manner at once, and stuttered out, as his manner was when moved, "You see, if Shakespeare entered, we should all rise; if *He* appeared we must kneel."[2] Or, not to multiply instances, as when Dante wrote what I will transcribe from my wife's Testament, wherein I recorded it fourteen years ago, "Thus I believe, thus I affirm, thus I am certain it is, that from this life I shall pass to another better, there, where that lady lives of whom my soul was enamoured."[3] Dear friend, I may have wearied you in spite of your good will. God bless you, sustain, and receive you! Reciprocate this blessing with

Yours affectionately,
ROBERT BROWNING.

1876 : 6

TO NORMAN MAC COLL

19. Warwick Crescent, W
June 13. '76.

Dear Sir,

I beg to thank you for your kind and flattering proposal. Many circumstances prevented me from taking—or trying to take—a very obvious way to public notice. It would hardly become me to mention why these ought to have little weight against a desire expressed on the part of the "Athenæum." If you were to refer to the volume of that Journal for 1833 you would find a notice of my first poem,—which gratified me and my people far beyond what will ever be the fortune of criticism now. I never knew by whom the notice was written, but one remembers such things—or rather, such a thing. I am relieved therefore of a real pain which I should feel if,—having any poem unpublished that might seem to suit your purpose,—I withheld it—by the simple fact that I am at this minute correcting the proofs of a volume containing the pieces to which Mr Furnivall must have alluded,—all and every one of such pieces, I assure you: and, I suppose, in a week or two you will, perhaps, congratulate yourself that your kind offer was made so late in the day, when you get "Pacchiarotto—

and how he worked in distemper: with other Poems," through the offices of Smith and Elder.

Pray believe me, Dear Sir,

Yours very sincerely

ROBERT BROWNING.

1876 : 7

To P. R. JACKSON

19, Warwick Crescent,
London, W.
June 28th, 1876.

Dear Sir,

I was not aware, nor I suppose can my publisher have been aware, that *Hervé Riel* had appeared in the *Royal Reader,* such an appearance without my knowledge and consent was a theft, and punishable. I consider the poem rather the publisher's than my property, because he gave me a hundred pounds for it, which I wanted for the starving French,[1] and it was only at his urgent request the other day that I included the thing in a volume, which has just passed through the press, and will be out in a day or two.[2] I could not, therefore, with propriety, allow that transfer to your collection, which the honesty and courtesy of your application would otherwise have induced me to permit.

I hope this explanation will satisfy you that it is in no churlish spirit that I am compelled to abide by what I wrote with reluctance.

I am, dear Sir,

Yours obediently

ROBERT BROWNING.

P. R. Jackson, Esq.

1876 : 8

To EDMUND GOSSE

19, Warwick Crescent, W.
July 25th, 1876

Dear Mr. Gosse,

Your goodness confuses me indeed. I am sure you have "looked to like, if looking liking move," and succeeded by virtue of your own generosity. Thank you very much.

I am on the point of leaving town; when I return, let me hope that I may turn our neighbourhood to better account than was possible in the few last weeks of social toil and trouble.

Ever truly yours,
Rob^T Browning.

P.S.—Let me tell you there are some odd pieces of oversight in the book[1]—attributable to my own carelessness, I believe. Especially, in a poem[2] written while the earlier sheets were passing through the press, read (page 194), for "aloft"—"from bier":[3] (213 for "crowns" —"crowned":[4] and (214) for "disbursed"—"unpursed."[5] There is also (page 164) in the 8th line a "who" for "how."[6] The punctuation—as is the way with printed verse—has been suffered to slip out of the endings, and confuse the sense in many instances. In *Numpholeptos* (p. 97) the 8th line should run: "So grant me—love—whole, sole," *etc.*[7]

1876 : 9

To H. Buxton Forman[1]

19, Warwick Crescent, W.
July 27, '76.

Dear Mr. Buxton Forman,

There can be no objection to such a simple statement of fact as you have inserted, if it seem worth inserting. "Fact," it is.—Next:—"aia" is generally an accumulative yet depreciative termination: "Cenciaia" —a bundle of rags: a trifle. The proverb[2] means "every poor creature will be for pressing into the company of his betters," and I used it to deprecate the notion that I intended anything of the kind. Is it any contribution to "all connected with Shelley" if I mention that my "Book" has a reference to the reason given by Farinacci, the advocate of the Cenci, of his failure in the defence of Beatrice? "Fuisse puni-tam Beatricem" (he declares) "poena ultimi supplicii, non quia ex intervallo occidi mandavit insidiantem suo honori, sed quia ejus ex-ceptionem non probavit ibi—*Prout, et idem firmiter sperabatur de sorore Beatrice si propositam excusationem probasset, prout non pro-bavit.*" That is, she was expected to avow the main outrage, and did not: in conformity with her words "That which I ought to confess, that will I confess; that to which I ought to assent, to that will I assent;

and that which I ought to deny, that will I deny." Here is another Cenciaja!

Yours very sincerely
ROBERT BROWNING.

1876 : 10

To EDMUND GOSSE

Blairbey, Lamlash, Arran. N B.
Aug. 19. '76

Dear Mr Gosse,

Your very kind and considerate letter follows me hither. I never fancied you were the author of the article to which you refer: it would have struck you that I must be thin-skinned indeed if I cared about the passages quoted by the "Examiner"[1] as "what Alfred Austin has done to deserve"—being even noticed for a moment. I had in my mind his anonymous writings in the "Standard" and other papers. The first of these which fixed my attention was a criticism on "Balaustion"—wherein, undertaking to give "specimens of Mr B's inability to write a line" (or some such phrase) the critic produced several isolated lines—seven, I remember—five of which he had altered by omission or addition: in the first were two omissions and one addition of a syllable: the remaining lines untampered with contained each a break in the rhythm which the context would have justified. If the "Examiner" can conceive of a gentler name than *littleness* for tricks of this kind persisted in up to the present time—*I* cannot. One particular piece of blackguardism headed "Men of Letters: R. B"—could only save its author from a kicking by the charitable hope that he was too small for that treatment. I never was unlucky enough to set eyes on the man: if he *is* physically as well as morally and intellectually a dwarf—you may be sure I should have considered him a pygmy had his stature been that of Goliath. But I really meant nothing except to enliven my visionary dance of chimney-sweeps[2] by a grotesque monkey-image which had been thrusting itself upon my notice this long while: and it seems that one fillip more than avenges fifty flea-bites. The "Examiner" may be sure, moreover, that Mr Alfred Austin will take his own part in every rag of a newspaper to which he has free access. What man of the ordinary size ever yet ducked down so low,—hooted from his hiding at what he presumed to call his "fellows,"—and then tried to stand on tiptoe by their side, as a "poet," just as if nothing had happened?

Ever truly yours

ROBERT BROWNING.

1876 : 11

To H. BUXTON FORMAN

19, Warwick Crescent,
London, W.
October 25th, 1876.

Dear Mr. Buxton Forman,

I find your note, and the kind gift of the book,[1] on returning home after a little absence, during the last weeks of which no letters were sent me—which will explain the delay in replying to this of yours. I have no objection whatever to your making what use of my poem[2] you please, if you really prefer "my own words" to a paraphrase. I got the facts from a contemporaneous account I found in a MS. volume containing the "Relation" of the Cenci affair—with other memorials of Italian crime—lent me by Sir J. Simeon, who published the Cenci Narrative, with notes, in the series of the Philobiblon Society. It was a better copy of the "Relation" than that used by Shelley, differing at least in a few particulars. You may refer to it at the Museum. I believe I have seen somewhere that the translation was made by Mrs. Shelley—the note appended to an omitted passage seems a womanly performance.

There is no allusion to the Cenci case in my *Book*,[3] except that which I furnished you with. I will give it in full, you can prune away the extraneous matter. Et in rei veritate adduximus in alia quamplurimas Supremorum Senatuum Decisiones, quibus liquet fuisse minoratam poenam Maritis qui etiam mediante Assassinio occidi fecerunt Conjuges, et vice versa nulla affertur Decisio Fisco favorabilis. Qualis sententia eò libentiùs amplectanda est quia à majori numero Doctorum canonizatur. Et licet Farinaccius, et Dominus meus Raynaldus contrariam sectari videantur, nihilominùs Farinaccius in suis "Quaestionibus" nimis se dubium reddidit, ut in alia ostendi: et in "Consiliis." 141. nimis inconstantem se praebuit, dum in "Consiliis." 66. *num*. 5. contrarium probavit. Quamobrem de hujusmodi inconstantia admonitus se excusando asseruit in dictis "Consiliis." 141. *sub*

num. 16. Beatricem, pro qua scripserat, in Cons. 66. fuisse capite ob-
truncatam quasi quod hujusmodi rigorosa sententia in practica serve-
tur: sed, parcat mihi tam eximius Doctor, nimis incongruè respondit
oblitus quae in fine dicti Consilii. 66. scripta reliquerat, hoc est fuisse
punitam Beatricem poena ultimi supplicii non quia ex intervallo
occidi mandavit insidiantem suo honori, sed quia ejus exceptionem
non probavit ibi—"Prout, et idem fermitèr sperabatur de sorore Beatrice si propositam excusationem probasset, prout non probavit."[4] (Il.
de Archangelis *pro Dom. Guidone Francischino,* marked in the
"Book," page 49.)

You may, by the help of the works of Farinacci referred to in the
above, hear more on the subject. They are in the Museum, where I
consulted them. The Defence of Beatrice exists, as you probably
know; indeed it was reprinted here some forty years ago by Sir George
Bowyer.[5]

Believe me, dear Mr. Buxton Forman,

> Yours very truly,
> ROBERT BROWNING.

1877 : 1

To H. Buxton Forman

> 19, Warwick Crescent,
> London, W.
> March 27th, 1877.

Dear Mr. Forman,

I beg you to forgive a little delay in replying to your letter of last
week. I saw and copied certain variations in Shelley's poem[1] when it
was in the possession of Mrs. Stisted, of the Bagni di Lucca. She is long
since dead, and I suppose her curiosities—for she collected such—were
dispersed at the time. The letter in Leigh Hunt's Biography[2] was
printed without leave, as was afterwards explained by the writer's
supposing I was not in England—though I had been applied to by him
for a letter from his father which I could not lay hands on at the
moment. I remember that the printing was "queer," as you say, but
I had no copy of the book.

Leigh Hunt told me that the *Lamia* was the only copy procurable
in Italy. That he lent it to Shelley with due injunctions to be careful
of the loan on that account, and that Shelley replied emphatically: "I
will return it you with my own hands." He told me also of the con-

solation there was to him in the circumstance that the book had been found in Shelley's bosom, together with the right hand—evidently thrust there, as his custom was, when, having been struck by any passage in whatever book he might be reading with a friend, he paused to enjoy and pronounce upon it. This circumstance Leigh Hunt considered decisive as to the suddenness and comparative painlessness of the death. It is altogether incompatible with the truth of the silly story put into circulation recently. On my asking Leigh Hunt if the book still existed, he replied: "No, I threw it into the burning pile; Shelley said he would return it with his own hands into mine, and so he *shall* return it!" I confess to having felt the grotesqueness of a spirit of a duodecimo as well as that of a man. I remember Leigh Hunt was standing by a piano when he told me this. He had been singing to his own accompaniment the old *Stanco di pascolar le pecorelle*. I observed: "Do you know Shelley has mentioned that air?"[3] He did not, though he said it had been a great favourite with Shelley. The mention, you know, is in a note to *The Triumph of Life*. Of course you may make what use you please of these nothings.

Yours truly ever,

ROBERT BROWNING.

1877 : 2

TO GEORGE BARNETT SMITH

19, Warwick Crescent,
London, W.
April 7th, 1877.

My dear Mr. Smith,

I have just seen your biographical notice of Tennyson, which is very good. You will be sure to do mine well enough without any help, but, if you send me either the MS. or a Proof, I will correct any mistake I may see, and add whatever occurs to me as necessary. Such of the notices of me and my works as I have seen were faulty enough.

You are quite at liberty to print nine of the poems you mention—the tenth, *Hervé Riel,* is properly not mine, but Smith's, who gave me a hundred pounds for the use of it—money I sent to the French, when a famine was apprehended in Paris.[1] I only included it in the volume published last year at his particular request, and, greatly as I should like to be of the least service to you (as I hope you understand without such assurance) I dare not encroach upon what seem to me his rights. I already have refused a person who applied for the poem a month or two ago. To be sure, he was quite a stranger to me. Indeed, I very well know that if he, Mr. Smith, chose to exercise his voice in the matter, he would lay an embargo on the rest of what we must smuggle out of harbour; but, for your sake, I will risk this much.

Ever truly yours,

ROBERT BROWNING.

1877 : 3

To H. BUXTON FORMAN

19, Warwick Crescent,
London, W.
July 2nd, 1877.

Dear Mr. Forman,

I was sorry to be absent on Saturday when you called. Thank you greatly for the new volume, into which I have only had time to dip. I notice what seems an error, page 316: the rainbow-bridge was surely "pieced by the masonry of heaven"[1]—just as presently the word occurs: "our minds piece the vacant intervals," page 318.

I prefer, in the *Stanzas at Naples,* "the noon's transparent light," to "might"—which isles and mountains hardly "wear." The line was first restored in a strange edition of Shelley published by Benbow in 1826; and Leigh Hunt, in 1828, quotes the poem without it, remarking on its loss: and it was myself who told him of its existence, to his surprise and pleasure. The notion of light as a *veil* and *transparent* is familiar with Shelley, and the Italian practice of making words rhyme which have the same sound but a different sense, not infrequent. Even in this stanza there is "delight" for "light" 's fellow.

Certainly, by the way, Leigh Hunt is alluded to in the 35th stanza of *Adonais;* I heard so from John Forster, an earlier friend of his. The "dark mantle thrown athwart the brow" is a characteristic touch. Hunt is seen cloaked, somewhat theatrically, in the portrait by Hayter engraved for the Byron Book.[2]

So, you bought my Manuscript the other day.[3] I made it for the use of Charles Kean and his wife, to whom I read it.[4] They would have acted the play—but in perhaps two or three years to come, and in the meantime I was to keep it unprinted—an arrangement which did not suit me—whereupon I withdrew it, and included it in my *Bells and*

Pomegranates. It was never in the prompter's hands, I think. The excisions were my own, also the pencil-marks, which emphasize any word in a passage. When it came back from the printer, my father caused the MS. to be bound, and I have no notion how it passed out of his or my possession. It is the single poem in the series that I copied with my own hand, my sister being my amanuensis in those days. I think this bit of comment your due, as the purchaser.

Ever truly yours,
ROBERT BROWNING.

1877 : 4

TO THOMAS CARLYLE

19 Warwick Crescent, W
Oct. 17. '77.

Dear Mr. Carlyle,

I beg your kind acceptance of the translation I ventured upon at your desire:[1] what it ought to be,—in justification of the honor which occasioned it,—I can hardly say;—what it probably *is* you will be indulgent to—taking the effort in place of that performance which were worthy of the affectionate gratitude and respect of

Yours ever
ROBERT BROWNING.

1877 : 5

TO THE EDITOR OF THE *Times*[1]

Sir,—I observe by a paragraph in *The Times* of today that, through some unaccountable misunderstanding, my name continues to be mentioned as that of a candidate for the Rectorship of St. Andrews. May I beg to say, by your intervention, that immediately on becoming informed that such an honour was proposed to me, I wrote to decline it with all gratitude, as I had found myself compelled to do on some former occasions?

I am, Sir, obediently yours,
ROBERT BROWNING.

19, Warwick-crescent, W., Nov. 19. [1877]

1877 : 6

To George Barnett Smith

> 19, Warwick Crescent,
> London, W.
> December 9th, 1877.

My dear Mr. Barnett Smith,

You have had reason to think me unmindful of your kindness, that is, of the need of promptly acknowledging it. But so many are the claims on my attention just now that, I assure you, this is the first time these two months that I can sit down early in the day (my only way of practising penmanship of any kind) and find myself at liberty to do what I please, and I *please,* most certainly, to thank you for your *Shelley,*[1] and the biographical notices. I am astonished at your working power, and had no notion you possessed such a mastery over the the materials for a Life of Shelley. Such energy (as well as ability) as you give ample proof of, cannot but have its effect and reward sooner or later.

Dear Miss Smith,[2] my old and precious friend, will no longer serve as your intermediary with *The Liverpool Mercury,*[3] but I daresay I can manage that future early notices of yours, whenever I print anything, will be inserted "for Auld lang syne." If it continue to be of service, you shall always have early proofs.

I hope Mrs. Barnett Smith's health is quite re-established, and that all goes prosperously with you in this world of chance and change.

> Yours very sincerely,
> Robert Browning.

1877 : 7

To H. Buxton Forman

> 19. Warwick Crescent, W
> Dec. 27. '77.

Dear Mr Forman,

When I returned, in the Autumn, to London, I found your kind gift of the concluding volume of Shelley: I was occupied by various matters just then, and wished to examine the contents, old and new, —which even yet has proved impossible: but it is easy enough to thank you very sincerely for your book, and I do so with all my heart.

A dip into the first leaves showed something on which I should like to observe. The poem "Similes," page 6, was first printed by Medwin in the "Athenæum" where I read it,—to remember it all my life. I am certain you will find, by referring to the "Athenæum," that the second line of the second stanza runs

> "From their bowers of deadly yew"

—altered with characteristic blundering by Medwin and Mrs Shelley into what you retain.[1] Consider the original superiority of the reading, and I think you will insert it some day.

Another dip alighted on the lines "Buonna Notte": they are so un-Italian that I can only suppose Shelley tortured them into accordance with some air: there are misprints too, as of *chi* for *che:* but the metre is altogether impossible.

Pray believe me, with best Christmas wishes,

Yours very truly

ROBERT BROWNING.

1878 : 1

To NORMAN MAC COLL

19. Warwick Crescent, W
Jan. 1. '78.

Dear Mr Mac Coll,

My correction is too obvious! You don't think for a moment I supposed that yourself would not have made it, had your eye fallen on the passage. You may well correct the error on your own authority—quoting, if you please,—out of a century of instances,—some such line as Martial's *"Personam capiti detrahat illa tuo."* Pray don't mention my name! If you like, while in the way of correcting the paper, you may observe that the "riddle of somewhat difficult solution" is no riddle at all. *"Et ecce"* means—"So noxious are the above three practices, that it is a wonder I—who have eschewed them all—should be dying all the same," a locution not unlike Mercutio's "No, 'tis not so deep as a well, nor so wide as a churchdoor; but 'tis enough, 'twill serve"—that is, "the hurt which cannot be much." Of course, the well-deep and churchdoor-wide wound would have served more than enough.

I take the opportunity of saying a word about another little matter, —wherein I have no fear that you will misinterpret my motive. There is just come out a remarkably close and clever translation of a poem of mine,—"the Inn Album,"—by a stranger to me: and I am told it is obtaining much notice in Germany.[1] I have procured a few copies, one of which I beg to send you: in the event of its seeming to be worth alluding to,—and I should be glad if it did so seem, for the translator's sake,—you will readily understand that any reference to my own share of the production, would vex me,—indeed, the fancy of appearing to invite such a reference prevented my begging your acceptance of the book before,—mere token of proper respect as it would have been. You know the proverbial "unintelligibility of the author,"—and I was the more amused to find how exactly I had managed to become intelligible to a foreigner who (of course) never submitted the M. S. or "proofs" to me for elucidation.

Believe me, with best New Year's wishes, Dear Mr Mac Coll,

Yours very truly

ROBERT BROWNING.

1878 : 2

TO THOMAS CARLYLE

19, Warwick Crescent, W
March 26, 1878.

My dear Mr Carlyle,

I hardly dare make the simple mention I am about to do of the fact that a picture by my son will be on view at my house till next Sunday: how much less can I dream of begging you to come and see merely *that!* But you did actually honour me by a visit, an attempted one, some time ago—and an abiding regret it has been to me that I was away at the time such a favour as you intended me. Only on this account I venture to say that, should any happy chance bring you to this neighbourhood any afternoon, my son's work would be rewarded indeed by your notice. You knew him when a child and were kind as he even yet well remembers: he is now some years older[1] than was his father when you were more than kind to

Your ever grateful and affectionate

ROBERT BROWNING.

1878 : 3

TO NORMAN MAC COLL

> 19. Warwick Crescent, W
> April 7. 1878.

Dear Mr Mac Coll,

I shall, of course, be very happy to see you whenever you please—on Tuesday, for instance, at no matter how early an hour before two o'clock, when I have an engagement.

> Pray believe me, very truly, yours
> R BROWNING.

1878 : 4

TO EDMUND GOSSE

> Hôtel Bodehhaus,
> Splügen.
> September 21st, 1878.

My dear Gosse,

Has your attention been directed to an article of last week's *Athenaeum,* on a reprint of some of the poems of Ebenezer Jones, in which my name was introduced as that of one who thoroughly "appreciated" the author? *That* is undoubtedly true: but I never saw nor heard anything of him except his one book,[1]—which was lent to me for a somewhat hurried reading. I remember speaking about it to W. J. Fox,—who told me he knew the writer personally, and shared in my opinion of his power: and, I *almost* think, it may have been from one of those "roughly-printed blue-paper books" that Eliot Warburton,[2] at breakfast once, declaimed to me an impassioned Chartist *tirade* in blank verse,—the speech of an orator addressing a crowd.

This is all I can say in answer to your first question; as to the second, I know nothing whatever. The year and the day of the death were given in the *Athenaeum* article: I suppose there is some doubt in your mind about their correctness.

With kind regards to Mrs. Gosse, believe me ever yours sincerely,

> ROBERT BROWNING.

1878 : 5

To Sir Frederick Leighton

19, Warwick Crescent, W.,
November 14, 1878.

Dear Leighton;—I wish you joy with all my heart, and congratulate us all on your election.[1] There ought to have been no sort of doubt as to the result, but the best of us are misconceived sometimes, though in your case never was a right more incontestable. All I hope is that your new duties will in no way interfere with the practice of your Art. I only venture to write, now, as one who, so many a year ago, saw your beginning with "Cimabue," and from that time to this remained confident what your career would be. But you know all this, and it required no answer, being rather a spurt of satisfaction at my own original discernment than any assurance which I can fancy you need from,—

Yours very truly,
Robert Browning

1879 : 1

To John H. Ingram

19, Warwick Crescent,
London, W.
March 12th, 1879.

My Dear Sir,
    I have most sincerely to beg your pardon for a seemingly unaccountable piece of negligence in failing to reply at once to your letter of some twelve days ago; I have only this moment found it misplaced amid a number of papers supposed to be done with. I make haste to say that whatever I mentioned to you about the statement (by no means "remark" merely) of Mr. Buchanan Read as to what Poe alleged to be the cause of his writing The Raven being true, and the responsibility for its truth resting wholly with Mr. Read himself, I can have no objection to being cited as your authority for such a statement having been made. Mr. Read did not appear so much convinced that there was any truth in it, as that—to quote his very words—the subsequent elaborate account of the matter was "every word a lie."

I, also, was in ignorance that my interlocutor at Mr. Rossetti's was a
gentleman with whom I had already become acquainted through
correspondence, and by other means. I should have been very glad to
have acknowledged your kindness.

Pray believe me, My dear Sir,

Yours very sincerely,

ROBERT BROWNING.

1879 : 2

To THOMAS CARLYLE

19, Warwick Crescent, W.
March 27, '79.

Dear Mr Carlyle,

You did indeed inaugurate most auspiciously Robert's first appearance as a would-be painter last year. I believe the kindness shown him
has been by no means thrown away. He is sending to London some
new pictures which, I am told, show decided progress. They are to
arrive to-day, and will be on view at a house much nearer your own
than that which you honored with a visit on the former occasion. If
therefore you could again so much indulge us,—the pictures will be
ready for your inspection next Friday and the three following days
from 2 till 5 p.m., at 17, Queen's Gate Gardens, South Kensington.
The house,—lent me by Mr George Smith,—is an empty one, and
the pictures will be seen on the ground-floor, nor cause any ascent.

I have been exceedingly unwell for the last three weeks, or I would
have begged this favor in person. I trust your own health is in a satisfactory state.

Believe me ever,

Dear Mr Carlyle,

Yours most respectfully and affectionately

ROBERT BROWNING.

1879 : 3

To ALFRED DOMETT[1]

Dear Domett, who knows but you might manage to look in? It would
greatly delight yours affy. ever

R B

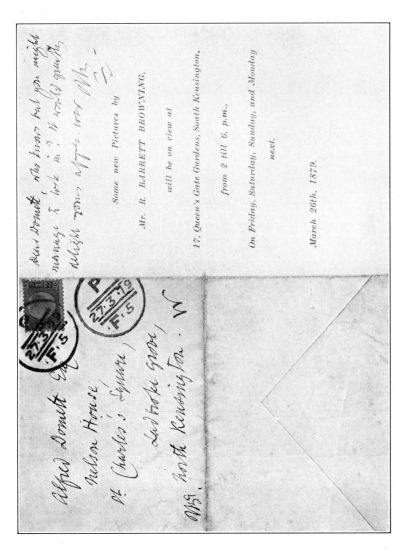

A PHOTOGRAPHIC REPRODUCTION OF LETTER 1879:3, pp. 186-187

[*The printed announcement on which this note is written is as follows.*]

Some new Pictures by
Mr. R. Barrett Browning
will be on view at
17, Queen's Gate Gardens, South Kensington,
from 2 till 6, p.m.,
On Friday, Saturday, Sunday, and Monday
next.

March 26th, 1879.

1879 : 4

To Norman Mac Coll

19. Warwick Crescent, W
Apr. 18. '79.

Dear Mr Mac Coll,

You are too good in acknowledging (even) such a trifle. Whenever any little fact of the kind occurs to me, I will always take the chance of your caring to notice it.

I know only that the poems[1] are announced for the 28th inst: I have a copy—but it is at the Binder's unluckily. The Publisher ought—and no doubt will be pleased—to give you whatever you may desire.

Ever truly yours
Robert Browning.

1879 : 5

To Edmund Gosse

19, Warwick Crescent, W.
June 4th, 1879.

Dear Mr. Gosse,

"Mansoor"[1] was one of the names of the third Fatemite Caliph, Biamrallah,—but the word "Hierophant" was used inadvertently. I changed the title to "The Return of the Druses," and the name to "Djabal." It is very good of you to care about the circumstance.

May I say how much I was delighted yesterday at the Grosvenor by the two jewel-like pictures[2] which I had somehow failed to observe before?

Ever truly yours,
Robert Browning.

1879 : 6

To Norman Mac Coll

19. Warwick Crescent, W
June 21. '79.

Dear Mr Mac Coll,

You are quite right, and take the course I should always prefer: I only mentioned a fact *in case* you happened to require it. What I see to-day is sufficient,—and words beyond *that* are wasted on their rascally subject.[1]

Ever truly yours
ROBERT BROWNING.

1879 : 7

To John H. Ingram

19, Warwick Crescent,
London, W.
December 29th, 1879.

Dear Mr. Ingram,

Thank you exceedingly for your little book[1]—which amused me greatly. I think Shenstone was the first to "wish to see Mrs. Somebody's handwriting that he might judge of her character."

Your guesses are only too good. I mean, you ought to pronounce upon the character with no previous knowledge of the character, which so shrewd an observer as yourself is sure to touch happily off.

Believe me, dear Mr. Ingram,
Yours very sincerely,
ROBERT BROWNING.

1880 : 1

To John H. Ingram

19, Warwick Crescent,
London, W.
March 21st, 1880.

My dear Sir,

I am much indebted to the kindness and considerateness of your letter; I hope you will see nothing to the prejudice of those qualities in myself when I assure you that, for reasons of insuperable force to me, I am compelled to refuse any assistance whatever to the writer of the biography which your publisher projects[1]—a thing impossible under existing circumstances, to be done properly, and in many respects improper to be done were it possible.

Had Miss Zimmern decided to attempt it, I would have so far strained a point in favour of a person for whom I have the very highest esteem as to correct any material error in her manuscript. Beyond this, even in her case, I could not go. I must decline this in the case of a stranger, poor assistance as it would probably amount to. I hope you will understand why I think it right to state what I am forced to do as explicitly as I can, and that you will believe with what regret I appear to deny a request you please to make.

Believe me, My dear Sir,

Yours very truly,

ROBERT BROWNING.

1880 : 2

TO THE REV. J. D. WILLIAMS

19. Warwick Crescent, W.

Apr. 21. '80.

Dear Mr. Williams,

I was delighted to get your newspaper with its details of your "high solemnity" (so I unaffectedly hold it to be) and I congratulate you as if I were an old friend—as perhaps, if we count earnestness as the equivalent of length of time employed in any experience, I may venture to say that I am. Your letter of the 31st ult. interested me greatly: and I really profit by your notice of the want of rhyme in "Pheidippides" which somehow never struck me. I change the last line's "too" into "rare,"—and the matter is mended as well as the case admits,—now that the poem has stiffened in the mould.[1] I am even more interested in your remarks on *The Inn Album,* which has been generally misunderstood in certain respects. It is curious that the German translator (a very competent one, but a stranger to me altogether) was told that such and such misunderstandings existed,—and replied "Having done what the Author's critics probably did *not*—read the passages carefully, none of these mistakes will be found in my translation." As to *"Athens"*—you very likely are right in your preference for the English form. In "Pheidippides," I conformed to the vulgar

"Miltīades,"—but in a new Greek little poem,[2] I revolted and write "Míltiadés": this serves as an excuse for saying (in my extemporized character of "old friend") that you must not procure any more books of mine except straight from the author—who, in a few weeks' time, will hope to send you a "novum libellum" ("lepidum" or otherwise) whereof the M.S. went to press yesterday.[3] "Corneli, tibi!"

My sister says you cared to ask if a photograph were to be got. One was taken the other day, and seems as good as any. I send it therefore. We both of us wish heartily to see you again, and you must gratify us whenever you can. I am sorry to hear of the ill health of Dr. Thompson:[4] whose amenities are very pleasant in my remembrance.

Pray believe me ever,
Dear Mr. Williams,
Yours cordially
ROBERT BROWNING.

1880 : 3

TO THE REV. HUGH REGINALD HAWEIS

19, Warwick Crescent, W.
May 11. '80.

Dear Mr. Haweis,

I have just got your book, and at once thank you very heartily for your kind sympathy and indulgence—conspicuous in the article concerning myself—which is all I have as yet read. I wish your printers would be more careful,—"fair, like my peers"—and "with his human hair"—for "fare like my peers" and "human air" do me wrong, you will confess.

On one point you are misinformed,—you will be glad to know instead of the poetry of E. B. B. being "almost forgotten," it is more remembered—or, at least, called for in order to be remembered—than it ever was. A note from the Publisher, four days ago, apprises me that the almost yearly new edition of the five volumes is out—and the corresponding edition of "Aurora Leigh"—while a second series of Selections from the Poetry is just printed. The demand for my own works is nothing like so large.

Pray believe me, Dear Mr Haweis,
Yours with all respect and much obligation,
ROBERT BROWNING.

1880 : 4

To John H. Ingram

19 Warwick Crescent,
London, W.
June 17th, 1880.

Dear Mr. Ingram,

I felt much obliged to you when, a few days ago, your kind present reached me.[1] On finishing the perusal of it, however, I find myself still more indebted to you for having cleared away so much misapprehension of the facts concerning Poe as I could not but lie under till such a truly pious work of rehabilitation should appear as the one I thankfully acknowledge.

Yours very truly,
ROBERT BROWNING.

1880 : 5

To John H. Ingram

Venice,
October 15th, 1880.

Dear Mr. Ingram,

It is quite true that I am, through a testamentary disposition of Mr. Kelsall's, the possessor of all the manuscripts—indeed, all the letters and documents now existing or attainable which relate to Beddoes: and I received them with an injunction to turn them to what account I best could in behalf of his memory, and increase of his readers.

For sufficient reasons, an adequate account of his life is hardly possible as yet; but I hope ere very long to say something about that, and his works also. These have been somewhat manipulated by cautious friends, and there are many omissions to restore.

It is needless to assure you that I have the matter really at heart, and do not appear to neglect it without good cause.[1]

I shall bequeath the MSS. to Balliol.

Believe, me, dear Mr. Ingram,
Yours sincerely,
ROBERT BROWNING.

1881 : 1

To Edmund Gosse

19, Warwick Crescent, W.
January 15th, 1881.

My Dear Gosse,

I fear I shall somewhat disappoint you—I know I am myself disappointed at finding I cannot comply with any request of yours—but here is the case. Robert[1] looked at the portrait from the heights of his six or seven months' experience since he painted it, and felt sure he could make certain improvements here and there; but he began these with a bad cold and cough beginning also, and the business of blotting out was done effectually before anything like substitution could follow, and the result is that the picture is quite useless for your purpose for some time to come—since, after keeping at home for a week under the doctor's hands, he started on Thursday evening, mummy-fashion as to wrappages, in the persuasion that he would only get well when away from London. He was very sorry on all accounts to leave his work in this state, but really was blameless in the matter. If on his return in April you still care to have a photograph for the purpose you mentioned, there shall be no delay in procuring one.

I have had no opportunity of wishing, or rather expressing, a very sincere wish appropriate to the season for Mrs. Gosse and yourself. It is hardly too late now, I hope.

Yours very truly,
ROBERT BROWNING.

1881 : 2

To J. O. Halliwell-Phillips

19, Warwick Crescent, W.
Jan. 27, '81.

Dear Sir,

I am sorry indeed to receive your letter of yesterday's date, and doubly sorry that there should have been occasion[1] for your writing it. I never saw the Preface in question, and altogether fail to understand the meaning or relevancy of the language you quote from it. My position with respect to the Society is purely honorary, as I stipulated before accepting it, nor have I been able hitherto to attend any one of its meetings; and should I ever do so, my first impulse will be to invoke the spirit of "gentle Shakespeare" that no wrong be done in his name to a member of the brotherhood of students combining to do him suit and service. Pray believe me,

Dear Sir,

Yours very respectfully,

ROBERT BROWNING.

1881 : 3

TO ALGERNON CHARLES SWINBURNE

19, Warwick Crescent, W.
Feb. 5. '81.

My dear Swinburne—for so I venture to waive formality in addressing your genius, though you cling to it in remembering my Age, I fear! —you are the kindest and most generous of poets. I shall treasure up your book,[1] but cannot pretend that I owe to this copy of it my delight in what it contains, seeing that I have, many days ago, read it at the "Athenæum." As for the great appreciation (I can't say, "tribute")— well, the recognition, if you like, of our dear Landor,—it went at once to my heart's intimate depths: but there are poems over and above which even you have never surpassed, I think, in power and beauty— but I won't be noisy where silence is wisest if not—certainly not easiest.

Indeed, I am no enemy of that Aristophanes—all on fire with invention,—and such music! I am confident that Euripides bore his fun and parodying good humoredly enough—as even Cleon did: but a friend of Euripides,—above all, a woman friend,—feels no such need of magnanimity: when I had done with her, I had *all but* done with anything like enmity to him—the reservation being simply due to the circumstance that Euripides was not triumphantly happy like Sophocles.

Well,—shall I never see you again? if ever accident brings you in this neighbourhood—and you apprise me of the good fortune—I shall renew the gratification which,—experienced now many years ago,— lives with me vividly as ever. Meanwhile, and ever—*I pede fausto,* and believe in the true regard

of yours affectionately

ROBERT BROWNING.

1881 : 4

To Edmund Gosse

19, Warwick Crescent, W.
March 21st, 1881.

My Dear Gosse,

It must be a slip of Horne's memory—no such performance ever took place.[1] I fancy he was thinking about a Play, with a "Duchess" in the title, written by Henry Chorley for Miss Cushman, and which she brought out—very likely at the Haymarket—while I was in Italy. I cannot in the least remember how I came to make those stage-directions—possibly for some projected performance by Helen Faucit,[2] to whom I read the play once. Other matters at that time put such as these quite out of my head.

Yours truly ever,
R. Browning.

I have just heard from America that the author of the parodies on Swinburne and myself is "a young girl named Jones."

1881 : 5

To Dr. F. J. Furnivall

Hôtel Virard,
St. Pierre De Chartreuse,
Isère, France.
August 29th, 1881.

My dear Furnivall,

I received your letter, and at the same time the proof-sheets of your *Bibliography*, in a parcel from home yesterday. What am I to say? This hamlet is close by, and a dependence on, the famous convent founded by St. Bruno as a necessary effect of his hearing a dead man declare "Justo judicio Dei condemnatus sum." Ought I not to set up a pillar, at least, on finding myself—quite as startlingly—called noteworthy; and brought into prominence after this fashion by the—never mind how partial—judgment of an extraordinarily generous friend?

I can only repeat—you startle me. Other feelings that are inevitable must continue unexpressed, though they are not easily kept down.

Were I in town, I could perhaps supplement your list of notices of the criticisms on my works by an instance or two you might like to preserve. I only remember the good natured ones however. The pencil notes of John Mill which he meant to construct an article upon—till he found he had been forestalled by a flippant line in the Review[1] which he was accustomed at that time to write for—are at the end of the copy of *Pauline* in Forster's Library at Kensington.[2] He had never seen me. *Paracelsus* was *first* reviewed by Forster, in the *Examiner*. He also wrote a paper on it in the *New Monthly Magazine*—in the same month that another by J. Heraud appeared in *Fraser*. The most curious notice I ever had was from Cardinal Wiseman on *Blougram*—i.e. himself. It was in the *Rambler,* a Catholic Journal of those days, and certified to be his by Father Prout, who said nobody else would have dared put it in. My friend Milsand reviewed me in the *Revue des deux Mondes,* and in another French review. But I have a huge shelf-full of reviews of my Father's collecting, which probably contain articles more or less to the point. Many I never read even at the time, and not one since. I only mention the few that rise in my mind as I read your list to show that when you please to say "you shall be grateful" for such an exercise of memory, I am not so ungrateful as to keep silence altogether. Well, you have not had much experience of any "steel"-like quality that may be in me, but let me say once for all, that whenever you have occasion to test it, you are entitled to look for "the ice brook's temper."

Ever yours truly,

ROBERT BROWNING.

Come, I ought to say something "sine ullâ solemnitate." Well bestowed as you are in Wales, you would be struck at the extraordinary picturesqueness and beauty of this wild little clump of cottages on a mountain amid loftier mountains. The "Hotel" is the roughest inn, and its arrangements the most primitive, I have yet chanced upon—but my sister bears them bravely. We stay two or three weeks longer, weather permitting, then go to Venice. Early in November you must come and see us, and we will compare our gains in travel. My sister desires me to give my best regards to you and to Mrs. Furnivall, my own accompanying them.

Thank you for the pleasant note which I return: "here are in all three worthy voices gained."

1881 : 6

To Dr. F. J. Furnivall

Hotel Virard, St. Pierre
de Chartreuse, Isere, F.
Sept. 15. '81.

My dear Furnivall,

Many thanks for your kind and pleasant letter: I am sure I ought to be "helpful" to you in such little matters when it is in my power. First, to its questions the replies are—*Karshish* is the proper word, referring as it does to him of the "Epistle"—*Karshook* (*Heb:* a Thistle) just belongs to the snarling verses I remember to have written but forget for whom: The other was the only one of the "Fifty." I wrote the Venice stanza to illustrate Maclise's picture,—for which he was anxious to get some such line or two: I had not seen it, but, from Forster's description, gave it to him, in his room, *impromptu.*[1] Maclise (a friend of my own) painted the whole thing—not the sky merely: when I did see it, I thought the Serenader too jolly somewhat for the notion I got from Forster—and I took up the subject in my own way. Metre: "Hervé Riel" goes mainly in anapaests and tribrachs—I fancy —On the sea/ and at the / Hogue / Fifteen Hund/red ninety / two / Did the Eng/lish fight the / French / Woe to France /. But the "Toccata" is purely Trochaic: O Gal/uppi / Baldass/ari,/ this is / very / sad to / find!/. What you tell me about the copy of "Pauline,"[2] interests me much: if "the entry was struck out of the catalogue," I suppose that means—the request I made to the Executor, Mr Chitty, that the book might be returned to me,—which he promised to attend to, but of which I heard no more,—was really complied with *so far*— I shall try if I can recover the copy: the odd thing is—that it was prefaced by some such notice as that given in the "Bibliography" page 16. I may have possibly repeated it for some friend. The "poems on a leaf in the Museum" are merely autographic copies of printed pieces. Looking hastily through the new "Proofs"[3]—I only see, to observe upon—Page 18. There might be a reference to Lady Martin's account of the circumstances under which the "Blot in the Scutcheon" was produced by Macready—the last of her papers in Blackwood on Shakspearian Characters, during the current year. 19. 23 years ago: I wrote in this and other instances with no copy at hand. 21. Alfred Domett, besides being the Author of the work mentioned, was Prime Minister in New Zealand. 28. "Shelley Letters." When I get home and have a copy before me, I will give you in a few words the true account of the whole transaction—and *perhaps* some remarks on the Essay by a very distinguished personage indeed:[4] (*Don't speak of this,* however.) Also, if on consideration I properly am able, I will give a list of the true names of men, things, and places in "Red Cotton Night-Cap Country."[5]—It is only just that I should do the little I can to show I am sensible of the favours done me—sensible I *am*.

And now, my dear Furnivall, you may hear of me again from Venice: this rough delightful country we leave on the 18th—the day when, by my calculation, this letter reaches you. Remember the address: "Albergo dell' Universo, Venezia": for about a month. I hope you have had weather like ours: to-day ends our five weeks' stay—during which only one rainy day confined us to the house. All congratulations to Mrs Furnivall on her climbing feat. What am I to say to Miss Lewis? I hope to do more toward justifying all this sympathy before I leave off.

My sister's cordial greetings to you and Mrs Furnivall.

Ever truly yours

ROBERT BROWNING.

1881 : 7

To Dr. F. J. FURNIVALL

Albergo Dell' Universo,
Venezia, Italia.
October 1st, 1881.

My dear Furnivall,

Just as I was leaving St. Pierre, in a wild mountain pass, the postman recognized me, and gave me your letter—and here I found another—"proofs" down to page 58—for all of which my best thanks.

Yes, the autograph was a mere quotation. The "W. M. the younger" was poor William Macready's eldest boy—dead, a few years ago. He had a talent for drawing, and asked me to give him some little thing to illustrate; so, I made a bit of a poem out of an old account of the death of the Pope's legate at the Council of Trent—which he made such clever drawings for, that I tried at a more picturesque subject, the Piper. I still possess the half dozen of the designs he gave me. If you cared to have the Legend of the Legate I am sure you are welcome to it, when I can transcribe it from the page of the old book it remains upon, unprinted hitherto—which I mention to show how equally welcome you are to reprint the other "unconsidered trifles" you speak of. I am bound to let any similar insignificances be of what use they may in giving a touch of, at least novelty, to a labour of love like yours.

A King lived long ago was given to the *M. Repository*.[1] You will find a strophe of a chorus out of Euripides in the book he gives name to, published lately by Mahaffy;[2] I translated it at his desire. Nothing else occurs to me at this moment. We are still in the disturbance of arrival here, and I must be brief: I shall not let your suggestions drop to the ground, depend upon it!

My sister repeats her kind regards, and all wishes that your Welsh excursion may have done good service to Mrs. Furnivall and yourself. We count on remaining here for a week or two. I did not know you had the glory of a "boy": I congratulate you, and am

Ever truly yours,
ROBERT BROWNING.

1881 : 8

To Dr. F. J. Furnivall

Albergo Dell' Universo,
Venezia.
October 3rd, 1881.

Ah, *no*—my dear Furnivall! Your proposal, kind and ingenious as it is, would give the notion of sending out a "sample," as is the wont of dealers in stuffs and Printed cottons. Your agency already does all that fair human endeavour can do: better be content with *that*.

I wrote two days ago. The notion of such a selection as you describe is well worth considering, and consideration it shall have when Smith and I can talk it over on my return.

Ever truly yours,
ROBERT BROWNING.

1881 : 9

To Dr. F. J. Furnivall

Albergo Dell' Universo,
Venezia.
October 11th, 1881.

My Dear Furnivall,

Your last letter, of the 6th, seemed in the main to have been answered by anticipation the day before—so I waited till we could regain the proper pace, my foot after yours.

You will let the "sample" alone, I know,—never mind how foolish I may be in my apprehensions, and I can go at once to the few *corrigenda* in the "proofs" which arrived this morning. Maclise's picture[1] undoubtedly *was* in the Academy Exhibition, together with my verse in the Catalogue, and you have missed it for the funny reason that it was printed as *prose!* I remember beseeching the secretary, Mr. Knight, at the Academy dinner, to get the lines into good order again, but to no purpose: or—*wait!* I am confounding—it strikes me all at once—the verse I wrote for Leighton's work,[2] when this accident befell, with the verse in question for Maclise's picture, which was exhibited in some more or less private adventure in the way of a Gallery—*what* Gallery might be found by referring to the periodical which Mr. S. C. Hall edited in those days, for there was a notice both of picture and verse therein. The mist cleared off from my memory on the circumstance starting up vividly in it that Mr. Knight excused his oversight by observing that Leighton was so very poetical a painter that there was no knowing whether the same quality might not have got the better of his prose!

Next. How have I overlooked hitherto that my school was at Peckham—not Dulwich—that of the Rev. Thomas Ready.

Last, about my being "strongly against Darwin, rejecting the truths of science and regretting its advance"—you only do as I should hope and expect in disbelieving *that*. It came, I suppose, of Hohenstiel-Schwangau's expressing the notion which was the popular one at the appearance of Darwin's book—and you might as well charge Shakespeare with holding that there were men whose heads grew beneath their shoulders, because Othello told Desdemona that he had seen such. In reality, all that seems *proved* in Darwin's scheme was a conception familiar to me from the beginning: see in *Paracelsus* the progressive development from senseless matter to organized, until man's appearance (*Part* v.). Also in *Cleon,* see the order of "life's mechanics,"—and I daresay in many passages of my poetry: for how can one look at Nature as a whole and doubt that, wherever there is a gap, a "link" must be "missing"—through the limited power and opportunity of the looker? But go back and back, as you please, *at* the back, as Mr. Sludge is made to insist, you find (*my* faith is as constant) creative intelligence, acting as matter but not resulting from it. Once set the balls rolling, and ball may hit ball and send any number in any direction over the table; but I believe in the cue pushed by a hand.

When one is taunted (as I notice is often fancied an easy method with the un-Darwinized)—taunted with thinking successive acts of creation credible, metaphysics have been stopped short at, however physics may fare: time and space being purely conceptions of our own, wholly inapplicable to intelligence of another kind—with whom, as I made Luria say, there is an "everlasting moment of creation," if one at all, —past, present, and future, one and the same state. This consideration does not affect Darwinism proper in any degree. But I do not consider that his case as to the changes in organization, brought about by desire and will in the creature, is proved. Tortoises never saw their own shells, top or bottom, nor those of their females, and are diversely variegated all over, each species after its own pattern. And the insects; this one is coloured to escape notice, this other to attract it, a third to frighten the foe—all out of one brood of caterpillars hatched in one day. No—I am incredulous—and *you,* dear patron and friend, are abundantly tired; so, thus much shall serve, scribbled as it has come to pass.

Our weather is mending somewhat, but continues a month behind hand, and very little characteristic of Venice. I walk, even in wind and rain, for a couple of hours on Lido, and enjoy the break of sea on the strip of sand as much as Shelley did in those old days. Good bye; all good wishes to you and yours, from

Yours truly ever,
Robert Browning.

1881 : 10

To Dr. F. J. Furnivall

Albergo Dell' Universo,
Venezia.
October 21st, 1881.

My dear Furnivall,

You very well know I can say nothing about this extraordinary halo of rainbow-hues with which your wonder-working hand has suddenly surrounded my dark orb. As with the performances of the mosaicists I see at work here—all sorts of shining stones, greater and smaller, which hardly took the eye by their single selves—suddenly coalesce and make a brilliant show when put ingeniously together—as my dazzled eyes acknowledge, pray believe! I will correct any mistake as to fact I may observe on going hastily through the proofs. Two thirds of the reviews and other notices I never saw till now, while many that stay in my memory are absent here, by the way.

Page 109: I am astounded at the notion, as to how it could possibly arise, that there was ever the slightest "falling out" between Carlyle and myself. Nothing of the kind ever happened during our long acquaintance.

Page 110: *Mrs.* Ritchie: her husband was not present. This minute incident took place not at *Freshwater,* where (for all Tennyson's repeated invitations of the kindest sort) I never yet have been, but at Twickenham, on the day of the christening of Hallam, whom his father trusted me with, straight out of the baby's bed.

I do not stop for misprints. Page 92: "Shirley"[1] is not Charles Lever, but a living writer [, whose] name escapes me at the moment: he sent me his book with a letter some time ago. Page 109: Miss Blagden: she was devoted to, but never in any way "nursed the poetess in her final illness." Page 106: All about the vernacular of the epitaph on *Pietro di Albano* is pure fun of Father Prout's. I told him of the thing at Florence, and did it *impromptu* into this doggerel:—

> *Studying my cyphers with the compass,*
> *I gather I soon shall be below ground,*
> *Because of my lore men make great rumpus,*
> *And war on myself makes each dull rogue round.*

He must have thought it worth remembering. In the text—*con* should be *col,*—sotterra, not *sotto terra,* sap*er,* for *ir,* gran, *without d,* m' hanno, for *nei h.*

And now, the stay here is hardly likely to last much longer. The weather is again abominable and *un-Venetian.* I suppose we may count on being back in London by the end of the first week in November—when we will talk by the fireside, I hope. Meanwhile and always, with truest regards to Mrs Furnivall and yourself from us two stay-aways, believe me, ever gratefully yours,

ROBERT BROWNING.

The pin-pointed iron pen, the table whereon my chin rests, and the seat from the depths of which I strain upwards must account for and excuse the scrawly scribble. The paper seems damp too.

1881 : 11

To Miss E. Dickinson West

19, Warwick Crescent,
W.
November 12th, 1881.

Dear Miss West,

I was in Venice when your letter reached me, after some delay. I thought I would wait till I got home quietly, and this is the first day I write to anybody—except to my son.

I have been in no danger of forgetting you; never shall be in that of mistaking you. I will tell you how I feel about the Society. It was instituted without my knowledge, and when knowledge was, I do not think acquiescence had need of being asked for. I write poems that they may be read, and—fifty years now—people said they were unintelligible. If other people, in the fulness of days, reply "we understand them, and will show that you may, if you will be at the pains," I should think it ungracious indeed to open my mouth for the first time on the matter with "Pray let the other people alone in their protested ignorance." I see a paragraph in *The World* to the effect that none of my personal friends figure in the list of members. Had I persuaded them to do so, the objection would have been more cogent, "only a clique—the man's personal following!"

Exactly what has touched me is the sudden assemblage of men and women to whose names, for the most part, I am a stranger, who choose to incur the ridicule sure to come readily to the critics who dispose of my works by the easy word "unintelligible," instead of saying safely to themselves "*I* understand it—or something of it—anyhow!" That there would be exaggeration in the approval was to be looked for, they reäct against a good deal.

As for Dr. Furnivall, I am altogether astonished at his caring about me at all. I suspect it is a late discovery with him, like that of Fontenelle when, chancing upon some out-of-the-way literature, he went about asking everybody "Do you know Habbakuk? He's a genius!" I think him most warm-hearted, whatever may be the mistakes about me of which his head is guilty; and as Lear's last instance of ingratitude is that of the mouth biting the hand for lifting food to it—so, it seems to me, would as signal an one be, the writer of books that are commonly pronounced unintelligible, objecting to the folk who propose to try that question.

There! It is unusual and uneasy, this talk about oneself: but it goes to you, and you will help it where it wants your friendly construction.

And now for your paper, the at least possible paper you may write. You know what I think of your writing, how deeply I shall be interested in this. Do honor me—and, let me say, benefit me—by writing on my poetry with the freedom and honesty which I hope I deserve! In whatever aspect, generally or in particular—*that* shall be at your pleasure. But I shall greatly appreciate your care to criticise me with whatever result. Your Sonnet is dear to me, you must know.

Farewell, dear Miss West. If you ever come to London, I might be privileged to see you face to face—who can tell? But my actual knowledge is a real possession, and I am,

Affectionately yours,
ROBERT BROWNING.

1881 : 12

TO ALBERT H. ORME[1]

19, Warwick Crescent,
London, W.
November 12th, 1881.

Dear Sir,

Forgive a little delay in replying, as well as I can, to your pleasant note of last week. I have only just returned to London.

I take it, Patience "holds a dulcimer in his hand," the left one—propping the instrument (as a lyre might be managed) against his side. There are many strings to it, and one hand suffices to evoke "harmonies" enough by help of the fingers and thumb. Paganini used the guitar for this purpose,—so he said; but that anybody, with the skill, may do as much is evident.

With all regards to your friend and yourself,

Believe me, Dear Sir,
Yours truly,
ROBERT BROWNING.

1881 : 13

TO NORMAN MAC COLL

19, Warwick Crescent,
W.
Nov. 24. '81.

Dear Mr Mac Coll,

There is a little matter on my mind, which—little as it truly is—I should like to remove. I told you some time ago that whenever I had any poems ready for printing I would inform the "Athenæum" of the fact—whether important enough to be noticed or not—for old acquaintance' sake. Now, there appeared in the "Academy" of last week a paragraph about "new Idyls" to come out soon—which you *might* think originated with me—(though you do *not* think, I hope, that any of the personal references to me, which I see there from time to time, do so originate directly or indirectly.)

This is mere conjecture or hearsay: I have written a poem or two, certainly, which may or may not go into a new volume of Idyls,—but whenever a volume of any sort there *is*—ready for press—I shall send exclusively to the "Athenæum" the particulars, such as they are,— quite irrespective of any sort of engagement on the part of the Journal to publish them. This is a word between you and myself,—pray,—and only written to avoid any possible misconception. I don't know whether there is any interest in knowing that two of my Son's pictures which the "Athenæum" spoke kindly about,—"The Secular Arm," exhibited at the Hanover Gallery, and the "Dinant Marketwoman," have just been purchased—the former for the Philadelphia Academy of Fine Arts,—the latter for the American purchaser's own satisfaction. Gossip about this—which happened last week—*might* get into print elsewhere, so I set it down,—begging you to

believe me ever yours truly
ROBERT BROWNING.

1881 : 14

TO ALBERT H. ORME

19, Warwick Crescent,
London, W.
November 24th, 1881.

Dear Sir,

I have no doubt the dulcimer was such an instrument as your authorities describe. My own most vivid notion of it must be caught from Coleridge and his "Abyssinian maid." So—*peccavimus!*

Yours very truly,
ROBERT BROWNING.

1881 : 15

To Dr. F. J. Furnivall

> 19, Warwick Crescent,
> London, W.
> December 8th, 1881.

Dear Furnivall,

I assure you I shirked no labour, but took down and piled up scores of dead and gone reviews as stale as the dust on them. "Read" them I could not pretend to attempt, so did the sight of their very outsides sadden me—the word is not too strong. So much misconception at best, ignorance at middling, and malice at worst, in those old slaps on my face in order apparently to keep some fellow's critical hands warm!

Yourself, and those like you, are the best suffumigators after this old smell; why keep a whiff of it to show how nastily I lived for a long while, sustained, abundantly, however, by many a kindlier breathing from various quarters—only, the "sweet south" "creeps" or "steals" silently, while the unpleasantness is, as Donne phrases it, "a loud perfume." No, let us bid good-bye to it all; not to real conscientious criticism by any means, but to mere mopping and mowing and such monkey-tricks. So, I only send you three characteristic samples, French, Italian, and American. Whether the writers praise or blame (which, on my honour, I absolutely forget), they at least have not taken up a book to get done with it on the easiest terms, laughing at what is worth no more serious notice. What a world of width between such people and Mr. Kirkman,[1] whose paper I return! The only *pain* I ever felt is the profitable one caused by such eulogy; I know *painfully* my own shortcomings and inadequate deserts. All I engage is, that in what of life may be left me, I will try harder than ever to deserve what my best efforts have hitherto failed to do. Enough!

As to the one volume edition of E. B. B.'s works, and Story's preface to the same, I never knew of the existence of either. Do not bring me in as if *parenthetically,* illustrative of her and her poems. These, I rejoice with all my heart to know and say, are in no need of any assistance; their popularity keeps ever far in advance of mine, as any bookseller will inform you; and, as Beethoven said of his music, "nothing but good can come to them."

Will you understand, and benignantly comply with, all this? Yes; and assure yourself I shall be more than ever

Gratefully as affectionately yours,
ROBERT BROWNING.

1881 : 16

To GEORGE BARNETT SMITH

19, Warwick Crescent, W.
Dec. 12. '81

Dear Mr Barnett-Smith,

Certainly you shall have any proofs of any poem as soon as *I* receive any—but that will be at a very distant time if at all: for the paragraph you mention was unauthorized and premature altogether: I may print such few things as I have, along with others yet unwritten, in a new volume,—and probably shall do so—but there is nothing designed, much less accomplished:[1] in all cases, you may depend upon my remembering your many instances of kindness.[2]

With respect to the other request—I will try and comply with it, when I can consider a little: you deserve that I should gratify you if I am able.

I rejoice to hear of your well-being: your literary achievements have greatly advantaged you, I make no doubt,—a success you deserve. My sister joins with me in kind regards to Mrs Barnett Smith, and I am ever yours sincerely

ROBERT BROWNING

1881 : 17

To DR. F. J. FURNIVALL

19, Warwick Crescent,
W.
Dec. 16. '81.

My dear Furnivall,

I return the Proofs: where do you find that the holiday of Hervé Riel was for "more than a day—his whole life-time?" If it is to be found I have strangely overlooked it. Yes, Landor was the Friend,[1] and his praise was prompt, both private and public—(in his Satire on Satirists.) "Eyebright"—i. e. "Euphrasia," an early sympathizer[2] still (happily) alive. I do not remember the "Eclectic."[3] Of course I shall be delighted to see Miss Lewis[4] on any day she may please to appoint. Once again, all thanks from

Yours truly ever

ROBERT BROWNING

1881 : 18

To Dr. F. J. FURNIVALL

19, Warwick Crescent,
London, W.
December 20th, 1881.

My dear Furnivall,

You are undoubtedly right, and I have mistaken the meaning of the phrase—I suppose through thinking that, if the "coasting-pilot's" business ended with reaching land, he might claim as a right to be let go: otherwise, an absolute discharge seems to approach in importance a substantial reward. Still, truth above all things—so treat the matter[1] as you please—believing me ever,

Yours,

R. BROWNING.

1882 : 1

To Dr. F. J. FURNIVALL

19, Warwick Crescent,
London, W.
January 12th, 1882.

My dear Furnivall,

I am beginning to enjoy the results of the institution of the "Society" (quite over and above the sympathy and kindness of its promoter and adherents) in the evident annoyance it is giving my dear old critics who have gone on gibing and gibbering at me time out of mind. If these worthies could point to a single performance in which they had themselves "read and studied" anything of mine, far less induced others to do so, there might be a reason for their wrath; but there has never been one such article in the *Saturday Review* since its existence. As for the *Pall Mall Gazette,* the late Proprietor's rule excluded any article upon any work published by Smith and Elder—on what principle I fail to see, inasmuch as he might fairly say: "since I publish nothing I do not believe to be of worth in its way, why should not the Editor of my Journal have the same opinion and express it?" But at any rate the mouth so reticent before needs not grow loquacious all at once on the other side of the question. I suppose these critics have their pets, and think loyalty to these demands irritation at any fancied intruder on the hero's little plot of ground, his τέμενος as the Greeks call it. All which amounts to—Pray don't imagine I can't understand the mock compliments to myself pretended to be involved in the censure of those who make so thoroughly-appreciated a person "ridiculous": the *ridiculus mus* is the inveterate nibbler at, and spoiler of, the fruits of a man's whole life's labour, which might otherwise go to the bakehouse and prove tolerable ship-biscuit. As for you, I shall not waste a word in bidding you mind this gabble as much and as little as does

Yours ever,

Robert Browning.

1882 : 2

To Dr. F. J. Furnivall

19, Warwick Crescent,
London, W.
January 23rd, 1882.

My dear Furnivall,

I return Mr. Radford's letter with many thanks. I never heard nor dreamed there had been any such notion at any time of a Moorish Front for the Duomo—it was altogether a fancy of my own illustrative of the feelings natural to Luria and Braccio each after his kind. As for *Aristophanes*—the allusions require a knowledge of the Scholia, besides acquaintance with the "Comicorum Graecorum Fragmenta," Athenaeus, Alciphron, and so forth, not forgotten. But I wrote in France, at an out of the way place, with none of these books.

How good you are, and how unable am I to do more than gratefully recognize it! I am reading Miss Lewis's novel—have got through only the first volume, and like it much: my sister promises me that I shall like the second volume still more.

Ever yours,

Robert Browning.

1882 : 3

To Dr. F. J. Furnivall

19, Warwick Crescent,
London, W.
February 17th, 1882.

My dear Furnivall,

Pardon a delay in replying to your first note, which this second shall not have to apologize for.

If "B" has no sense of humour he ought to shut up poetical shop, or better, never have opened it. The mistake grew out of a word on the want of sympathy and understanding he confessed to respecting "practical jokes," wherein he failed to see "humour" at all. He rather fancied his love of humour led him into scrapes of indecorousness occasionally, when occupied on serious matters—who knows?

The little pamphlet[1] was printed by Arabel Barrett, for a Bazaar to benefit the "Refuge for young destitute girls" which she set going all those years ago—the first of its kind, I believe, and still in existence.

Ever truly yours,
ROBERT BROWNING.

1882 : 4

To Dr. F. J. Furnivall

19, Warwick Crescent,
London, W.
March 11th, 1882.

My dear Furnivall,

The story of "Old Tod," as told in Bunyan's "Life and Death of Mr. Badman," was distinctly in my mind when I wrote Ned Bratts—at the Splugen, without reference to what I had read when quite a boy. I wrote Ivan Ivanowitch at the same place and altitude.

The "Saint" by "Haste-thee-Luke";[1] i.e. "Luca-fu-presto," as Luca Giordano was styled, somewhat disparagingly, from his expeditious way of working.

No "bother"—so, no forgiveness from

Yours ever,
ROBERT BROWNING.

1882 : 5

To John H. Ingram

> 19, Warwick Crescent,
> London, W.
> May 5th, 1882.

My Dear Sir,

I must have failed to make myself understood on the matter in question.[1] I have neither the right nor the wish to withhold my consent to the appearance of the volume. What I am compelled to refuse is, any co-operation with its author, however illustrious or friendly, in so far as that implies giving information or allowing letters to be inspected, in any case where I have any control.

I seemed bound to permit the publication of Mr. Horne's book,[2] inasmuch as the correspondence was literary only, between persons who had never seen each other, and before I could pretend to any sort of guardianship. In every other instance I have kept a resolution to which I came on sufficient grounds, I beg of your kindness to believe,

Ever truly yours,

ROBERT BROWNING.

1882 : 6

To John H. Ingram

> 19, Warwick Crescent,
> London, W.
> May 18th, 1882.

Dear Mr. Ingram,

I am truly sorry if my inability to render you the particular assistance[1] you might not unnaturally expect should have caused you any inconvenience; a word to me, in the first instance, would have prevented this. You may not be aware that five brothers of my wife are still alive, and still to be considered in the matter which mainly concerns their family—though I confess that the feelings of my wife, perfectly known to me, render any attention to those of others superfluous.

Yours very truly,

ROBERT BROWNING.

1882 : 7

To John H. Ingram

> 19, Warwick Crescent,
> London, W.
> May 22nd, 1882.

Do believe me, dear Mr. Ingram, ever disposed to be never so little helpful to you when it is fortunately in my power: how should it be otherwise?

There can hardly have been any other "misunderstanding" than that, when I promised to *correct* any errors which the writer might, or rather would certainly fall into should the performance attempt to be biographical and not critical merely, my promise was supposed to involve the supplying any original information or allowing the inspection of letters over which I have any power. This engagement to a valued friend¹ was little enough, but all I was justified in making; indeed, my business would only have been to run the pen through the "facts" of such notices, which are such as the following in a paper of *Tinsley's Magazine* for the current month: "That Mr. Barrett was an East India merchant," instead of "a West India proprietor." "That the boat catastrophe happened in the sight of my wife," instead of miles away; that "I had admittance to her through the blunder of a servant," instead of my visit being the natural consequence of much intimacy long before, brought as naturally about by her cousin, my father's school-fellow, and my own friend, John Kenyon.

> Yours very truly,
> Robert Browning.

1882 : 8

To Dr. F. J. Furnivall

> 19, Warwick Crescent,
> London, W.
> October 7th, 1882.

My dear Furnivall,

I have got, I believe, all the letters with which you obliged me at Venice; the last arrived yesterday.

Why do you always manage to give me so much pleasure, as by the account of Miss Beale's paper; and why cannot I reciprocate by at least doing some poor little thing that you think is in my power? Indeed the Preface,[1] for which you are so kindly urgent, is quite out of it. Tell Mr. Bell so, pray, with many thanks for thinking better of my abilities than they deserve—or, at all events, of my "sweet reasonableness" when wise counsels would benefit me.

How glad I am that you so evidently enjoy yourself! This fine summer of Saint Martin does indeed cast the other half of his charitable cloak around us: I am too warm in the sun at this moment.

Come and see us when you can, and whenever you can. We are disappointed doubtlessly at this stop to our progress,—and certain people, whom we much wanted to see, are flatteringly sorry they do not see us; but we did well to return, I believe. Don't return before you can help; and get your collating work done. I like the samples of it I have seen—in the *Academy*—very much indeed.

Ever yours affectionately,

ROBERT BROWNING.

1882 : 9

To Edmund Yates

19, Warwick Crescent,
London, W.
[*ca.* 1882.]

Dear Mr. Yates,

The Browning Society, I need not say, as well as Browning himself, are fair game for criticism. I had no more to do with the founding it than the babe unborn; and, as Wilkes was no Wilkeite, I am quite other than a Browningite. But I cannot wish harm to a society of, with a few exceptions, names unknown to me, who are busied about my books so disinterestedly. The exaggerations probably come of the fifty-years'-long charge of unintelligibility against my books; such reactions are possible, though I never looked for the beginning of one so soon. That there is a grotesque side to the thing is certain; but I have been surprised and touched by what cannot but have been well intentioned, I think. Anyhow, as I never felt inconvenienced by hard words, you will not expect me to wax bumptious because of undue compliment: so enough of 'Browning,'—except that he is yours very truly, 'while this machine is to him.'[1]

Yours,

ROBERT BROWNING.

1883 : 1

To Dr. F. J. Furnivall

19, Warwick Crescent,
London, W.
January 9th, 1883.

My dear Furnivall,

I have been overwhelmed with your kindnesses in these last weeks: the papers, the illustrations[1]—and now comes this really charming print.[2] I probably saw the original picture in a favourable *darkness;* it was blackened by taper-smoke, and one fancied the angel all but surrounded with cloud—only a light on the face. By the bye, that picture of Lippi's, mentioned by Mr. Radford, with the saints in a row, has—either *that* or its companion, the *Annunciation,* also in the National Gallery—the arms of the Medici above the figures; and in all likelihood both pictures were painted during Lippi's stay, enforced or otherwise, in the Medici Palace.

I have given, this afternoon, Smith my new book to print. It is a collection of things grav*ish* and gay*ish*—hence the title *Jocoseria*—which is Batavian Latin, I think. There are some eleven of these pieces, little and big; the main of them being the Deer-stalking poem, you remember, *Donald—Solomon and Balkis—Christina and Monaldeschi—Ixion—Mary Wollstonecraft and Fuseli*—and a long *Hakkadosch Jochanan,* a Rabbinical story; eleven pieces in all.[3] May some morsels of this Olla Podrida take your taste!

Ever truly yours, with belated but very sincere New Year wishes,

Robert Browning.

1883 : 2

To the Rev. J. D. Williams

19 W. Warwick Crescent, W.
March 10, '83

Dear Mr. Williams,

How many days have I said, on beginning to write answers to the half-dozen letters requiring them—"Just despatch these tiresome table-encumbrances, and I will take my pleasure having done my business"! And as often—when the pen is laid down at last—there it lies in reserve for the morrow that never comes. But you probably understand and forgive—as one, I dare say, who get through thrice the work and get spare time to delight a friend when you ought to be rewarding labour by amusement: the really idle cannot allow for idleness—not that my sins have been of that nature,—no! First then, I read the felicitous Latin version[1] with surprise at the achievement,— *yours* though it be! It would be presumptuous in me to praise what yourself best know the worth of. Next, you will have received to-day, I hope, the little book with the Dutch-Latin Title—taken, by an odd coincidence, from a little old rare book which my Father gave me so long ago, and which, to my amazement, was noticed at length in the "Blackwood" of last month—some three days after my own title[2] had been announced. It was of course written by somebody who never had heard of my knowledge of the book. The poems that solicit your indulgence are light enough,—probably the last of the kind I shall care to write.

In another direction quite—I repeat my trust that the—on the whole —not unsatisfactory news of your son continue—at the very least—to be so. I thought of you—may I say, affectionately—as I directed the book to you yesterday—my own son's birthday: that event was a joy soon enough dashed with grief, for, one week after, my Mother died suddenly: and the news, she had been anxious to learn, reached England when she was just passing away. If misfortune should also be unstable, and joy succeed to your sorrow!

Come, can I amuse you never so little? Just after the termination of the "Belt Trial," I was looking into Pindar, and came upon the 3ᵈ Epode of his seventh Olympian. I made this rough translation at once —to match the Judge's quotation from Aristotle.

> *And to these Rhodians She, the Sharp-eyed One,*
> *Gave the supremacy,—to rule in Art,*
> *And, nobly labouring, play the craftsman's part*
> *Beyond all dwellers underneath the sun.*
> *So that the very ways by which ye pass*
> *Bore sculpture-living things that walk or creep,*
> *Like as the life: whence very high and deep*
> *Indeed the glory of the Artist was.*
> *For, in the well-instructed artist, skill*
> *However great receives our greeting*
> *As something greater still*
> *When unaccompanied by cheating!*

Enough of this. My sister wrote lately, I know. She is not in the house at this moment, but I may safely give her kindest regards along with my own to Mrs Williams and yourself.

Ever yours most truly
ROBERT BROWNING.

1883 : 3

To EDMUND GOSSE

19. Warwick Crescent, W.
March 21. '83.

Dear Mr Gosse,

I hear that you are about to become a candidate for the recently-appointed Clark Lectureship at Cambridge. May I be permitted to say, from a real knowledge of your various qualifications for the Post, that I believe you to be, in every respect, thoroughly competent to the discharge of its duties: and that I am anxious to testify my own gratitude to the University which, a year or two since, so deeply obliged me by the bestowment of a signal honour,[1] when I attempt—never so humbly—to enlist among her servants one so efficient as yourself. Believe me, Dear Mr Gosse,

Yours very sincerely
ROBERT BROWNING.

1883 : 4

To CHARLES D. BROWNING[1]

19. Warwick Crescent, W.
March 22. '83

My dear Mr. Browning,

Pray forgive some delay in replying to your kind letter of last week. I had so little to say that I might have said at once—there is *no* historical incident whatever commemorated by the Poem[2] you mention,—which I wrote at sea, off the African coast, with a merely general impression of the characteristic warfare and besieging which abound in the Annals of Flanders. This accounts for some difficulties in the time and space occupied by the ride in one night. I rejoice—without much surprise—at the "Good news from"—Sydney.

Yours very truly,

ROBERT BROWNING.

1883 : 5

To Dr. F. J. Furnivall

19, Warwick Crescent,
London, W.
April 10th, 1883.

My dear Furnivall,

I did indeed translate that little song for Mrs. Bell, never dreaming anybody would suppose there was "another hand" in her work. See now! I should have thought it very mean had I told anybody "that's mine!", and she herself unnecessarily tells it—from sheer honesty, I have no doubt, on somebody observing "what, you versify?"

You amuse me by what Mr. Garnett[1] proposes to do with that No. 9 of the *Railway Indicator*:[2] we have all of us been obliged to him in our time. Will he accept for the Museum all the numbers I possess, from 1 to 18 inclusive, the missing links being No. 2, and that same No. 9 which he possesses? They shall be put aside here for you when you next please to call. I could send them, but, you may as well call!

Innocent XII. was not the first to be tolerant in that direction; but if his predecessor's clemency had been sufficient, there would have needed no supplementary "Bull" on the subject, you see! A Pope *adds* to the efficacy of another Pope's measure; does something on his own account.

I got an American paper, last night, wherein there is repeated that Jochanan revived by "a transfusion of blood." There is not a word about such a thing; on the contrary, the account in the poem makes it impossible. How could the "transfusion" bring experiences with it? or how could the boy's gift, "which he threw and it stuck," be taken in that manner? This comes of the critics reading attentively the criticisms of their brethren, and paying no attention at all to the text criticized. The writer of the article in *The Times* made the mistake first, and even the *Academy* article must needs follow him. The whole story is a fiction of my own, with just this foundation, that the old Rabbins fancied that *earnest wishing* might add to a valued life. Could you say a word on the subject?

Ever yours,
R. BROWNING.

1883 : 6

To Dr. F. J. FURNIVALL

19, Warwick Crescent,
London, W.
April 15th, 1883.

My dear Furnivall,

By all means, if Miss "Teena"[1] kindly cares to come, bring her next Sunday, and don't be under any apprehension that we shall kill a fatted calf on your account or on hers. We shall as easily content you both as we shall ourselves be contented, and much more, by your visit.

My poor friend, Miss Haworth, was the first to call my attention, long ago, to the existence of the old ballad of *Johnnie Fad*—which I was in total ignorance about when I wrote the poem some years before. There was an odd circumstance that either mended or marred the poem in the writing, I fancied the latter at the time. As I finished the line (which ends what was printed in *Hood's Magazine*) "and the old one—you shall hear!" I saw from the window where I sat a friend opening the gate to our house, one Captain Lloyd, whom I jumped up to meet, judging from the time of day that something especially interesting had brought him—as proved to be the case, for he was in a strange difficulty. This took a deal of discussing. Next day other interruptions occurred, and the end was I lost altogether the thing as it was in my head at the beginning, and, subsequently, gave it to Hood as a fragment. Some time afterwards I was staying at Bettisfield Park, in Wales, and a guest, speaking of early winter, said "the deer had already to break the ice in the pond." A fancy struck me, which, on returning home, I worked up into what concludes the story—which originally all grew out of this one intelligible line of a song that I heard a woman singing at a bon-fire Guy Faux night when I was a boy—*Following the Queen of the Gypsies, O!* From so slender a twig of fact can these little singing birds start themselves for a flight to more or less distances.

Ever yours,
R. BROWNING.

1883 : 7

To the Rev. J. D. Williams

17. April, '83. 19. Warwick Cr.

Dear Mr. Williams,

You overloaded me with your goodness and, Issachar-like, I lay down under them,—like the ungrateful long-ears which I am *not*—oh, no! Your two translations[1] strike my poor scholarship as admirable; and, in the one matter which I could make pretence to speak authoritatively about—my own meaning in the original—it is a bit of a triumph to me that you express it so thoroughly: for the "Spectator" had—what Rochester called "great qualms" concerning the sense of "where is the blot?"—opining, on the whole, that it referred to some break in the blue above head: your "Mundi numqua pars" etc is just the thing. In the capital—(if I dare so pronounce)—capital Hendecasyllabics (I keep, as my way is, seeing one word while writing or spelling another, and in this instance had before my mind's eye the old edition of George Buchanan's Poems I used to read when a boy—with its "Hendecasyllabωn Liber,"—good reading it is or was)—well, in these I find nothing but first rate work: those "venti inhospitales" —"vox in aure furtiva cessans" "Aversus ocellus" and the rest, typify exactly the doubts and fears which beset one and are to be repelled. In fine, my verses get clothed in purple and fine linen by your generosity, and certainly will continue to wear their new clothes whenever they present themselves to their author for the future.

How are you, and dear Mrs. Williams, and your family?

This little "Jocoseria" (joking even in the title) has had the usual luck of the little-deserving,—got itself sold (as Carlyle would say) at the rate of 2000 very early, and is now reprinting. It all comes of the Browning Societies. I cannot have been sufficiently grateful for Dr. Westcott's paper—one of the most valued honors of my life. As to your translations—I shall append them (in M.S. at least) to the text, one day, as the best of "new editions."

My friend Gosse is a candidate for this new Professorship of Literature at Cambridge. He is an exceedingly fit man for the post, I think, —as men now go and are in evidence: Tennyson thinks the same. I hope he has a chance.

You will certainly come to Town for the Wordsworth meeting in May, and I shall see you, I trust: the promise is excellent,—why do you not contribute a paper? Rather—why do you not get tired of many things, and, among them, of helping—by your sympathy—the daily tasks of

Yours affectionately ever
ROBERT BROWNING.

1883 : 8

To Edmund Gosse

19, Warwick Crescent,
W.
July 11th, 1883.

My dear Gosse,

Will you look in here next Sunday morning,—after your "early" wont? I mean to make a thorough examination of the contents of that dismal Box,[1] and to see how much of them I can give you with a free conscience: all I can give:—for there is a particular fact which is painful enough,—and I fear that it must remain a secret—at least for some time longer;—but the other matters shall be at your disposal, and with all my heart.

Yours very truly,
ROBERT BROWNING.

1883 : 9

To Edmund Gosse

19, Warwick Crescent,
W.
July 16th, 1883.

My dear Gosse,

Mrs. Procter will be happy to see you and give you all the information[1] in her power whenever you please to call on her at Albert Hall Mansions, No. 19. She is at home on Tuesdays and Sundays—people do not arrive to interrupt you till 4, or thereabouts, and if you go at 3—you find her at home. "She has not much to tell," she bids me say: but I am sure you will get a good deal out of her,—at all events, more than from anybody else.

Ever yours truly,
ROBERT BROWNING.

1883 : 10

To William Sharp

St. Pierre de Chartreuse,
Isere, France.
[*ca.* 1883.]

Dear Mr. Sharp,

Rossetti's *Pauline* letter was addressed to me at Florence more than thirty years ago.[1] I have preserved it, but, even were I at home, should be unable to find it without troublesome searching. It was to the effect that the writer, personally and altogether unknown to me, had come upon a poem in the British Museum, which he copied the whole of, from its being not otherwise procurable—that he judged it to be mine, but could not be sure, and wished me to pronounce on the matter—which I did. A year or two after, I had a visit in London from Mr. (William) Allingham and a friend—who proved to be Rossetti.[2] When I heard he was a painter I insisted on calling on him, though he declared he had nothing to show me—which was far enough from the case. Subsequently, on another of my returns to London, he painted my portrait, not, I fancy, in oils, but water-colours, and finished it in Paris shortly after.[3] This must have been in the year when Tennyson published *Maud,* for I remember Tennyson reading the poem one evening while Rossetti made a rapid pen-and-ink sketch of him, very good, from one obscure corner of vantage, which I still possess, and duly value.[4] This was before Rossetti's marriage.

Yours,
Robert Browning.

1883 : 11

To Dr. F. J. Furnivall

Hotel Delapierre,
Gressoney St. Jean,
Val D' Aosta.
August 29th, 1883.

My dear Furnivall,

I have just got my letters from London and yours among them. Of course, I was sure some reason was for your silence, and that you would have kindly given me a farewell sight of you had it been in your power.

We arrived here a week ago, and are in a beautiful place indeed, a paradise of coolness and quiet, shut in by the Alps; just under Monte Rosa with its glaciers. The reaching this rest was rough work however. From Jura to Port St. Martin by two hours carriage-drive, and thence seven continued hours of clambering and crawling on mule-back; even our luggage needing to be carried on a couple of the poor creatures after the same fashion. And just so shall we have to descend, when time comes and snow falls—which, they say, will be soon enough. We are very well off, however, in a quite perfect "Hotel"— with every comfort desirable, and no drawback of any kind. When the snow comes, whither we go is uncertain. I greatly hope the determination will not be forced on us before another fortnight.

My sister sends her kindest regards with mine. I wish you may be in the enjoyment of anything like our glorious weather.

Ever affectionately yours,
ROBERT BROWNING.

My very handwriting is affected by the lumpy ink and skewery pen. You will decipher it, I daresay. I have received *from home* some newspapers, but no literary journal of any kind—*yet*.

1883 : 12

To Dr. F. J. Furnivall

Hôtel Delapierre,
Gressoney St. Jean,
Val D'Aosta, Italia.
September 17th, 1883.

My dear Furnivall,

Let me first of all get rid of a trifle on my mind; and yet no trifle if it indicated carelessness on my part, as it might seem to do.

In my hurry to send off an answer to your letter I got some stamps from the people of the house, and, by candle-light, the proper *blue* was undistinguishable from the *green*—one fifth of the proper value. I had stamped and despatched my letter when the mistake was discovered, which *you* have been mulcted for.[1] You will forgive the blunder, which I was sufficiently sorry about.

Your new letter is very affecting, and the portion of it which relates to myself, well, I don't know whether it pains or gratifies me the more. It is useless to consider; if those little endeavours to please were so successful, how willingly would one have redoubled or centupled them! As to the wish of the poor parents that I should write something on the sad subject, all I can say is, if such an exceptional experience should happen to me as that I could put the feelings I am undoubtedly full of into verse which should be worthy of the name, I should hardly require an instigation from the outside to do so. But in the two or three great sorrows of my life it has been the last thing that occurred to me. *Incidentally,* I am quite sure, and as I told you, this dreadful accident will have its influence more or less remarkably on what I write. I should hate any mechanical attempt to do what would only acquire worth from being a spontaneous outflow. Understand all this; indeed, I know you will; but tell the amount of it to the parents with whom I sympathize from my inmost heart.[2]

My sister again desires to condole with you in all sincerity. We purpose remaining here for at least another week, after which, as the weather may allow, we shall descend into the lowlands and move towards Venice, where we hope to arrive about the 1st of *October*. The weather continues surprisingly fine for the place and time of year.

Ever affectionately yours,
ROBERT BROWNING.

I return the melancholy newspaper account.

1883 : 13

TO DR. F. J. FURNIVALL

Gressoney St. Jean,
Val D'Aosta, Italy.
September 29th, 1883.

My dear Furnivall,

Six weeks in this delightful solitude, with one day only to prevent our[1] leaving the house! On every other morning and afternoon we have walked right and left, never less and often more than five hours a day—and the good to us both, I hope, certainly to myself, is in proportion. At Venice we shall be social, however, and I cannot expect to return with as florid a pair of cheeks as I occasionally get glimpses of in the glass.

That was indeed a—*Godsend,* is hardly the appropriate word, to Dowden, whom I never cease wishing well to. I wonder if he has had access to the correspondence of the first Mrs. Shelley with—what was the bookseller's name, he of Bond Street, Shelley's intimate friend?[2]

He put them into my hands, and a very decided impression they left with me, the reverse of what I had been prepared for by the biographers of Shelley. Hookham (where was my memory?) offered them to me unreservedly on the only occasion of our interview, and they are all-important for a right view of the case as between wife and husband; the latter being, I hold, at that time of his life half crazy and wholly inexcusable.[3]

So to Venice, if weather allow, for we *walk* the first six hours of the descent; and there, and everywhere, remember me as

Ever affectionately yours,

ROBERT BROWNING.

1883 : 14

To Professor Edward Dowden

Palazzo Giustiniani-Recanati,[1]
Venice, Oct. 12, '83.

My dear Mr Dowden,

I get a letter of yours addressed to Mr Furnivall containing a request that I would give you some further explanation of the matters I mentioned to him. As to what Mr Hookham told me in the only conversation we had, I prefer keeping silence about stories for the truth of which he only was responsible, and which I heard some twenty five years ago. But the letters which he showed me were good evidence on certain points—misunderstood or misstated in every account I had previously seen.

Harriet—represented as either uneducated or incapable of becoming so—said that, in compliance with her Husband's desire, she was learning Latin and could already make out the Odes of Horace: she was, for the same reason, practising music, and commissioned Hookham to procure for her pieces—"especially by Mozart": The most striking letter was the last one—written to enquire where Shelley might be—whether, as the writer thought probable, with Hookham, —altogether conceived in such a state of surprise and bewilderment at his disappearance as to completely dispose of the notion, hitherto accepted by Shelley's biographers, that they had parted by common consent—the wife proving in the sequel unable to bear the separation as philosophically as her husband. I was not the authority for Rossetti's statement about the destitution in which she was left.

Hookham said Shelley was suffering from intense bodily pain at the time,—"would roll himself writhing on the ground, pulling the sofa-cushions upon him"—and, to alleviate this, "he would actually go about with a laudanum-bottle in his hand, supping thence as need might be." The letter containing the account of the imaginary noc-turnal attack was begun, for perhaps three lines, by Shelley and the rest added, from his version of it, by the wife: all the letters were well written in every respect. This is all I am able to say—and, of course, is for *you* and not the public: my object in saying it is to refer you to documents which must still be in existence, and ought to be produced if the controverted subject of Shelley's relations with his first wife is to be revived.[2]

I write in great haste, but with all the good wishes which go to you in leisure from

yours truly ever
ROBERT BROWNING.

1883 : 15

To Dr. F. J. FURNIVALL

Palazzo Giustiniani-Recanati,
Venice.
October 15th, 1883.

Better not, my dear Furnivall, for it is in the lazy blood of the whole people, and telling them of their faults rather saddens than irritates them, besides doing no sort of good. Everybody who can block up a window, brick over a moulding, or other apparently useless ornament, does so; or, better, disposes of it—a balcony, well, or such like fixture— to the Jew antiquity-mongers. It is really an argument against the throwing open museums and galleries to the people on Sundays that here, where the works which glorify such institutions were originally produced, and where similar excellences may be still seen every day, the inhabitants have the worst taste in the whole world. I believe that remonstrating with the pigheaded authorities here would merely con-firm them in their obstinate determination to Liverpoolize Venice. Let them be, poor pigs with the devil in them!

I wrote a word or two to Dowden, and have no doubt he may get at the letters if he tries; they cannot well have been destroyed.

I never saw that book of Powell's[1] to which you allude, and should refuse to accept a line of it as true, unless I *did* see it, the author being

late into a simply polite thanking and declining of a very flattering proposal.

Yes,—I saw the letter of my unknown advocate in the "Daily News"—a paper I take in regularly. The fussy foolish gentleman who put his little person forward so officiously is laughed at throughout Venice for his pains. The anecdote was even mentioned in the "Times'" notice of Rawdon Brown—written, I am told, by L^y East-lake: don't give the silliness another word, pray.

Ever truly yours
ROBERT BROWNING.

1884 : 2

To J. DYKES CAMPBELL

19, Warwick Crescent, W.,
March 15, '84.

Dear Mr. Dykes Campbell,—I observe that you have done the Browning Society the honour of becoming its Secretary,[1] and there seems to occur a good opportunity for saying just a word on a subject which is borne increasingly on my mind, the more than doubtful expediency of the monthly abstract of proceedings *being sent to me in a "proof."* I have the appearance of thus authorising whatever notice it may contain, considerable or otherwise, since I receive it—and say nothing, which is as good as consenting to the ordinary apprehension: and it would save me many inconvenient enquiries, as to things done or contemplated, if I could answer—"I have in no way authorised this intelligence." As the Secretary of the Society, you are, I suppose, the proper recipient of this very intelligible request, and I am sure you will indulge me by complying with it.[2]

I am, dear Mr. Dykes Campbell, yours very sincerely,

ROBERT BROWNING.

1884 : 3

To J. DYKES CAMPBELL

19, Warwick Crescent, W.,
March 18, '84.

Dear Mr. Dykes Campbell,—I was very sorry to miss your kind visit on Sunday. I have, as usual, expressed myself badly in giving you the notion that anything amounting "to annoyance" has been occasioned by my receiving the proofs in question. All I meant was that it was inexpedient that I should get "proofs" that I might naturally be expected to authorise by keeping silent about them. There is much difference between leaving any comparatively unimportant statement, concerning one unreplied to; and seeming to desire unmistakably that it should go forth to the world. I saw in a newspaper that among the people who witnessed Salvini's performance on Friday was observable—myself! Well and good; but if a slip had been forwarded to me beforehand, I should probably have struck out *that,* as of little interest to anybody: whereas if I had really been absent instead of present, there would be no need of calling attention to an error of trifling consequence indeed.

Believe me, dear Mr. Dykes Campbell, yours ever truly,

ROBERT BROWNING.

1884 : 4

To Dr. F. J. Furnivall

19, Warwick Crescent,
London, W.
April 25th, 1884.

My dear Furnivall,

I don't see that, because a clown's conception of the laws of the Heavenly bodies is grotesque and impossible, that of Newton must be necessarily as absurd; or that the writer of *La Saisiaz* must see through such horny eyes as those of Caliban: besides, in each case, there is a faculty of reason which should be employed in correcting and adjusting the first impressions of the senses—and, I hope, the two make a very different use of their respective faculties; one doubts and the other has no doubt at all, "sayeth" so and so, as if Prospero could say no otherwise. Then, as to the divergence from Shakespeare's Caliban—is it so decided? There is no "forgetfulness of his love for music," since he makes a song and sings it; nor of his "visions of Heaven," for he speculates on what goes on there; nor of his resolve to "learn wisdom and such grace," seeing that he falls flat and loveth Setebos, and was a fool to gibe at a Power he had miscalculated. True, "he was a very different being at the end of the Play from what he was at its beginning"—but my Caliban indulges his fancies long before even that beginning. All the same, "fire away!"

I have hardly had a minute, of late, to be quiet in. My son is here,

Milsand is here also; and I have been away, as you know, and much engaged in matters of a teasing nature about—well, let me forget them! Your young lady was abundantly welcome to the song. I hope to see you on Sunday, of course.

Ever truly yours,
ROBERT BROWNING.

1884 : 5

TO MADAME PERUZZI (NÉE EDITH STORY)

19, Warwick Crescent, W.
Aug. 7, '84

My dear Edie, What else am I to say? Your kind letter arrived two days ago, and the Book[1] has followed quickly. It is not so very "little" an affair; and, in the fear that, when my sister has finished it, I may have to begin my own reading, and end it so late as to lead you to suppose that either book or letter has gone wrong, on this account I write at once to thank you most heartily. My sister says the autobiography is *fascinating*. I can well believe it, for I never knew such a work to be without interest, and this of Dupré must abound in precisely the matters that interest me most—but it happens also that your father read aloud to me, at Venice, a considerable portion of your performance, and very greatly was I delighted by it. To be sure, I should welcome any work of yours and be disappointed indeed if it were otherwise than I have a right to expect. When I have thoroughly gone through the book, I will write again, if you permit me— as I know your old memories will be indulgent in the case. I was most happy to hear from your father's friends the Curtises of Venice, who are here, that his health is greatly improved; that of your mother has not suffered, I believe. There is not much likelihood of our going to Italy this autumn, the silly quarantine regulations effactually hinder our attempting that; and in no case should I—probably—trust myself in Florence again—but such an event might be, and if you are within reach, you will be certain to see the old friend—who always rejoices when he hears of your well-being, and trusts it may continue.

Pen is very well, at Dinant, just now, painting landscape in the open air. I have told him already of the book which I know he will delight in reading. I am occupied this very day in sending his statue of Dryope to Brussels, where the exhibition will give it a chance of being judged by better knowledge than is found here. Your own brothers' works are capital—Julian's picture at the Grosvenor is admirable, in many respects, above the works on each side of it; and Waldo's statuette is exceedingly good also. They have, each of them, enjoyed a better education than is easily obtainable here.

My sister sends her kindest love to you. She had, some weeks ago, a serious attack of *peritonitis* which gave us alarm at one time—but she is herself again—after five weeks' confinement to bed. We are ordered to find mountain air for her, and must somehow manage it —but our Gressoney in the Val d'Aosta is a barred paradise at present. Switzerland is our resource, I suppose. What do you think? We get, this moment, a word from your mother to say she—or "we"—may be seen in town this day only, as she leaves early tomorrow. I shall contrive to call this evening, and will keep my letter open to make it worth your reading by my news.

Friday, Aug. 8. I spent the evening very pleasantly with your father and mother at the York Hotel. They are, both of them, perfectly well and in excellent spirits. Their plan is to go somewhere for a week or two's refuge from the heat, and thence, returning to London, get to Rome as soon as the difficulties on the frontier are removed. For ourselves, we hope to leave in a day or two for St. Moritz, where Mrs. Moore[2] offers us lodging in a villa she rents there. My sister's state is beginning to require immediate change, and I have apparently no alternative. So, once more, goodbye and God bless you, dear Edie! Offer my best respects to your husband and believe me ever affectionately yours

ROBERT BROWNING

1884 : 6

To Dr. F. J. FURNIVALL

Villa Berry,
St. Moritz, Switzerland.
September 28th, 1884.

My dear Furnivall,

We leave for London next Wednesday, October 1st, and count upon arriving there in a couple of days; so that if you are in Town, and chariotably minded, you will come and "batten on cold bits" with us this day week, and hear all our news. We had not been here a fortnight when our kind hostess was summoned to America, to her great vexation. Imperative as the summons was, she only obeyed it on condition of our remaining her guests to the end of our visit's natural term; and we have done so. There was no avoiding the quarantine established at all the Italian passes till a short while ago, and long before then (our beloved Mrs. Bronson being at Kreuznach, and, similarly shut out apparently from return, determined to go on to Paris and London) our mind was accordingly made up to forgo Venice and return to London when the wonderful friend telegraphed to us that she should greatly prefer changing her plans, going back to Venice, and receiving us there, "if we did not fear the cholera." The cholera, above all, at Venice where, I believe, it has never yet entered, does not frighten us at all—but the notion of our friend's making such a sacrifice on our account was unendurable, and we keep to our determination. There are also many matters which want attending to personally in London; and our seven weeks here have passed so profitably that we must be content without the usual Italian supplement.

Nothing could exceed the delightfulness of the weather. I write at this moment (not 9 A.M.) in a blaze of sunshine which I shrink from at the unluckily most convenient table in the room. And so it has been uninterruptedly for the last two weeks; not a symptom of cloud in the blue to-day. Yet the "season" is over long ago, the hotels are shut up, and the place deserted mostly. We have walked every day, morning and evening—afternoon, I should say—two or three hours each excursion, the delicious mountain air surpassing any I was ever privileged to breathe. My sister is absolutely herself again, and something over: I was hardly in want of such doctoring.

Well, I saw an advertisement, in last week's *Saturday Review,* of my new Poem[1]—somewhat to my surprise, for there are reasons for keeping back the publication for at least a week or two. My part is done, however, and the last corrected "proofs" are at the printers. I can't at all guess how people will like it, but I have managed to say a thing or two that I "fancied" I should like to say.

Since I began this I have walked on and up the mountain for three hours. The splendour of the day is indescribable. To be sure, you have a fine St. Martin, by all accounts, and so much the better! But you cannot have the air of these altitudes, nor, alas, can I—next week! It would have been pleasant to feel oneself gradually *let down* into the winter by a two-months' sojourn in Venice.

My sister sends her kindest regards. She, at all events, will witness your great doings in November.

Ever truly yours,
ROBERT BROWNING.

1884 : 7

To Norman Mac Coll

19, Warwick Crescent,
W.
Oct. 31, '84.

Dear Mr Mac Coll,
I have just heard from Mr Smith that my book[1] will be published, simultaneously with the American edition, *on Nov. 21st—a Friday,* pray observe!

Yours very truly
ROBERT BROWNING.

1884 : 8

To J. Dykes Campbell

19, Warwick Crescent, W.,
Dec. 24, '84.

Dear Mr. Dykes Campbell,—Thank you very much for the kind note which preceded the arrival of the beautiful reproductions of Sir F.'s picture.[1] I had no notion till the latter reached me that the gift to the society had included the permission to make use of the picture for such a purpose. It is a piece of generosity, however, in thorough accordance with his habitual practice. All good wishes appropriate to the season. So heartily say we all here! Pray believe it on the word of yours truly ever,

ROBERT BROWNING.

1884 : 9

To the Storys

19 Warwick Crescent W
Dec. 25, 1884

Dear friends,—
I make haste to say that I have just received your letter with its enclosures, and will give them to Mrs. Moore at once—she having arrived from America last week. I read them, according to your desire, and can judge what has happened, plainly enough, through an

unfortunate mental peculiarity of seeing only, for the time present, the desirableness of an acquisition—and afterwards discovering that this looks otherwise in another light, and forgetting what has been said and done—and, in this case, written—under the first impulse. Nothing could cause much greater inconvenience, or subject the author of it to more serious misconception—a lighter word than you would naturally use to qualify it—but I have had considerable experience, and should hardly entertain very seriously any proposal to acquire a work of art which was not acted upon at once and past mistake—that is, a mistake in Mrs. Moore's mind as to what she had originally—beyond question—intended to do: it is a sort of "thinking aloud" instead of thinking in silence, and speaking definitely at last. I have a real sorrow that a lady, whose nature I know to be generous in the extreme, should, by a failing of this kind, cause—in other cases than the present—a doubt of the existence of generosity and something more important: but so it is.

In my letter of a week ago, I forgot to say how grieved I was at the death of poor Hamilton Wild[1]—of which I had been informed by Mr. Field[2]—those were good days when we foregathered at the Villa in Siena! But this is Christmas Day, and I have many unopened letters lying beside me. I thought it best to acknowledge yours at once. So, with true Christmas good wishes for you and all with you, believe me ever

Affectionately yours,

ROBERT BROWNING.

1884 : 10

To W. W. STORY

19 Warwick Crescent W,
December 28, 1884

My dear Story,—

I called yesterday afternoon at the house of Mrs. Moore to deliver, as you desired, the two letters—hers and your own—but she was not visible, being confined to her bed by a bad cold, and I left the papers in an enclosure. By the evening post, those which you now receive came here—with no other word in the envelope,—and I have the simply unpleasant business of returning them. I heard about the misunderstanding some three years ago,—hardly, if at all, since,—and am very sorry to find matters are no better but apparently worse than before. Indeed, I gathered, from what I heard at the time, that Mrs. Moore was still ready to buy any new work of yours, of which no "replica," by consequence, could already exist—the difficulty being in that respect, and not so much as to subsequent copying. If the fact of the statue being itself a "replica" was duly explained to her, I fail to conceive what the objection could be to abiding by the terms of her agreement. I understood, besides, that if she had seen and been satisfied with the statue, as she endeavoured to do at Paris, she would have accepted it in spite of what she considered disadvantageous circumstances,—but the owner was away, and her dissatisfaction had no chance of being removed. I can only be (once again) very sorry for what seems past remedy.

Mrs. Hurlbert has just written to me concerning the Hawthorne calumnies. I can have no objection to anybody hearing that I think them monstrous. The bringing in my wife and myself as witnesses of the spiritualistic experiments at the Villa Montauto is absurd—as might have been known by Mr. Julian had he looked at his father's "notes"—wherein no mention of our names will be found, though he dwells on the minutest incidents: We had left Florence a month before he took the Villa, nor returned there until long after he was out of it. This piece of inexactitude,—the first bit of the book I fell upon, —warned me effectually off the premises. So much may be said "on my authority"—but I object to making any statement which may give Mr. Julian the happy chance of an altercation in the newspapers: letters and letters!

Pen came here nearly a fortnight ago very unwell—but we doctored and nursed and brought him round again. His love goes with mine and my sister's to you and all with you.

I am, my dear Story, ever affectionately yours,

ROBERT BROWNING.

1885 : 1

To LAWRENCE BARRETT

19, Warwick Crescent, W.
Feb. 3, '85.

My dear Mr. Barrett:—

Although I received your most kind and in every way satisfactory letter a full fortnight ago, yet the packet of newspaper notices which it mentioned as "sent" did not reach me till this morning and I wish to say at once, however hurriedly, how much I feel your gracious and effectual goodness in the whole matter from beginning to end. I gather from the various reports this one certain fact, that as a stage-manager you have done your utmost for the play, and, as an actor, have completely realized whatever was worthy in the character of Tresham. When I look back to the circumstances under which the piece was brought out in London—forty-two years ago—I may well wonder whether,—if my inclination for dramatic writing had met with half so much encouragement and assistance as you have really gratuitously bestowed on it,—I might not have gone on, for better or worse, play-writing to the end of my days; and the conditions of the stage were so much simpler then than at present, that it would not follow necessarily that, because I constructed a piece then with a view to its performance in the little Haymarket Theatre, I should not now attempt to employ more elaborate means to an end than seemed advisable when an audience was rather "all ears" than "all eyes." "It has seemed otherwise to the Divinities" as the Poet says; and I am all the more grateful that your will and power have been so benevolently employed in keeping my (theatrical) head above the waters even now that a rougher tide has come in. And whether the most of your efforts shall go on or stop short—in any case, I am privileged indeed to have known a nature so sympathetic and intelligent as your own.

With every best wish in your behalf, believe me, Dear Mr. Barrett,

Yours most sincerely,
ROBERT BROWNING.

1885 : 2

To EDMUND GOSSE

19, Warwick Crescent,
W.
March 15th, 1885.

My dear Gosse,

"Four Poems, of moderate length, which represent their writer fairly": if I knew what moderation exactly meant, the choice would be easier. Let me say—at a venture—

Lyrical: *Saul* or *Abt Vogler.*

Narrative: *A Forgiveness.*

Dramatic: *Caliban on Setebos.*

Idyllic (in the Greek sense): *Clive.*

Which means that, being restricted to *four* dips in the Lucky-bag, I should not object to be judged by these samples,—so far as these go,—for there is somewhat behind still!

Ever truly yours,

ROBERT BROWNING.

1885 : 3

TO W. G. KINGSLAND

19, Warwick Crescent,
W.
March 27th, 1885.

Dear Sir,

I will answer your questions as well as I can briefly do so. I frequently attended the service at Mr. Jones's Chapel[1] about twenty years ago. I am somewhat ashamed to have troubled my head for a moment, and interrupted my proper occupation, by taking notice of so contemptible a person as the one you mention; and beg you to leave the indiscretion alone, all the more that you kindly profess to have gone on to something better in my verses.

I have no sort of influence with my publisher, and no knowledge whether, much less when, he will bring out a cheap edition of my works. There is, however, a cheaper edition lately published, in two volumes, of *Selections* from them. As for collecting the original editions of books, of many of which I paid the expenses of printing, and as good as gave away, these are now fetching enormous prices I am told, having attained to be curiosities.

Yours obediently,

ROBERT BROWNING.

1885 : 4

TO MRS. MARY CARLYLE

19, Warwick Crescent, W.,
Apr. 7, '85.

Dear Mrs. Carlyle,

I shall be as willing as ready to submit to you and Professor Norton[1] every letter that I possess by your Uncle. They were offered to Mr.

Lento dolente.

à tempo d'un canto

Robert Browning.
Apr. 16.'85.

Froude but not seen by him, nor apparently needed; certain of them, written to me when I was abroad, are astray and missing—for the moment only, I hope—but they shall be diligently searched after.

Believe me, Dear Mrs Carlyle,

Yours very sincerely

ROBERT BROWNING.

1885 : 5

To EDMUND GOSSE

19, Warwick Crescent,
W.
July 1st, 1885.

My dear Gosse,

I was away last week—hence the delay in returning to you the letter,[1] which could not but deeply interest me. It is much to have been privileged to render what his kindness calls help to such a man, and I am very grateful to you for the knowledge of it.

I had a letter from Mr. Lawrence Barrett some days ago, with as much geniality and friendliness as he could put into it. There was a scrupulous account of his doings,[2] and a handsome cheque, as their result,—all in strange contrast with my English experience so many years ago. One lives and learns—and the learning is not invariably a sad business. I shall be happy to see him next year, as he promises shall be the case.

Always affectionately yours,

ROBERT BROWNING.

1885 : 6

To JOHN W. FIELD[1]

19, Warwick Crescent, W.
Aug. 16. '85

My dear Field, I really could not answer at once; the letter was a severe shock to me. It seemed impossible that one I so vividly remember as full of youth as well as life, should announce to me, as you have done, the dismal news that it may suddenly come to an end—all that gaiety and goodness which make up for me, and for all your friends, the dearly beloved image of John Field. But, at the last, something must be attempted, and I shall just say that if I—your elder—am destined to survive you,—the few years which can be left will keep as freshly the remembrance of all your loving-kindness as when we parted two short seasons ago. And yet, with the plentiful experience I have that the judgments of the best doctors are being perpetually re-vised or reversed by the mere operation of nature, I am far from re-signing myself to a patient acceptance of their verdict in your case. It is however presumptuous in me to speak on this subject. I will sim-ply repeat—unnecessarily enough—that, whatever be the event, you will be accompanied throughout my own life with the sincerest love and gratefullest affection of your friend

ROBERT BROWNING

My sister has never ceased to think and speak of your letter, previously recalling and enjoying over again your benevolence to us both. I will not say that she "sends" you her love—it will continue with her, as mine with me. But you can help us by offering our thorough sym-pathy and truest of kind wishes to Mrs. Field. We purpose going to Venice in the autumn—it will never be old Venice if it is to sadly re-mind us, at every turn, of a happiness existing no longer.

1885 : 7

To Dr. F. J. FURNIVALL

Hotel Delapierre,
Gressoney St. Jean,
Val D'Aosta, Italy.
September 7th, 1885.

My dear Furnivall,

I was just going to thank you for your pleasant letter from the Moors when your second arrived. I will begin with the proposal in the latter.

Certainly nobody will ever treat of my wife and myself more graciously and partially (if that is desirable at all) than you; so, by all means biographize about both of us. For my own part, I will do what I can in the talk over the matter that is to be. I have nothing to keep back, and will answer any question to the best of my power. But in the other case, the little I confidently can profess to *know* I am forced to be silent about; and how very little that little is appears extraordinary to me, and may seem almost incredible to anybody else. The personality of my wife was so strong and peculiar that I had no curiosity to go beyond it, and concern myself with matters which she was evidently disinclined to communicate. I believe I discovered her birthday—the day, not the date—three weeks ago, when engaged in some search after missing letters. But I can set right certain errors which appear in the printed notices that I have seen. Any help in that way, which is in my power to give, I will give you readily.

I rejoice that your Yorkshire visit was so successful. You speak of bad or indifferent weather; ours here has been, and continues, all we could desire. We are all but alone, the brief "season" being over, and only a chance traveller turning up for a fortnight's lodging. We take our walks in the old way; two and a half hours before breakfast, three after it, in the most beautiful country I know. Yesterday the three hours passed without our meeting a single man, woman, or child; one man only was discovered at a distance at the foot of a mountain we had climbed.

Yes, I am writing another poem. It may give you a notion of this place when I tell you that on the 17th of Last January an avalanche destroyed two houses close to this Hotel, and a third on the other side of it, crushing six people at their morning meal, one child escaping through a couple of beams falling cross-wise over her head. The snow lay four *mètres* deep, so effectually blocking up the Hotel that it was two days before the inhabitants became aware of what had happened. They had provisions enough, but were reduced to melted snow and ice, which kept cows and a mule alive. The Doctor and the Priest were imprisoned in the house, having sought shelter there.

I did not know that Pen's projected trip was so notably recorded in the papers. He leaves Dinant for Venice at the end of this week, takes a studio there, and tries his hand at something different, I hope, from the conventional work. Did I tell you of the success of his *Dryope* at the Paris Salon, where it obtained a *mention honorable*—a great distinction for sculpture in the best sculpture-producing country? They proceed grade by grade there, and this is all he could hope for as yet. Please do not, in your kindness, mention this, which I am glad to have never seen in print. The *Academy* is unfriendly enough without need of further exasperation!

I suppose we shall stay here till the end of the month. One good storm, with thunder, threatened to break up the genial autumn's beginning (for it is no more than that, we have greenness everywhere), but it only deposited snow on the mountain tops, and left a sky bluer than ever.

Good-bye, dear Furnivall; my sister summons me—taking occasion to send her best regards. I rose at half past five, and am ready for our walk. Do write whenever the happy mood is upon you; your letters are cheery to us both. Don't think I forget to wish your son a triumphant cycling. And believe me

Always most truly yours,
ROBERT BROWNING.

1885 : 8

To J. DYKES CAMPBELL

Palazzo Giustiniani Recanati,[1] Venice,
Nov. 9, '85

Dear Mr. Dykes Campbell,—You are ever the kindest of the kind. I can think of nobody who deserves a ticket; all the deserving must be members of the Society. Seriously, no name of a friend occurs to me at this moment. I wish I could myself be present. It is impossible, however, and I stay here for a little matter of business, and not pleasure. You are very kind to care about the lines I wrote in a hurry one morning from a wish I had to "stand to my guns" on being appealed to. I expected that a "proof" would be sent, but nothing came, and I can only hope that no egregious blunder is in the printed copy. The Editor—quite a stranger to me—may have fancied I was out of reach, as I said nothing about where I meant to go when I left Gressoney. In a week or two I trust to turn my face homewards, and the first employment of a Sunday afternoon will be to see you, and, however insufficiently, thank you. My sister begs to send her kindest regards to you and to Mrs. Campbell, who will also accept those of, dear Mr. Dykes Campbell, yours most truly,

ROBERT BROWNING.

1885 : 9

To Dr. F. J. Furnivall

Venice.
November 17th, 1885.

My dear Furnivall,

I find that at last I can get away and go home—as I hope to do next Monday; arriving thus in London two or three days after. I write at once to apprize you of this, knowing that your good nature would prompt you to give me an account of *Colombe*—which needs must be, would reach Venice on Monday, and so fail of reaching myself. Address whatever news, good or bad, there may be, to the London place,[1] and I will read it gratefully the moment I arrive—probably on Wednesday.

"The London Place": well, your friendliness now must know that I have been kept thus long here by the business of buying a Venice Palace, the Manzoni Palazzo, of which you may see an account in the Guide Books. I think, with many or most of them, that it is the most beautiful house—not the biggest nor most majestic—in Venice. I buy it solely for Pen, who is in love with the City beyond anything I could expect, and had set his heart on this particular acquisition before I joined him, quite unaware that I had entertained a similar preference for it years ago. Don't think I mean to give up London till it warns me away; when the hospitalities and innumerable delights grow a burden, even as we are assured the grasshopper will eventually do in the case of the stoutest of us. Pen will have sunshine and beauty about him, and every help to profit by these, while I and my sister have secured a shelter when the fogs of life grow too troublesome. We cannot enter into possession for some months, and Pen returns in our company to resume work in Paris. I should have mentioned that I was in the thick of this affair of a purchase but that the owner was abroad, and I needed to first negotiate with him in person; and, oh the slips between cups and lips! so that I closed mine till the cup's last contents were fairly inside them.[2]

What sort of weather are you having to-day? We walked two hours just now, with abundance of sunshine, a blue sky, and a bracing wind—pronounced by our servant to be "stupendously cold." Pen—who drops in while I write—sends his best regards, and congratulations on the successes of your son,[3] which he appreciates as a connoisseur should.

My sister joins me in the hope of soon a pleasant meeting. So does Pen, for he too, is only minded to stay here occasionally; by no means to detach himself from the England of us all—and assuredly of

Yours truly ever,

ROBERT BROWNING.

1885 : 10

To J. DYKES CAMPBELL

19, Warwick Crescent, W.,
Dec. 4, '85.

My dear Mr. Dykes Campbell,—I signed and sent off the paper concerning Ruskin as soon as I found it on my return: however, there being no harm in an emphatic repetition of readiness to do what one is desired, I very willingly sign a second time. I feel exactly about Ruskin as yourself besides having a particularly affectionate feeling for him personally. I enclose the other papers, as you may want to use them for some other application.—Ever truly yours,

ROBERT BROWNING.

1885 : 11

To Dr. F. J. FURNIVALL

19, Warwick Crescent,
London, W.
December 8th, 1885.

My dear Furnivall,

You are, as always, very good in wishing to invest me with new honours, but the acceptance of this last[1] is impossible; it would be tantamount to a profession of belief that what the Browning Society has done so helpfully in my case—mine, who stood in need of it— should now be repeated in the case of Shelley who, for years, has tasked the ingenuity of his admirers to leave no scrap of his writing nor incident of his life without its illustration by every kind of direct or cross light—not, I very much suspect, to the advantage of either. For myself, I painfully contrast my notions of Shelley the *man* and

Shelley, well, even the *poet,* with what they were sixty years ago, when I only had his works, for a certainty, and took his character on trust.

Moreover, I am frightened, just a moment after reading your proposal, by learning that I was last night "unanimously elected Honorary President of the University of Edinburgh in the room of Lord Bury—see *The Times* of to-day. No hint of such an intention had reached me. What is expected of such a President I have no notion; and, if anything more is required than the thanks for the honour, that honour will be assuredly declined.

I shall not say a word about my feeling in your case; you know it.

Remember we expect you and your son next Sunday. I returned, at 2 p.m., from Cambridge; the playing was admirably done.

Ever yours,

ROBERT BROWNING.

1885 : 12

TO ALMA MURRAY (MRS. ALFRED FORMAN)

19, Warwick Crescent, W
Dec. 29. '85

I could not have expected that the year would all but run out before I had written even a single word of the many I was minded to send you when, on returning to London, I heard from friends I could trust and strangers whose testimony there was no reason to doubt—how admirably you had done honour to my play by your performance of Colombe. There has been no attempt at the poor piece of flattery supposed acceptable to a playwright; that 'his poetry had hardly been done justice to' and so forth: it thoroughly delighted me to hear and to believe that you had realized my idea and probably added graces of your own. When I observe what preparations for a theatrical venture are supposed requisite for success,—the thousands of pounds spent on scenery and costume,—the hundreds of rehearsals—and the dozens of paragraphs-preliminary,—I look with wonder and no little satisfaction on the circumstance that an old play composed under the old conditions and brought out in the hope of living through one night only,—should have rewarded the efforts in its favour, as it has more than satisfied the author's ambition, I am sure. Take my renewed thanks, dear Mrs. Forman, and believe that you will be followed in your career by the deep interest of

Yours truly ever,

ROBERT BROWNING.

1885 : 13

TO EDMUND GOSSE

19, Warwick Crescent,
W.
December 29th, 1885.

My dear Gosse,

I do not exactly remember Thrupp's statue in the Abbey,[1] but I well keep in mind the statuette of Woolner which I have not seen for many years.

I cannot conceive why a *replica* should be thought of: why not state the case as pointedly to the Professor as you have done in the letter to myself? I shall not send it him, of course—no danger of that!—but your own repetition of the advice would certainly do good.

Ever truly yours,

ROBERT BROWNING.

1886 : 1

TO THE EDITOR OF A BOSTON MAGAZINE[1]

[London, *ca.* 1886.]

[Dear Sir:]

If I would write in that way for any one, I would consider this request from Boston, but I simply can't. An English magazine offered me a large price, which I refused, and then a still larger, which I again refused. Then they sent me a blank cheque, and asked me to fill it out to my own satisfaction. But I returned that also.

I cannot bring myself to write for periodicals. If I publish a book, and people choose to buy it, that proves they want to read my work. But to have them turn over the pages of a magazine and find me—that is to be an uninvited guest. My wife liked it. She liked to be with the others; but I have steadfastly refused that kind of thing from first to last.

ROBERT BROWNING.

1886 : 2

To J. Dykes Campbell

19, Warwick Crescent,
Jan. 19th, '86.

Dear Mr. Dykes Campbell,—I return, with very many thanks, the interesting excerpts from Lowell's clever speech: as you bid me retain the "slip" with Mr. Berry's article I do so. There is one minute error in it, which may lead to a confusion in the mind of the reader; in the quotation—(I see, I must send it back, after all, or you may miss the truly minute objection I make)—"How rose smit earth will rise"[1] I should avoid the jumble of "rose" and "rise" by being printed with a hyphen—rose-smit—i. e., "smitten with rosiness." I suppose it is past correction now. It was Marguerite of Navarre who passing by Chasselain, the poet, found asleep in the gallery, stooped and kissed him. When her attendant ladies expressed surprise that she could kiss "so ugly a mouth," she answered: "No—the mouth that has uttered such beautiful things." There was no love in the case, but my queen forgets the precise facts, and—wanting an illustration of love under difficulties—turns the kiss-complimentary into a more demonstrative one —the mere "kiss" serves her turn well enough. But the story is told, with variations, of other princesses than Marguerite.—Ever yours truly,

ROBERT BROWNING.

1886 : 3

To J. Dykes Campbell

19, Warwick Crescent, London, W.,
March 1, 1886.

My dear Mr. Campbell,—I will go to you next Saturday with the greatest pleasure.

I was about to thank you for the note, which I enclose, and the "psychological curiosity," such as it is, which I return also.

What weather! I was invited to visit a friend in Yorkshire this very day—the day on which, by the bye, I started for St. Petersburg many a year ago.[1] Since then a fireside has got to be dearer to me, too naturally.

My sister's kind regards go with those of yours very truly,

ROBERT BROWNING.

1886 : 4

To THOMAS J. WISE

19, Warwick Crescent,
London, W.
March 3rd, 1886.

Dear Mr. Wise,

You are certainly right, and I spoke too hastily on a very imperfect recollection, for I afterwards did remember having heard that some such poem[1] was in existence. "Hope End" was built as well as inhabited by Mr. Barrett, and the other circumstances mentioned in your letter are conclusive enough.

Believe me, dear Mr. Wise,

Yours very sincerely,

ROBERT BROWNING.

As for the early editions of Shelley. They were obtained for me some time before 1830 (or even earlier) in the *regular way,* from Hunt and Clarke, in consequence of a direction I obtained from the *Literary Gazette.* I still possess *Posthumous Poems,* but have long since parted with *Prometheus Unbound, Rosalind* and *Helen, Six Weeks' Tour, Cenci,* and the *Adonais.*[2] I got at the same time nearly, *Endymion* and *Lamia,* &c., just as if they had been purchased a week before, and not years after the death of Keats![3]

1886 : 5

To THOMAS J. WISE

19, Warwick Crescent,
W.
March 10. '86,

Dear Mr. Wise,

I would be glad to oblige you, were it in my power, with respect to the little book[1]—but I have given away one of the copies already to a friend of mine,[2] and must keep the other for my son,—who expects me to think of him in such a case.

With all thanks for your kind interest, believe me,

Yours very truly

ROBERT BROWNING.

1886 : 6

TO DR. F. J. FURNIVALL

19, Warwick Crescent,
London, W.
May 12th, 1886.

My dear Furnivall,

Congratulations, first and foremost, on your victory of Monday[1]—and your smart letter in the *Pall Mall,* the day before. In each case the "scull" has been well employed, and whether better employed in "rōwing" or "rŏwing" is a moot point.

Next, I am heartily glad if my little word of appreciation gave any pleasure to the lady we are so much indebted to. You see the charge of inflicting boundless *ennui* on the audience is insisted on in the *World* —"It shall to the barber's with the critic's beard: he's for a jig or, &c., or he sleeps"—I daresay.

By the way, you spoke of making use of my *Essay* for the Society, and also of the little poem. If you can do any good with the *Cenciaja* it is at your service, of course.

I am ashamed at the objection taken by some of the critics to the Eve-like simplicity of Pen's peasant-girl, who before going on to saintliness (which the Church still withholds from her) was satisfied with the proverbially next step to it—cleanliness.[2] If they knew anything of Joan's habits even when advanced in her saintly career, they would remember she was no prude by any means. Her favoured young cavalier, the Duc d' Alençon, mentions that he had frequently seen her undress, and that "aliquando videbat ejus mammas quae pulchrae erant"—in his very words.

Ever truly yours,

ROBERT BROWNING.

1886 : 7

To Dr. F. J. Furnivall

> 19, Warwick Crescent,
> W.
> May 25. '86.

My dear Furnivall,

You are quite at liberty to make the use you mention of "Pauline"[1] —taking care that it is no infraction of the copyright,—as indeed it can hardly be. Don't give me a single copy "for my friends"—but keep them for the more than friendly subscribers to the Society.

I don't understand what Mrs Dall can mean by saying that "Sordello" has been "re-written": I did certainly at one time intend to re-write much of it,—but changed my mind,—and the edition which I reprinted was the same in all respects as its predecessor—only with an elucidatory heading to each page, and some few alterations, presumably for the better, in the text—such as occur in most of my works: I cannot remember a single instance of any importance that is "re-written"—and I only suppose that Mrs Dall has taken project for performance, and set down as "done" what was for a while intended to be done.

Well cycled, you and your worthy son both! All congratulations from

> Yours truly ever
> ROBERT BROWNING.

1886 : 8

To Edmund Gosse

> 19, Warwick Crescent,
> W.
> June 1st, 1886.

My dear Gosse,

For very many reasons I would most readily and gladly go to you this evening, late or early. But consider my case! At 8 I dine to meet an American family who leave England to-morrow. This is in Hans Place, and thence I am bound to go to the Rallis' entertainment, who bring over the Coquelins for their friends. What chance of doing what I wish with all my heart I could do? I believe you will understand me in this matter; that the admirable and beloved Autocrat[1] will also understand that the loss of any opportunity of seeing him during his stay here is regarded by me—as by every one privileged to know him —in the light of a great misfortune—of *that,* I am certain. Pray tell him the substance of so much. And believe me ever, my dear Gosse,

Yours truly,

ROBERT BROWNING.

1886 : 9

To W. W. Story

19, Warwick Crescent, W.
June 19, '86

My dear Story,

I received last night the packet of M.S.—all thanks to your kindness. Had I mustered courage enough to look at the originals—undisturbed in their repose of fourteen years since I copied them for you—I should probably have given neither you nor myself further trouble in the matter—but my memory was hazy as to the precise charge which I intended they should meet—and fancied they were more than what they prove to be—a simple answer to the assertion (if it was really made) that I had been making endeavours to renew a relation of even ordinary acquaintance, instead of resisting cajoleries and pathetic appeals, for two years together, that I should do so. As bearing upon the writer's veracity this was evidence enough. And even with respect to the calumnies which Lady A.[1] exploded in all the madness of her wounded vanity—I was not aware at that time of what I have had abundant knowledge of since—how thoroughly her character as a calumniator was understood by those most intimately connected with her—and how little credit would be given to assertions of this sort in my case. I retained exactly as much as I was disposed to value of the esteem and attention of every one of our common friends and acquaintance,—and in two instances—when I chose to volunteer an explanation of the causes of my feeling with regard to her,—I found that her nearest relatives had undergone precisely similar treatment. One of these,—whom I only became acquainted with a few years ago,— told me she herself had been treated as—and called to her face—"a thief." There would seem therefore little use in casting about for means of defence against such a charge from such a person—*posthumous,* as her cowardice would take care that it should be. I shall nevertheless abide by your advice, and retain the original letters—giving such directions for their ultimate disposal as you very properly suggest, and indeed as I had always intended. So, enough of an odious experience—which had, however, the effect of enabling you and Mrs. Story to prove yourselves effectually and admirably my friends, as there is no need that I should gratefully acknowledge now.

Last week, my sister was on the point of going to Paris—where Milsand is unhappily far from well. My own engagements would not allow me to leave with her, but I was to fetch her back in a week. On the evening before her departure she had a severe return of the inflammatory attack which she suffered from two years ago. By prompt remedies the danger was averted—and she is convalescent, though weakened by ten days spent in bed. She is to get up for half an hour, this morning. Pen who was to have accompanied her to Boulogne, stayed till we had assurance that he might do so without apprehension. He left on Sunday for Dinant. "Our Palace"² will belong to us in due form, if there be any justice in the law-courts whither the case is relegated. My lawyer has no doubt of the event. He considered that I paid too much for the property and that as the Vendors' conduct "left them bound but myself free" I might preferably get a better bargain elsewhere—hence his hesitation to proceed against the Montecuccoli who, moreover, if I withdrew from the agreement, would no doubt intreat me to fulfil the same. But I decided to try conclusions with these "mascalzoni," and the proper "citazione" has been issued, and my advocate selected. The delay will be tiresome, as the Montecuccoli are entitled to some forty days' grace, when a Venetian could claim a week only, or thereabouts. Moreover these people know that, whenever they please to take it, my money is waiting—meanwhile they collect the rents from the existing tenants. I leave myself no room for such news as are at hand. It is bitterly cold here—beyond example in June. I will give your message to Lowell, whom I saw two days since,—and shall see next week at Oxford, where Jowett's vice chancellorship ends in a festive bouquet of fireworks at Commemoration—wherein a degree will be conferred on Dr. Holmes—whom I have seen much of lately. Mrs. Bronson and Edith are here enjoying themselves and greatly adding to our enjoyment. They too go to Oxford. The Curtis family will be here presently, I am glad to say. They were at Amsterdam when I heard last. You know the strange turmoil of politics in which we are engaged just now, and which will be intensified in a week or two. I met Gladstone at dinner the day after his defeat—and never saw him in higher

spirits. I am dead against him, however. All true love to you both—
from

yours affectionately ever,
R B.

1886 : 10

To Thomas J. Wise

19, Warwick Crescent, W.
July 6. '86,

My dear Mr. Wise,

I hardly know what you may be thinking of my negligence and indeed want of common gratitude: but when I tell you how it has happened that your kind present has been so long unacknowledged I feel
sure that I shall right myself in your eyes. My Sister has been dangerously ill,—is only just convalescent: and while our anxiety was at the
height, I conjecture by the date of your letter which accompanied the
parcel, the parcel itself was laid away, with several others, for subsequent examination, for I supposed it was an ordinary book. Judge of
my confusion when I find that the present was so valuable, and yours
beside. I can only thank you exceedingly, and assure you that, on every
account, I trust that no communication from you, of whatever the
nature, will be kept waiting thus unworthily a second time.

If it really *does* interest you to have my statement "in black and
white," I willingly repeat that to the best of my belief no single copy
of the original edition of *Pauline* found a buyer; the book was undoubtedly "stillborn,"—and that despite the kindly offices of many
friends, who did their best to bring about a successful birth.

Believe me, with repeated thanks,

Dear Mr. Wise,
Yours very sincerely
Robert Browning.

1886 : 11

To Dr. F. J. Furnivall

July 20th, 1886.

My dear Furnivall,

In the Royalist rhymes entitled *Vanity of Vanities,* or *Sir Harry*

Vane's Picture, wherein Vane is charged with being a Jesuit, occur these lines:—

> *" 'Tis said they will give him a Cardinal's hat*
> *They sooner will give him an old nun's twat!"*

The ballad is partly quoted in the Appendix to Forster's *Life of Vane,* but the above lines are left out. I remember them, however, and the word struck me as a distinctive part of a nun's attire that might fitly pair off with the cowl appropriated to a monk.[1] To "twattle" was used for "tattle" sometimes—as in Croxhall's *Fables,* where the birds that object to carrying the tortoise who is to hold a stick in his mouth, do so because "he will be twattling"—and let it go thereby.

Ever truly yours,

ROBERT BROWNING.

1886 : 12

To J. DYKES CAMPBELL

19, Warwick Crescent, W.,
August 8th, '86.

My dear Mr. Dykes Campbell,—I ought to have earlier (by a little) apprised you of my sister's returning health and strength. She only needs the tonic of fresh air, and we propose going in a day or two for what good may be gotten at Llangollen—near which place we have friends. There must be no such adventure for us, this year, as we have undertaken again and again in the autumn, and it is very doubtful if, later, the customary visit to Venice can be paid: we shall see, however. You know there is a spoke in Fortune's wheel as regards the Palazzo, and that I am forced to take legal means of obliging the late owners to receive the purchase money which was duly transmitted six months ago; they apparently continue to collect the rents of the people who reside there, knowing that, when needs must, they can take my money and go off so much the better by their rascality. My lawyer conjectures that the other members of this noble family will plead that their representative, the vendor, had not the requisite authority he alleged in our agreement—in other words, was punishable under the criminal rather than the civil law. We shall soon see,— "soon" for an Italian Court of Justice, where suits are all but interminable.

I wish your account of Mrs. Campbell were altogether satisfactory, and that you had no need to leave the retreat you enjoy so much: we also are advised that a dose of sea-air might be advantageous bye-and-bye. You must send no roses, to die in our rooms with closed shutters, —but my sister gratefully accepts the will for the deed.

I congratulate you on what must be an extraordinary godsend—that little book of Beddoes': I never saw it.[1] Who knows but "the Box" may hold it? When I return here (say at the end of September) you shall have box and its contents at your own house, and examine the latter to heart's content.[2] Meanwhile and ever, dear Mr. Dykes Campbell, believe me, with all regards to Mrs. Campbell, in which my sister participates cordially, yours truly ever,

ROBERT BROWNING.

1886 : 13

To THOMAS J. WISE

19, Warwick Crescent,
London, W.
August 8th, 1886.

Dear Mr. Wise,

I really have said my little say about the little book[1] elsewhere, and should only increase words without knowledge. An introductory sentence or two of your own will be better in every way.

There was a note of explanation in the copy I gave John Forster—which contained also a criticism by John Mill. It is not included in the Catalogue of his books, however,—but may turn up, some day.[2]

Believe me, Dear Mr. Wise,
Yours very sincerely,
ROBERT BROWNING.

1886 : 14

To LAWRENCE BARRETT

North Wales
Aug. 17, '86.

My dear Mr. Lawrence Barrett:—

I got your letter with its enclosure at this pretty place where I am staying for as many weeks as the weather will allow—my sister was dangerously ill in the summer, so as to prevent our usual journey abroad,—she is comparatively well now—this hinders me from sending you at once the portrait you care to have, and the book too: as soon as I return, I will forward you whatever face of me seems fittest to look at you from your library table; and, I think the book shall be this one I am just engaged upon, which ought to be my best. In any case, book and face will go to one whose friendship I shall ever be proud of, whether I am destined to enjoy it many years or few. Now the Play which caused me much disappointment and vexation half a century ago, or thereabouts, has compensated me a hundred times over by your association with it; and the knowledge I have gained of a character which its very qualities stop me from attempting to eulogize. My dear friend, if you can indeed come to England next year, it will delight me to see you, if that may be; whether or no, my truest wishes will accompany you. How other than a thoroughly successful career should one noble as yours become or rather continue?

Ever yours cordially,
ROBERT BROWNING

1886 : 15

TO DR. F. J. FURNIVALL

Hand Hotel,
Llangollen, N. Wales.
September 6th, 1886.

My dear Furnivall,

I had thought to say something before this of our stay here, and the good effect it continues to have on my sister's health—but the object of this letter is different indeed. I should be sorry if you heard incidentally from another than myself that my friend Milsand died two days ago—on the 4th, at his place, Villers la Faye, in the Cote d'Or. We had been long aware of his declining health; and the last letter, of August 28, spoke of increasing bodily weakness, "the head remaining strong." We were unprepared for what has followed so fast, and which we are apprised of by a telegram this morning.

It is due to your kindness to say this much.

Ever truly yours,
ROBERT BROWNING.

1886 : 16

To Dr. F. J. Furnivall

Hand Hotel,
Llangollen, N. Wales.
September 12th, 1886.

My dear Furnivall,

Often enough, or too much, you have said kind things of me, done kind things to me, and if I have not in every case straightway told you how I was impressed by your kindness it has been through a confidence that you would understand easily how, while feeling much, one seems to need little speaking. This time, however, you have so thrilled me through with gratitude for your notice of Milsand that I am as willing as able to thank you from my heart. You did all I could wish in the way of sobriety and succinctness as well as adequate recognition and handsome appreciation—adequate for the "public"—who will never know what only an intimate of thirty-five years knows and never will attempt to put into words. Your notice was so excellently devised, you see, that *The Times* at once transferred it to its columns, so giving it all the circulation desirable. I sent it to Ma^de Milsand, and others will of course see what they would have probably missed. I do not "inform" you that Milsand liked you greatly, little as was the intercourse between you permitted by circumstances—your own penetration and sympathy must have divined that.

Truest thanks once again and always from

Yours affectionately,
ROBERT BROWNING.

1886 : 17

To Thomas J. Wise

19, Warwick Crescent,
W.
Oct. 24, '86

Dear Mr. Wise,

I have again to thank you, and very sincerely, for your Shelley Gift-Books. I am only just returned to Town, or this kind attention of yours would have been earlier acknowledged, but no book-parcels were forwarded to me.

Ever truly yours
ROBERT BROWNING.

1886 : 18

To Thomas J. Wise

> 19, Warwick Crescent,
> London, W.
> November 5th, 1886.

Dear Mr. Wise,

I do not require to see the "Proofs,"[1] which no doubt you have kindly supervised.

The "King"[2] is Agamemnon, in the Tragedy of that name by Æschylos, whose treading the purple carpets spread before him by his wife, preparatory to his murder, is a notable passage. "The boy"[3] is Orestes, as described at the end of the *Choephoroi,* by the same Author.

V.A.XX.[4] is the Latin abbreviation of *Vixi Annos*—"I was twenty years old"—that is, the imaginary subject of the poem was of that age.

> In haste, but
> > Yours very truly,
> > > Robert Browning.

1886 : 19

To Walter B. Slater

> 19, Warwick Crescent,
> London, W.
> November 6th, 1886.

Dear Mr. Slater,

I "remember your existence"—as also your kindness—very well indeed, and will answer your questions to the best of my ability.

The Book[1] which I return is an example of the practices of Thomas Powell, its original owner, which consisted in affecting to forge, in sport, the signatures of his acquaintance in order to subsequently induce the belief, when his serious forgeries should be discovered, that he was simply a monomaniac on the matter of an irresistible itch at imitating other folks' writing—which he did only too adroitly, as the Mercantile Firm which employed him found by experience. The signatures in the present case are very like indeed—although with, to my eye, a discernible difference—a slight one, certainly. He was well acquainted with all the persons supposed to have written on the fly-leaf, and had letters &c. from each of them. My own hand-writing has, no doubt, changed somewhat in the course of years, and at the time when I knew Powell, much resembled what you see intended for it. He was forced to fly the country, thereby avoiding the punishment he richly deserved—and he may still be alive for aught I know. He at once, on arriving in America, wrote a description of his "literary friends." This I never saw, but was assured, at the time, that it was a sort of revenge on every one of them for being of good repute,—a tissue of lies, in short. This precious farrago was referred to, in *The Academy,* a short while since, as containing "notable information respecting my wife which deserved the notice it had not found in the article just out in the new *Biographical Dictionary":* the fact being that he never saw her in his life, nor had any other means of informing himself than by what he could glean from her correspondence with Mr. Horne, on purely literary subjects. Dickens exposed the poor fellow at the time—myself was abroad. Thus you have all I can well communicate on a disagreeable subject.

By the way, the last letter I ever received from Powell, with whom I had ceased to hold intercourse, was impudently written throughout as if by the brother of Dickens, Henry, long since dead—that is, since that time.

Believe me, dear Mr. Slater,

Yours very sincerely,

ROBERT BROWNING.

1886 : 20

To JOHN H. INGRAM

19, Warwick Crescent,
London, W.
November 24th, 1886.

Dear Mr. Ingram,

You write very kindly, and I am sorry indeed that I shall disappoint you—unable as I am to comply with any one of your requests. I have given all the help I was entitled to do, on the occasion of the Memoir of Mrs. Ritchie[1]—a distant kinswoman of my wife, and one who knew her a little in old days. I engaged to verify any dates she had furnished, and I did so—no more. Only those are to be depended upon if you resolve "to use printed material."

The "two or three dozen ladies" who volunteered (I can well believe) to compose a biography would have achieved the feat "out of their inner consciousness," and the printed material aforesaid.

One authority you mention, that of Powell, I have purposely avoided knowing or hearing about. This person was a consummate rascal, who but for the leniency of his employers would have been transported for his enormous forgeries on their name. He obtained credit with Talfourd, who introduced him to various friends and myself, on the ground of his contributions to the necessity of poor Leigh Hunt, and his civilities to Wordsworth and Dickens. On taking refuge in America he at once published an account of his "Contemporaries," among which I figure; the single instance of his veracity that has been reported to me being that "all my love poems were written to a portrait of my grandmother" that he had seen in my house. As this literary abortion had never in his life seen my wife, and could only have got any intelligence concerning her from Horne, who also had never seen her till after her marriage and in my company— I conclude the "quality of lying is not strained" in this particular case, but "droppeth" as should the wringings of a felon brain for the sake of a dollar.

You will therefore use your own discretion as to making any new use of the "facts" already in existence; I have no right to hinder you or anybody. But it *may* happen, as adverse things will, that I shall myself, on compulsion, endeavour as briefly as possible to substitute fact for fiction—since I possess several hundred letters and documents which alone could help me abundantly.

Yours very truly,

ROBERT BROWNING.

1886 : 21

To PROFESSOR EDWARD DOWDEN

19, Warwick Crescent,
W.
November 27th, 1886.

Dear Mr. Dowden,

Your kind intention has been carried into effect, and I got this moment your two beautiful books; no work will interest me so much. It will take time, I am glad to think, before I can possess all the contents. I will not delay a moment, therefore, but thank you most heartily at once.

It is long since I saw you. If you ever revisit London, will you not apprise me? I trust all goes well with you, that Mrs. Dowden (whom I by no means have forgotten) finds life as I would wish.

My sister, who remembers also, begs to send her true regards to both, with those of,

Dear Mr. Dowden,
Yours truly ever,
ROBERT BROWNING.

1886 : 22

To Dr. F. J. Furnivall

19, Warwick Crescent,
London, W.
December 13th, 1886.

My dear Furnivall,

I return Alma Murray's letter with great regret that she should have been obliged to write it. Tell her how sensible I am of her good-will in the matter, and how thoroughly she is justified in not attempting an impossibility.

Do not you think this is a very proper occasion for postponing the representation?[1]

You see the judicious remarks of the Critic in this morning's *Daily News:* not a doubt as to whether the bankrupt management of that day did what was requisite for the success of the piece, whether the wretched acting of the inferior people might not have done harm (a stone-deaf Charles, a silly, simpering Carlisle, &c.), and whether the management "that dressed the Scots Commissioners in kilts" might not refuse, as it did, "one rag for the new piece." The only conclusion to draw is that a play which did not obtain the enthusiastic praise of the critics *then,* cannot deserve a better fate *now,* under quite other conditions. I would strongly advise that you run no such risk, but let a thing which has so long lain dormant, sleep a little longer. Of course I do not know what the engagements are, and whether it is not too late to recede, but surely with the loss of Alma Murray goes the last chance of a gratifying result.

In haste, but ever truly yours,

ROBERT BROWNING.

1887 : 1

To Thomas J. Wise[1]

> 19, Warwick Crescent,
> London, W.
> January 8th, 1887.

Dear Mr. Wise,—

I have seldom met with such a strange inability to understand what seems the plainest matter possible: "ball-goers" are probably not history readers, but any Guide-book would confirm what is sufficiently stated in the poem. I will append a note or two, however.

Yes,—thank you—I am completely myself again—as I was *not,* unfortunately, when you so kindly called, a fortnight or more ago. I hope you will repeat your visit, and believe me,

> Yours very sincerely
> ROBERT BROWNING.

1. "This story the townsmen tell": "when, how, and where," constitute the subject of the poem.

2. The lady was the wife of the Riccardi, and the Duke—Ferdinand —just as the poem says

3. As it[2] was built by, and inhabited by the Medici till sold, long after, to the Riccardi,—it was not from the Duke's Palace, but a window in that of the Riccardi,[3] that the lady gazed at her lover riding by. The statue is still in its place, looking at the window under which "now is the empty shrine." Can anything be clearer? My "vagueness" leaves *what* to be "gathered" when all these things are put down in black and white? Oh, "ball-goers"!

1887 : 2

To Thomas J. Wise

> 19, Warwick Crescent,
> W.
> Jan. 8. '87.

Dear Mr. Wise,

Since I wrote the hasty answer to the enquiry in your letter, this morning, I had the curiosity to refer to the "Handbook" of Mrs. Orr in order to see whether the information I had just given was not to be found there. All and every particular to the minutest are given with the greatest care and preciseness: and I think the author's pains have been altogether thrown away if every idle "ball-goer" requires instruction which is already abundantly in reach. If you will consult the book at pages 205–6 you will feel that it is useless to go on informing people for whom the information has been long ago furnished as completely as possible.

Yours very sincerely
ROBERT BROWNING.

1887 : 3

To Thomas J. Wise

19, Warwick Crescent,
W.
Jan. 19. '87.

Dear Mr. Wise,

It is very kind of Mr Kingsland to reprint his Lecture[1] and very generous of you to guarantee his immunity from any expense the publication may entail. As for me, I am most happy to allow as many extracts from my poetry as he pleases to make—a very trifling reward of his constant goodness.

Ever truly yours
ROBERT BROWNING.

1887 : 4

To a Correspondent[1]

19, Warwick Crescent,
London, W.
February 10th, 1887.

Dear Sir,

I am quite sure you mean very kindly, but I have had too long an experience of the inability of the human goose to do other than cackle when benevolent, and hiss when malicious; and no amount of goose criticism shall make me lift a heel at what waddles behind it.

Believe me, Dear Sir,
Very sincerely,
ROBERT BROWNING.

1887 : 5

To Dr. F. J. Furnivall

19, Warwick Crescent,
London, W.
March 4th, 1887.

My dear Furnivall,

Don't trouble yourself about Smart on my account—unnecessarily, since, after nearly fifty years, I remember the whole pretty well. I think it was the reprint in Chambers that I saw—not in Chalmers; indeed I am sure of it, although I discovered it there on an occasion that would excuse much mistiness in my memory. Depend upon it, no goody-goody writer ever conceived or executed the stanzas I could repeat—as I did, with all the effect I supposed would follow—to people of authority enough: Tennyson, the present Bishop of London, and, last year to Wendell Holmes, who had asked me innocently at Oxford, "whether I knew the wonderful poem."[1] Weak passages there undoubtedly are, but the strong ones are decisive as to Smart's power and right of place. You hear what Rossetti thought and said; I was not aware of it.

I am surprised at an edition appearing so early as in 1819; that which I bought professed to be just out some years later.

"O Lyric Love."

"Human"—so as to be *ready,* at the first summons to general service, to drop down &c.; the *readiness* implied as a necessary quality of the humanity.

Ever yours,
Robert Browning.

1887 : 6

To W. G. Kingsland

19, Warwick Crescent,
London, W.
March 17th, 1887.

My dear Kingsland,

How can I be other than most grateful to you for your generous belief in me?—unwarranted as it may be by anything I have succeeded in doing, although somewhat justified perhaps by what I would fain have done if I could. But it is now a long time indeed since I have been assured of your sympathy, and proud of your friendship.

As for the book[1]—it seems to me sufficiently pretty on the outside to require no "large paper" or other enhancement of its attractiveness. I have no doubt that whoever reads it will be the more disposed to think favorably of my general writings: your extracts are calculated to excite interest in the poems of which they are such good samples. You know how happy I shall be to see you.

Meantime, and always, remember me as

Yours affectionately,
ROBERT BROWNING.

1887 : 7

To J. Dykes Campbell

19, Warwick Crescent, W.,
March 30, '87.

My dear Mr. Dykes Campbell, (if your kindness will permit me to drop the more formal prelude of a letter), there seems nothing to object to in what you please to have written. The book (Rosalind and Helen) was lent to Eliza Flower (Lizzie) who managed to lose it, as described[1]—and very likely in the course of the excursion described by Fox—the "someone," who thus noted the circumstance. It was through the intervention of Miss Flower,—a very remarkable person, —that I became known to Mr. Fox in my childhood or just emerging from it.—Yours very truly,

ROBERT BROWNING.

1887 : 8

To the Storys

19, Warwick Crescent, W.
Apr. 4, '87

Dear Friends, I got the letter of which I enclose a copy, two days ago, under the following circumstances. A Mr. Shortall, of Chicago,—with whom I had some correspondence last year concerning the representation there of one of my plays by an amateur company,—wrote to me, last week, to say he was just arrived in London and about to depart thence, but wished first to see me for a few minutes. I replied I should be happy to see him, and on Friday he called accordingly,—a pleasant kindly person. He had—you will observe—no need of anybody's intervention on his behalf. The writer of the letter I subjoin chose to address me in the way you will see; and I think it due to you—hardly necessary as it may be—to show how far impudence can go. Pray do not even reply to this recurrence of mine to a hateful subject—but as you have so lately looked over the letters etc. of Lady Ashburton,[1] you may as well know how the chief agent in that business professes to feel for me whom she slandered. Of course, I never have said a word about her to Lady Marian—whom indeed I have only met once, at poor Houghton's, since I saw her in your rooms at London, as you remember, when Lady A. "tried on" conciliation—not quite with such effrontery however.

Although this is no letter-proper, only a brief notice I think necessary, I cannot help sweetening the page by mentioning that Pen writes in warm terms of Julian's picture for the Salon,—full of cleverness, he says. I trust you are both well. Our winter has been abominable, and I found myself decidedly the worse for the want of my customary dose of the divine Italian air.

Ever affectionately yours
ROBERT BROWNING.

[Copied by Robert Browning]

Copy

Churchside
Denmark Hill
March 31 [1887]

My dear Friend,

Here comes a very affectionate ghost from the Past. This ghost, however, has very often been with you in spirit though absent in shadow, and it was glad you had not forgotten her,—as Lady Marian assured her not long since, your enquiries proved. Now she is coming in the flesh to explain its long seclusion. In the meantime, pray smile kindly upon my friend Mr. Shortall who presents you this, and believe that I am as always

Affectionately yours
HATTY HOSMER

1887 : 9

To Edmund Gosse

19, Warwick Crescent,
W.
June 4th, 1887.

My dear Gosse,

Many thanks for the very interesting notice,[1] which I return.

Mr. Harvey's[2] derivation of "crusion" from κροῦσις is absurd,—the word meaning simply a "knocking"—he must have meant χρυσίον— "a bit of gold"—and the connection with "silverlings" probably came from Smart's having in mind the Greek equivalent for our phrase "silver and gold"—ἀργύριον καὶ χρυσίον: they were likely to express χ by c—not ch.

Ever truly yours,
ROBERT BROWNING.

1887 : 10

To Robert Barrett Browning

Villa Berry, St. Moritz, Aug. 19. '87.

Dearest Pen,—I waited for the letter in reply to my last,—which I knew would be on the way,—before answering the more important one—which took me by surprise indeed,—but a very joyful surprise. I think you could not do a wiser, better thing than marry the in every way suitable lady whom you have been fortunate enough to induce to take such a step, and who, you are bound to feel, behaves with the utmost generosity. You know very well I have never had any other aim than your happiness in all I have done: the kind of life you have been forced to lead for these last years always seemed comfortless and even dangerous to me,—whatever might be said for it as helpful to your art (and *that* it no doubt was)—you must know it had lasted long enough for the purpose, and could not, in the nature of things, continue as you advance in years: "no home"—is sad work,—and with a home, and *such* a home as [with] *such* a wife as yours will be, your further progress will be infinitely more easy and rapid. I do approve of your choice with all my heart: there is no young person I know at all comparable to Miss C.[1] She has every requisite to make you happy and successful, if you deserve it—as I believe you will endeavour to do. If the lady had been unknown to me,—or one of the innumerable pleasant parties to a flirtation and utterly useless for anything else, I should have given you up for lost. As it is, you are just at the time of life when you may "take a fresh departure" with the greatest advantage. You can bring all your acquired Continental knowledge to bear on an English enterprise: take a house and studio here, and try what may be done when your work may have the chances which you never yet enjoyed—of being seen, as you produce them, in your own Studio, with the advantage of acquaintance with all the artists you care to know. Miss C. has spoken to me with the greatest frankness and generosity of the means she will have of contributing to your support—for my part, I can engage to give you £300 a year: this, with the results of your work—if you manage to sell but a single picture in the year—will amply suffice. Of course, at my death you will have whatever I possess: and meantime if any good fortune comes to me—well, it will be, as it ever has been, your good fortune also.

I write very temperately about all this—but it makes me really happy—as I should not be, if I doubted you would not do your utmost to deserve such a blessing as God seems disposed to give you: may He bless you, I pray from my heart.

Ever affectionately yours
ROBERT BROWNING.

It is hardly worth while, just now, to discuss the merits of the subject I suggested. You do not see that you must accept the "données"—the story as told by Homer. He "gives you" a Goddess of human appearance, only greater and stronger than human, though not so much so as to be impossible: for instance, in the same battle, Diomede *wounds* this Goddess in the wrist, and sends her shrieking away. A hero might be made of smaller proportions than such a being, and yet not "puny" at all. But enough on this point. I told you Bellot had sent me his Bill, which I returned with a Cheque,—desiring him to send me a receipt: he has done so. Would it be worth while to write and ask if he has received it?

[*Continued by Sarianna Browning*]

Dearest Pen,

I am very happy indeed to think you are going to be married. Hôtel life is very comfortless as well as very expensive, and you have now had quite enough of it. You will not, I trust, work less well for having a happy home. I am sure I shall be very fond of Fannie, and altogether approve of your choice. This afternoon I went over to her, and we had a long talk. She is very different from the fast American girls who abound here. You have every prospect of happiness—God bless you. The weather has changed to sharp cold. We have had thunder-storms, sleet, snow on the mountains, and an earthquake, though I was not fortunate enough to perceive it. Mrs. Moore's stay here is uncertain; her daughter has been worse, and to-day she has sent her away to a warmer place: probably she may soon follow. Your papa is so well here that I am anxious to remain as long as possible. We both of us like the bracing air. Mr. Natorp complains that it does not agree with him, yet he stays on at the big hôtel where he says the food is very bad, chiefly for the sake of the dancing which is constantly going on there. The C.s are at a nice quiet hôtel.

Ever your affectionate
Sarianna.

1887 : 11

To Dr. F. J. Furnivall

Villa Berry,
St. Moritz, Switzerland.
August 21st, 1887.

What do you think, dear Cyclist? We are "snowed up" this morning; cannot leave our house to go to the Hotel opposite, close by, where we get our meals! Such is Alpine treatment of travellers! Our amends is in the magnificence of the mountain, and its firs black against the universal white. The natives assure us that this little summer-interlude only heralds a particularly fine September; and so it may, let us hope, for both my sister and myself have greatly benefited by our month's stay in these altitudes.

So you, for your part, have managed to enhance the enjoyment of your holiday by an overset—damaged wrist, and so forth! When I read in a newspaper that an adventurous somebody had chosen to skate down a steep incline and break his neck, I thought of Dr. Furnivall literally riding his hobby to death, and ruining the Browning Society—a climax only equalled by one I had from the mouth of my old piano-forte master, Abel: said he "Yes, I am in love; it destroys my appetite, interferes with my sleep, and considerably breaks in upon my practising."

But to brighter matters. I had not been here a week before I was altogether my old self with perhaps an addition; quite well: and my sister, who needed rest and change far more than I, profited conspicuously. We had three perfect weeks of blue sky and living air; last Sunday the weather broke up, but mended next day. Some days ago we were surprised by an earthquake, so those say who felt it past mistake, and they are in such a number that one cannot doubt it, I suppose. To-day comes exactly such a snow-storm as I happened to read of this morning in the *Iliad,* the only book I brought with me; but Homer expressly makes it fall on a winter's day, while we are in mid-August. I shall stay, I hope, a week or two longer.

Oh, for your subject—the young lady stripping for humanity's sake, or rather that of the Blue-Ribbon Cause.[1] Really it is not versifiable—sufficient to the deed is the prose description thereof. Besides, since she could swim a mile with ease, the reward of the feat was surely in itself during the hot weather of last month:

> *"Accoutred as she was not, plunging in,*
> *She watered, so to speak, the boatman's gin."*

The days glide away uneventfully, *nearly,* and I breathe in the pleasant idleness at every pore. I have no few acquaintances here—nay, some old friends—but my intimates are the firs on the hill-side, and the myriad butterflies all about it, every bright wing of them under the snow to-day, which ought not to have been for a fortnight yet. Moral: flutter out your own life while you can, and don't crush it with the "wheels"!

My sister sends a cordial greeting, and I am

Ever affectionately yours,
ROBERT BROWNING.

1887 : 12

To Dr. F. J. FURNIVALL

Villa Berry,
St. Moritz, Switzerland.
August 30th, 1887.

My dear Furnivall,

You forget that I know nothing of Brown or of his book.[1] All I take for granted is that he is poor and meritorious in his endeavours, whatever may be the worth of his attainment—on the strength of which knowledge I will at once write and press his claims, if you will be kind enough to state them succinctly: his age, condition, experiences in life, literary labours, and the fruit of it all, such as it is—which *you* can do, and I cannot by any means. Let me have such a summary of work done, and I will let Lytton have it "with what flourishes I may"; Lytton, the intended backer-up of my petition, being altogether as ignorant on the subject as I. If we simply prayed "Give Brown a sum of money," we should be "sure to be despised."

I did not think of the mere feat of the lady when I wrote; is it so wonderful? I think I could have managed it once upon a time, but I gave up swimming because of a peculiar affection of the throat—real strangulation—if the salt water got into it; and I rather aimed at long continuance in the sea, than going away from shore. Pen could have performed the feat with ease. But I thought your, approbation went to the fact that Miss MacNaughten stripped and swam to win over a sottish fellow to leave his bestiality, and I hold that if he were unamenable to the ordinary reasons why he should cease to make a beast of himself, his life was not worth saving at any price; and I, for my part, would have refused "accoutred as I was, to plunge in"—unless I bade him follow, sure that he would go to the bottom. Such a fellow, after exacting such a sacrifice, would be sure to get drunk the next day on the strength of his having made a fool of her.

Our weather is glorious. I shall probably move off in a week to Raugatz, but—Here is an interruption, a visitor, "but none in the affection I bear to" (old style, wanting to us moderns!)

Kind genial paper, that you sent me!

Ever yours,
ROBERT BROWNING.

1887 : 13

To Miss Fannie Coddington

[September, 1887.]

Dearest Fannie,—all I can say is, I trust I shall have you for a Daughter. You must know I love you as one. All love to dear Marie also—from

Yours ever affectionately
R B.

I have a delightful letter from Miss Sewell which I will acknowledge to-morrow.

1887 : 14

To Mrs. Henry Schlesinger

Villa Berry, St. Moritz.
Sept. 9. '87.

Dear Mrs Schlesinger,

I got your kindest of letters this moment, and make haste to say how grateful I am for your sympathy and that of Mr Schlesinger and your whole family, of which I have been duly informed,—and I am apprised also of all the invaluable help you have so generously offered to the young people[1]—which I know they appreciate as it deserves.

Few things could have surprised me more than the proposed marriage—nothing in the world could delight me more thoroughly. I have had fortunately an opportunity of becoming acquainted with Fannie and her Sister during their stay here,—and, knowing as I do the nature and disposition of Pen, I can say with all confidence that I never have fallen in with a person more qualified to make him happy. I believe he is fully aware of his good fortune, and will endeavour to deserve it. The prospect of his and Fannie's taking up their abode near me seems too good to be true—but I am confident of Fannie's excellent sense, and will hope for what so lately appeared to be impossible. In all this, I speak for my Sister as well as myself: she has always, from first to last, been devoted to Pen's interests—and consequently is very happy in this realization of her warmest wishes.

We leave here next Monday, and hope to get home by Thursday E^g. A letter from Fannie, received along with yours (delayed in London) tells us—(what probably you know from herself) that she leaves to-day for Paris, and Pen for a short visit to Venice, where he wishes to make a particular study of *sea* for a nearly-finished picture. Give something better than my formal "love"—my very real love and thanks to your Husband—and to Mary—and believe me ever Affectionately

yours
RobᵀBROWNING.

To day is the anniversary of my own wedding day! It was a deliciously fine and warm morning, I well remember: here it is raining hard and abundantly cold—the weather having broken only yesterday after a series of wonderful weeks—this being the seventh of our experience.

1887 : 15

To Miss Fannie Coddington

Hôtel de L'Univers
Jouzeau
Amiens
Sept. 15. '87.

Dearest Fannie,—on arriving at Bâle, on Tuesday E^g, I at once got your letter, of which I had been advised by the Telegram at Coire. As I shall be in London to-night, I can myself call on the Clerk at Kensington, and direct that the Banns be published next Sunday, and on the two following Sundays, as you direct. I presume that you have either communicated with the Clerk at Pembury, or will do so. I think all your arrangements excellent. I expect to find a letter from Pen on arriving in London,—there has been no time to communicate with him, nor hear from him. I write in utmost haste: we arrived after nearly 14 hours continued journeying—from Bâle to Amiens— by a longer route than we were prepared for,—but we are both quite well,—and full of hope and joy at the prospect before us. The drawback is in the illness of poor Marie,[1]—I trust—and my sister trusts— she is better. All love to you both from S. and

Yours affectionately ever
R B.

1887 : 16

To Henry Schlesinger

29, De Vere Gardens.
W.
Sept. 17. '87.

My dear Schlesinger,

We arrived here on Thursday evening, and, the next morning, I applied in person at the Vestry of St. Mary Abbotts for the publication of the Banns to-morrow, Sept. 18—and the two following Sundays. No sort of objection was made to Pen's momentary absence (which I somewhat incautiously mentioned,—not supposing it was of any moment,)—the Clerk only observing that "he would probably be back in time,"—to which I replied that he might arrive any day. The Clerk added—"You will hear the publication next Sunday if you go to Church"—and directed me to call for the Certificate on the morning of the 3ᵈ October,—I shall therefore bring it with me in the afternoon, according to Mrs Schlesinger's most kind invitation to my Sister. I heard from Pen last night, and conclude he is soon about to return. You only do justice to my feelings in believing that this event makes me—and makes my sister—happy indeed. I cannot conceive of a better, fitter wife for Pen than this choice he has been privileged to make,—one whom already I love with all my heart, as I think she knows.

And what am I to attempt to say to *you* and to your dear Wife and Daughter?—who have laid me, on this occasion, under a debt of gratitude I can never repay, but certainly will never forget.

I retain the Vicar's kind and helpful letter, in case of any quite unforeseen necessity of profiting by the advice it contains. Pray tell him how much obliged I feel by his assistance in the matter.

I wrote a few lines to Mrs Schlesinger from St. Moritz: I shall enclose a word or two to Mary. It is truly delightful to obtain such generous sympathy where I should be most desirous of its existence,—from the old and ever-valued friends I have always found in you.

My Sister's best love goes to you all with that of

Yours affectionately ever
ROBERT BROWNING.

1887 : 17

To EDMUND GOSSE

29, De Vere Gardens. W.
Oct. 8. '87.

My dear Gosse,

I am always sure of your kind sympathy and that of all your Family: this time, the circumstances warrant your liberality in the matter, which satisfies me in every way. I was altogether taken by surprise when informed, perhaps two months ago, of Pen's desire to marry— but the rest of my feelings were pleasurable indeed. He could not have chosen a wife more fitted to make him happy.

It is possible I may see you this afternoon at the Grosvenor Gallery, but I want to tell you without delay how much I feel your goodness and am ever

Gratefully yours
ROBERT BROWNING.

1887 : 18

To Mrs. Fannie Barrett Browning

29 De Vere Gardens.
W.
Oct. 10. '87.

Dearest Fannie, I shall not attempt to tell what needs no telling—
what intense delight I felt on getting your letter on Saturday evening,
—and now a second comes to my Sister, adding, if possible to our
joy. Every word that assures us of your happiness and that of Pen
which is dependent upon it is a comfort beyond expression. All that
you say of your relationship to me is what I trust you will find, so long
as I live, the strictly simple truth. Dear Marie called yesterday afternoon,—looking well, and making herself more and more lovable at
every visit. But I must speak of a few matters about which you are less
informed. I sent, in an envelope, some letters from Mrs. B. M—there
is little doubt that she has been suffering from some strange fancy, or
hallucination—from which she is recovered: what the letters contain,
I don't know: it will be for Pen to reply properly as the case may be.
Marie, as your natural Custodian, opened the packet, which produced
two pretty diamond-stars,—those, no doubt, which she had originally
intended as a present: and which, if given at once, would have saved
all the talking and writing. F. Locker, Pen's old acquaintance, sends
a quaint pretty little silver ornament (a match-box, perhaps),—apolo-
gizing for the scarcity of fit objects at Cromer, where he is staying.
Mr and Mrs F. Lehmann send an extremely useful and pretty clock:
I will enclose the kind letter which accompanied it; and which himself
must attend to. Above all, Edith Bronson has forwarded a charming
little Birthday Book in which the names occur of the Mother and
Daughter; of Ch. Forbes, Olga Ker, and other friends. Furnivall
called yesterday,—was full of kind congratulations, and saw Marie,—
I was glad of *that*. Marie dines with us alone to-day,—so your ears
will burn! I am not so conversant with news from Hawkwell[1] as she
must be,—and you will get more in her letters than in mine.

Dearest Fannie,—Your Aunt is out—on a charitable call, at Mrs.
Fitz Gerald's: but I know and you know how she loves you, and is
gladdened by the good account of yourself. Take all care that your
health continues—don't attempt too much. Pray is my minute *intimate* writing, with which I am accustomed to try Pen's eyes, too much
for yours?

Do remember me most kindly to all friends—to Mrs B.² and Edith, to the Curtis family,—to everybody, in short, and keep me ever in mind as most affectionately yours

ROBERT BROWNING

Scarcely room to put in my big love to you both. I will write to Fannie to-morrow. Love to the dear Bs.

1887 : 19

TO THE REV. J. D. WILLIAMS

29. De Vere Gardens.
W.
Oct. 21. '87.

Dear Mr. Williams,

I rather supposed that my Sister had already given Mrs Williams the particulars, few as they are, of Pen's engagement and marriage. We were altogether in ignorance of his desires until perhaps two months ago, when our quietude at St. Moritz was startled by a letter —the least expected possible—to inform me, after a good and proper fashion, of what he proposed doing—but fortunately all the rest was abundantly compensative of the startle, for we well knew the lady, and had long ago known her estimable parents—great friends of Dean Stanley, in whose company I met them first. It appears that the attachment is fourteen years old,—Pen having made up and spoken out his mind so long ago! Then came a long separation—then, only the other day, by the accident of the lady's return to England for the benefit of the health of her sister, an immediate renewal of both feeling and its expression,—whereof the end was—the letter aforesaid. Now, it happens that I could have chosen, within the circle of my acquaintance, no young person more qualified, so far as I can judge, to make Pen eminently happy—the match presenting every advantage without a single drawback: what was to be done, therefore, but accept and be thankful? Fannie, my daughter in love and law, is good, true, sympathetic in every way,—a few years younger than Pen,—very pretty, we think, very devoted to him, we know,—and having been an admirable daughter and sister will presumably become as fitting a wife. She has all the ambition for his sake which I could wish, and is eminently distinguished for common sense: so that—I repeat—how can I be other than thankful? I ought to add that the means of comfortable life are abundant in this case—indeed Pen might become independent of my own assistance, did either he or I permit of such an arrangement. The Couple are at Venice,—will return here next week, thence proceed to America, where the lady must needs settle her affairs before returning to Europe: the aftercourse, and eventual subsidence,—that I leave to their own judgment—sure that a well-weighed and all-considerate judgment there will be somehow.

Oct. 22.—I was interrupted yesterday, just where interruption came naturally—but there was more to say—first, grateful recognition of Mrs Williams' efficacity in fitting us with so good a servant as Rolph (Richard) proves himself hitherto: his quiet intelligent and obliging ways suit us perfectly, and we hope to attach him to us: he seems to wish the same thing. Of the Engadine,—well, we enjoyed the pure air and beautiful surroundings—and I, for my part, got rid in a trice of all the ugly consequences of some nine months' stay in London: our absence was shorter than we could have wished,—there was a need of looking after matters at home—our "new surroundings" wanted much supervision, and we are only now beginning to "take our ease in our Inn": it does commend itself to us more and more, and I have had not one of the usual twinges which follow a decisive measure for better or worse: I believe I have done well in a worldly sense, and made my intercourse with friends here more practicable—consequently, theirs with me: this is a direct challenge to *you,* who must put the assertion to proof, by coming to us the moment you are able. My sister will have it, your way is easier than of old,—straight, too, not circuitous. Solvitur ambulando, seu te in curriculum conjiciendo!

By the way, I have two invitations to go to Cambridge for the Greek Play,—one from the master of Trinity, the other from Mr. Stanford: I provisionally accept the hospitality of the latter,—but reserving for myself the power of staying at home, should there be some possible hindrance at the end of November,—I shall go if I can. I observe that the "Œdipus" is brought out under the auspices of Professor Kennedy   yet the text to be used is that of Jebb: now, last year I read, in Wales, the edition of the play just issued by the Professor—every one of the notes being, it would seem, an arrow directed at the edition of Jebb—somewhat perversely, I fancied. It shows magnanimity that there has been allowance on this occasion of the rival text. Mr. Stanford writes the music, which went very well in the case of the "Eumenides." No interruption, this time,—at the bottom of a page: I must put in just something of my sister's and my own gratitude to Mrs Williams, who has done such wonders for us again and yet again. She and yourself must ever remember me as

Affectionately yours
ROBERT BROWNING.

1887 : 20

To Pen and Fannie Browning

29, De Vere Gardens.
W.
Nov. 26. '87.

My dearest Fannie and dearest Pen, we were overjoyed to get the letter on Thursday night: it was thoughtful indeed to make sure of its arriving at once, unhindered perhaps by the inevitable distractions of next day's landing—about which, next letter will instruct us, and anxiously we look for it. The surprising circumstance is that the passage should have been so good—when, according to all accounts, boats crossing the same weather-line suffered greatly. It is a comfort to think that you both of you prove good sailors and will not consider future voyages as formidable as we here do. Now, what news can I give you? Poor Mrs B. M's[1] good intentions about the picture have failed lamentably—as I expected would be the case: the enthusiastic friends who were certain to want anything which had once had a place on her walls, proved for once insensible: so she transferred the picture to the Hanover Gallery—where a purchaser would be found at once: after a fortnight's trial in vain, back comes the picture, "by Mrs B. M's desire," to its old place here—and here it is: *why* she returns the thing which she declared herself so happy to possess, there is no guessing: we have not seen her this long while, nor know if she is in London. I sent a bill, for Pen, from the Paris frame-maker,—and a letter for Fannie. I dined with the Schlesingers, two days ago: Janotha played very finely, perfectly indeed: and Emmy[2] played extremely well. Mary is recovering from her horse-accident, which might well have been worse. She and her mother looked,—each of them,—as pretty as possible. The Douglas Murrays were there—He desired me to tell you that the best of his pups is "laid down" for you. He says that Joe was a representative of the purest breed of Dachshund—and that Count Münster (the German Ambassador) told him there were no such specimens out of England—the very short-legged and over-crooked sort being a product of the old "turnspit" which got the shape of its limbs from over-work. Natorp is working away at a "Medallion-head" of myself: I have given him three sittings, and the thing promises to be tolerably like—if he can keep his hands from chopping and changing. I am sorry not to go, to-day, to Cambridge for the Greek Play: I dreaded the long hot business,—not to speak of the hospitalities of next day, and the business of my return: I dine with the Balls—and, I hope, have a holiday all next week. We have had calls here from Mrs. Alma Tadema, L^y. Wentworth, and L^y. Colley. I have hung the "Tan Yard" and the Pig—and they look capitally. Our House continues to please us,—so warm and comfortable. How sorry I was to hear of the death of poor Miss Lazarus,[3]—that is, sorry for the dreadful cause of what, in itself, can only be a blessing. There was a paragraph about her in the "Times," in which they mentioned that I appreciated her talents,—as I did. Our weather is fairly good,—mild enough, and reasonably free from fog just now. Do you see anything of friends of mine,—Irving, Chamberlain? Oh, I must tell Pen that Dykes Campbell, a great understander of old and rare books, wrote on my account to the Librarian of Chetham's Library, Manchester—where the *uniquely* perfect copy of the "Crudities" is to be found: and he has been good enough to send a collation of the same: by which it appears that my copy is very slightly defective,—having all the plates but one, and wanting the "printed title" (not the engraved one) and another of less importance: it is very valuable therefore.

Give dearest Marie my true love: you will naturally tell us constantly how she is. Boughton's adopted daughter is to be married at St. Mary Abbotts: I shall be obliged to go—but I like him. So, good bye, my dear ones, for the present, and bless you both!

Ever affectionately yours
R_{OB}^T B_{ROWNING}.

1887 : 21

T_O P_{EN} _{AND} F_{ANNIE} B_{ROWNING}

29 De Vere Gardens.
W.
Dec. 17. '87.

My two dearest ones, this will be a short letter, for I have a very busy morning before me,—the business with you being the most important, however, though it is mainly to say we are quite well, and happy indeed when Monday brings us your news—every particle of which is delightful. First let me tell Pen that I received a letter from the Brussels Exhibition requiring to know whither the Bust and the Picture were to be sent: I replied, giving the Paris address: a second letter informed me that the objects would be packed and sent, on the assur-

ance that somebody there would be authorized to receive them and
pay the charges for packing and sending: Natorp, kind as usual, undertook to manage a matter he "probably understood better than I,"
and wrote two letters—to the Concierge, giving instructions and sending a cheque on a Paris House for 75 f^{cs}, as likely to meet the expense
—engaging to send more if more were required—and another letter
to the Secretary of the B. Ex. telling him what had been done,—which
letter I signed. I suppose all will come right. I told the Secretary that
you were in America. Well, the weather is very mild, and fine. My
medallion-portrait ought to be "getting on"—N. works conscientiously
at it. I have dined out several times in the course of the week: everywhere people enquired about you with much interest. At the Academy
affair, I met Tadema, Fildes, many others—all kind exceedingly.
Leighton read a learned and instructive discourse, quite "over the
heads" of the students and probably the Academicians: the distribu-
tion of the prizes was a striking affair: for the first time in the history
of the Academy, the gold medals for the best Historical Picture, and
best Landscape, were obtained by the same person: I am assured that
the event is not made known until the announcement is made in the
Room—so that the hearts of the competitors must palpitate considerably. Mrs Orr was to have accompanied me—and the best seats were
engaged by Leighton for her and myself—but she is very unwell—
quite unable to receive company. Frampton pronounces on the case,
—weakness of the heart, affecting the nerves: no organic disease but
general debility: he will do what he can, but I am very anxious about
the result—and she is very despondent. Mrs F. G. is in town, but unable to see me,—Keane's affairs are in a terrible state of confusion—
perhaps his estate will be insolvent, in spite of all his efforts,—shameful burden to be laid on an old mother "who can now neither sleep nor
eat in consequence," is selling books &c—all through the selfish indulgence of one who should have known better. She sent yesterday
for the Venice Book of Prints—to sell it! I have condensed some facts
furnished by George Barrett into a prefatory note—to be printed along
with the little edition of E. B. B's collected poems—correcting the
misstatements in a recent memoir:[1] we dined with Smith yesterday,
—he thinks it will have an useful effect. I have sent a "Proof" for
George to add to, if he thinks fit. Hallé and Carr have secured a large
Hall in Regent Street for the opposition Gallery[2]—"three times as big
as the Grosvenor"—not an advantage, if that means—admission of
thrice the number of pictures. He says, all the opposition came from
the Painters—B. Jones, Tadema, Watts &c. and Herkomer, whom I

met at Colvin's two days ago, said the same thing. I suppose you may exhibit at either Gallery. Do your gaieties altogether preclude painting,—as your project was to embrace? I was pricked to the heart (poor human nature!) on hearing Herkomer and Colvin vie with each other in glorifying Gilbert. Fannie, darling, "stir him up with a long pole"—as we used to say at school! and leave my love alone, for *it* wants no arousing, being ever employed about you both—whom God bless!

Yours affectionately
R B.

An application from Oxford to join in the Ox^d. U^y. Home Rule League!!—Have replied very decidedly. Dolly Tennent, last eve^g, said Gladstone names her pictures for her. She feels as I do about him.

[Upside down, at the top of the fourth page.]
All love to Marie—squeezed up as is the space to say so.

1887 : 22

To Pen and Fannie Browning

29, De Vere Gardens.
W.
Dec. 24. '87.

My two beloved ones, this will be a short and shabby letter, for my morning is claimed by very many matters I am forced to attend to: while you have been dear and good indeed—twice did your letters make us happy in every respect. All you say about your plans—so far as they are partly determined upon—is just what I should expect of your good sense on a due consideration of the matter. A year's residence at a place which may possibly not suit you after all will be safe and well in every way: while if it does prove really desirable, nothing is lost, not even time spent elsewhere. It is an immense comfort to feel confident, as I do, in your always endeavouring for the best—your "best" being assuredly mine also.

I have very little news. Smith is about to bring out my works in 15 or 16 monthly volumes—at somewhat of a sacrifice to himself but, I think, a decided advantage to me. He will advertise about it. There is just come out a very noticeable book—"Studies on RB." by a Mr. Fotheringham whose name, even, I never heard before. I obtained the loan of a copy two days ago,—not having been graced by the gift of one from the Author or Publisher,—and it is a very remarkable instance (so far as I have read—perhaps one tenth of it) of the interest a complete stranger can take in my "unintelligible works." Our weather is excellent, for the time of year: mild, at all events, and not too rainy. We are having the wires for the electric light laid down before our line of houses: we shall probably not avail ourselves of it,—but it may be useful one day. Natorp is working away,—good fellow,—and I believe with real success at my portrait—it is far from finished after 22 sittings! We dine to day with the Schlesingers, whom I shall be very glad to see. I go out as seldom as I can,—but dined two days ago pleasantly at Lʸ. Colleys—Ld. Wolseley, Fitz James Stephen, the Jeunes, Dr. Cloncurry, Smalley and Elinor Tennyson: Fitz J. S. and I go home together in a Hansom, on these occasions. I am hurried and must end—with a great desire to continue talking! S. will make amends. Dearest Fannie, Dearest Pen, I wish you all best Christmas wishes from the bottom of my heart, and am ever most lovingly yours

ROBERT BROWNING

Archdeacon Farrar applied to me, this day week, to write a "quatrain" for the Jubilee window[1] about to be put up in his church—Tennyson, Lowell, and Whittier having done the same for three windows in honor of Caxton, Raleigh and Milton. I could not refuse, and it will be "cut in marble and inlaid with brass" forthwith—says the Archdeacon, who seems pleased with what I sent.

1887 : 23

TO MISS MARIE CODDINGTON

29, De Vere Gardens.
W.
Dec. 24, '87.

So, my dearest Marie, you must needs be trying to show yourself more dear and good than I know you to be, and I am to thank you for a huge turkey and supremely delicious apples—as I know they will be when they arrive—just as if I need assurance that I have got a sister in you—no more and no less—as I felt from the beginning was the case. Thank you, Dear, not a little for the gifts but more than all for the love that induced you to send them. Who know but that on next

Christmas Day—if we all should be suffered to see it—the beloved Trio[1] may assemble here and try the merits of an English bird? Yours shall beat him, if you please—but our love shall at least try hard to carry off the victory from yours. Dearest Marie, I wish from the bottom of my heart, being, in all affection,

Ever yours
ROBERT BROWNING.

Miss Marie Coddington.

1888 : 1

To Pen and Fannie Browning

29. De Vere Gardens. W.
Jan. 14. '88.

My two beloved ones, I am far from well,—you shall always have the truth from me as nearly as I can give it,—but I am better,—quite cured of what was a new symptom, the rheumatic pain, and really in the way to get rid of the cough, which is *spasmodic,* not originating in anything worse than my old trouble of the liver. I have kept house for the whole week—with small temptation to seek amusement elsewhere: to-day and yesterday,—simple darkness: the gas lit everywhere—of course here in my room at midday. Under these circumstances I have but little news to scrape together and offer. We were happy to get your letters after a day's delay, caused by the fog which delayed the ship. Dear Fannie, you must bear being martyrized for the glory of us all, and Pen must feel how much he is bound to love and be helpful to the mother of his child, if God please. Oh, Fannie, if you knew how certain women I have known would have gone joyfully through any amount of suffering to be in the condition that costs so much but promises to bless you in the end. What a comfort to us here that we are absolutely certain that *your* part will be played gallantly and heroically,—that we need not concern ourselves with advice that you will be careful: it sounds like a mockery to write it, yet you are not indifferent to the fact that we have you here present in our minds,—feeling for you in every conceivable way. Well,—I have, as I say, been nowhere, nor seen anybody. Alma Tadema's Birthday occurs on the 8th,—he likes it to be held in remembrance by his friends: and I sent him a little old print of satyrs dancing a merry round beneath the sun of the 8th (where it *was,* I don't know.) So, yesterday brought him, with his warm bright face and manner. He wanted all the news about you: came up here expressly to see your bust of my-self[1]—and admired it over again, up to the height. There were some lady visitors down stairs,—whom otherwise I should not have seen—and he was much struck by the high civilization of these inhabitants of the Australian bush,—to find how much they knew of modern Art. Mrs Fitz G. called soon after,—looking very well: if she said any-thing noteworth it was to S. who will report it. And this morning we have a short letter from Mrs Moore, yet written at three *reprises*—very affectionate, fully confirmed in Keelyism,[2] who is to thunder-strike us all *next* February: there is great good about her, spite of the nonsense.

Natorp comes to enquire, like the kind fellow he is: my sittings are interrupted but far enough from an end: every now and then the face looks very like mine: but he works by himself,—has "new lights" &c. By the bye, he says he fears a letter written to you,—as I conjecture, about some business of his own,—may have miscarried: is it so?

More bills, Pen—Austin, Beale, the Bootmaker!

I have had so many kind cards, almanacs, remembrances from American friends—all which I hope and intend to duly reply to in time: I think that the same goodness which remembers me will un-derstand if the multitude of calls on my time, just now, cause more delay in doing so than I could wish. In honour to a sort of improve-ment in the light of day I have just put out the gas. What weather for painters here! S. met Rudolf Lehmann yesterday in the street, look-ing truly "unemployed."

Night back again, at 2 o'clock, gas lit, and all to say a hearty good bye! How we look forward to Monday's post! By the "Times" we have ascertained whether or no the packet has arrived on Saturday. Dearest Marie, a word with *you*—all the love possible in it! How much we rejoice in the notion of eventually seeing you,—there is no need to say. Cannot you too write occasionally—not letting those two curious ones overlook you, but telling us *yourself* about yourself and them? Bless you, all precious three! Fannie and Pen,—I must make the fine distinction when I address you that Ly. William Russell did when she wrote under the portraits of her two sons, Arthur and Odo, (in Spanish) "The One has my soul, the Other my heart." Which is the better possession, I don't know so share it impartially between you, my two dearest!

Yours ever

R B.

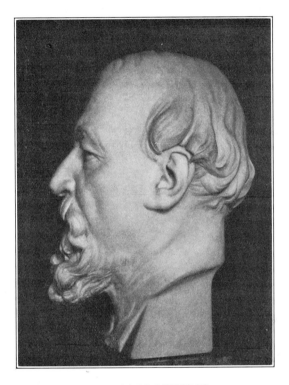

ROBERT BROWNING

PORTRAIT BUST BY HIS SON; NOW IN THE POSSESSION
OF MR. THOMAS J. WISE

1888 : 2

To Pen and Fannie Browning

29, De Vere Gardens.
W.
Jan. 21, '88.

My two dearest ones, I am, of course, more anxious to hear about you than ever—and probably Monday will bring news. It is needless to say how much I feel for poor Fannie, prevented from going to Boston and the kind friends there: fortunately one knows that the difficulties will not last too long. She is never out of my thoughts.

I myself was unwell enough, as I told you—and kept the house for ten days: but all the inconveniences left me,—under the judicious doctoring of Frampton,—and I am quite in my ordinary condition—though I take more precautions against cold and fog than were necessary of old. Our weather is—this year, at least,—far milder than elsewhere, even in Italy—where they bitterly complain of snow and frost—of which we experience nothing in London. Alma Tadema called the other day, and wished to see your Bust of myself—he praised it greatly. Henry James did the same, two days ago, when he called, and mounted to my room.[1] I have had a letter from the Committee for giving a dinner to Coutts L.[2] in March, asking me to put my name with theirs—and I consented, of course: he has always been most kind to you and to me; and with the quarrels of other people I have nothing to do. I had a pretty letter,—I rather think with an intention in it, besides the apparent one of offering me the loan of a book,—from Mary Drew—née Gladstone: and I was not sorry to have the opportunity of saying that, while I rejoiced at what she told me of her Father's fine health in Florence, I was forced to say I had altogether parted company with him in politics. The Schlesingers (that is, Mrs S. and Mary) are at Torquay. I enclose,—as desired,—two letters, and a card, from our poor friend—who really seems madder than ever on this subject. Keeley announces his publication of the discovery for next month; I tell her let us have that, and nothing else either for or against the thing. But one might as well talk to the winds: and much better to the Oran-outang you very properly cultivate. I cannot have news unless I go abroad for them, and when I shall "dine out" again seems very uncertain indeed. Natorp is well, and working in his way: my portrait is not finished yet—but he is an exceedingly good fellow. Now, bless you all—all three, dearest Marie included! S. will probably have more to say—no more love to send than goes to you with this from yours

ever affectionately R B.

1888 : 3

To Robert Barrett Browning

29. De Vere Gardens. W.
Jan. 25. '88.

Dearest Pen, you know very well how we have been feeling for you and poor darling Fannie. The telegram was a great blessing, coming as it did on the 23^d at night—while the letters, for which it prepared us, only arrived this morning. I shall write on Saturday as usual, but cannot help sending this at once. We trust that Fannie is "convalescent" indeed—and it is useless to say how anxious we must be till we hear next. Don't be disappointed at this first failure of your natural hopes—it may soon be repaired. Your dearest Mother experienced the same misfortune, at much about the same time after marriage: and it happened also to my own mother, before I was born. I am not going to write a formal letter,—indeed I have no news of any importance, or that cannot wait: but give dearest Marie my truest love and thanks for her letter, and the assurance it gives that all possible assistance is rendered to our darling Fannie. You will like to know that I am myself quite well again: I avoid engagements, but only as possibly hurtful. God bless you all, dearest ones.

Yours ever affectionately
R B.

1888 : 4

To Robert Barrett Browning

29. De Vere Gardens. W.
Jan. 28. '88.

Dearest Pen, We were very glad indeed to get your letter of the 17th. We wrote on the 25th when the earlier letters arrived, finding it too hard to wait till the regular Saturday. How thankful we are that matters are no worse, I shall not need to say. The great business now will be for dearest Fannie to lay in all the stock of strength that will assist her on a future occasion: when, with no previous irritation from sea-voyages, all is likely to go happily. I can well conceive how anxious you and Marie have been,—give her my truest love and thanks. Here we have no news—I do not go out to get any: but my own ailments are completely gone, and I have only to do what I can to hinder them from returning. The weather is most favourable: at this moment, the sun is shining brightly, and although it is cold, yet the general feeling is of early Spring: it is strange to hear of your snow and frost—that is, hard or serious frost of which we have had no specimen. Natorp has finished my portrait,—at least so far as to cast it in bronze,—a process it is now undergoing: he really took prodigious pains with it, and I willingly co-operated by sitting day after day: and I think the result is highly satisfactory: Mrs Orr and Sarianna agree that, on the whole, no better likeness exists. With earlier thorough training he would undoubtedly have proved a good painter—and one quality by no means common—that of inventiveness—he possesses in a marked degree. The wrangle (on the Hallé and Carr side) about the Grosvenor keeps up its noise—and, by the correspondence they have printed, they by no means improve their position—Coutts L. plays the superior and gentlemanly part throughout. Smith is taking much pains with my forthcoming edition—in monthly volumes—, sixteen, I believe. In the "Pall Mall" two days ago, appeared a paragraph to the effect that Miss Alma Murray would play in the "Blot in the 'Scutcheon," at the Olympic on March 8: and later, with Mrs Kendal, in "In a Balcony"—meaning to bring out the "Return of the Druses" next year. Very good of her! I got a somewhat melancholy letter from Heyermans,[1]—to congratulate you on your marriage—which he wished to have heard of from yourself. His wife has been ill—has undergone a serious operation. He is unable to come to London, but would greatly like pupils in Antwerp. Moscheles says the circumstances are materially altered since there were advantages in going to study there: in London, for instance, we have Herkomer, the Slade School, and other places where proper instruction is given. I daresay he is in a forlorn way—so easy is it to let the main opportunity slip, and never regain the chance. Dearest Pen, I end as I began, with the truest love to you all. We trust to hear the good news confirmed by the next letters.

Ever yours most affectionately
R BROWNING.

1888 : 5

To Thomas J. Wise

29, De Vere Gardens,
London, W.
January 31st, 1888.

My dear Mr. Wise,

I shall be happy to see you whenever you do me the favour to call; if on a Sunday, as you propose, may I ask that you make your visit an early one, as I am generally away in the afternoon.

Of course I will cheerfully do what you please to require so kindly with the copy of *Pauline*,[1] which you have purchased, as far as I can remember, at about two thirds of the price paid for printing the whole edition fifty-five years ago.

Many thanks for the promised *Epipsychidion*. I possess somewhere one of the original copies.

Believe me, Dear Mr. Wise,
Yours very sincerely,
ROBERT BROWNING.

1888 : 6

To Dr. F. J. Furnivall

29, De Vere Gardens,
London, W.
February 12th, 1888.

My dear Furnivall,

I was sorry indeed to find, on getting home, that you had just left. I miscalculated the distance, and supposed I could return much earlier. I had more than one thing I was wanting to say. My sister tells me your reason for not coming to luncheon was that you fancied we might be inconvenienced by making the hour *two* instead of *one*. Nothing of the kind! Do believe in our utter indifference in the matter, so you but apprise us by a word beforehand. I have a letter of yours which came when I was far from well, and when I got better there was an accumulation of minor worryings, which I found in the way both of work and pleasure. Do manage to come soon and have a talk as in the days of old—for they seem "old" already!

I was looking over the account of that paper[1] concerning my treatment of the Jews. It was remarked[2] I mistook a Rabbi for a High Priest! This comes of forgetting that one writes dramatically. The speaker, Baldinucci, is a typically ignorant Tuscan, and makes the gross mistake already noted in Arbuthnot's *Martinus Scriblerus*—of whom it is said, at the very beginning: "Those who had never seen a Jesuit took him for one, while others thought him rather to be some High Priest of the Jews." Somebody objected to a Jewish burying-ground being in the neighbourhood of any habitation, but Baldinucci tells the story, and describes the locality as he knew it—and I follow him, of course.

I shall not comment on the disgraceful issue of the Trial,[3] the grotesque perversion of equity, whatever may be the ruling of law—or rather, the lawyers. I have always had a supreme contempt for the profession, and the lawyers in my poems get the benefit thereof. I believe you have the thorough sympathy of everybody worth caring for, and as for your adversary—pity it is that you ever wasted a word on him. He was just the fellow to make money out of a kick, the beggar!

This is a sad case of the poor man whose letter you enclose; my unlucky absence from the Club prevented my attempting to help. Could there be a second application? I would try and make up for the past.

> Ever, my dear Furnivall,
> Yours most cordially,
> ROBERT BROWNING.

1888 : 7

To Dr. F. J. FURNIVALL

> 29, De Vere Gardens,
> London, W.
> February 17th, 1888.

Dear Furnivall,

Very glad to hear we shall have you on Sunday week.

As for the "Trial," everybody I have seen takes the right view of the subject.

The "Correspondent" may complete his answer to objections by mentioning that, in *Holy Cross Day,* Ben Ezra is not supposed to acknowledge Christ as the Messiah because he resorts to the obvious argument "even on your own showing, and accepting for the moment the authority of your accepted Lawgiver, you are condemned by His precepts—let alone ours."

I shall do my best to be present at the Play. I wish Pen would accompany me, and bring his wife. Excellent news of her, three days ago.

Yours truly ever,
ROBERT BROWNING.

1888 : 8

To WALTER B. SLATER

29, De Vere Gardens,
London, W.
February 22nd, 1888.

Dear Mr. Slater,

In reply to your kind letter, I may say that I certainly shall be present, if possible, at a performance[1] got up with so much generous trouble and expense of every sort. If you can reserve the smallest of the boxes for my sister and myself we shall be much obliged to you. I am not aware, at this moment, of any friend whom I could recommend to your obliging attention; but if I should hear of one who both desires and deserves a ticket, I will avail myself of your goodness.

I never have seen Miss Alma Murray in any play but the *Cenci*—wherein her acting was most admirable. I shall be highly interested in whatever she can do for my piece.

Believe me, Dear Mr. Slater,

Yours very sincerely,
ROBERT BROWNING.

1888 : 9

To EDMUND GOSSE

29, De Vere Gardens.
W.
Feb. 23. '88.

My dear Gosse, (You *will* over-Master me, but I won't imitate you). I never heard of any connection of my Father's family with that of the illustrious Playwright:[1] we came out of Dorsetshire.

I am glad you are so good as to lend the Portrait.[2] My Sister,—a better authority than myself,—always liked it as resembling its subject when his features had more resemblance to those of his Mother than in aftertime when those of his Father got the better—or perhaps the worse—of them.

I sent photographs of the drawing to her from Rome,—and supplied one of these to Smith,—who preferred applying to you directly.

With all regards to Mrs Gosse,

Ever truly yours
ROBERT BROWNING.

Do look in upon us here some propitious day that brings you in our direction. It is long since we have seen you.

My Grandfather told me that in consequence of the notoriety of Mrs. Brownrigg "the 'Prenticecide,"[3] most of those unlucky enough to be her name-sakes changed *r* and *g* to a couple of *ns,* and so apparently increased our tribe.

1888 : 10

To PEN AND FANNIE BROWNING

29. De Vere Gardens. W.
March 16. '88.

Dearest Fannie, Dearest Pen,—I hug both of you in anticipation, even at this distance: how glad I shall be to see you soon, in the flesh not in the spirit, there is no need to say. You will be reading newspapers all the evening of your arrival, and learn all that has happened since the 18th—the Emperor's Death, the new Emperor's accession and behaviour—also the terrible and unprecedented storm of snow from which you have just escaped at New York: if your passage has been bad, it can hardly have affected you more than the dreadful "blizzard" with which New York makes acquaintance for the first time. Here the weather is (to-day, at least) cold and rainy, but Spring has unmistakably set in. Yesterday, they acted my play ("The Blot &c") very well, and apparently to the satisfaction of the audience. I am delighted to hear of the coming alligator—but fear the news is too good to be true. We (S. and I) go tomorrow to a party which Professor Flower gives at the S. K. Museum: he is the director at the Zoölogical Gardens, and will tell me how to keep the creature: there are several large ones in the collection. Leighton has sent both of you an invitation for his *matinée* on the 28th. Joachim always does his best there. Yes, we are all delighted at Chamberlain's success, as it is surely to be considered. He was received with much cordiality by the House of Commons last night. I was prevented from going to the Speaker's for lunch yesterday by having to attend the Play: I should like to have seen who might be there. You are all too late for the Royal Academy exhibition—not for that at the Grosvenor however. I duly sent off the Picture and Bust, and hope they arrived in time: we made enquiries, and found that Natorp was—*more suo*—fidgety and un-necessarily apprehensive: they would easily get to Paris, *par petite vitesse,* in three days or so: and if they arrived yesterday, it was in time enough: the bust could go in much later,—in April indeed. But we shall talk of all things better than write now. Mrs Schlesinger has got you the rooms you require at the Hotel: the neighbourhood will be delightfully near. S. will tell you about our visit from Mrs Moore. All love to you both, all trust that you may have arrived safely,—and the best welcome imaginable when you do really arrive.

Ever affectionately yours
Robert Browning.

1888 : 11

To Pen and Fannie Browning

29, De Vere Gardens.
W.
May 14. '88.

My dearest ones, the letter from Paris, the post-card from Milan, and this morning's letter from Venice are good, better, and best. I am chiefly anxious now to learn how the climate of Venice suits Fannie, whether the heat is not oppressive. All you told me about the "Salon," and the Picture in the Studio was very interesting. The R. A. exhibi-tion is good, perhaps above the average: and the general judgment on the principal pictures pretty just. The remarkable success is of a view of the "Pool," (the Thames by London Bridge) which is fine—as are two landscapes by Leader. There are no "figure"-pieces worth notice, except as singularly bad, for the most part. The Grosvenor is alto-gether bad,—so bad that it is believed that it will not be attempted a second time. At the R. A. Dinner I saw C. Lindsay, who first told me he had not answered my letters because of the number of pictures arrived already,—then—that he had only received one letter—then, that Dechamps had called, and lastly that he had called himself,—in other words, so many falsehoods. He evidently has lost all interest in the Gallery, does not answer letters, sends back pictures he has asked for,—is "gone to the bad" in short. The New Gallery is a decided success, both as a Gallery and for the show there—certainly very remarkable. All the pictures look well, and the poetical element abounds. Yes, I heard of a portrait by Carolus Duran being refused at the Academy: but *two* are well hung there: and since the rules limit the number of pictures allowed to Foreign Artists—only some twelve, I think— surely no one artist ought to place three on the walls,—take for himself one quarter of the whole available space—what he has got admittance for are *very* fine,—as is Sargent's work. Natorp's Medallion is in the best possible place,—even he is satisfied with it. Dearest Fannie, you are too good to say what you do about the book[1] I am keeping for you; for whom was my copy to be reserved if not for you? There will be this much interest attached to it that it is already *rare*—every copy being disposed of *before* publication: I asked Smith if he would not print more of the same sort—but he said that the restricted number was one of the circumstances which give value to books published in this way. The other Edition is doing very well, I believe. I go out as usual,—too much, indeed: met the Layards several times last week. Mrs Bronson wrote to us last week—we answered at once. She told us about Edith's intended departure. I go to-day to John Murray's, where, I am sorry to say, I shall meet Gladstone—but I shall take care of myself. Mrs Moore is back—full of kindness: I saw her yesterday. Clare Montalba's pictures were refused at the Academy. Poynter's *portraits* are dreadful—vulgar to the last degree, and,—one at least,— with hands altogether shamefully drawn. S. shall go on: I am altogether yours affectionately

ROBERT BROWNING.

[Continued by Sarianna Browning]

Dearest Fannie,

Your last letter from Paris reached us on Monday night (7th). I had not understood that you would leave quite so soon, and on Saturday afternoon (the 5th) had forwarded to the hôtel du Louvre two letters for you and Rosalie, enclosed,—and what I take to be a bundle of photographs—I hope it arrived on Sunday before you left in the evening. With this post, I forward two letters in one envelope, and a paper from Mrs B. M. a notice of Pen's painting. This morning I have been to my bookseller and will despatch the book to Paris to Mrs F. G. He had not one of the very cheaply bound copies, so I sent a better one, price 1 s. 6—and as he deducted 4 pence for ready money, it cost only a shilling and two pence—two pence more postage—not ruinous! Father's birthday went off in an avalanche of flowers—We have received a parcel for Pen containing field-glasses. Lady Frances Baillie left a card for you. Did you see the announcement of the re-marriage of Mrs Lionel Tennyson to Augustine Birrell, author of Obiter Dicta. Do not forget to send the address which your papa has mislaid for the letter Pen wished him to write. Now, darling, take great care of yourself, and avoid fatigue. Go to bed at reasonable hours and don't take to smoking! We shall all of us be delighted to see dear Marie. We long for your letters. Ever your own affectionate

SARIANNA.

Our kind love to the Curtises; we have written to Mrs Bronson.

1888 : 12

To Pen and Fannie Browning

29, De Vere Gardens.
W.
May 21, '88.

My two dear ones, we were looking anxiously for the news of you which this morning fortunately brings us: how happy we were that you, both of you, are well—(Fannie *so* well) there is no need to say. It is pleasant to know exactly where you are—the "Dario" being as present to my mind's eye as the house opposite. Here we are also well —and myself am at last quiet for a day or two, all my engagements having come to their natural end: (with two exceptions I have dined out for the last sixteen days.) On Monday, I met Gladstone at John Murray's, and, to my discomfiture, sat next him,—nobody could be more agreeable: on Friday I sat as close to Bright, at Chamberlain's, —and few people could show themselves so ignorant of English Literature: "he was convinced Shakespeare could not have written the plays,—a man who could hardly write at all, and was known, in his own age, to nobody." I could not stand *that,* and let him know what I thought of it. Chamberlain is very interesting and delightful indeed.

I have a kind invitation from Ly. Pembroke to go to Wilton—where she would make a party for me: I will not accept, however: but Jowett invites me for Commemoration Week, and I go gladly. Our weather is very fine and inspiriting after the prolonged cold. Mrs Orr is back again—not much better, I fear. We—or rather S. had a call from Miss Levitt yesterday. It is melancholy to hear how poor Story has been bothered about his house,—so badly built, that the Municipality refuse to sanction proceeding with it,—so unsafe does it appear. I have seen the Layards several times of late—we dine with them before very long. There was a picture of Heyermans' rejected at the R. A.: now at Moscheles' studio,—not a strong work. Vicat Coles' fine picture is bought for the Chantrey Gallery—as is one by Logsdail, and another by Gow. S. will tell you about the Schlesingers. I am going out, and may hear something to subjoin—but should I be unable to do so—Give my love to Mrs Bronson and Edith, and believe me— dearest Fannie and Pen—ever yours

most affectionately
ROBERT BROWNING.

[Continued by Sarianna Browning]

Darling, I am glad to hear that you are, for the present, at anchor. I remember the beautiful outside of the Dario, but Miss Ker said that she found the inside very uncomfortable. Tell us all your doings, for we have no greater pleasure than getting a letter. We always write immediately,—though there was a longer interval than usual last time because we knew you were on the wing, and were not sure of the spot where you would alight. The weather just now is beautiful,— and the Gardens and Park, perfect: the former a mass of flowers and Verdure,—and the latter, all glowing with budding trees and green grass. I enjoy walking there. Our own house looks very well—the shrubs in the windows make it gay, and the sun streams in the rooms. Herewith, I send a letter for Rosalie. Tell me the state of your pets— Max—Jocko &c. If I lived in Venice I would tame some sea-gulls—if you took them infants, they would make a home chez vous, without cutting a wing, or depriving them of a pleasure. I could not enjoy them as prisoners. All the news must come from you—tell us quantities. Our love to the dear Bronsons and Curtises. We shall soon be welcoming Marie, I hope.

Ever your affect^e

Ever your affect^e
SARIANNA.

1888 : 13

To Miss Marie Coddington

June 6, '88.

Dearest Marie, There is little need that I should put into words what you must know I feel in my heart, if speaking could do any good! but it may be of some little use if it makes you know how much you are loved, and, of necessity, sympathized with in this unfortunate accident and its consequences. We shall not see you, nor the dear ones at Venice, after all our counting upon that delight: still it is a comfort to think that you are temporarily disabled at home and not abroad where such helpful attention as you are receiving would be impossible to find. An out-of-the-way place, inexperienced treatment,—this might have turned what I trust is only a passing inconvenience into confirmed lameness perhaps. So let us be truly thankful that, great as is our disappointment, there will be all the more joy at the recovery we have every reason to hope for. Dearest Marie, you will not forget how anxiously we shall wait for news. My sister writes, but I could not let anyone say for me just this—that I am ever

most affectionately yours

R. B.

1888 : 14

To W. G. Kingsland

29, De Vere Gardens
London, W.
June 15th, 1888.

My dear Kingsland,

There is not a word of truth in the passage you have the kindness to send me. I never at any time had the least notion of writing my "Reminiscences," nor ever shall do so; consequently the other "account" is not likely to be furnished. The stanza quoted is from my poem of The Statue and the Bust, towards the end.

It will give me, and give my sister, great pleasure to see you whenever you are able to call. I spend next week at Oxford—though that circumstance needs not interfere with your calling, after the 23rd.

We are both of us quite well, and hope that you and all your family are in good health likewise. With best regards to them and to you.

Believe me,

Affectionately yours,

Robert Browning.

1888 : 15

To Thomas J. Wise

29. De Vere Gardens.
W.
June 18. '88.

Dear Mr. Wise,

I have too long delayed thanking you for the very interesting Fac-simile of Shelley's Poem,[1]—indeed I have even been unable as yet to examine it as carefully as it deserves, and you will understand my desire to do so—as well as to express my sense of your great kindness.

Believe me, Dear Mr. Wise,

Yours very sincerely

Robert Browning.

1888 : 16

To William Archer, Esq.

William Archer, Esq.
26, Gordon Square,
W. C.

29 De Vere Gardens
W.
June 29'. '88.

Dear Sir,

I have commented with a word or two, and as gently as was consistent with truth, on the paragraphs you submit to my notice. If I must do so at all,—the truth is the truth, and must be told—partly, perhaps.

Macready was *"fuori di sè"* from the moment when,—in pure ignorance of what he was driving at,—I acquiesced in his proposal that a serious play of any pretension should appear under his management with any other protagonist than himself. When the more learned subsequently enlightened me a little, I was angry and disinclined to take advice—but it is happily over so long ago! Believe me, Dear Sir,

Yours sincerely

ROBERT BROWNING.

Browning's Notes on Macready's Diary.[1]

1. Nov. 27. 1835. *Browning's first meeting at Rev. W. J. Fox's. Bayswater.*

Note "I found Macready, as I left—and, happily, after a long interval, resumed him—so to speak, one of the most admirable and indeed fascinating characters I have ever known: somewhat too sensitive for his own happiness, and much too impulsive for invariable consistency with his nobler moods."

2. DEC. 31. 1835. *Browning visits Macready at Elstree, where he first met Forster.*

Note "(To see the old year out—and how pleasantly!)"

3. FEB. 16. 1836. *Browning proposes to Macready to write a tragedy on Narses.*

Note "a passing fancy: one difficulty in the subject was insuperable, I soon saw"

4. MAY 26. 1836. *The supper at Talfourd's house after the production of Ion. Browning meets Wordsworth and Landor. Browning asked to write a tragedy.*

Note "a memorable supper at which Talfourd, the most generous of men, proposed the health of 'the youngest poet present'! On descending the staircase, Macready said, with an affectionate gesture, 'Will you not write me a tragedy and save me from going to America?' In reply, I sent the Note* in question to say I would do all in my power to effect this."

[*This letter from Robert Browning, Macready calls "one of the very highest—may I not say the highest?—honour I have through life received."]

5. AUG. 3. 1836. *Forster tells Macready that Browning had settled on* STRAFFORD *for his play.*

Note "I was engaged on other work, hence the delay in determining on a subject fit for Macready's purpose."

6. MARCH 30. 1837. *Macready reads Strafford to Osbaldiston (Manager of Covent Garden) who accepts it with avidity.*

Note "From first to last Macready did his utmost to ensure the

success of the play—superintending the rehearsals carefully. Vandenhoff was engaged in the place of Elton."

7. APRIL 28. 1837. *Macready remarks that the only chance of success
for* STRAFFORD *would be "in the acting."*

Note " 'the acting'—that is, his own performance—the other actors,
with the notable exception of Vandenhoff and Miss Helen Faucit,
being incompetent. The theatre was in a bad way, about to close, and
the Manager economized accordingly."

8. MAY 1. 1837. *Production of* STRAFFORD *at Covent Garden.*

Note "He [Macready] acted very finely—as did Miss Faucit. Pym
received tolerable treatment,—the rest,—for the sake of whose in-
competence the play had to be reduced by at least one third of its
dialogue,—*non ragionam di loro!* Nevertheless it met with no 'opposition' at all, ran for a few nights, was displaced by some 'Benefits'—and
was finally brought out, with the substitution of Elton for Vandenhoff—the former undertaking to study the part of Pym on condition
that he should play it "next season"—which was never to be, the
management decamping a week after."

9. FEB. 4. 6. 11. 1843. *Macready's brief entries on the rehearsing and
production of the* BLOT.

Note "This play was brought out under circumstances I have been
forced to animadvert upon and would willingly forget. Macready had
engaged to produce it after two other pieces: the second proved a
failure, and it would seem, by all the evidence I had afterward, that
I was supposed to myself understand the expediency of begging to
withdraw, at least for a time, my own work—saving Macready the
imaginary failure to keep a promise to which I never attached particular importance. As so many hints to my dull perception of this,
Macready declined to play his part, caused the play to be read in my
absence to the actors by a ludicrously incapable person—the result
being, as he informed me, 'that the play was laughed at from the beginning to the end'—naturally enough, a girl's part made comical by
a red-nosed one-legged elderly gentleman:—then, after proposing to
take away from his substitute the opportunity of distinction he had
given him,—to which I refused my consent—leaving the play to a
fate which it somehow managed to escape. I thought differently of
this behaviour than now, when, by the publication of Macready's
diary, I am made aware of the extreme difficulty of his financial position at the time:—one friendly straightforward word to the effect that
what was intended for an advantage would, under circumstances of

which I was altogether ignorant, prove the reverse,—how easy to have spoken, and what regret it would have spared us both!"

R B.

1888 : 17

To Thomas J. Wise

29, De Vere Gardens,
London, W.
August 1ˢᵗ, 1888.

Dear Mr. Wise,

Tht *Runaway Slave at Pilgrim's Point* was given by its author to the Boston *Liberty Bell,* and was afterwards comprised in the collective edition of Chapman and Hall, 1850.

I never heard of a separate publication, and am pretty certain such a circumstance never happened. I fear that this must be a fabricated affair, and, moreover, *have* a doubt whether the *Battle of Marathon,*[1] of which I never have seen a copy, may not be a fabrication also. As the poem (*The Runaway Slave*) was first printed in America, no copyright could be claimed for it in England. It is possible some of the "friends of Freedom" may have used a certain "freedom" in reprinting the poem, for the sake of the good cause, nor thought proper to refer to the author at all.

Believe me, Dear Mr. Wise,
Yours very sincerely,
ROBERT BROWNING.

1888 : 18

To Thomas J. Wise

29, De Vere Gardens,
London, W.
August 3ʳᵈ, 1888.

Dear Mr. Wise,

I daresay the fact has been that, on the publication of the Poem in America, the American friends (in London) who had been instrumental in obtaining it, wrote to the Authoress (in Florence) for leave to republish it in England, and that she of course gave her consent— probably wrote the little advertisement. The respectability of the

Publisher and Printer is a guarantee that nothing surreptitious has been done. You may observe that no price is affixed, and no advertisements are to be found on the cover,—the pamphlet[1] was clearly a private issue for "friends." The appearance of the pamphlet convinces me that things were as I say.

I possess a copy of the *Liberty Bell,* and when I disinter it from the chaos of my books I will refer to any notice that may be there in reference to your acquisition—which I return with many thanks.

Yours very sincerely,

ROBERT BROWNING.

1888 : 19

To EDMUND GOSSE

29, De Vere Gardens,

W.

August 3rd, 1888.

My dear Gosse,

You are, as ever, kind indeed: I shall read and enjoy your book[1] very soon, I hope, but I will not wait to thank you for the pleasant gift.

I by no means repudiate the relationship of Congreve's mother—only doubt whether I could establish my claim to such an honour.

Ever truly yours,

ROBERT BROWNING.

1888 : 20

To H. BUXTON FORMAN

29, De Vere Gardens.

W.

Dec. 26. '88.

Dear Mr Buxton Forman,

I know nothing, nor ever wished to know, of Landor's wretched squabble[1] with the people who rightly or wrongly gave him offence. It all took place while I was in Italy, and only on his arrival there did I hear anything about it. From the time when we became intimate I was careful to prevent his dwelling on what had happened,—his intentions of resuming his attacks,—and so forth. I believe the name you refer to was that of his prosecutrix.

Ever truly yours

ROBERT BROWNING.

1888 : 21

To Miss Marie Coddington

29, De Vere Gardens.
W.
Dec. 28. '88.

Dearest Marie, Far beyond even your lovely apples, which came to rejoice us, do I and my sister welcome the news that you are really better. Of course, we heard of you constantly the whole of the last four months, with relief or anxiety according as the accounts affected us. I do indeed trust that the plan for the Spring, which you mention, may be carried into effect; and that, after those German Baths you purpose to visit, there may be the meeting with those dear ones at Venice who live in the hope of seeing you. I am certain that their happiness is "catching" and would communicate itself to you—as it did to us who have been close to it for so long. I never remember (to speak of another advantage) such a succession of wonderful days of the finest weather imaginable: three months of glory with only two rainy days—in sad contrast to the grim aspect of things in London. You will be amused, and I think greatly interested when you see the famous palazzo their property, which Pen is doing his best to make as comfortable as it is magnificent. They have charming friends too— no few Americans—and are altogether in an enviable condition— would but that dearest Fannie's health continue, as it is described to us in a letter received yesterday. But you have all the accounts, I know, and need none at second hand; all I can furnish, unfortunately.

Dearest Marie, you know how thoroughly I reciprocate your good wishes—how deeply delighted I shall be to see you again when you come to London: I shall not dwell on it. My sister says she will write for herself, and she may easily put in words something I have over-looked: but the simple truth must serve that I love you most heartily and beg you ever to remember me as most fraternally and affection-ately yours

ROBERT BROWNING.

1889 : 1

To Dr. F. J. Furnivall

29, De Vere Gardens,
London, W.
February 23rd, 1889.

My dear Furnivall,

By really an unpardonable oversight, I forgot to reply to your question of the day before yesterday, a multiplicity of matters having diverted my attention from it.

The meaning of the passages is much as you say—entirely so, indeed. "Neither body nor mind is born to attain perfect strength or perfect health at its first stage of existence respectively, in each case, by the want of and desire for the thing as yet out of reach, they get raised towards it, and are educated by the process—as would not happen were the body strong all at once—or the soul at once perfect in apprehension.[1]

"Wishing what I write may be read by their light"—*viz.* of Shakespeare, Dekker, Heywood and the others mentioned in the preface to *Vittoria Accorambona* by Webster.

Ever, in haste as in leisure,

Yours truly,
R. Browning.

1889 : 2

To Dr. F. J. Furnivall

29, De Vere Gardens,
London, W.
March 2nd, 1889.

My dear Furnivall,

I should prosaically state the meaning[1] thus: I do not ask a full disclosure of Truth, which would be a concession contrary to the law of things, which applies equally to the body and the soul, that it is only by striving to attain strength (in the one case) and truth (in the other) that body and soul do so—the effort (common to both) being productive, in each instance, of the necessary initiation into all the satisfactions which result from partial success; absolute success being only attainable for the body in full manhood—for the soul, in its full apprehension of Truth—which will be, not *here,* at all events.

The sense is much the same whether you place a comma after "effort," or leave it out as I have done. "Effort whereby," or general effort, the result of mind's striving to urge the body to get strong all at once.

And now, I have to beg you to do me a very serious favour. Read this letter and the accompanying summary of the writer's husband's services.[2] I should be happy to help the poor fellow in the way he wants were I able, but I am not. I cannot apply either to Gladstone or Buckle[3] just now for very certain reasons, nor to Bright either.

Can you contrive simply to bring the matter under Gladstone's notice, he being the person the parties evidently most count upon—I fear, hopelessly? He has not the power now, if he had—as he probably may have—the will; but I can only do, or attempt to do, what is prescribed by the letter. Only, something I am anxious to do, and I want a more efficacious hand than mine to make the effort. I know you will help me if you can. Mr. Barnett Smith wrote many good-natured notices of me in *The Times,* and other newspapers—which, at least as early advertisements, did good to my books, I have no doubt. At all events forgive my troubling you and believe me,

Ever truly yours,

ROBERT BROWNING.

I was much pleased by Mr. Robertson's article. There is another— an essay in a book of which I never heard till the other day, *Cross Lights,*[4] by I don't know what person, which highly interested me.

1889 : 3

TO NORMAN MAC COLL

29, De Vere Gardens.
W.
March 10. '89.

My dear Mr Mac Coll,

May I venture to bespeak your kind attention to a request I have to make—one, I hope, permissible—at least, encouraged by your sympathy and good-nature. My young friend Mr Sidney Thompson, who has published a volume of poetry which may have come under your notice, and which, I think, evinces considerable power of various kinds,—this gentleman is anxious to have employment as a reviewer of poetry, works of fiction and the like. I well know how efficient a "staff" you possess: but there may be occasions when you might, at all events, give a trial to a new writer on such subjects. In that case, may I refer you to Mr Sidney Thompson, whose address is—1. Talgarth Road, W. You would make acquaintance with a gentleman in every way worthy of your notice—as well Editorial as social.

Believe me, Dear Mr Mac Coll,

Yours very truly

ROBERT BROWNING.

1889 : 4

To T. J. NETTLESHIP

29, De Vere Gardens,
W.
March 10th, 1889.

My dear Nettleship,

I return the article and the review. Putting aside what you shall never persuade me to be other than a far too generous appreciation of what I have really done, you are quite right as to what I intended to do. From the first I notified the poems were each and all,—with afterward an exception or two,—purely *dramatic,* with no sort of attempt at esoteric meaning, moreover besides the self-display—just the thing I was bent upon avoiding. Mr. Sarrazin sees this clearly enough. I am astonished at his exuberant generosity, which, coming half a century after the appearance of some of the works he considers successful, is in such strange contrast with the treatment they mostly met with then and long after. I think you are hard on the Society,— *not* on the vagaries of the gnostic papers—those marked by the "over-knowingness" you animadvert upon most justly—but because I never understood that the Society was originally instituted for the purpose of even elucidating dark passages or disinterring deep meanings; but rather from a desire to get together certain people likely to sympathise in obtaining more interest than existed for works generally supposed to be unintelligible or nearly so. As for wishing to get behind any plain sense that might be discoverable, Furnivall, the founder, strikes me as going to the other extreme; disparaging anything but plain facts. Is it not so? Nor do I account the circumstance that whenever a paper is read which happens to be fantastical, the

Society is bound to suppress it—or even pronounce judgment upon it: the member used his right and said his say. The others may differ from it—and either pronounce their opinion, or keep silence, as seems best. When all is done—I cannot but be very grateful for the institution of the Society; for to what else but the eight years' persistent calling attention to my works can one attribute the present demand for them?

If Johnson showed his good sense in telling somebody who deprecated the appearance of an adverse criticism on something he had just brought out "Sir, if the critics did not notice me, I should starve,"—well, I am justified in fancying that, but for what was done by Furnivall and his colleagues, I should have no more readers than ten years ago,—that is, what is called a "Public" of a sort,—for I never was without the man or two whose "allowance for the care my labouring spirit took in this—poetry—" proved to me "a theatre large enow—and their applause only sufficient was"—if I may thus quote Daniel—and give thanks to Nettleship—of whom I shall ever be proud as a critic—and to whom, as a friend, goes all the affection of his truly ever,

Robert Browning.

1889 : 5

To Dr. F. J. Furnivall

29, De Vere Gardens,
London, W.
March 27th, 1889.

My dear Furnivall,

1st question—you answer rightly—except perhaps that the lady, a passionate Italian, means "Whether I shall find a new lover and bestow on him all you despise, and even more—forgetting all else; or whether I shall not rather bethink myself of taking a thorough revenge on you—that is for after consideration: you are not 'out of the wood yet' "!

2nd. St. Mark's is constructed out of various objects originally intended to illustrate some other cult than that which, by the superior power of the Christian symbol, has exclusively appropriated earth's homage.

Ever truly yours,
Robert Browning.

1889 : 6

To Robert Barrett Browning

29. De Vere Gardens.
W.
March 30. '89.

Dearest Pen,—the best news is that Fannie is "wonderfully well"—
and yourself have got rid of that troublesome rheumatism: after that
comes the satisfaction of hearing that your doings in the house have
been successful, and that we may hope to see you soon. I had a letter
this morning, from Leighton to Mrs Orr, about the wording of your
paper to the Committee,—"he had thought you wished to go into the
French Section"—though, in that case, I don't see what he would have
to do with your application. I have written to say that what I presume
you to want is to be included among the English exhibitors, not figuring as a Frenchman,—and that you only mentioned that the works
had been seen at the Salon to show that there was no likelihood of
their being disapproved of: they had all been previously exhibited in
London,—an essential requirement. At the same time, I suppose your
works will not be placed otherwise than with the English. I hope the
portrait will arrive in time: I have received a notice from the Grosvenor that the receiving days are April 8–9: I hardly think it likely that
the passage can be expeditious enough for *that:* I shall write and explain if necessary. I met Fildes at dinner last week, and he said the
resemblance was great,—he had only seen it at an early stage, you
know. I was at Leighton's morning party on Wednesday (Joachim,
Pialli and others) and shall meet him to-morrow at the Freshfields'.
We are very sorry for poor William Grove, whose wife died this
morning (of *dropsy*) after giving birth to a child some days before
—dead also. Her condition had long ago been judged,—without reference to her childbearing,—as quite certain to end as it has done. He
suffers terribly, as is inevitable. Well,—did you hear of my wonderful
stanza to illustrate Moscheles' really pretty and indeed imaginative
picture? He urged me to give it a name and find a motto descriptive
of it[1]—and I threw off a line or two,—which so delighted him that, I
cannot but think, he sent it to the "Pall Mall" and "Star"—which put
it in with a flaming puff! I should say, the picture was refused, before I did this, by the "Grosvenor." I went yesterday to see Nettleship's

pictures—fine and forcible, I thought—especially a life-size tiger. He is a clever fellow but "wanting is—what?"

I have had a letter from George,[2] giving me a few dates and facts. The blunder of Ocky[3] is inexplicable,—the birth place (proved by the family-bible's record) was quite other than he supposed,—and I was *just* on the point of sending his drawing to be engraved: and the Uncle, whose seat he supposed it to be, was only 18, at the time—neither an M. P. nor a county seat inhabitant. He has sent me many interesting MSS: poetry written at eleven years of age, and diaries &c. I shall give—if anything—merely the facts, without a word.

Dearest boy, I quite understand what you say about the inconvenience to both of us were I to prevent you from having your bills addressed here, by letting you know I should pay them myself—nor shall I do so: only, on this occasion, when you must naturally have an use for your money, it struck me as the best way of making you a birthday present: you can lay it out on a piece of furniture and consider that the little gift takes that form: so go on as before, and don't fear that I shall impoverish myself by too wanton a generosity! I had been intending to ask you to buy no lantern for me: when I spoke of it, I was expecting that the men here would put up *two* supports, one on each side of the wall, and the unused one would seem unseemly: they have only fixed a single one,—so that there is no sort of need for another lantern to correspond. Thank you, all the same, for your trouble. We had Nelly here, looking cheerful and well. I dine with the Schlesinger's this evening and shall meet her. Give my truest love to dearest Fannie: I can well believe you enjoyed your trip to Abano with her. I have had a letter from Mrs Margaret L. Woods, daughter of Dean Bradley, who is going to Venice "about April 4." She is very clever and agreeable—the author of that extremely interesting "Village Tragedy" which excited such attention, and also of some poems, privately printed, which have been highly praised by Fred: Harrison. She particularly wants to see Fannie and yourself during her short stay, and you would like her much. I give her, as she desires, a letter. Also, there will be a "personally-conducted party" of youths, sent by Toynbee Hall, to have their minds opened by a week spent in Venice —the conductor being Albert Ball, son of our friend: I assured him you would gladly show them over your palazzo.

Good bye, dearest Pen and dearest Fannie, God bless you both.

Yours affectionately ever

ROBT. BROWNING.

1889 : 7

To Robert Barrett Browning

29. De Vere Gardens.
W.
Apr. 11. '89.

Dearest Pen,—We heard last evening that "the marbles had arrived and would be delivered in due course"—which is not yet: you did most properly therefore in expediting the passage of the picture—which was on view for a clear week, and gave entire satisfaction. The utmost effort of criticism on Alma Tadema's part was—that a touch of shadow on the collar reflected from the beard would be advantageous,—and a broader shade on the pedestal to the left, of use to balance the light on the opposite side. He thought too the hand wanted a little modelling to explain its action better: I think there is something in that. Joachim, and the others were prodigal of praise: and Leighton told me he had heard it was a great success. L^y Millais came,—S. will tell you, for I was hardly ever present: she is prevented from going to Paris by an accident which has befallen somebody who was to have joined the party. Don't forget that Mr Ball's son, Alberto, will conduct a number of young men from Toynbee Hall, who are anxious to see Venice: and I have promised that you will do the honours of the Palazzo. Last evening I dined with the Leslies—and met Gordon, who spoke warmly of your kindness and that of Fannie to him—also of the capital effect of your doings in the Rezzonico. His wife did not accompany him—being oppressed, on returning to London, by the sorrow of her father—which seems to have been in abeyance during her stay in Italy. Millais was there—genial as ever. He has a fine landscape, they say: I went to the shows of Leighton, Val, Fildes, Dicksee, and Boughton—not to forget Poynter—whose small pictures are very pretty. I saw Woods for a moment in the street,—he had no show. If your picture needs varnishing I can desire it to be done at the "Grosvenor." The manager there is *Prange*—who wrote to me that he knew you in Dinant, and desired to be remembered to you. I am glad Fannie likes Mrs Woods. I wrote to M. Deschamps—giving the dimensions again: these people like making themselves of importance. By a paragraph in the Pall Mall it would seem that there is no room among the English exhibits for any sculpture,—and it will be placed with the French works. I told M. Deschamps you would give the necessary orders. Whenever all your arrangements on the outside of the Palazzo are complete, you may get executed for me—in large—the two photographs I have in little,—the front view only,—and the view in connection with the other palaces, ending with the Foscari: I will frame and hang them up. 4½ p. m./ The case arrived with the marbles capitally packed: I have just seen *one* opened safely, and Richard is busy with the other. They have been cleaned and look very well. The strange thing is—that, by this long route, they cost exactly *elevenpence* less than the much larger case with the picture—those being charged £4. 17″. while the picture came to 4. 17. 11.—so for elevenpence more, you saved a month's delay! I shall put them up where they will look effectively, I think: you have superintended the work, I am sure, so carefully has it been done. We went to see young Burne Jones' pictures,—clever but rather "finicking." We met there George Howard, now Lord Carlisle, who asked particularly after you. Our weather yesterday and this morning till past midday was very bad—I lit the gas, or could not have seen to write. All this about matters of little importance beside the fact of your being well, both of you, and enjoying the society of your friends—I am happy they are so contented with your performances,—the appearance of the Palazzo &c: it will be such good news for Fannie's friends at home. I shall leave off here, and let S. who is out but will return shortly, add a word if she pleases. I saw Natorp this morning,—he is going away for a change of air till after the holidays. Dearest Fannie, dearest Pen, bless you both! Yours

ever affectionately
R B.

I will write to Dr. Brinton as he desires.

It is near post-time and I will not wait for S. The marble with the heads is broken in two at one end. Was it so when packed? The joining will be very easy, and not discernible.

1889 : 8

To T. J. NETTLESHIP

29, De Vere Gardens,
W.
May 16th, 1889.

My dear Nettleship,

First of all let me say how glad we are, my sister and myself, to hear from you.

There was a report, or something more definite, that you had been ill; and I looked in vain for any picture on the walls of the Academy, and other Galleries. At the former are lions enough—but none to make up for the absence of yours. I hope that, if you have really suffered at all, the worst is over, and the good weather, when it shall be confirmedly good, will have due effect on you.

I believe it was as you say with the poem in question.[1] I heard, first of all, the merest sketch of the story on the spot. Milsand told me that the owner of the house had destroyed himself from remorse at having behaved unfilially to his mother. In a subsequent visit (I paid one every year while Milsand lived there) he told me some other particulars, and they at once struck me as likely to have been occasioned by religious considerations as well as passionate woman-love,—and I concluded that there was no intention of committing suicide; and I said at once that I would myself treat the subject *just so*.

Afterward he procured me the legal documents. I collected the accounts current among the people of the neighbourhood, inspected the house and grounds, and convinced myself that I had guessed rightly enough in every respect. Indeed the facts are so exactly put down, that, in order to avoid the possibility of prosecution for Libel—that is, telling the exact truth—I changed all the names of persons and places, as they stood in the original "Proofs," and gave them as they are to be found in Mrs. Orr's Hand-book.

But it is long ago, now, since I wrote the poem; which I have never read till I was obliged to run through it, for corrections, a few weeks ago; and I cannot remember at this moment any but the general state of the case, as I give it to you—for what it may be worth—and very hurriedly.

> Ever affectionately yours,
> ROBERT BROWNING.

1889 : 9

To Miss Alma Lehmann[1]

> 29, De Vere Gardens,
> London, W.
> July 6th, 1889.

My beloved Alma,

I had the honour yesterday of dining with the Shah, whereupon the following dialogue:—

"Vous êtes poète?"

"On s'est permis de me le dire quelquefois."

"Et vous avez fait des livres?"

"Trop de livres."

"Voulez-vous m'en donner un, afin que je puisse me ressouvenir de vous?"

"Avec plaisir."

I have been accordingly this morning to town, where the thing is procurable, and as I chose a volume of which I judged the binding might take the imperial eye, I said to myself, "Here do I present my poetry to a personage for whom I do not care three straws; why should I not venture to do as much for a young lady I love dearly, who, for the author's sake, will not impossibly care rather for the inside than the outside of the volume?" So I was bold enough to take one and offer it to you for your kind acceptance, begging you to remember in days to come that the author, whether a good poet or no, was always, my Alma,

Your affectionate friend,

ROBERT BROWNING.

1889 : 10

TO W. G. KINGSLAND

29. De Vere Gardens.

W.

July 7. '89.

My dear Mr. Kingsland,

Will you be good and kind enough to forgive me under the circumstances which you are to hear. I received a letter from you enclosing one from a friend you wished me to see—as I shall be happy to do. But the letter came just as I was on the point of leaving for Oxford—where I stayed a week—and I had no time to do more than glance at what I was intending to notice particularly on my return,—before which it was useless to do so. Well, on my return some days ago, I searched everywhere for the letters and could not find in what safe place I have laid them away—so safe a place, that I am sure they will soon turn up—possibly as soon as I make this confession—but meanwhile I am distressed to think you are awaiting an answer so unaccountably delayed. I therefore discontinue a hitherto fruitless search to say that if you will grant me an indulgence I greatly need, and write—in two lines—what you desire on the part of your friend, I will take care that, this time, you shall not be kept waiting one minute longer than is necessary to say I will (I repeat) be happy to receive your friend—to whom pray make what excuse you can,—and indeed could you know the vexation my apparent carelessness has caused me, your pardon and his also would be cheerfully granted.

Ever, my dear Kingsland,
Yours most truly
ROBERT BROWNING.

1889 : 11

To NORMAN MAC COLL

29. De Vere Gardens.
W.
July 9. '89.

My dear Mac Coll,

The incident I have recorded in verse[1] took place last Sunday. If you consider that the feeling I gave some faint expression to in the accompanying stanzas is discordant with the general tone of the poetry in your columns—pray let me have them again for publication elsewhere. Remember I never saw the man, nor did my wife ever know of his existence.

Ever truly yours
ROBERT BROWNING.

1889 : 12

To ROBERT BARRETT BROWNING

29. De Vere Gardens.
W.
July 13. '89.

Dearest Pen, with this you will get to-day's "Athenæum," and see what I have said in reply to Fitzgerald's brutality. I opened the book, at just this place, as I have said. There was more abuse of "Aurora Leigh" and women-writers generally, but *that* he had a right to say, and take the consequences of being a fool and worse: but the shocking notion of thanking God for the death of a person who never saw him (any more than did I) and never heard of his name—(as was only the case with me, a few years ago)—*this* was unbearable, and I was not going to let the people who are reading the book suppose for a moment that I am inclined to let such a ruffian insult the dead with impunity. The main thing will be to get the Editor, Aldis Wright, duly blamed for his stupidity—which is inconceivable—in letting such a blackguardism pass, when he could have simply dropped it out and done harm to nobody—least of all to the wretched Irish fribble and "feather-head," as his own friends allowed him to be. I was dreadfully afraid that the letter might have been written to Tennyson, whose adulatory lick-spittle he always was: but the critique in the "Athenæum" mentions that no letters to him are published. I shall not look at the book again: in all likelihood he has delivered himself of the usual impertinences about *me:* and if that is the case, I should be sorry to even seem in the least moved by any other than contempt for the poor envious creature, and might wish I had let him alone, as the more dignified way: as it is, all I know is that the fellow insulted one unable to defend herself—who yet is able to express his loathing for such a scamp. I shall now try and forget it all—having really been the worse, physically, for this outrage.

I wrote a long letter you must have got by this time.

Ever affectionately yours
ROBERT BROWNING.

I have received a singularly fine large photograph from Watts, of his portrait of myself. I shall give it to Fannie: it is better than the Picture itself—that is, without its colour,—so we think. I had a long talk with Millais two days ago: he had been informed I was certainly meaning to write the laudatory lines for his portrait of G. about which I told you: he said to himself "That's if B. *will.*" He approved, of course. All love to Fannie—every hope that she will soon be herself. I send the "Pall Mall"—now that Miss F. G.[1] is going to marry a Home-Ruler, they notice her poems favorably!

1889 : 13

TO DR. F. J. FURNIVALL[1]

29, De Vere Gardens,
London, W.
July 16th, 1889.

My dear Furnivall,

Yes, it is sad to think, as Keats says, that "Honey can't be got without hard money,"[2] and literary honey, of whatever the sort, any more than the bee's product. But Smith sells "Collections," and pays me for the right of doing so, while he cannot hinder the Americans from taking them and paying nothing at all—so that you cannot wonder if he is disinclined to allow the payers-of-nothing there to compete with his publications here, and pay nothing into the bargain. So, "curse nobody, but grin and bear it."

As to my own utterance after receiving unexpectedly an outrage, why, like all impulsive actions, once the impulse over, I believe I might preferably have left the thing to its proper contempt. But there was something too shocking in a man, whom my wife never even heard of, "feeling relieved at her death, he must say"—and I too said what I must. The people who tell you "his opinion was really on the woman question" talk nonsense. He might have uttered any amount of impertinence about women's work in general, and that of my wife in particular, without getting a word out of me—but, "to be relieved at the *death* which would stop the work, thank God."

How Editor and Publisher could let this passage remain in the letter which a pen-scratch would have left unobjectionable, passes my power of understanding. It is noticeable that the passage is immediately preceded by a sign (. . .) that something considered really objectionable has been omitted: this might pass!

I have your XVth volume, but the XVIth will follow so soon now that I may send them in one packet.

Ever truly yours,
R. Browning.

The answers to the Examination paper are perfect: "lasagne"[3] are the long broad ribbon-like strings of macaroni.

1889 : 14

To Robert Barrett Browning

29. De Vere Gardens.
W.
July 17, '89.

Dearest Pen, I got both your letters, one after the other. You are wrong in supposing that such expressions as that of Fitzgerald, "recoil sufficiently on those who use them": the praise of the book was unbounded in the papers,—nobody thinking it worth while to say a word about Fitzgerald's little slip of the tongue or his editor's trifling mistake in printing it: and here was a piece of brutality to go on circulating without the least objection from anybody. People, with their usual perspicacity, would be just as likely, or more so, to suppose *I* was quite indifferent about it, as that I felt merely contempt for its author: and "contempt" is not exactly applicable to a man of such wide and high reputation as Fitzgerald—whose opinion is likely to be of *real* influence just now—when a new edition is coming out, of the works he "thanks God are at an end." There are so many falsehoods told about me,—of a gossiping kind,—that I believe my silence would have been considered very natural. The Publisher has written to express his "pain and grief at the outrageous words" and the fool of an Editor gets blamed all round for his stupidity—the secondary cause of it all. One may decline any painful duty on very specious grounds—letting the thing recoil &c—but I said a little of my mind and there it will remain—I expect as long as Fitzgerald's recorded "relief"—the blackguard. I have inspected the book since: *my* name only occurs once in it—he calls me a "great man": people would have understood why *that* caused me to placable. And now enough of him. I enclose a letter just to show how another kind of man feels on the subject; and now dismiss it.

No, it was Leighton who, I *know,* was disappointed terribly at getting nothing of importance: I don't know the difference between the awards of the English and the French Jury: Millais told me *he* had not competed. Anyhow, if the Jury pleased to give a medal *over the heads* of the regular Jury,—whichever it was Leighton desired to be excused from appealing to,—they have not given him the same honor as Moore and others. I am glad Julian[1] has the medal: Story's work is exactly as I described it to you when I saw the photographs at St. Moritz: this comes of wanting to be universally a smatterer—just as if he had got to the end of all to be done in sculpture thirty years ago—as I believe was the case with all *he* was able to do. Waldo and his wife called here, some days ago,—S. called in return, but did not see them.

How happy I am at the restored health of Fannie there is little need to say. I daresay she will write. I am glad she was able to see somewhat of the exhibition.

I have some rather large bills from Austin Beale and Sampson which I will pay next week or earlier (I have paid Austin) Austin, 61.18.9. Beale 17.10.10. Sampson 12.10.6.—total 92.0. 1. You must remember the Palace, and take care.

Ever affy. yours R B.

[*Continued by Sarianna Browning*]

Dearest Pen,

Fannie is kind in wishing to blame our servants rather than me, but the fault of the delayed letter was entirely mine. I see now how it occurred. I am extremely sorry for it,—servants are often blamed for their master's faults.

I need not say I knew nothing of the verses, or their cause, till I saw them in print—Your papa was quite ill with the pain it gave him. It was shameful of the editor of F's Life, to insert such a letter.

Henrietta Corkran talks of going over to Paris, and has asked me for your address. Mrs. Bronson tells us, she has bought a small place at Asolo. If you leave Paris, say to what address the newspapers ought to be sent. The man is Wade, 25, High St. Kensington.

Your aff

S.

1889 : 15

To Alfred, Lord Tennyson[1]

29, De Vere Gardens,
London, W.
August 5th, 1889.

My dear Tennyson,

To-morrow is your birthday—indeed a memorable one. Let me say I associate myself with the universal pride of our country in your glory, and in its hope that for many and many a year we may have your very self among us—secure that your poetry will be a wonder and delight to all those appointed to come after. And for my own part, let me further say, I have loved you dearly. May God bless you and yours!

At no moment from first to last of my acquaintance with your works, or friendship with yourself, have I had any other feeling, expressed or kept silent, than this which an opportunity allows me to utter—that I am and ever shall be, my dear Tennyson, admiringly and affectionately yours,

Robert Browning.

1889 : 16

To Robert Barrett Browning

(Glass at 66°)
29. De Vere Gardens.
W.
Aug. 16. '89.

Dearest Pen, I got your kind letter two days ago but refrained from answering it till I could get one from Mrs Bronson to whom I had written—and her answer came next day. I daresay she will have told you that we mean to go to Asolo where she promises to get us good rooms at the Inn. All you say is affectionate and considerate,—but you must not suppose my weariness and indisposition to undertake a long journey were trifling hindrances to the great delight of seeing you. At the end of the season,—which dates from my last "Dinner out"—July 26th three weeks ago—I profited remarkably by the entire rest—also by the pleasant weather, now that I could enjoy it my own way; and the difficulties naturally seem diminished. I *did* fancy that a day's journey only, to some quiet place in Scotland, might answer my purpose of getting braced-up. But for the last fortnight the cold (for *Summer*) has been remarkable, as you may have heard,—for *that* and the rain threaten to ruin the harvest of which such great hopes were entertained: and Scotland seemed a very undesirable place even now—while to remain there for more than a few weeks would be impossible. Meanwhile, treating London as the bracing-place, I took plenty of exercise—walking, for the last week two hours daily, and the result is I am in an altogether different condition from this time last year—the day, I believe, when we arrived at Primiero. There is no need of trying to escape heat now,—two days ago, S. remarked she would "like to have a fire, except for the shame of the thing,"—but a change is an advantage of another kind and perhaps as necessary,— certainly for S.,—and I concluded that the best way would be to go to Asolo, my old attraction—now immensely increased by the prospective company of Mrs Bronson—and, if the weather does not suit, we shall be close by Primiero as a resource: and, say at the end of September go to Venice for a month at least. Nothing can possibly give me so much pleasure as being with you and my dearest Fannie (and her Sister too) in your own beautiful house, and seeing for myself all you have done and intend to do—and this enjoyment I trust to obtain—but you ought not to fancy that a little inconvenience stood in the way of my joining you this year: it was worse than *that*. So, I shall hope to set out in a few days—breaking the journey at Berne—for a day: if I start *well* there is no fatigue before Basle: of course I will write and apprise you of everything: Mrs B. has engaged to write in a day or two.

For the rest, there is no news: through Fannie's goodness, we hear from her often, and satisfactorily—so too, as concerning Marie. I am more oppressed by letters from all sorts of people than I can describe with patience,—also, I have work of my own to do. I had a pleasant cheerful letter from Miss FitzG. last evening—she spoke of a letter from Fannie which had much gratified her. She and her mother are at Pontresina. I cannot resist the temptation of copying a letter I received a few days ago from Tennyson: I had written to congratulate him on completing his 80th year on the 6th (people say it should be the 5th) He acknowledged the general correspondence in the "Times"— but wrote to me as follows: "Aug^t '89. My dear Browning, I thank you with my whole heart and being for your noble and affectionate letter, and with my whole heart and being I return your friendship. To be loved and appreciated by so great and powerful a nature as yours will be a solace to me, and lighten my dark hours during the short time of life that is left to me. Ever yours, Tennyson." I am not to tell you, whom I can trust and who understand besides that I would on no account have anybody see a word of this letter—(Fannie and you are one)—it would literally be the death of me in a sense: but I want you to know that T. is not the man to sympathize with a poor creature like Fitz Gerald, whom I punished no more than he deserved—heartily wishing he were alive in the body—not, for the first time, alive in his words which only now go forth to the world: I *did* nothing—only said what I would certainly have done had they been spoken in my hearing. I find the excuse of the friendly reviewers who loaded the book with praise was—"they hoped the passage would be unobserved!"

Ever affectionately yours
ROBERT BROWNING

How is Lady Layard?—if she arrived at Venice.

[Continued by Sarianna Browning]

Dearest Pen, you need not be told I am glad your papa resolves on Asolo and Venice. Dear Mrs. Bronson assured him we could find rooms at the hôtel. I wish he would start at once before waiting till he falls ill. There is not the slightest reason that I can see that Mrs. B. should write again, but as she kindly said she will do so, I hope she will, that we may set off. Your papa is in good health now—but he may change. I am sure I feel as if I should enjoy getting away. London is very empty. You know how delighted I shall be to see you later on. I do not think Asolo will be much too warm. We can stay there the longer—which involves, staying the longer at Venice.

Ever your aff^{te}
SARIANNA.

1889 : 17

To Miss Edith Adams

29, De Vere Gardens,
London, W.
August 28th, 1889.

Dear Miss Adams,

I have much to beg your forgiveness on account of—here is the fact, which I can only commend to your kind consideration.

Through some inadvertence, your poems[1] and the accompanying letter only came under my notice this morning—this all but last morning of my continuance in England for the rest of the year. Consequently, I could only give a hurried attention to what, I feel sure, deserves careful reading.

Hasty as my examination has been, it satisfies me that you possess music and fancy in a high degree. I shall remember your name, and be on the watch for the appearance if not of these yet of abler proofs, that still "There is room in the blue for a new Song-Bird."[2]

Believe me,
Yours very cordially,
ROBERT BROWNING.

1889 : 18

To Fannie Barrett Browning

Asolo, Oct. 4., '89.

Two years ago since your Wedding-Day, dearest Fannie! If I was happy then in the belief that you would be a blessing to me and to us all,—how must I feel now when assured by experience that you are all I could possibly hope or desire? So it is, and so I pray it may continue to be. I trust you also are as happy as you deserve: if your Husband's love and ours can make you so,—but what is beyond human power to effect, may God grant,—is all I am able to say.

Pen's visit was a true benefit to us. I suppose he reached you surely and safely. Tell him, we went afterwards in order to purchase the articles he had wished to acquire: but the man was obdurate,—refused to abate a farthing: and as I concluded that Pen thought his demand too high I would not then agree to it. If he should think it reasonable after all,—of course I can close with the old fellow: but there must be many similar articles to be found at Venice where we shall soon find ourselves.

I wish with all my heart we could hear that dear Marie's health was completely re-established. Give her my true love and that of S. (who writes herself).

And, once more, God bless you, my own dearest Fannie! I am ever most

affectionately yours
ROBERT BROWNING.

1889 : 19

TO ROBERT BARRETT BROWNING

Asolo, Oct. 21., '89.

Dearest Pen, I am happy to see your handwriting again, as I was to read Fannie's letter received two days ago. I feel sorry indeed that we had no opportunity of seeing Marie before her departure: it was quite right to accompany her so far as to ensure her easy travelling for the rest of the journey: and though Fannie feels the absence naturally, she must be consoled by knowing that the visit to Venice has done evident good. Yes, I am surprised too at the stupidity of the Custom House People about the direction which they call "insufficient": S. took the greatest care that it should be accurate in every respect. I shall be anxious to know that you have received the picture safely. It was a pity though unavoidable that you missed the sights during the Prince's stay at Venice: I have no doubt your lights and flags cut a good figure. As to the Asolo affair, the Sindaco at once called on our landlady Nina and informed her that he had called all the Giunta what his

brother-in-law had called him—"Asini" for not knowing who I was—
which he laid to blame of Nina who had only told him it was a
"poeta"—"e non qual poeta"—which was not to be wondered at: but
from the profusion of honors he bestowed on me ("Doctor in so many
universities" &c. &c.) I can see friend Marcato has been "laying it on"
pretty thickly—for which, pray tell him, I am duly grateful. We have
not allowed a word to transpire and the matter could not be more
advantageously laid in any other hands than yours and Marcato's—
though we are intimately acquainted with an influential member of
the Giunta here, Count Loredano, who will certainly be helpful in
the matter whenever it is in his power. My own desire to get the house
is rather increased than abated by my greater experience of the country: you may take my word for it, you have not half seen the capabilities of enjoyment in the place. Every fresh drive we take shows us
new beauty: the day we took you to Bassano we returned by a new
route, close under the mountains comparatively, with Romano to our
right, and we all agreed it exceeded in interest what we had hitherto
seen: and since then it has been the same with other unexplored roads
—the only drawback is the persistent bad weather—which the inhabitants say is unexampled: "last year was one uninterrupted series
of fine days &c." Still, when the fine exceptions do occur they are fine
indeed: we walk in a blaze of sun under a bluest of skies, S and I, for
above two hours—and have no wish to change the roads, now so
glorified by the Autumn tints on the verdure everywhere. For the
last two days we got very tolerable walking, and yesterday a drive too
—but the rain overtook us. A few days ago we drove to S. Zenoni,
the scene of that tragedy we told you of: and I ascended the tower
where Alberico and his five sons and two daughters were shut in till,
starved out, they surrendered and were tortured to death: a peasant
showed us some iron arrow-heads found in digging—certainly of that
time: and I bought them, 6, for 2 f^{cs}. In fine, I and S could enjoy ourselves here for any length of time did but our lodgings admit of it:
but there are no fire-places and the cold is what you may suppose. Mrs
B. continues to do her very utmost to make us comfortable in every
possible way: she is remarkably cheerful and satisfied with staying
on—to our surprise, for she must miss the conveniences of Cà Alvisi,[1]
—and I was not prepared for her giving up so readily those afternoon
and evening callers and the smoking tea-parties: yet so it clearly is.
But this life of ours cannot last for ever, and, if you are ready to receive
us, I suppose we ought to go at the month's end. I sent off my new
Volume[2] last Tuesday, and this morning, with yours, comes a pleasant

letter from Smith announcing its safe arrival—about which I had some fears, though I registered the big parcel. It will be put in type at once. The first vol. of E. B. B's works will appear next Saturday. There may be some trouble and delay (not *very* much) if I am not in England a little later on. I had a good-natured letter, two days ago, from George (directed to London) who "fancied I must be returned from the Tyrol"—however *that* got into his head. He wanted to know all about you, and the palazzo, very kindly—said that "Charlotte Altham, Surtees' daughter by his second wife, is shortly to be married to Mr Stewart, the Rector of the Parish in which Timbercombe is situated." But the best thing he says is the following: after speaking of you and F.—"By the way, the more I look at her photograph which your Sister so kindly sent me, the more winning it becomes. It is full of intellectual character, and also captivating from a singular softness and gentleness of expression." Fannie informed us of the Storys' gift—very kind and good of them. I wish we could have seen them before the bad weather set in. Give them our affectionate regards—also every kind remembrance to the Curtises, one and all: how different was the weather when, this time last year, I took those delightful walks with them on the Lido! It is rainy to-day. I observe by the "Venezia" that the "Galleggiante" was to be stationed at the Rezzonico: it rained here—and I suppose the music was none of the most cheerful. That poor Mrs Moore! You see—what I always saw—what a set of *canaille* she has been befooled by! and how exquisitely foolish she makes herself, as usual. There is no possibility of influencing her for her own good, and I am glad to be away. Dearest Pen, dearest Fannie, all love to you both: I trust soon to see you. Tell us if the picture has come safely: any news however is precious, for I am

ever yours most affectionately

R B.

ROBERT BROWNING AND ROBERT WIEDEMANN
BARRETT BROWNING

VENICE, 1889

APPENDIX

APPENDIX

Browning and Lady Ashburton

(Reprinted from *The Yale Review*, Autumn, 1932.)

AMONG the hitherto unpublished letters of Robert Browning is one of prime interest. It takes the central place in a chain of evidence regarding his relations with Louisa Lady Ashburton, with their highly important bearing upon his later life and work. It was addressed to Edith Marion Story, daughter of the American sculptor, William Wetmore Story. Browning had known her from her infancy, when he and his wife had first become intimate friends of the Storys in Rome. The letter was written at the country house of Lady Marian Alford. It refers to her house in Park Lane, where Browning was a frequent guest. "Hatty" is Harriet Hosmer, the American sculptress, "Pen" is Browning's son, and "Lady A." is Lady Ashburton. The people to whom the poet refers may best be introduced more fully after the letter itself has been given. It reads:

> Belton House,
> Grantham
> April 4, 1872

Dearest Edith,

Thank you very much for your letter and all its kindness. I have only a short quarter of an hour at my service, but I want to answer it with no more delay than I can help—and, to get done with the one unpleasantness first,—what you tell me about Hatty and the "intimate friends" and their report of me which made her cut our old and long friendship short, is the one touch wanting to confirm my impression of her behaviour in that matter. I suggested that her authority *might possibly* be Mrs. Sartoris's, not at all because I saw reason to suspect her of anything worse than a little disliking, with or without reason, which she had, and still may have for aught I know, but from a remainder of respect to Hatty—who *might have* paid attention to any story reported by somebody who, at all events, was intimate with all three of the parties concerned,—myself, Hatty and Lady A.—she turns out, however, to have thought it quite just and proper to listen to people I never by any possibility can have mentioned Lady A's name to (for I *know* well to whom, and under what particular circumstances, I ever was induced to mention the name) and then, without giving me a hint of what the story was, how I might explain it or expose it, to take on herself to write that letter: that is,—to say she took it on herself,—for I don't believe any such nonsense, or that she was anything but the cat's paw of Lady A. in the business,—who, knowing she had only succeeded, after nine or ten months' teazing with her invitations, to get me to promise to visit her for one day, and so get handsomely done with it all,—wanted to have the air of shutting the door in my face with a final bang,—fancying that she could coax me round the back-way the very next day,—as she did by sending a servant and a letter of invitation to the house in Park Lane. I have told her my mind so thoroughly about *that,* and so effectually relieved myself from any further bother of the kind, that I need not bring up the nauseating remembrance. She and I have met once since, and I felt excused from even looking at—much less, speaking to her. But I should like to know,—whatever the story may have been,—what business Hatty had with my behaviour to Lady A. in Lady A's house? I suppose that Lady A. did not suppress what she considered the capital point of her quarrel with me when she foamed out into the couple of letters she bespattered me with,—yet the worst she charged me with was,—having said that my heart was buried in Florence, and the attractiveness of a marriage with her lay in its advantage to Pen—two simple facts,—as I told her,— which I had never left her in ignorance about, for a moment, though that I ever paraded this in a gross form to anybody is simply false; but had it been true,—does Hatty instantly practise impertinence on any friend of hers who intends to make an ambitious or mercenary marriage? As for her devotion to Lady A., begetting this chivalrous ardour in her,—Lady A. has got plenty of friends quite as intimate, who never fancied for a moment that they were called on to fight her battles. For instance, I have been a week here with Lady Marian Alford, whom I was especially invited to meet,—she, I fancy, received the utmost of Lady A's confidences, and heard whatever there was to hear; and nothing can exceed the friendliness with which we converse day after day; which is only to say, that she is a rational woman of the world, valuing her own independence, and understanding that there are two ways of telling a story. So, now, I have done with Hatty, for once and always. Had I believed stories about her, many a long year ago, and ordered her away from people's houses on the strength of them, I should have lost a friendship I used to value highly; but I have gained some pleasant memories by being less ready than she to believe slanderous gossip,—and, as she has elected to know me only through the reports of others, though I would have shown what they were worth in a minute, had she given me the opportunity; so shall our relation be, and no otherwise, to the end of time. I scribble all this as fast as the pen can drive, but you will understand, and help with your sympathy and intelligence, I know.

Well, I am glad of all you tell me,—of the statue's news, of your approaching visit to London, of the enjoyments, in various ways, you tell me about so pleasantly. I have come here for a little change and relaxation, my six month's stay in town having begun to get the better of me. Pen is with his kind friends in Scotland, whence he writes in good spirits to-day. I shall return soon, having to go to "prep"—prepare, indeed! All my love to you all—don't let this very indignant letter hide the true feeling that is under it. This, I trust will be the last of my returning to that detestable subject.

Ever affectionately yours, dearest Edith,

R. B.

This long letter serves to bind together many circumstances and details in the story of Browning's proposal of marriage to Lady Ashburton. The bare fact of the proposal which it mentions has also been preserved by oral tradition. It was known to a few scholars in 1927 when Professor William Clyde De Vane, Jr., in his book on Browning's "Parleyings," first showed that the stanzas in the "Parleying with Daniel Bartoli" about the "she-shape" which troubled the duke had an autobiographical significance. With regard to the story Mr. De Vane wrote, "Intimate friends of Browning knew that . . . he had proposed to, and been refused by, a certain lady of title," and drew the inference that the "bold she-shape" was the poetic representation of this woman who had intervened between Browning and the memory of Elizabeth Barrett.

Lady Ashburton, the "lady of title" whom Mr. De Vane was not authorized to name in his discussion of the poem, was a most remarkable person. In Griffin's and Minchin's *Life* of Browning we read: "In July [1869] Browning was out of sorts. 'I was unwell,' he writes to Mrs. Frederick Lehman, 'having been so for some time—and felt the grasshopper a burden all day long in the house, from which I never stirred.' In this mood northern latitudes attracted him. In company with the Storys and their daughter he set out for Scotland, staying first at a little inn on Loch Achnault, near Garve, where the old style of life was renewed—luncheon amid the heather, followed by chapters from *Rob Roy*—and afterwards at Loch Luichart Lodge, where Louisa, Lady Ashburton, a brilliant if somewhat overpowering personage, was their hostess. Lady Marian Alford, a friend in Roman days, was among those who listened to the readings from *The Ring and the Book*."

Henry James has given us a more detailed description of this "overpowering personage" in *William Wetmore Story and his Friends,* written in 1903, the year of Lady Ashburton's death. His record, which throws a kindly haze about her, begins: "We wander here still amid shades—not the less, I feel, at a moment when the late Louisa Lady Ashburton, one of the most eminent of the friends from early years, joins the company. This so striking and interesting personage, a rich, generous presence that, wherever encountered, seemed always to fill the foreground with colour, with picture, with fine mellow sound and, on the part of every one else, with a kind of traditional charmed, amused patience—this brilliant and fitful apparition was a familiar *figure* for our friends, as, throughout, for the society of her time, and I come, in my blurred record, frequently upon her name." James devotes several hundred delightfully subtle words to her personality in connection with his account of the visit of Browning and the Storys to her at Loch Luichart in 1869. And he ends thus: "The delayed visit took place, with compensations abounding, with, in fact, for the consciousness of the present chronicler, more interesting passages of personal history than may here be touched upon."

The "interesting passages of personal history" are obviously the relations—his proposal of marriage and the ill feeling its terms caused—between Browning and this splendid lady, disclosed to Henry James by the letters from Browning to the Storys which were then in his hands.

At this point we turn to Harriet Hosmer, then at the height of her career as sculptress. She was of the circle, a central figure, indeed—an American friend of the Brownings in the Roman days, and a particularly intimate comrade of the Storys during winters of work in Rome and summers in England, a protégé of Lady Ashburton's and as intimate a friend as she could well have had. Harriet Hosmer, the "Hatty" of these letters, becomes "the chief agent" in the affair. Her first meeting with Lady Ashburton had been in Rome, in 1867. Her account of the incident is worth quoting, both for its description of Lady Ashburton and for its feminine flattery. If Henry James's account of Lady Ashburton's charm were not sufficient to establish her right to Browning's special admiration, Miss Hosmer's would be.

"On an eventful day of the year 1867," she writes, "came a lady to the studio bringing a note of introduction from a mutual friend. I have a distinct recollection of stonily gazing at the lady when she presented herself, and of so remaining, gazing, with no thought of advancing to greet her, for, as I gazed, it seemed to my bewildered senses that the Ludovisi Goddess in person, weary, perhaps, of the long imprisonment of Art, had assumed the stature and the state of mortals and stood before me. There were the same square-cut and grandiose features, whose classic beauty was humanized by a pair of keen, dark eyes, lovely smile, and then a rich, musical voice of inquiry, arousing me to the situation. And here I may add, by way of parenthesis, as greatly amused was I, but less surprised, when, in after years, the lady laughingly characterized my deportment that day as 'most pe-

LOUISA LADY ASHBURTON

(WIFE OF THE SECOND LORD ASHBURTON) AND HER ONLY
DAUGHTER MAYSIE

From a portrait painted by Sir Edwin Landseer in 1862.

culiar.' Did no wave from the Fortunate Isles bear to me a prophetic whisper of this beautiful woman? No! and we talked of art, and of Rome, and of our common friend, as strangers talk who meet for a pleasant hour, then go their ways.

"Those who at that period of her life knew Louisa, Lady Ashburton, for she it was, then in the height of her splendid beauty, will recognize the portrait. Born of a great race, she looked her greatness, but her chief charm lay neither in her nobility of presence nor in her classic outline of feature, but in the ever varying radiance of expression, which each moment wrought undiscovered charms in the lovely face, as sunlight playing over a flower renders it ever more beautiful than before. And to those rare gifts was added the perhaps still rarer one of an exquisitely modulated voice, rich and musical, with every inflection of which the human voice is capable. Such was the personality of the lady whose acquaintance I made on that auspicious day, and which ripened into a friendship that throughout her life knew no shadow of change."

At the time when Browning proposed to Lady Ashburton she was at the height of a brilliant social career. She was third daughter of the Rt. Hon. James Alexander Stuart Mackenzie, and heir to the Mackenzie estate of nearly 30,000 acres in Rossshire. In 1871 her lands alone amounted to about 33,000 acres worth about £6000 a year. At her death in 1903, at the age of seventy-six, her will probated over £285,000 gross. Her husband, William Bingham (Baring), Baron Ashburton, had died in March, 1864, five years after his marriage to her.

Such was the lady who became the central figure in this story. Besides her friend Harriet Hosmer, the others who had a part in it were William Wetmore Story, Browning's disciple in writing and teacher in modelling, more a comrade of the poet's than any other man in all the fifty years of his later life; Emelyn Story, his wife; and his daughter Edith Marion Story—all of them knew well not only Browning but Lady Ashburton and Harriet Hosmer, and all remained Browning's stanch friends. There was also Lady Marian Alford, fully as great and popular a figure in London as Lady Ashburton, a patroness too of Harriet Hosmer, a friend of Browning from the Roman days, and a friend indeed in the matter of Lady Ashburton. In the background was the brilliant Mrs. Sartoris (Adelaide Kemble), another friend from Roman days, at this time, apparently, ranged somehow on the side of Lady Ashburton and Harriet Hosmer.

One other person played at once the least conspicuous and the most important part in the whole affair—the poet's son Robert Wiede-mann Barrett Browning, "Pen." At the time of his mother's death in 1861, he appeared as a strangely talented and charming boy of twelve; from that moment he became his father's main concern in life. The boy failed to secure admission to Balliol under Jowett, and finally on January 19, 1869, matriculated at Christ Church. He was now twenty. In college he took an interest in boating and billiards. His attendance was interrupted by sickness, and he presently abandoned the struggle. Certainly by the summer of 1869, Pen was a very real problem to his father. In February, 1868, Browning wrote that the boy might "want no end of money." In August, 1871, he wrote, "Pen won't work." Apparently Browning had in Pen not merely a great "worry" but a strong motive for considering a marriage of convenience in 1869.

The story of Browning and Lady Ashburton begins soon after the poet's return to London, when he picked up the broken thread of his life and assumed a place in society. As early as November, 1863, he had written to Story of forwarding a parcel to Lady Ashburton for him. In a letter to Isa Blagden from Loch Luichart, in August, 1869, when Browning was Lady Ashburton's guest at Loch Luichart Lodge on her estate in Rossshire, he writes, "Here at an old friend's, I am comfortable altogether." (It is perhaps worth noting that he avoids mentioning Lady Ashburton's name, and that in no extant letter of Browning's to Miss Blagden does he actually mention it.) One early item, perhaps the earliest, is the name of Lady Ashburton in his ad-dress-book, among the A's, four lines below that of Lady Marian Alford—a dear friend of Lady Ashburton's, and doubtless one of Browning's first hostesses in London—and just above the names of "Matthew Arnold," "Mr. Austin" (Alfred Austin), and "Mr. Adams, American Ministre, 5 Upper Portland Place," bracketed with "Henry B. Adams." Browning wrote of calling on Arnold in November, 1866. Charles Francis Adams and his son left England in May, 1868. These bits of evidence suggest the social circles in which Browning came to know Lady Ashburton, and the approximate date of their first meeting, doubtless before the death of her husband, in March, 1864.

The central episode in this story—Browning's proposal, with its dramatic consequences—may be traced through a succession of letters beginning with one from the poet to Miss Blagden from Audièrne, dated October 19, 1868. The part which concerns us is as follows: "I rejoice at your pleasure in Scotland; no doubt it is a beautiful place; I have at least half a dozen invitations from friends to go there this year; one letter lies by yours, describing just such another lovely place in Rossshire, but I can't get up the steam. Pen is with Mr. Jowett and his reading party at St. Andrews,—quite well and in spirits." Lady Marian Alford and Harriet Hosmer were guests of Lady Ashburton's in October, 1868, at Loch Luichart, on the estate in Rossshire. If the letter lying beside Isa's was not from one of these three women— perhaps from Hatty Hosmer, as probably most influential with the poet, and written with the knowledge and approval of Lady Ashburton—all signs fail.

Loch Luichart Lodge, at any rate, was in the following year the scene of the visit famous in Browning biography and described at length in James's Life of Story. The party at Loch Luichart included Lady Marian, her son Lord Brownlow, the Storys, and Sir Roderick Murchison, besides the Brownings (Robert, his sister Sarianna, and his son Pen). Of course, Hatty Hosmer was missed, and desired. A letter of hers to Mrs. Carr, published by the recipient in her *Harriet Hosmer Letters and Memories,* makes plain the circumstances:—

Rome, Sep. 1869

Dear C.:

Oh, I have just had a document, Browning's last unpublished poem! It seems that the Storys, Mr. Browning and his sister (Sarianna), Lady Marian Alford, and Sir Roderick Murchison, all found themselves staying with Lady Ashburton at her place in Scotland, so they got up a Round Robin, written by Browning, which was despatched to me. Here it is:

Loch Luichart, Dingwall, N.B.

> Dear Hosmer; or still dearer, Hatty—
> Mixture of *miele* and of *latte,*
> So good and sweet and—somewhat fatty—
>
> Why linger still in Rome's old glory
> When Scotland lies so cool before ye?
> Make haste and come!—quoth Mr. Story.
>
> Sculpture is not a thing to sit to
> In summertime; do find a fit toe
> To kick the clay aside a bit—oh,
> Yield to our prayers! quoth Mrs. Ditto,
>
> Give comfort to us poor and needy
> Who, wanting you, are waiting greedy
> Our meat and drink, yourself, quoth Edie.

Nay, though past clay, you chip the Parian,
Throw chisel down! quoth Lady Marian.

Be welcome, as to cow—the fodder-rick!
Excuse the simile!—quoth Sir Roderick.

Say not (in Scotch) "in troth it canna be"—
But honey, milk and, indeed, manna be!
Forgive a stranger!—Sarianna B.

Don't set an old acquaintance frowning,
But come and quickly! quoth R. Browning,
For since prodigious fault is found with you,
I—that is, Robin—must be Round with you.

P.S.
Do wash your hands, or leave the dirt on,
But leave the tools as Gammer Gurton
Her needle lost,—Lady Ashburton
Thus ends this letter—ease my sick heart,
And come to my divine Loch Luichart!

W. W. STORY, his mark X
EMELYN STORY,
EDITH MARION STORY,
I am,   M. ALFORD,
RODERICK MURCHISON,
SARIANNA BROWNING,
ROBERT BROWNING,
L. ASHBURTON.

Sept. 5th, 1869.

At the time of the visit to Loch Luichart in August, 1869, Browning wrote to Miss Blagden: "Through circumstances unforeseen and quite out of my control I am not in Brittany but here, having been bothered in the last three weeks beyond most folk's bearing. Never mind, the worst is over and here at an old friend's, I am comfortable altogether. Sarianna and Pen (for whose sake I came) are here, I don't know for how long. I *could not* write till now, in the hideous confusion of three weeks' constant inconstancy, and flitting from bad place to worse. However, all goes well now in this beautiful place. Pen has got what he wanted, shooting and deer-stalking; he began operations the day before yesterday and much to his credit as a hunter, shot a splendid stag—'royal'—the head of which will glorify his rooms at Christ Church."

On September 19, he wrote to Isa from Naworth Castle, Brampton, in Cumberland, "Lord Carlisle's beautiful place": "Pen and my sister are gone, she to London, he to Hampshire. My 'worry' is increased to pretty nearly the last degree, but there is no need to put it on paper yet, or perhaps ever, so, only be prepared to 'comfort' me when there is absolute need. Be certain I should prize your comfort at more than anybody else's gift of that sort, anybody's in the world. Of course, that I have been, or am 'worried' is, as usual wholly between me and your dear self. Yes, Scotland is divinely beautful, and I was in perhaps the most beautiful part of it. I saw beside all the Lakes, Glenore, etc. I am due today, for a week's visit to the Ds. of Cleveland at Raby, but recoil from going and perhaps or probably shall excuse myself. After that, I ought to go to Ly. Marian Alford's, and after that, whither do you suppose? This is pretty well for one who, for eight years, has gone on steadily refusing all such interruptions of a quiet life; so little was I prepared for this, that I came without the commonest belongings of a civilized man, and have had to supply myself with neck-ties etc. on the road!"

The winter of 1869–70 was apparently very trying to Browning, with much "worry" about Pen. June found him full of troubles. In July he made a flying trip to Scotland, remaining there only five hours, to attend the funeral of Lord Lothian; but in August he and Sarianna were with Milsand at St. Aubin, while Pen was at Ollerton with his tutor. On August 19 he wrote to Miss Blagden, "I shall escape if I can all visits in England this year: people are very kind, but the country-life does not suit me, and I prefer the utter roughness of this hamlet to the finery of that and the other great place where I might be."

Perhaps Loch Luichart was one of those great places. The next incident in the story, at any rate, is a visit to Loch Luichart planned for October 2, 1871. On the first of October he wrote to Isa Blagden from Glen Fincastle, Perthshire, "The country is exquisite, far from as wild and grandiose, however, as Loch Luichart where we hope to be tomorrow night." This is probably the "final visit" to which he refers in the letter of April 4, 1872, to Edith Story which has already been quoted.

Before that date, there is one earlier letter mentioning Lady Ashburton to Edith Story, which may be given though it serves only to suggest some strain in the relations between Browning and Lady Ashburton in the autumn of 1871.

19 Warwick Crescent,
Jan. 1, '72

Private

Dearest Edie,

First and last of all,—truest good wishes to you and everybody yours, for this year and whatever years are to follow after! Then, thank you very much for your letter, and the kind things you say about me and the little book; only, I don't think, when you have read more, you will find I have "taken the man for any Hero"—I rather made him confess he was the opposite, though I put forward what excuses I thought he was likely to make for himself, if inclined to try. I never at any time thought much better of him than now; and I don't think so much worse of the character as shown us in the last few years, because I suppose there to be a physical and intellectual decline of faculty, brought about by the man's own faults, no doubt—but I think he struggled against these; and when that is the case, depend on it, in a soliloquy, a man makes the most of his good intentions and sees great excuse in them—far beyond what our optics discover! I really wrote—that is, conceived the poem, twelve years ago in the Via del Tritone—in a little hand-breadth of prose, now yellow with age and Italian ink, which I breathed out into this full-blown bubble in a couple of months this autumn that is gone—thinking it fair so to do. What is the poem you allude to, which "I talked about at L. L." I have absolutely forgotten—if you tell me, and I still am of the same mind about it, I will try and keep alive what you will have helped me to recover—when this thing I am now engaged upon (half-done, now) is out of hand.

And now, with respect to the "question quite between ourselves." I only know of one person in London, not "whom I would call my enemy," but who openly professes herself such,—Mrs. Sartoris. Three years ago, I found she was complaining to people that I had quarreled with her, she didn't imagine why—while, all I knew was that she had discontinued inviting me to her house. *I* didn't imagine why. I met her a year after at Wrest, passed some days in her company, thought all was right again. She accused me of "dropping her," I replied that she had "dropped me"—for the kindness was all of one side, in the nature of things, I had no home to invite her to, and could only accept her invitations—which ceased to come. To be sure, I might have "called"—but I never was one of the intimates she kept aware of her movements,—as to when she would be in town for a day or two, and as suddenly away again,—and, moreover, I never feel inclined to take much trouble to pick up a friendship anybody lets fall for so little reason, to dirty my hands by so doing. Last season, just before May's marriage, I met the whole family at dinner,—sat by Mrs. S. and found her friendly as of old,—and I took the occasion, from something she inquired about, to write a friendly little note next day. But then happened this that I shall tell you. Two years ago, *just* before we went to Scotland, Miss Gabriel gave me an account of her grievances against Mrs. S.—which account I received, never forgetting first that it was a one-sided account, and secondly that if the conduct she complained of were truly described, there was nothing in it, which, *a la rigueur,* could not be excused after a fashion into a fault of judgement and temper,—nothing therefore which prevented the friendly feeling I showed, and, in turn, wished to get again at Wrest as I have mentioned—but this last year, Lady A. began upon me one day about the "utter falseness of Miss G."—"having just heard the whole story from Mrs. S." We got no further in the story than the first sentence "Miss G. wrote to Mr. Greville, with whom she had little or no previous acquaintance"—because I interposed—"with whom she had an intimate acquaintance." That was a point necessary to be cleared up, because all Miss G's veracity would have disappeared, were the facts otherwise. Accordingly I called on Miss G.—picked out a couple of the shortest notes from a heap she had retained,—for a purpose,—and sent them to Lʸ A. that she might see for herself whether the writer was "intimate" or not with Miss G. The letters were returned to me with an expression of convenient wonder how—but I will transcribe from the letter itself—"The world is out of joint"—and "I can't imagine how two tales so entirely different can both be true." Both could not, indeed, "be true," but, with that evidence, it was pretty clear which was false. I make no doubt this was at once reported to Mrs. S. who is consequently, I have as little doubt, from many circumstances that are come to my knowledge, "an enemy of mine"—for which, be assured, I care not three straws, nor do I trouble myself to inquire what she has said, written, or done in return for my "making the two tales look so very different." If poor Hatty heard some third tale, and at once threw up her old friend, I am sorry for her. The whole business has turned out too blessedly for me to much concern myself as to how it happened, and by means of whom.

Ever affectionately yours,

R. BROWNING.

The letter quoted at the beginning of this article ties together all the circumstances thus far mentioned. Two years later, on June 9, 1874, Browning wrote to Story at some length, giving him news of many common friends and of himself. He devotes a sentence to the lady: "I see every now and then that contemptible Lady Ashburton, and mind her no more than any other black beetle—so long as it don't crawl up my sleeve." And in 1887, in the "Parleying with Daniel Bartoli," appeared the stanzas about the "she-shape" in which Mr. De Vane recognized the likness of Lady Ashburton. The lines themselves confirm our impression of her dark, Olympian beauty; and the story they tell harmonizes with Browning's expressions in his letters to the Storys.

Once more, in 1886, Browning in writing to Story refers to Lady Ashburton:

> 19, Warwick Crescent, W.
> June 19, '86

My dear Story,

I received last night the packet of M.S.—all thanks to your kindness. Had I mustered courage enough to look at the originals—undisturbed in their repose of fourteen years since I copied them for you—I should probably have given neither you nor myself further trouble in the matter—but my memory was hazy as to the precise charge which I intended they should meet—and fancied they were more than what they proved to be—a simple answer to the assertion (if it was really made) that I had been making endeavours to renew a relation of even ordinary acquaintance, instead of resisting cajoleries and pathetic appeals, for two years together, that I should do so. As bearing upon the writer's veracity this was evidence enough. And even with respect to the calumnies which Lady A. exploded in all the madness of her wounded vanity—I was not aware at that time of what I have had abundant knowledge of since—how thoroughly her character as a calumniator was understood by those most intimately connected with her—and how little credit would be given to assertions of this sort in my case. I retained exactly as much as I was disposed to value of the esteem and attention of every one of our common friends and acquaintance,—and in two instances—when I chose to volunteer an explanation of the causes of my feeling with regard to her,—I found that her nearest relatives had undergone precisely similar treatment. One of these, —whom I only became acquainted with a few years ago,—told me she herself had been treated as—and called to her face—"a thief." There would seem therefore little use in casting about for means of defence against such a charge from such a person—*posthumous,* as her cowardice would take care that it should be. I shall nevertheless abide by your advice, and retain the original letters—giving such directions for their ultimate disposal as you very properly suggest, and indeed as I had always intended. So, enough of an odious experience—which had, however, the effect of enabling you and Mrs. Story to prove yourselves effectually and admirably my friends, as there is no need that I should gratefully acknowledge now.

The last entry in the chronicle concerns Miss Hosmer.

> 19, Warwick Crescent, W.
> April 4, 1887

Dear Friends,

I got the letter of which I enclose a copy, two days ago, under the following circumstances. A Mr. Shortall, of Chicago,—with whom I had some correspondence last year concerning the representation there of one of my plays by an amateur company,—wrote to me, last week, to say he was just arrived in London and about to depart thence, but wished first to see me for a few minutes. I replied I should be happy to see him, and on Friday he called accordingly,—a pleasant kindly person. He had—you will observe—no need of anybody's intervention on his behalf. The writer of the letter I subjoin chose to address me in the way you will see; and I think it due to you—hardly necessary as it may be—to show how far impudence can go. Pray do not even reply to this recurrence of mine to a hateful subject—but as you have so lately looked over the letters etc. of Lady Ashburton, you may as well know how the chief agent in that business professes to feel for me whom she slandered. Of course, I never have said a word about her to Lady Marian—whom indeed I have only met once, at poor Houghton's, since I saw her in your rooms at London, as you remember, when Lady A. "tried on" conciliation—not quite with such effrontery however.

Although this is no letter-proper, only a brief notice I think necessary, I cannot help sweetening the page by mentioning that Pen writes in warm terms of Julian's picture for the Salon,—full of cleverness, he says. I trust you are both well. Our winter has been abominable, and I found myself decidedly the worse for the want of my customary dose of the divine Italian air.

> Ever affectionately yours,
> ROBERT BROWNING

The letter from Harriet Hosmer, Browning copied and enclosed with the foregoing letter. It runs as follows:

> Churchside,
> Denmark Hill,
> March 31, [1887].

My dear Friend,

Here comes a very affectionate ghost from the Past. This ghost, however, has very often been with you in spirit though absent in shadow, and it was glad you had not forgotten her,—as Lady Marian assured her not long since, your enquiries proved. Now she is coming in the flesh to explain its long seclusion. In the meantime, pray smile kindly upon my friend Mr. Shortall who presents you this, and believe that I am as always

> Affectionately yours,
> HATTY HOSMER

Thus the episode ends. For himself, Browning probably did not really welcome the idea of marrying again. One letter, in Mr. Wise's collection, to Isa Blagden, of September 19, 1867, is vigorous and definite on this point. Browning is dealing with the wholly false report that he was to marry Jean Ingelow, the novelist and poetess. "No goose," he says, "tells you I *am* married,—only, that I *shall* be,—and six years hence, the same goose can cackle "So it *was* to be,—only, it was broken off"! . . . It is funny people think I am likely to do nothing naughty in the world, neither rob nor kill, seduce nor ravish,— only honestly *marry*—which I should consider the two last,—and perhaps the two first,—naughtinesses united, together with the grace of perjury. Enough of it all."

The story is thus clear enough in main outline. "An odious experience" it must indeed have been to Robert Browning and no doubt to Lady Ashburton, who was the soul of generosity and kindness. She seems unfortunate in having unavoidably and really innocently been the cause of this wretched episode in Browning's life. Through it all Browning moves before us in a natural but dangerous and rather bitter course; and through it all, the golden tradition of his memory of Elizabeth Barrett remains intact. In August, 1871, six weeks before his final little visit of a day to Lady Ashburton, he wrote of Elizabeth Barrett to Isa Blagden: "All is best as it is, for her, and me too. I shall wash my hands clean in a minute, before I see her, as I trust to do."

NOTES

NOTES

In setting together the following notes, the editor has borrowed the notes prepared by Mr. Wise and by the late Professor W. Hall Griffin for many of the letters privately printed by Mr. Wise. He has not attempted to distinguish his own contributions from those he has thus borrowed. Among the topics with which it has been his privilege to deal independently are John Stuart Mill's remarks on *Pauline*, the history of the writing of *The Ring and the Book*, Landor's Will, Browning's break with Chapman, the dispute with Alfred Austin (carried on in *The Examiner*), and the matter of Browning and Lady Ashburton. For errors and omissions he apologizes, trusting that the sympathy of Browning students, of which he has had abundant experience during the course of his research both in England and in the United States, will enable them to forgive the mistakes for the sake of the few discoveries that shed light on the life and work of Robert Browning.

The letters in the text are numbered in sequence, by years; e.g., 1865 : 3 designates the third letter of the year 1865 in this volume. In the notes, the century figures are left off, and the number of the note is added; e.g., 65 : 3–1 refers to the first note on the third letter of the year 1865.

30 : 1–1. The holograph of this letter is believed to be the earliest now extant in the handwriting of Robert Browning. A *facsimile* of it forms the frontispiece of *Letters from Robert Browning to Various Correspondents*, edited by Thomas J. Wise, Second Series, Vol. I, London, Privately Printed, 1907.

Christopher Dowson, Junior, married, in 1836, Mary Domett, sister of Alfred Domett. Dowson became one of Browning's closest friends. He died of consumption in 1884.

30 : 1–2. Captain Pritchard ("Dear old Pritchard"), an old friend of the Dowson family. One of his whims was never to let any one know where he lived. It was probably he who was the means of introducing Browning to the Dowson circle. He died in 1860, and by his will left to Miss Browning £1000, to Miss Emily Dowson £500, and to Miss Walton £500.

30 : 1–3. Captain Charles Walton, R.N. See *The Letters of Robert Browning and Elizabeth Barrett*, 1898, II, 39–40.

30 : 1–4. Joseph Dowson, a younger brother of Christopher Dowson.

38 : 1–1. The play cannot be singled out with certainty from among several. In March, 1840, Browning was busy on "some plays," probably *Pippa Passes, King Victor and King Charles*, and *Mansoor the Hierophant* (later published as *The Return of the Druses*), all of which had been announced as nearly ready. At about this time he was interested in at least one other subject for a play, connected with the ballad of *The Atheist's Tragedy. A Blot in the 'Scutcheon* was completed before the end of 1840. It was written in five days.

38 : 1–2. *Sordello*, Book III, ll. 967 ff.

40 : 1–1. Eliza Flower, sister, one year older, of Sarah Flower (afterwards Mrs. Adams), author of the drama *Vivia Perpetua* and the hymn *Nearer, my God, to Thee*. Eliza Flower was a musical composer, and often set her sister's hymns to music. She died in 1846, at the age of forty-three; the younger sister died in August, 1848.

40 : 1–2. The Rev. W. Johnson Fox—he wrote appreciative reviews of *Pauline* in *The Monthly Magazine* (New Series, vol. vii, 1835, pp. 254–262) and of *Paracelsus* in *The Monthly Repository* (No. 107, November, 1835, pp. 716–727). He was M.P. for Oldham for several years.

40 : 3–1. *A Blot in the 'Scutcheon.*

40 : 3–2. "My own notion"—*i.e.,* in *The Return of the Druses,* written after a search for "a subject of the most wild and passionate love," involving "self-devotement, self-forgetting." See Griffin and Minchin: *The Life of Robert Browning,* p. 113.

41 : 1–1. This letter describes Browning's journey from Camberwell to Bond Street, in quest of Laman Blanchard's first published volume, *Offerings,* the publisher being William Harrison Ainsworth, in Old Bond Street. The letter has been printed in the "Memoir" by Blanchard Jerrold in *The Poetical Works of Laman Blanchard,* London, 1876, pp. 6–8.

41 : 2–1. The dinner with the Carlyles referred to in this letter was probably that of the end of December, 1841. See D. A. Wilson: *Carlyle on Cromwell and Others,* 1925, p. 152.

41 : 2–2. The scene of Andromeda described in *Pauline,* lines 656–667, is that of a picture by Polidoro da Caravaggio, an engraving of which Browning had in his study. Sharp states in his *Life:* "It is strange that among all his father's collection of drawings and engravings nothing had such fascination for him as an engraving of a picture of Andromeda and Perseus by Caravaggio. The story of the innocent victim and the divine deliverer was one of which in his boyhood he was never tired of hearing: and as he grew older the charm of its pictorial presentment had for him a deeper and more complex significance." Andromeda as a subject of portraiture is alluded to in the "Parleying With Francis Furini."

41 : 2–3. *King Victor and King Charles.*

41 : 2–4. "The Serenade." Cf. 81 : 6–1.

42 : 1–1. The Countess Pepoli, once Elizabeth Fergus of Kirkcaldy, a very dear friend of Mrs. Carlyle's.

42 : 2–1. In a letter of December 13, 1842, to Domett, Browning wrote "Who, do you suppose, wrote that article in the *C. of E. Quarterly?* Horne! Judge of my astonishment. But was it not generous of an unappreciated man, so to write?" (*Robert Browning and Alfred Domett,* p. 50.) The article on Browning, by Richard Henry Horne, appeared in the *Church of England Quarterly* for October, 1842. (*Ibid.,* ftn., p. 45.)

44 : 1–1. *Colombe's Birthday.*

44 : 2–1. "In the midst, however, of this sickness and distress [May, 1844], my father's friends rallied round him. Mr. F. O. Ward installed himself as unpaid editor [of *Hood's Magazine*], and corrected proofs and arranged matter for the press."—*Memorials of Thomas Hood,* 1860, II, 200.

44 : 2–2. The "proof" was that of "Sibrandus Schafnaburgensis," contributed to *Hood's Magazine* in July, 1844. The "gossamer," &c., alterations suggest that the poem was revised considerably in its proof stages. The "gossamer" doubtless refers to the spider's web, spun over the crevice in the plum-tree, after the book had been dropped in it.

44 : 2–3. A prose paper, "Sensations of Sixteen. By a very old man." *Hood's Magazine,* Vol. II, July, 1844, pp. 36–44.

44 : 2–4. Uncle Silverthorne, the Camberwell brewer.

44 : 2–5. In July, 1844, Browning contributed to *Hood's Magazine* the two "Garden Fancies" (pp. 45–48). For the August number (pp. 140–142) he furnished "The Boy and the Angel." He contributed respectively in March and April, 1845, "The Tomb at St. Praxed's (Rome, 15—)" (pp. 237–239) and "The Flight of the Duchess" (pp. 313–318).

45 : 1–1. This letter has been printed in Henry Fothergill Chorley's *Autobiography, Memoir, and Letters,* compiled by Henry G. Hewlett, 2 vols., London, 1873, II, 25–26.

45 : 1–2. *Pomfret; or Public Opinion and Private Judgment,* a novel in two volumes, was published in 1845.

46 : 1–1. Richard Henry Horne—author of *Orion* (the famous "Farthing Epic"), *The Death of Marlowe, Judas Iscariot, Cosmo de' Medici, The Dreamer and the Worker, A New Spirit of the Age,* &c. &c. In 1844, in *A New Spirit of the Age,* Horne reprinted a long and favorable article about Browning (Vol. II, pp. 153–186). Browning supplied some of the mottoes, and Miss Barrett supplied others, for this volume. The two poets had not yet become acquainted.

46 : 1–2. The book referred to here is *Ballad Romances*, 1846, containing some of Horne's best minor work.

46 : 1–3. "The Noble Heart."

46 : 1–4. "Ben Capstan; a Ballad of the Night-Watch."

46 : 1–5. "The Elf of the Woodlands; a Child's Story."

46 : 1–6. "The Ballad of Delora" had first appeared in *The Monthly Repository*, with side-notes in the manner of Coleridge's *Ancient Mariner*.

46 : 1–7. "The Good-Natured Bear; a Story for Children of All Ages," was published anonymously by Horne (Cundall, 1846) in the same year as the *Ballad Romances*.

46 : 2–1. In *The Letters of Robert Browning and Elizabeth Barrett Barrett*, 1899, Vol. I, p. 563, Browning writes [post-mark, March 18, 1846] that Archer Gurney is coming to see him. Apparently, as both letters are dated "March," and as the visit seems to be a first one, this letter may be taken as referring to that visit of March, 1846, and may be dated accordingly.

46 : 2–2. *Paracelsus*, published in 1835.

46 : 3–1. This letter has been printed in *Letters of Elizabeth Barrett Browning addressed to Richard Hengist Horne*, London, 1877, II, 182–183.

47 : 2–1. Mrs. Anna Brownell Jameson (1794–1860), a prolific and authoritative writer on the history of art. She befriended the Brownings, aiding them greatly during their first days in Italy.

47 : 3–1. This letter and the others to Carlyle in this volume appeared in an article entitled "Correspondence between Carlyle and Browning," in the *Cornhill Magazine*, May, 1915.

48 : 1–1. Sarah Flower Adams died in August, 1848. See 40 : 1–1. The MS. copies by Miss Eliza Flower here referred to are probably the same as the *Incondita* the burning of which Mr. Wise witnessed (see the Introduction). The original *Incondita* Browning probably destroyed soon after a friend had shown it to the Flower sisters. See the *Cornhill Magazine* of January, 1914, and *New Poems by Robert Browning and Elizabeth Barrett Browning*, Macmillan, 1915, pp. 13–20, for Bertram Dobell's account of "The Earliest Poems of Robert Browning."

48 : 1–2. *A Blot in the 'Scutcheon* was very successfully revived by Phelps at Sadler's Wells theatre on Monday, November 27, 1848. See the *Athenaeum* of Saturday, December 2, 1848; and the *Examiner* of December 9.

48 : 1–3. *Poems by Robert Browning. In two volumes. A new Edition. London: Chapman and Hall, 186, Strand. 1849. [Only Paracelsus and Bells and Pomegranates.]* The author's statement, dated December, 1848, is as follows: "Many of these pieces were out of print, the rest had been withdrawn from circulation, when the corrected edition, now submitted to the reader, was prepared. The various Poems and Dramas have received the author's most careful revision."

48 : 1–4. Concerning Thomas Powell and his rascality, see 83 : 15–1; 86 : 4–2.

49 : 1–1. This letter is written in an extremely minute, but wholly legible, hand, on a tiny piece of paper, the whole folded to about the size of a modern postage stamp. It is a "baby" letter, indeed! To his last years, Browning enjoyed such exercises as writing the Lord's Prayer on a bit of paper the size of a shilling.

49 : 1–2. Flush, a toy spaniel, was a gift to Mrs. Browning from Miss Mitford. See E.B.B.'s poem "To Flush, My Dog."

49 : 2–1. The Rev. George Clayton, pastor of York Street Chapel (now called Browning Hall) in Walworth. On June 14, 1812, he baptized Robert Browning.

49 : 2–2. The poet's mother, Sarah Anna Wiedemann, had died a week after the birth of the poet's son, Robert Wiedemann Barrett Browning.

49 : 3–1. This letter has been printed in Alexander Gilchrist's *Life of William Etty, R.A.;* 2 vols.; London, 1855; II, 280–281.

49 : 3–2. The "Sirens" is a poem by Etty. Cf. 41 : 2.

50 : 1–1. This letter from Carlyle is that referred to by Elizabeth Barrett Browning in a letter to her sister Henrietta of July 9, 1847: "By the way, I ought certainly to tell you of a delightful letter which Carlyle sent to Robert the other day, which when I had read I kissed for gladness and gratitude, it gave me so much of both. He says that not for years had any marriage, occurring in his circle, given him an equal pleasure to our marriage. Here are his words as he goes on:—

" 'You, I had known and judged of: *her* too, conclusively enough, if less directly; and certainly if ever there was a union indicated by the finger of Heaven itself, and sanctioned and prescribed by the Eternal Laws under which poor transitory sons of Adam live, it seemed to me, from all I could hear and know of it, to be this! Courage, therefore; follow piously the Heavenly omen, and fear not. He that can follow there, he, in the loneliest desert, in the densest jostle and whirlpool of London fog, will find his haven. Perpetually serene weather is not to be looked for by anybody; least of all by the like of you two—in whom precisely because more is given, more also in the same proportion is required: but unless I altogether mistake, there is a life-partnership which, in all kinds of weather, has in it a capacity of being blessed to the parties. May it indeed prove so. May the weather on the whole be moderate; and if joy be ever absent for a season, may nobleness never! That is the best I can wish. The sun cannot shine always; but the places of the *stars,* these ought to be known always and these can.'

"Isn't that full, full of kindness? We had had kind messages from him before, but it is the first letter—and I have copied more than I could becomingly perhaps. If so, you will make allowance, knowing my reverence for Carlyle, and the natural pleasure which words like these from him must overflow me with."—*Elizabeth Barrett Browning: Letters to Her Sister, 1846–1859;* London; John Murray, Albemarle Street, W.; 1929; pp. 33–34. Carlyle's letter, dated June 23, 1847, is printed in full in *Letters of Thomas Carlyle to John Stuart Mill, John Sterling, and Robert Browning,* 1923, pp. 281–284.

50 : 2–1. Some particulars of this two-volume edition of Elizabeth Barrett Browning's poems are given in a letter to Miss Mitford of September 24, 1850 (*The Letters of Elizabeth Barrett Browning,* 1910, I, 462): "The two volumes are to come out, it appears, at the end of October; not before, because Mr. Chapman wished to inaugurate them for his new house in Piccadilly." The first two-volume edition of her poems had appeared in 1844.

50 : 2–2. Miss Bayley was a friend and companion of John Kenyon's, who nursed him during his last illness. She remained a friend of the Brownings after the death of John Kenyon. She is mentioned several times in Mrs. Browning's letters.

50 : 2–3. Henry Fothergill Chorley (1808–1872), a critic on the *Athenaeum* until his retirement in 1866.

50 : 2–4. Probably F. O. Ward. See 44 : 2–1.

51 : 2–1. The *Memoirs of Margaret Fuller Ossoli* (2 vols., 1852) were edited by R. W. Emerson, W. H. Channing, and J. F. Clarke.

51 : 3–1. Carlyle's account of the expedition, entitled "Excursion (futile enough) to Paris, Autumn, 1851," was published in *Last Words of Thomas Carlyle,* London, 1892. He put off his journey a day that he might travel with the Brownings.

51 : 4–1. Dr. W. C. Bennett,—author of *My Sonnets,* 1843; *Poems,* 1850; *Songs for Sailors,* 1872, &c. "Our friend Bennett of Blackheath."—*Letters of Robert Browning and Elizabeth Barrett,* 1899, Vol. II, p. 364.

51 : 4–2. The present letter refers to the *Poems* of 1850. In 1846 Browning wrote, "I found a new litter of poetry in a letter of our indefatigable Bennett,—the happy man!"—*Letters of Robert Browning and Elizabeth Barrett,* 1899, II, 364.

51 : 5–1. Carlyle had visited twice at Paris. The quotation seems to be a paraphrase of a speech of Falstaff's (*Merry Wives*, V, 1): "This is the third time; I hope good luck lies in odd numbers."

51 : 5–2. "Mazzini can at once afford you and Mrs. Browning, without any difficulty, the required introduction to Madame Dudevant; only he says this sublime Highpriestess of Anarchy is seldom now in Paris, only when there is some Play coming out or the like: so you will require to be on the outlook for her advent, if you do not like to run out some time by railway (if there is a rail), and see her among her rustic neighbours,—within sound of the 'Church Bell' she has lately *christened,* at her Curé's request. After all, I participate in your liking for the melody that runs thro' that strange 'beautiful incontinent' soul,—a *Modern* Magdalen, with the 'seven devils' mostly still in her! At any rate, the introduction is most ready, the instant you write to me for it."—From the letter from Carlyle to Browning of October 10, 1851, printed in Alexander Carlyle's *Letters of Carlyle to Mill, Sterling, and Browning*, 1923, pp. 287–289.

51 : 5–3. This refers to the volume of twenty-five spurious Shelley letters, published, with a prefatory *Essay* by Robert Browning, by Moxon in 1852. These letters, together with a number of spurious Byron manuscripts, were produced about 1848 by one de Gibler, who assumed the name of George Gordon Byron and proclaimed himself to be a natural son of the poet. The Shelley letters were purchased by William White, a bookseller of Pall Mall, who consigned them to Messrs. Sotheby's rooms for sale by public auction. They were there purchased by Mr. Edward Moxon, who at once proceeded to publish them, and at whose suggestion Browning undertook to supply a suitable Introduction. Browning was then (December, 1851) in Paris. He told Mr. Wise that he never saw the original holographs, having been provided either with manuscript copies of the letters, or printed proofs of the book, he was uncertain which. Upon ascertaining that the documents were forgeries, Moxon withdrew the volume from circulation. The whole of the facts were commented upon by the *Athenaeum,* and White replied in a pamphlet (which ran to two editions) entitled *The Calumnies of the "Athenaeum" Exposed,* etc. The original letters were presented by Moxon to the Manuscript Department of the British Museum.

53 : 1–1. Baron Seymour Kirkup. Julian Hawthorne's description of Kirkup, in *Hawthorne and his Circle* (New York and London, 1903), pp. 345–348, is memorable. It begins thus:—"There was a magical old man in Florence named Kirkup, an Englishman, though he had dwelt abroad so many years that he seemed more Florentine than the Florentines themselves. He had known, in his youth, Byron, Shelley, Hunt, and Edward Trelawney. . . . Kirkup, in the course of his researches into the past, came upon the books of necromancers, . . and began to practise their spells and conjurations; and by-and-by, being a great admirer and student of Dante, that poet manifested himself to him in his lonely vigils and told him many unknown facts about his career on earth, and incidentally revealed to him the whereabouts of the now-familiar fresco of Dante on the wall of the Bargello Chapel, where it had been hidden for ages beneath a coat of whitewash. In these occult researches, Kirkup, of course, had need of a medium, and he found among the Florentine peasants a young girl, radiantly beautiful, who possessed an extraordinary susceptibility to spiritual influences. Through her means he conversed with the renowned dead men of the past times. But one day Regina (such was the girl's name), much to the old man's surprise, gave birth to a child. She herself died, in Kirkup's house, soon after, and on her death-bed she swore a solemn oath on the crucifix that the baby's father was none other than Kirkup himself. The poor old gentleman had grown so accustomed to believing in miracles that he made little ado about accepting this one also; he received the child as his daughter, and made provision for her in his will." There follows an account of a visit by the Hawthornes to the queer old palace of Kirkup, close to the Ponte Vecchio, in which he lived among his dusty treasures, with the child, Imogen, who was "a powerful medium" at the age of four or five. Nathaniel Hawthorne "wrote it all down in his journal, and it evidently impressed his imagination; and she and Kirkup himself—*mutatis mutandis*—appear in *Dr. Grimshawe's Secret,* and again, in a somewhat different form, in *The Dolliver Romance."* Cf. 67 : 1–1.

53 : 1–2. Hiram Powers was an American sculptor who lived for many years in Florence. Julian Hawthorne gives a vivid account of him in *Hawthorne and his Circle,* 1903, pp. 337–338.

53 : 1–3. Mr. and Mrs. Fraser Corkran. Mr. Corkran was Paris correspondent of the *Morning Chronicle.* From the apartment of the Corkrans in the Rue Basse des Remparts, Boulevard des Italiens, the Brownings witnessed the progress of Louis Napoleon through the city.—Griffin and Minchin: *The Life of Robert Browning,* 1910, p. 188.

53 : 1–4. See 47 : 2–1.

53 : 1–5. Mr. and Mrs. Bryan Waller Procter ("Barry Cornwall").

53 : 2–1. William Burnet Kinney was United States Minister to the Court of Sardinia at Turin; he was commissioned chargé on April 22, 1850, and served until October 8, 1853. He was often consulted by Cavour regarding the practical workings of the American governmental system. His wife was Elizabeth Clementine (Dodge) Stedman Kinney (1810–1889). In 1853, the Sardinian mission having ended, the Kinneys moved to Florence, where they lived for more than ten years. Mrs. Kinney was the mother of Edmund Clarence Stedman. She wrote *Felicità* (1855), a metrical romance based on an incident in Italian history.

53 : 2–2.

"To his good friends thus wide I'll ope my arms;
"And, like the kind life-rendering pelican,
"Repast them with my blood."

Hamlet, Act IV, Scene V.

55 : 1–1. *The Mystic,* by Philip James Bailey, published in 1855.

55 : 1–2. *Men and Women,* 1855.

55 : 1–3. These corrections have all been made except the two in "Cleon," in the later editions of the poems: "Old Pictures in Florence" (pp. 34–37), "Cleon" (188–189), and "One Word More" (p. 231).

56 : 1–1. This letter was in response to Carlyle's request for assistance with materials for his *Frederick the Great.*

56 : 1–2. On December 4th, 1855, Carlyle had written in a letter to Browning . . . "it is verily one of my sorrows that you cannot be seen from night to night by me, but live on the other side of the seas.—I got a glimpse of your *Men and Women;* and will not rest till I have read it; there! That old 'corregidor' is a diamond—*unequalled* since something else of yours I saw.

"Courage ever, and stand to your arms!"

The corregidor figures in "How It Strikes a Contemporary," *q.v.*

56 : 2–1. This letter has been privately printed in *Some Lamb and Browning Letters to Leigh Hunt,* for Luther A. Brewer, Cedar Rapids, Iowa, 1924.

57 : 2–1. Edward Robert Bulwer-Lytton, later First Earl of Lytton (1831–1891) ("Owen Meredith"). He was nursed through this dangerous attack of gastric fever by Miss Isabella Blagden, and some thought evidently arose in the minds of the Brownings that a marriage might ensue. In Browning's letters to Miss Blagden he frequently mentions Lytton after this time. "Robert has been up with him eight nights, and Isa Blagden eight nights. Nothing can exceed her devotion to him by night or day. We have persuaded her, however, at last to call in a nurse for the nights."—*Letters of Elizabeth Barrett Browning,* 1919, II, 269–270. "I have a letter from Isa Blagden with a good account of Lytton. He goes back to Villa Bricchieri, where they are to house together, unless Sir Edward comes down (which he may do) to catch up his son and change the plan."—*Ibid.,* II, 272.

57 : 2–2. *Aurora Leigh,* 1856.

57 : 2–3. Mrs. Stisted, "Queen of the Baths" (*i.e.,* Bagni di Lucca). See T. A. Trollope: *What I Remember,* Vol. II, Ch. 8. *"That Book"* was found in Shelley's hand after his death, and burned with his body. Cf. 77 : 1–1.

57 : 2–4. Leigh Hunt had shared with the Brownings a lock he possessed of Milton's hair. In later years, at Warwick Crescent, Browning kept Hunt's gift in a glass-topped table cabinet near his desk, along with other precious keepsakes.

57 : 2–5. John Kenyon, in whose house *Aurora Leigh* had been completed, and to whom it had been dedicated, died on December 3, 1856. Mrs. Browning wrote to Mrs. Jameson on December 26, "You will have heard (we heard it only three days ago) how our kindest friend, who never forgot us, remembered us in his will. The legacy is eleven thousand pounds; six thousand five hundred of which are left to Robert, marking delicately a sense of trust for which I am especially grateful. . . . It has been a sad, sad Christmas to me. . . . He has been to me in much what my father might have been, and now the place is empty twice over."—*Letters of Elizabeth Barrett Browning,* II, 246–247.

58 : 1–1. In an action for libel brought against Landor by the Rev. Morris Yescombe and his wife, and decided at Bristol on August 23rd, 1858, he was condemned to pay heavy damages. The *Times* on August 25th, 1858, had a leading article on the case, reprobating in the severest terms the defendant's conduct and finding no excuse for it. With few if any exceptions, the English newspaper press took the same line.

58 : 1–2. Harriet Goodhue Hosmer (1830–1908), American sculptress.

59 : 1–1. See 57 : 2–1.

59 : 1–2. This note is printed in the *Letters of Elizabeth Barrett Browning,* 1910, II, 320. It is dated "Wednesday," and on the basis of Browning's statement, August 10 is the date.

59 : 1–3. Elizabeth Sophia Landor. Two addresses are entered for "Miss Sophia Landor" in the earlier of Browning's two address-books. The first entry, "Miss Sophia Landor, 3 Belmont, Bath," is paired with "Walter Savage Landor, 2671, *Via Nunziatina.*" She later acted as her cousins' and her uncles' *"Pen"* in negotiating with Browning about administering Landor's Will.

59 : 1–4. Miss Annette Bracken, a companion of Miss Blagden and a most intimate friend of Browning's.

60 : 2–1. This letter has been printed in Chorley's *Autobiography, Memoir, and Letters,* 1873, II, 169–174. Cf. 50 : 2–3.

60 : 2–2. *Roccabella,* by Chorley, was published in 1859 under the pseudonym of *Paul Bell.* The work was dedicated to Mrs. Browning, but was an attack on revolutionists in Europe trying to win English sympathy.

61 : 1–1. The death of Cavour, on June 6th, 1861, hastened Elizabeth Barrett Browning's death. The conclusion of this letter is believed to be the last bit of extant correspondence from her hand.

61 : 3–1. Macready married, for the second time, on April 3, 1860, Cecile Louise Frederica Spencer (1827–1908). See 67 : 2–6.

61 : 4–1. Arabel Barrett, sister of Mrs. Browning, seven years her junior.

62 : 1–1. An arrangement for a regular correspondence had been made by Browning with Miss Blagden; she was to write to him on the 12th of each month, his wedding date, and he was to reply on the 19th.

62 : 1–2. John Gibson, famous English sculptor. He had taken Harriet Hosmer as a pupil in 1852, though it was not his custom to take pupils. His studio was at No. 4, Via della Fontanella, in Rome. Miss Hosmer made a striking medallion portrait of him, a photograph of which is reproduced facing p. 218 of *Harriet Hosmer: Letters and Memories,* edited by Cornelia Carr, London, 1913.

62 : 1–3. This is one of the recurrent allusions in Browning's letters to Miss Blagden to the Song of Callicles in Arnold's *Empedocles on Etna:*—

"Far, far from here
"The Adriatic breaks in a warm bay
"Among the green Illyrian hills; . . .
"And there, they say, two bright and aged snakes,
"Who once were Cadmus and Harmonia,
"Bask in the glens or on the warm sea-shore,
"In breathless quiet, after all their ills." . . .

Cf. 65 : 9–2; 67 : 5–3; 67 : 7–1.

62 : 2–1. Landor's letter to the *Times,* to which Browning refers, was the one printed in its issue of June 26th, 1862, p. 7. According to an article in *The Times Literary Supplement,* April 10th, 1919, this was his last accepted contribution to the paper. The letter purports to be written from Leghorn during the return journey from Rome to Florence. Landor says he had gone to "the Eternal City, as it is the fashionable slang to call it," "not to be a spectator of the canonization of Roman Catholic Missionaries put to death in Japan early in the seventeenth century," but "to see other suits of scarlet than I found . . . one about the ardent breast of Garibaldi."

This visit to Rome has nowhere else been mentioned, and it would appear to have been an imaginary excursion. Why the publication of Landor's letter should have given Browning so much annoyance is hard to understand. One assumption, however, would be that, having done all that he could to find a comfortable home for his aged and infirm friend in the Via Nunziatina, Florence, where all possible care would be taken of him, Browning had been put to the trouble of explaining, in reply to the inquiries of Landor's relatives, that the old man had not really been wandering about the country and that the visit to Rome was a fiction.

It was doubtless Dr. Arthur de Noé Walker who sent on Landor's letter to the *Times* office; and the anything but polite terms in which he is spoken of by Browning point to ill feelings about which it is needless to speculate. It must suffice here to say that Browning had grievously misjudged him.

62 : 2–2. "Hookey," *i.e.,* Dr. Arthur de Noé Walker. Browning made a playful use of the slang phrase *"Hookey Walker"* then current. The book referred to was *Heroic Idyls,* published in 1863.

62 : 2–3. Thomas Adolphus Trollope, elder brother of Anthony, married Theodosia Garrow. She died on April 13, 1865.

62 : 3–1. See 63 : 1–2.

62 : 4–1. *Selections from the Poetical Works of Robert Browning. London: Chapman and Hall, 193, Piccadilly. 1863.* The Preface is dated "November, 1862." It was edited by John Forster and B. W. Procter ("Barry Cornwall").

63 : 1–1. Cf. 62 : 4–1.

63 : 1–2. The chapter on "The Evil Eye and Other Superstitions" in W. W. Story's *Roba di Roma,* first published serially in the *Atlantic Monthly,* April, 1859, to June, 1860; then in book form, by Chapman and Hall, London; and afterwards by Houghton, Mifflin & Co., Boston. The Greek quotations did not appear in the original publication in the *Atlantic Monthly.* Cf. 62 : 3–1.

63 : 2–1. The letter is written on the stationery of the Athenaeum Club.

63 : 2–2. *The Cost of a Secret, by the Author of "Agnes Tremorne,"* 3 vols., London, Chapman and Hall, 1863. The British Museum copy was received on January 2nd, 1863. See 66 : 8–2.

63 : 2–3. George Eliot. She and her husband George Henry Lewes had been in Florence in 1860.—*Letters of Elizabeth Barrett Browning,* 1910, II, 400.

63 : 2–4. The monument to Elizabeth Barrett Browning in the English Cemetery, Florence.

63 : 2–5. The tablet on Casa Guidi, Via Maggio, 9, Florence, to the memory of Elizabeth Barrett Browning. The inscription was written by the Italian poet, Tommaseo.

63 : 2–6. Probably John Brett, whose address appears in the earlier of Browning's address books as "6 Pump Court, Middle Temple, E.C." Thus we may infer that Browning did come to know his "kind understander."

63 : 4–1. Edward George Earle Lytton-Bulwer, First Lord Lytton. The house was No. 1, Park Lane. "L" is his son, Edward Robert Bulwer-Lytton, First Earl of Lytton. See 57 : 2–1.

63 : 4–2. In the *Athenaeum*, December 19, 1863, p. 840, appeared a letter from W. W. Story, written at Rome and dated "November, 1863," defending Harriet Hosmer against the accusation that Signor Nucci (one of her workmen) did her "Zenobia" for her. The charge had been made in the *Art-Journal*, quoting from *The Queen*.

63 : 4–3. Hume (D. D. Home) was the original of Mr. Sludge, in *Mr. Sludge, the "Medium."* See Griffin and Minchin: *Life of Robert Browning*, pp. 203–206. Browning caught Hume cheating on one occasion, and subsequently ejected Hume from his house, when he had the temerity to call on Browning in Dorset Street.

63 : 4–4. Willy Bracken. With his mother, Willy Bracken frequently accompanied Browning and his son Pen in later years on summer vacations in France. The two boys were fast friends.

64 : 1–1. Major William Surtees Cook (after 1862 surnamed Altham), Henrietta Barrett's second cousin. They were married in 1850. They named their eldest boy Altham.

Illustration facing p. 80. The Pas de Roland. W. M. Rossetti entered in his diary the following account of a conversation with Browning on March 15, 1868. . . . "Browning's forthcoming poem exceeds 20,000 lines: it may probably be out in July, but he would defer it if he finds that more conducive to the satisfactory completion of the work. He began it in October '64. Was staying at Bayonne, and walked out to a mountain-gorge traditionally said to have been cut or kicked out by Roland, and there laid out the full plan of his twelve cantos, accurately carried out in the execution. He says he writes day by day on a regular systematic plan—some three hours in the early part of the day; he seldom or never, unless in quite brief poems, feels the inspiring impulse and sets the thing down into words at the same time—often stores up a subject long before he writes it. He has written his forthcoming work all consecutively—not some of the later parts before the earlier."—*Rossetti Papers*, p. 302, March 15, 1868.

The handwriting in the sketch is Sarianna Browning's. All the handwriting in the sketchbook from which it is taken is hers. But some of the sketches in the book may be by Browning himself,—among them sketches of Robert Browning, Senior, Pen, and Sarianna. The fact that Sarianna and Robert were never separated in long morning walks during their summers in France makes it safe to assume that he was with her at the Pas de Roland on August 27, 1864. Two other sketches in the book were apparently (surrounding dates indicate) made on the same day, though they are not dated. This one seems to be the first of the three, and the most carefully done. On August 19, Browning wrote to Isa Blagden from Cambo Près Bayonne, without mentioning the Pas. A letter to Mrs. Story from Cambo, printed without date in Henry James's *William Wetmore Story and his Friends*, II, 153 ff., contains the statement, "I went two days ago to see a famous mountain-pass, *le pas de Roland,* so called because that paladin kicked a hole in a rock, which blocked the way, to allow Charlemagne's army to pass. Very striking and picturesque it was, while the meadows by the riverside were delightful."

On September 19, 1864 (misdated 1862 by Mrs. Orr), he wrote to Isa Blagden from Biarritz, "I stay till the end of the month, then go to Paris, and then get my neck back into the old collar again. . . . For me, I have got on by having a great read at Euripides—the one book I brought with me, besides attending to my own matters, my new poem that is about to be; and of which the whole is pretty well in my head,—the Roman murder story you know."—

64 : 2–1. The designs by Sir Frederic Leighton for Mrs. Browning's tomb at Florence. See 63 : 2–4 and 63 : 3.

64 : 2–2. From letters (unpublished) written by Landor's niece, Elizabeth Sophia Landor, to Browning after her uncle's death (September 17, 1864), we learn that Browning and Sophia Landor's cousin, Mr. Robert Landor, were co-executors of Landor's Will. A "so-called" Will was made later than the true one, on December 23rd, 1862, and committed to Browning's care. Sophia Landor writes "I hope I shall not be in any way doing wrong, if I show him [Mr. Robert Landor] the paper in my Uncle's writing, which you sent me. Most likely it is worthless, but as it purports to be the last Will, it ought not to be put aside without proper authority, and as Mr. R. Landor is both Executor under the previous Will and also the Trustee and legal adviser of the family, it seems to me that he should be made aware of it: of course I shall not leave it with him."

This second Will was witnessed by Landor's sons, Walter Savage Landor and Charles Savage Landor. It contains the following clause:—"I bequeath my upright Salvator Rosa, and my Holy Family by Taddeo Gaddi, and my S. Peter by Guido (next to it) to my friend, Robert Browning, and all my Latin books to his son Robert." A copy in *facsimile* of this document (excluding only the signatures of the witnesses, which are on the reverse) was among the illustrations to an article on Landor in the *Bookman*, July, 1916. Seeing that in a further clause, other pictures were bequeathed to Landor's two younger sons, who signed as witnesses, the Will by English, if not by Italian, law would be held invalid so far as the witnesses were concerned.

No Will is to be found at Somerset House. Mr. Robert Landor was willing to have the later (illegal) Will proved in Italy, as Browning proposed doing, where the Yescombes could not enforce a claim on the estate. (See 58 : 1–1.) What apparently happened was that Browning turned over this later (illegal) Will to Landor's son Walter, in Italy, and Landor's bequests were carried out without proving either Will. Landor's wife and sons were generously provided for. Certain pictures, including one very large one, were sent by Browning, after keeping them safe for some time by special request, to Robert Landor, a brother who especially desired them. The property in Italy was of small value. With the exception of some pictures and personal belongings, his unentailed property, before he came to Browning, had been transferred to his sons and his wife in Fièsole ("the amiable people at the Villa," Browning calls them, with intensest irony).

64 : 2–3. See 59 : 1–4. Miss Annette Bracken had lived with Miss Blagden in Italy for a long time. Browning recorded her address as changed from "43, Grosvenor Place, Hyde Park," to "28, Harbourne Road, Edgbaston, near Birmingham," perhaps at this time, but the significance of this change is unknown.

64 : 2–4. Robert, Earl Lytton—"Owen Meredith." See 57 : 2–1.

64 : 2–5. Frances Power Cobbe: *Italics: Notes on Italy in 1864.*

64 : 2–6. Jessie White, daughter of J. Meriton White, married Alberto Mario. She was the authoress of a *Life of Garibaldi.*

64 : 2–7. This poem was to become *The Ring and the Book.* Browning began writing the poem at this time. George Murray Smith, mentioned above, was to be the publisher.

64 : 2–8. *Edinburgh Review,* October, 1864, Article VIII, pp. 537–565.

64 : 2–9. "A Tuscan Village—A Tuscan Sanctuary," in the *Cornhill Magazine,* October, 1864. The article is unsigned, but the identification of it seems certain. It includes an account of a visit to the monastery at Vallombrosa, which the Brownings had visited in 1847, and which Miss Blagden no doubt visited with some of her friends from Florence or the Bagni di Lucca.

65 : 1–1. The boys were W. W. Story's sons Thomas Waldo, born in 1854, and Julian Russell, born in 1856. Edith Marion, Story's only daughter, was born in 1844.

65 : 2–1. James Bertrand Payne, manager of the business of Moxon & Co. after the death of Edward Moxon.

65 : 2–2. *Moxon's Miniature Poets: A Selection from the Works of Robert Browning;* London; Edward Moxon & Co.; 1865. Payne issued the Browning Selections in sixpenny numbers, as he had done with the Selections from Tennyson in the same year.

65 : 2–3. Probably some of the numerous Moxon publications of Shelley. Browning expected to prepare a volume of Selections from Shelley, for *Moxon's Miniature Poets*.

65 : 3–1. "Mr. Cartwright, who spent a night or two at Warwick Crescent, about 1864 or '5, remembers that Browning then told him he was engaged upon a poem based on the Franceschini affair, as to which, he added, he had procured further information: this would be that contained in a reprint of a contemporary manuscript pamphlet, sent him by a friend, containing an account of the murder and of Guido's trial and execution."—Griffin's and Minchin's *Life,* p. 230. Professor Griffin is apparently referring to the *Secondary Source* of *The Ring and the Book,* which was not printed until Browning gave his MS. of it to Sir John Simeon, who prepared it for publication in the *Philobiblon Society Miscellanies,* xii, 1868–69, Item 3. Browning read the proofs, he states in a preliminary word to this issue, on the day when the news of Sir John Simeon's death reached him. The *Secondary Source* was in manuscript in 1865, and it was probably the document he had secured from Mrs. Baker, through Isa Blagden, in 1862. The opening words quoted in this letter are those of the *Secondary Source.* It seems likely that Cartwright had learned from Mr. Craven of still another account of the murder case, which Browning was naturally eager to see. At any rate, there is in existence such another account, entitled (in Italian) "The Trial and Death of Franceschini for Murder," etc. This narrative was discovered in 1900 by Signor Dottore Ignazio Giorgi, Librarian of the Royal Casanatense Library in Rome, in a volume containing material about the Cenci; and published in translation, by Professor Griffin, in the *Monthly Review,* November, 1900. This translation is reprinted in Griffin's and Minchin's *Life,* Appendix B, pp. 309–327. The special analogies between the poem and this document are sufficiently striking to be most readily explained only on the assumption that Browning drew somehow from this third source. Cartwright, to whom Browning had once offered the *Old Yellow Book* (the primary source) in Rome, was no doubt interested in the subject for his friend's sake, and therefore on the watch for fresh material. The Mr. Craven referred to was, fairly certainly, Augustus Craven, son of Keppel Richard Craven, and husband of Pauline Marie Armande Aglaé Craven, at this date (1865) still maintaining his residence in Naples, but on the verge of moving to Rome. He was interested in Italian history, and would have been a likely person to discover this account of the case of Franceschini in the Royal Casanatense Library. At any rate, it is clear that Cartwright was able to inform Browning of the existence of some manuscript account with which he was not personally familiar, and that apparently Browning reproduced in *The Ring and the Book* some details of the Casanatense document. These circumstances establish strong probability that Browning knew the contents of this document, and that he secured the knowledge of it through Mr. Cartwright's mediation with Mr. Craven.

65 : 4–1. *The Ring and the Book.* In the first edition, the first five books amount to 8355 lines, as numbered, with half-lines counted as whole ones. Browning's manuscript had twenty-eight lines on a page; he had probably used almost exactly three hundred sheets at this time.

65 : 5–1. The Storys lived, when in England, with Mr. and Mrs. Russell Sturgis, at Mount Felix, Walton-on-Thames.

65 : 6–1. Story made a bust of Elizabeth Barrett Browning, after her death, as a companion-piece to his bust of Robert Browning.

65 : 9–1. *The Ring and the Book.*

65 : 9–2. See 62 : 1–3.

66 : 1–1. "Elys," cf. *Sordello,* II, lines 139 and 151.

66 : 1–2. The two "moods of mind" are those of two kinds of poets described in *Sordello*, I, lines 466 ff.: . . . "you can believe / Sordello foremost in the regal class," etc. The second "mood" begins with line 523: "For there's a class that eagerly looks," etc. The quotation in the letter, "Thrusting in time eternity's concern," occurs in line 566.

66 : 1–3. *The Ring and the Book.*

66 : 2–1. Browning's hopes of securing his son's admission to Balliol were disappointed. Robert Barrett Browning failed in the matriculation examinations for Balliol, but later secured admission to Christ Church, where he matriculated on January 15, 1869, at the age of nineteen. Cf. 66 : 9; 67 : 1–2; 67 : 2; 67 : 3–3.

66 : 2–2. *The Ring and the Book.* See 67 : 4–2.

66 : 3–1. Robert Browning, Senior, the poet's father.

66 : 5–1. Mrs. Bracken, mother of Willy. The Brackens were companions of the Brownings on several vacation trips to France.

66 : 8–1. Le Croisic, a sea-port town of the extreme south of Brittany, situated on a peninsula of salt-marshes at the northern extremity of the estuary of the Loire, was the autumn retreat of the Brownings in 1866 and 1867. It was at Le Croisic (September 30, 1867) that Browning wrote "Hervé Riel," in which a local hero is celebrated. It was here also that the poetaster Paul Desforges-Maillard wrote those verses, under the pseudonym of Mlle. de Malcrais, which "brought Voltaire upon his knees" to a non-existent lady of high Breton birth. Here, too, lived another and earlier poeticule, René Gentilhomme, and the adventures of these two oddities Browning has immortalized in the second half of his volume of 1878, *La Saisiaz: The Two Poets of Croisic.* He is understood to have found these stories in the book of a local antiquary, Caillo's *Notes sur le Croisic.*

The "men in white, with baggy breeches," who attracted the poet's notice at Batz, were the famous *paludiers* or salt-marsh workers, a colony of some four hundred persons, who lived in complete isolation and spoke a different patois from their neighbors. It has been supposed that they were Scandinavians. Cf. 67 : 1.

66 : 8–2. The book was *Nora and Archibald Lee,* published in March, 1867, by Chapman and Hall. *Agnes Tremorne,* Miss Blagden's first novel, had been published by Smith, Elder, and Co., in 1861. Chapman and Hall published *The Cost of a Secret* in 1863; and *The Woman I Loved and the Woman Who Loved Me,* in 1865. The "delay" was in payments to Miss Blagden for this book, which was apparently issued later than was planned. It came out in midsummer of 1865, though it contained advertising dated October, 1864. Miss Blagden apparently was ready to try Chapman once more, though Browning had broken with him on her account. *The Crown of a Life,* her last novel, was published by Hurst and Blackett, in 1869. One suspects that her novels were never popular enough to make a publisher eager for them. The copies in the British Museum had until recently never been fully opened. See 66 : 7; 66 : 9–2; 67–2; 67 : 2–1.

66 : 8–3. *Poems and Ballads* [First Series], Moxon & Co. See *Athenaeum,* No. 2023, August 4, 1886, p. 137.

66 : 9–1. The Brownings were married on September 12th, 1846. Miss Blagden had agreed to write on the 12th of each month, and in this month fell the anniversary of the wedding.

66 : 9–2. *Nora and Archibald Lee,* 3 vols. See 66 : 8–2. The copy in the British Museum was received on March 25, 1867.

66 : 10–1. The "revelation he describes" had suggested to Browning the similar revelation of Swedenborg; hence, "Swedish." Mrs. Browning was a professed Swedenborgian.

66 : 10–2. "Instead of studying, he did nothing but spoil his books with scribbling faces in them." Cf. Poem:—

"I drew men's faces on my copy-books,
"Scrawled them within the antiphonary's marge," etc.

66 : 10–3. "If the paintings in the Cloister and Church of the Carmine were done by Lippo, while he still remained a Carmelite, it would be only reasonable to infer that these paintings were later studied and copied by Masaccio."

66 : 10–4. "He worked at the Carmine, always following the steps of Filippo."

67 : 1–1. Seymour Stocker Kirkup had been made a Barone of the Italian Kingdom in recognition partly of his conspicuous achievement, with his friends Bezzi and Wilde, in uncovering from whitewash, on July 21, 1840, the portrait of Dante ascribed by tradition to Giotto, in the chapel of the Palazzo del Podestà, in the Florentine Bargello. He asserted that the spirit of Dante had revealed to him the location of the picture. Browning had in his album a photographic copy of the picture. Cf. 53 : 1–1.

67 : 1–2. See 66 : 2–1.

67 : 1–3. Bibi was probably Kirkup's daughter Imogen. Cf. 53 : 1–1.

67 : 2–1. *Nora and Archibald Lee,* which appeared in March, 1867. Cf. 66 : 8–2.

67 : 2–2. James Bertrand Payne was manager of Moxon's. The trouble arose over the inclusion of certain copyright poems by Landor in Locker's *Lyra Elegantiarum.* The book was suppressed, and reissued in amended form.

67 : 2–3. "Hatty" is Harriet Hosmer. It is interesting to find this unfavorable judgment of her character not long before Browning's permanent break with her. See Appendix, "Browning and Lady Ashburton."

67 : 2–4. Browning's spelling of the name of George Henry Lewes was uncertain. He is probably meant here.

67 : 2–5. See 62 : 1–3.

67 : 2–6. See 61 : 3–1.

67 : 3–1. See 66 : 9–2.

67 : 3–2. Matthew Arnold. The spelling is confused with that of the name of Browning's early and very dear friend, Joseph Arnould.

67 : 3–3. Pen was not destined to pass his examinations at this time. See 66 : 2–1; 67 : 1–2.

67 : 4–1. This letter is quoted from *Proceedings of the Massachusetts Historical Society,* October–November, 1926, LX, 35–36. Cf. 68 : 4.

67 : 4–2. Browning had probably asked, and been promised, £200 for the American rights to *The Ring and the Book.* Cf. 66 : 2–2.

67 : 5–1. On Wednesday, June 26, 1867, the M.A. degree was conferred on Browning by diploma at Oxford. Browning regarded it properly as "a very rare distinction said to have only happened in Dr. Johnson's case!" He valued it because it gave him the rights of the University, with a vote in Council. The plan was, once this degree was conferred, to make Browning an Honorary Fellow of Balliol. This was done, in the following October. Browning's acceptance was "purely for Pen's sake," and "the advantage it will be to me to be in that position while Pen is there." But cf. 66 : 2–1.

67 : 5–2. Cf. 66 : 8, in which Browning writes of a "decisive" letter, consequent upon his resentment against Chapman for his treatment of Isa Blagden. That was the end of Browning's business relations with Chapman and Hall. Cf. 66 : 8–2; 66 : 9; 67 : 2–1.

67 : 5–3. See 62 : 1–3.

67 : 6–1. Theodosia Garrow, first wife of Thomas Adolphus Trollope, died on April 13, 1865. Their daughter was Beatrice. His second wife was Frances Eleanor Ternan, whom he first met at Riccorboli (his recently purchased house) in the spring of 1866.

67 : 6–2. A slip of the pen for "Empedocles on Etna." The misplaced quotation marks at this point in the letter indicate hasty writing.

67 : 7–1. See 62 : 1–3.

67 : 7–2. *The Crown of a Life*, published in 1869 by Hurst and Blackett. Cf. 66 : 8–2.

67 : 8–1. An article on *Sordello*, by Professor Dowden, was accepted by Charles Kingsley as temporary editor of *Fraser's Magazine* during the absence of Mr. J. A. Froude, and printed in the number for October, 1867, pp. 518–530. The second part was declined by Froude, on the ground that a poem which requires an explanation is no poem at all. It accordingly remained unprinted until its inclusion, together with the first part, in *Transcripts and Studies*.

67 : 8–2. *The Ring and the Book*. A passage in point appears in Book X, lines 272–275:—

> "For I am ware it is the seed of act
> "God holds appraising in His hollow palm,
> "Not act grown great thence on the world below,
> "Leafage and branchage, vulgar eyes admire."

In *Browning*, p. 147, Dowden writes, "The principle, again, by which he determined an artist's rank is in harmony with Browning's general feeling that men are to be judged less by their actual achievements than by the possibilities that lie unfolded within them, and the ends to which they aspire, even though such ends be unattained."

67 : 9–1. See 67 : 8–1.

67 : 9–2. Professor Dowden's study of *Sordello* was printed entire in *Transcripts and Studies*, pp. 18 ff.

67 : 9–3. *Essays on Robert Browning's Poetry*. By John T. Nettleship. London: Macmillan & Co., 1868.

67 : 9–4. *I.e.*, the Third Collected Edition of 1868. With regard to the "blunders," see 66 : 10.

67 : 9–5. *"Booming"*: the carroch being the car on which the flag of a City or State was mounted, accompanied by trumpeters, etc.—hence the "boom." The "somebody" must have bungled, or his memory must have been at fault, when speaking to Browning. The word occurs in *Sordello*, Book I, line 317 (p. 14, line 17 of the First Edition, of 1840), and is quite correctly printed: "The carroch's booming; safe at last! Why strange" . . .

68 : 2–1. Arabel Barrett, after leaving the Wimpole Street house, lived for many years at 7, Delamere Terrace, not far from 19, Warwick Crescent, where Browning took up his abode on his return to England. "There was much in her nature that resembled that of her sister Elizabeth. Browning felt her death keenly; it was long before he could bring himself so much as to pass the house where she had lived."—Griffin's and Minchin's *Life*, p. 237.

68 : 2–2. Elizabeth Barrett died on June 29th, 1861.

68 : 2–3. Elizabeth Barrett.

68 : 4–1. This letter was first printed in a catalogue issued by an American firm of autograph-dealers; it was reprinted in the *Daily Chronicle*, July 19th, 1895, p. 3 d. Cf. 67 : 4.

68 : 4–2. *The Ring and the Book*, published in four volumes, one each month, November to February, 1868–69.

68 : 4–3. The fact that George Murray Smith read the manuscript of *The Ring and the Book* constitutes an exception to the procedure ordinarily established. See 84 : 1, on Browning's usual practice in submitting MSS. at this date. The question of the most advantageous way of issuing the work had been raised, no doubt, by Browning's proposing a two-volume issue.

68 : 5–1. Eneas Sweetland Dallas, leader writer in the *Times;* author of *The Gay Science*, etc. He was the husband of Miss Glyn, the actress. This letter is probably a reply to a request for a contribution to a short-lived weekly newspaper, *The Mirror*, launched about this time by Mr. Dallas.

68 : 5–2. *The Ring and the Book.*

68 : 6–1. Mr. William G. Kingsland, author of *Robert Browning, Chief Poet of the Age,* 1887.

69 : 1–1. Buchanan's first "Reading" was given at the Queen's Concert Rooms, Hanover Square, on January 25th, 1869. "In front of him sat Lord Houghton, on his right was Robert Browning, near him sat Dr. Westland Marston and the Rev. Newman Hall."—Miss H. Jay's *Robert Buchanan,* 1903, p. 158. The second, and last, reading was given in the following March.

69 : 1–2. Probably chosen from *North Coast and other Poems,* 1868, but possibly from earlier volumes as well.

69 : 2–1. Three volumes had appeared by this date; but the whole imprint had evidently not yet been bound. It is a peculiar circumstance that the backstrips of the volumes of the first edition of *The Ring and the Book,* in those specimens the editor has examined, have Roman numbers on Vols. I and III and Arabic numbers on the other two volumes. This letter perhaps offers a clue to the mystery.

69 : 2–2. The misprint occurred in line 1617 (on p. 166 of Vol. III) of Part VIII, in the First Edition.

> . . . "defray its cost
> "By money dug out of the dirty earth,
> "Mere irritant, in Maro's phrase, to ill?"

In the edition of 1872, the line (1626) is changed to

> "Irritant mere, in Ovid's phrase, to ill."

The Latin line is from the *Metamorphoses,* I, 140.

69 : 3–1. This letter has already been printed in *The Athenaeum,* No. 3559, January 11, 1896, p. 52, where it was introduced by the following note:—

> "15, Cranley Place, S.W.

> "Looking over old letters—that *via dolorosa* which leads one through death and loss—I have lighted on the enclosed. It is in reply to some remonstrance I had ventured to make on the quantity which Browning somewhere assigned to the word *metamorphosis,* the penultimate syllable of which is long in Greek.
> "F. T. Palgrave."

The Ring and the Book, X, 1615, in the first edition, read "The immeasurable metamorphosis"; in the edition of 1872, it read (line 1616), "Metamorphosis the immeasurable."

69 : 4–1. Browning had spent the summer in Scotland with the Storys. See Appendix, "Browning and Lady Ashburton."

69 : 4–2. Theodore Tilton was editor of *The Independent,* in which in former years some of Mrs. Browning's poems had appeared.

70 : 1–1. *The Life of Mary Russell Mitford . . . Related in a selection from her letters to her Friends,* was edited by the Rev. A. G. L'Estrange, in 1869, and published in 1870. A Second Series of her letters was edited by H. F. Chorley, in 1872. The Rev. William Harness was the recipient of many letters from Miss Mitford.

70 : 1–2. *The Holy Grail and Other Poems.*

70 : 1–3. *The Earthly Paradise,* Part iii.

70 : 2–1. This letter reminds us of the prolonged hostility between Alfred Austin and Browning. In 1870 was published *The Poetry of the Period,* by Alfred Austin. The paper on Browning occupied pp. 38 to 76. It had originally appeared in *Temple Bar* for June, 1869 (vol. xxvi, pp. 316–333). Ten years later, the author stated that this volume had long been out of print, and that he would never consent to its reappearance. See 72 : 3 and 76 : 10–1.

70 : 3–1. In the *Times* of May 14, 1870, appeared an account of the "Vandalism at Oxford." "A wanton destruction of valuable marble busts at Christ Church a few nights ago is the theme of general indignation at Oxford. It appears the perpetrators of the disgraceful outrage, who are believed to be undergraduate members of Christ Church, entered the library of the College by breaking a pane of glass in the dead of night, and conveyed the figures into Peckwater Quadrangle, where a fire was made of faggots and doormats which did its work without creating much blaze. Among those destroyed was a bust of the late Dean, Dr. Gaisford, by Woolner, which is an irreparable loss to the Society." Etc.

Pen Browning had matriculated at Christ Church on January 15th, 1869, but was absent during the term in which this episode took place. His chief activities during the next year (his last, apparently, in college), aside from his studies, were billiards, in which he won a cup, and rowing. In Browning's album in the Hall at Balliol are several photographs of Christ Church crews of which Pen was a member.

70 : 7–1. Lord Stratford de Redcliffe.

71 : 1–1. *Napoleon Fallen*, reviewed in *The Athenaeum*, January 7, 1871. Reissued later in the year (the dedication is dated May) as the second of the three plays in the Dramatic Trilogy called *The Drama of Kings*.

71 : 1–2. The poem appeared in 1871 as *Prince Hohenstiel-Schwangau, Saviour of Society*.

71 : 2–1. This letter appeared in the *Daily News*, February 10, 1871, p. 6 b.

71 : 2–2. The poem was "Hervé Riel." Cf. 76 : 7–1.

71 : 5–1. Ernest Benzon. During the summer, Browning was the guest of the Benzons at Little Milton, in the hills above Loch Tummel. He was at work on *Prince Hohenstiel-Schwangau, Saviour of Society*.

71 : 5–2. *Balaustion's Adventure*, which Browning had written as "a May-month's amusement," appeared in August, 1871.

71 : 6–1. The letter refers to "Browning as a Preacher," two papers by Miss E. Dickinson West in *The Dark Blue*, October and November, 1871, Vol. II, pp. 171–184, 305–319. In the Browning Society's first published volume, in Appendix IV, pp. 98–99, Professor Dowden gives more than a full page of quotations from these papers; and on p. 98, ftn., remarks that the article is "among the very best articles written on 'Browning,'" and on p. 99 that it is "an admirable essay." Miss West later became Mrs. Dowden.

71 : 8–1. *Balaustion's Adventure.* See 71 : 5–2.

71 : 9–1. See 71 : 6–1.

71 : 9–2. *Prince Hohenstiel-Schwangau, Saviour of Society.* The name was suggested to Browning by Mr. W. C. Cartwright.

71 : 10–1. *Prince Hohenstiel-Schwangau, Saviour of Society.*

72 : 1–1. *Prince Hohenstiel-Schwangau, Saviour of Society.*

72 : 1–2. *Fifine at the Fair* was Browning's next work.

72 : 1–3. Louisa Lady Ashburton. See Appendix, "Browning and Lady Ashburton."

72 : 2–1. Belton House, Grantham, was the estate of Lady Marian Alford in Surrey. "The house in Park Lane" was doubtless the town house of Lady Marian Alford, whose address appears in Browning's address book (the earlier one) as "Park Lane." Lady Ashburton's address in the same book was "Bath House, 82, Piccadilly."

72 : 2–2. See Appendix, "Browning and Lady Ashburton."

73 : 1–1. *Red Cotton Night-Cap Country, or Turf and Towers*, 1873; at the end the poem is dated "January 23, 1873." Tailleville was called Clairvaux in the poem, in which the names were altered to forestall action for libel. See 89 : 8. "When once the raw material had been collected and absorbed, the process of composition was very rapid. The whole poem was written in seven weeks, and printed off from the first draft; and in May, 1873, it was published."—Sir Frederic G. Kenyon's Introduction to Vol. VII of the Centenary Edition of the *Works*, p. xv.

73 : 2–1. Isabella Blagden died at her home in Florence—Piazza di Bello Sguardo, No. 5—on January 20th, 1873, aged fifty-five.

73 : 4–1. See 71 : 5–1. The Benzons' house in London was at 5, Kensington Park Gardens, W. Mr. Benzon was a brother of Mr. Henry Schlesinger; Mrs. Benzon was a Lehman, of the family of Browning's dear friend Rudolf Lehman, the artist. The Benzons were among the most intimate of Browning's friends. Mr. Benzon bequeathed to Browning a valuable collection of arms.

74 : 1–1. Lily Benzon, adopted daughter of Ernest Benzon.

74 : 1–2. Jean-Arnould Heyermans, born at Antwerp, was Pen's master in painting. His portrait of Pen at work in the studio at Antwerp is in the Browning Collection in Browning Hall, at the Browning Settlement in Walworth.

74 : 1–3. Beatrice Trollope, daughter of Thomas Adolphus Trollope and his first wife, Theodosia Garrow.

74 : 2–1. An unsuccessful application had in 1871 been made to Mr. Gladstone to grant a Civil List pension to Mr. Horne, in recognition partly of his literary claims, and partly of his Government services in Victoria. Among the signatures to the petition were those of Tennyson, Browning, Carlyle, William Morris, Swinburne, D. G. Rossetti, and Matthew Arnold. In June, 1874, Lord Beaconsfield granted the pension.

74 : 3–1. This letter appeared in the *Daily News*, November 21, 1874, p. 6 a. It deals with a phrase in "The Grammarian's Funeral."

75 : 1–1. *The Inn Album*, published in 1875.

75 : 2–1. Swinburne's *George Chapman*, 1875, contained (pp. 15–32) a most skilful, sympathetic, and just defense of Browning's work against the charge of obscurity, pointing out analogies between Browning's work and Chapman's. It would be difficult to find higher or more skilful praise of Browning. The tone of Browning's letter reflects the subtle quality of Swinburne's criticism.

75 : 3–1. Previously printed in *The Prose Works of William Wordsworth*, edited by the Rev. Alexander B. Grosart, London, 1876, Vol. I, p. xxxvii.

75 : 3–2. "The Lost Leader."

75 : 4–1. An announcement of the wedding of Mr. and Mrs. Edmund Gosse.

76 : 1–1. *Verses by E. D. W. Printed for Private Circulation.* 1876.

76 : 2–1. *King Erik. By Edmund Gosse.* London: 8vo, 1876. The Tragedy is prefaced by a Dedication, in verse, to Robert Browning.

76 : 3–1. "With a murmurous stir uncertain," etc. The Conclusion to *Lady Geraldine's Courtship,* Stanza 4, line 1.

76 : 3–2. Of course, as Mr. Ingram suggests, "someone had blundered" in this circumstantial account. Poe was not the man to have made the alleged confession to Mr. J. B. Read or, indeed, to anyone else. The manuscript of Mrs. Browning's poem, *Lady Geraldine's Courtship*, left England about the last day or so of July, 1844, and, as it was the last piece in the second volume of the American Edition of her poems, it is scarcely likely to have appeared in print until the end of the year. Although *The Raven* was not published until January 29, 1845, it had been in print some time already; and as it is known to have been in existence long previous to its acceptance for *The American Review,* it is scarcely possible that Poe could have seen the English poem until after his own poem had been written, if, indeed, until after his *Raven* had been printed.

The second account is equally faulty, and is a very inaccurate reminiscence of Poe's *Philosophy of Composition.*

76 : 5–1. This letter has been previously printed in *The Non-conformist,* and also in *Robert Browning: Chief Poet of the Age,* by W. G. Kingsland. It was written by Browning to a lady who, believing herself to be dying, wrote to thank him for the help she had derived from his poems, mentioning particularly "Rabbi Ben Ezra" and "Abt Vogler."

76 : 5–2. Browning no doubt had in his mind a passage in Hazlitt's Essay "Persons one would Wish to have Seen." There is no evidence that the story is other than apocryphal.

76 : 5–3. Two years after the date of this letter, appeared Mr. Browning's *La Saisiaz*, in which the following lines occur:—

> "I take upon my lips
> "Phrase the solemn Tuscan fashioned, and declare the soul's eclipse
> "Not the soul's extinction. Take his—'I believe and I declare—
> "Certain am I—from this life I pass into a better, there
> "Where this lady lives of whom enamoured was my soul.' "

76 : 7–1. "Hervé Riel" appeared, against Browning's usual custom, in *The Cornhill Magazine*, March, 1871, pp. 257–260. Browning desired to give a subscription to the Fund raised on behalf of the French after the siege of Paris by the Germans in 1870–71, and accordingly sent the £100 given by Mr. George Murray Smith for the poem to that fund. Cf. 71 : 2–2. The manuscript of the poem is dated September 30, 1867.

76 : 7–2. *Pacchiarotto and How he Worked in Distemper: With other Poems*, London, 1876.

76 : 8–1. *Pacchiarotto*, etc.

76 : 8–2. "Filippo Baldinucci on the Privilege of Burial. A Reminiscence of A. D. 1676." The MS. of this poem is dated "May 19, '76." Browning wrote on the first sheet of the MS. of "Filippo," "Print this poem *the last but one* in the volume—i.e., immediately before 'Cowslip Wine.' " The pages of that poem in the MS. were renumbered to make room for the insertion of "Filippo." The next poem before "Filippo" in date is *Pacchiarotto*, put first in the volume after the Dedication; the MS. of it is dated "Apr. 15, '76. May 1, '76." "Epilogue," entitled "Cowslip Wine" in the MS., is dated April 24 '76. The MS. of "Pacchiarotto" has the following note on the first sheet: "(The original copy. R. B.)." These particulars of the MSS. in the volume are of some interest in connection with the conflict between Browning and Alfred Austin. See 70 : 2 and 76 : 10–1.

76 : 8–3. Stanza 16, line 2: "In just a lady borne aloft [from bier]." The manuscript was accurately followed by the printer. Browning made the change in the edition of 1889.

76 : 8–4. Stanza 45, line 2: "Resolve me! Can it be she crowns,—[crowned,—]." The manuscript was accurately followed by the printer. Browning made the change in the edition of 1889.

76 : 8–5. Stanza 45, line 7: "Only for Mary's sake, disbursed [unpursed]." The manuscript was accurately followed by the printer. Browning made the change in the edition of 1889.

76 : 8–6. "Cenciaja." Page 164, line 8: "Relating who [how] the penalty was paid." The printer did not follow copy. Browning made the correction in the edition of 1889.

76 : 8–7. As printed the line reads: "Love, the love whole and sole without alloy." The MS. read: "Love, old love whole" etc. In the edition of 1889, Browning made no change in the line as originally printed.

76 : 9–1. This letter has been printed in the *Poetical Works of Shelley*, edited by H. Buxton Forman, II, Appendix II, "Mr. Browning on the Santa Croce Case and on Farinacci's Failure in the Defence of the Cenci," p. 420. Browning's *Cenciaja* deals with the episode of Paolo Santa Croce, the matricide, whose crime had so disastrous a bearing on the Cenci tragedy.

76 : 9–2. The title of "Cenciaja" is followed by the Italian proverb, *Ogni cencio vuol entrare in bucato*.

76 : 10–1. Cf. 70 : 2–1 on Browning's feeling about Alfred Austin's treatment of him in 1870. It is perhaps worth noting here than in a Memoir of Isa Blagden by Alfred Austin in an edition of her poems in 1873, he does not mention Browning's name. This is an *argumentum ab silentio* that he was hostile, despite his later statements that he suppressed his volume of criticism in 1873. 76 : 8–2 shows that *Pacchia-rotto*, in which Browning attacked Alfred Austin personally, was dated just before the volume containing it went to press, though put at the front of the volume. (See Professor William Lyon Phelps's article on "Browning and Alfred Austin," *Yale Review*, April, 1918.) Since the ensuing controversy has never, so far as the editor is aware, been dealt with, he desires to present here three items from *The Examiner*, the first being Alfred Austin's public disclaimer of any guilt such as Browning attributed to him, the second being an answer by Browning in verse (not reprinted in any of his published works), and the third being an unsigned editorial rather too precisely informed to have been written without Alfred Austin's direct assistance.

The first of the three items is as follows, in *The Examiner*, June 10, 1876:—

A Disclaimer.

Sir,—Will you kindly afford me the opportunity of removing a misconception of whose prevalence I am continually receiving fresh proofs, and which I think you will agree with me I should, in ordinary justice to myself, no longer allow to pass uncorrected.

Some few years ago I published a volume of essays on the poetry of our own day, whose object was not so much to estimate the merits of living poets, as to indicate, and, if possible, correct what I conceived to be the mischievous tendency of current criticism to exalt the incidental blemishes and peculiar shortcomings of works of incontestable genius and no little distinction, at the expense of dead poets, whose writings display in my opinion, yet greater because more masculine qualities. I still think it was desirable that some one should have undertaken this task, and as I happened to express not my own view merely, but the view entertained, I fully believe, by most of my countrymen who interest themselves in the higher concerns of literature, the work had some success. Nevertheless, had I not at that date mistakenly persuaded myself that I should never again in my lifetime invite the public to a perusal of any verse of my own, I should have abstained from the duty I somewhat unwillingly undertook. Before publishing "Madonna's Child" I made arrangements with Mr. Bentley for the transfer of the entire copyright of the volume to me, and, the edition being exhausted, I have not since allowed it to be reprinted.

The fact, however, of my having written these essays has not only exposed me, as the author of them, to no little animosity in certain quarters, of which it would be idle to complain, even if I were disposed to do so, but has caused me to be saddled with the responsibility of a number of anonymous criticisms, more especially with several that have appeared in the columns of an influential morning journal, which I no more wrote or inspired than, Sir, did you yourself. It has repeatedly been brought to my knowledge that I am set down in literary circles as the writer of notices which have appeared in the *Standard* newspaper of "Queen Mary," "Aristophanes' Apology," "The Inn Album," Mr. Morris's "Translation of the Aeneid," "Erechtheus," and I know not what beside; and now, by way of climax, a considerable poet writes to me, "I was most roughly handled in the *Standard*, apropos of my '——', and people keep assuring me that you are its only poetical critic."

Will you, therefore, allow me to state, once for all, and in order to put an end to these random assertions, made sometimes, I daresay, in perfect sincerity, but too frequently, I suspect, in a spirit of excessive sensitiveness and selflove, that I did not write one syllable of the notices I have named, nor have I the remotest idea who did; that I have nothing to do with the poetical reviews and notices in the *Standard,* save as one of the general public, occasionally to admire and sometimes utterly to dissent from them, that the only two poems I have for years past reviewed in its columns, by special and exceptional request of its editor, are Mr. Swinburne's "Bothwell" and Lord Lytton's "Fables in Song," of both of which I spoke with the enthusiastic admiration with which they inspired me; and that I have a letter from Mr. Swinburne, in which he was good enough to say that no review of any work of his ever gratified him more deeply?

I may add, as the attempt is being perpetually made to lay at my door reviews likewise of books in the *World,* that I have never reviewed any book in that paper, whether of verse or prose, from the day it was started to this hour.

Thanking you, by anticipation, for your courtesy, I have the honour to be, Sir, your obedient servant,

Alfred Austin.

Swinford House,
    June 5.

The second item, Browning's retort, is in the same vein as the passage about the dance of the sweeps in *Pacchiarotto,* and particularly carries on the idea of the *skoramis* passage in which Alfred Austin was personally attacked, as explained in the third item, the editorial, here presented after the poem. It appeared in *The Examiner,* August 5, 1876, p. 879.

TO MY CRITICS.

(WRITTEN SINCE MY LATE PUBLICATION.)

So, Master Critic, I'm told you think
    I should lend you my loving cup,
And fill it too with the best of drink,
    Give you in short both bite and sup.

No doubt you fancy yourself clever,
    And fit to tell me what to say.
You have perhaps a strong enough lever,
    To hoist me into the light of day?

You'd have me stand upon a stage
    Like a naked Spartan acrobat,
And go through my tricks. You'll then engage
    To send about the begging hat?

You say I should sing, I should not prate,
    But which knows best what each should do?
You say my large poems are only a spate
    Of dirty brown water, a hullabaloo!

Then when I issue a volume of short,
    You snigger and sniff as if you'd got
Something to show up for Philistine sport,
    A flea in my ear, a bug, a bot!

But I am a favorite of the Numphs,
    And if you knew your place, you'd drop
Upon your knees, you niggery sumphs,
    In the back slum of the editor's shop.

You would like, no doubt, to knock and ring,
    To be just hail fellow well met, with me,
But I've slops dirtier still to fling
    About you, and I shall, you'll see!

R———— B————

The third item is the judgment of *The Examiner* in the matter. It appeared in the issue of August 12, 1876, pp. 904–905.

Mr. Browning and His Critics

We have spoken very highly of the literary merits of Mr. Browning's "Pacchiarotto," and we see no cause to alter our opinion that it is the wittiest and most successful poem of its kind since "Hudibras." But the language which Mr. Browning incidentally applies to such of his critics as are also writers of verse, raises a moral question as to the limits of fair retort. We do not think it is for the public entertainment, or even for the public good, that those limits should be unduly confined; but Mr. Browning has at one point stepped so flagrantly beyond the limits commonly accepted that it becomes necessary to make some attempt to rectify the frontier. For much of the abuse which Mr. Browning heaps upon his critics he can plead the established practice of poets in all ages. No man likes to be criticised, and no poet likes to take criticism silently. What is the good of having all language as one's province, if one cannot use it to vex and confound one's enemies? and a poet's enemies are all who venture to dispute the intuitions of his genius. It is perfectly natural that Mr. Browning should try to place his critics in the most contemptuous light that he possibly can, more particularly when those critics aspire to teach him by example. In "Pacchiarotto" he imagines them as chimney-sweeps, whose work it is to "sweep out his chimbly." That is their proper function, but they came, he says, one May morning under his window with drums, fifes, triangles, tongs and bellows, blown with Saturnalian insolence, to show him how to make music. This was very different from the salutation which poets in old time were accustomed to receive from rival songsters on May morning; but Mr. Browning did not, he tells us, lose his temper. He thanked God that he was not as his critics were—dingy, dirty wretches, who did not sing all the year round like himself, but could only allow themselves one holiday, and misspent that in insulting their betters. He did not kick them out of his grounds, but chucked them some halfpence, told them that they were ignorant, impudent, envious, and malicious, and bade them be off, because his housemaid had her eye upon them, and suspected them of bringing more filth into the house than they took away. A terrible person is this housemaid of Mr. Browning's. "Quick march!" he cries to the chimney-sweeps,

> for Xanthippe my housemaid,
> If once on your pates she a souse made
> With what, pan or pot, bowl or *skoramis,*
> First comes to her hand,—things were more amiss!
> I would not for worlds be your place in—
> Recipient of slops from her basin!

There is not much to be said against this. There is little sweetness and light in it, certainly; but there is a rude primeval humour, and if Mr. Browning chooses thus to express his view of the relations between himself and his poet-critics, there must be some of his readers who will be more amused than disgusted. It is an attribute of poetic greatness to be childlike; the great poet deals with primeval feelings; and there is probably no conception which would appeal more cordially to children and savages than that of emptying a *skoramis*—even Mr. Browning does not venture to translate the word—on the head of an enemy. "Poetry hath in it," Bacon says, "some participation of the divine," but it hath also in it some participation of the vulgar; and in these self-distrustful days it is well that the sentiment of personal elation and inflation should be kept alive. Then, too, it is to be noted that Mr. Browning does make some concession to modern refinement. It is his housemaid, not himself, whom he glories in imagining as the active instrument in inflicting the indignity. He would not touch a *skoramis* himself with a pair of tongs; he gathers his "garland and singing robes about him," and points at the means of revenge with a jewelled finger.

We should be sorry to deny Mr. Browning the imaginary use of the *skoramis,* with these delicate refinements, if it gives him any satisfaction. But in the vindication of his high rank as a poet, Mr. Browning goes farther, and has recourse to more questionable weapons of offence. He singles out one of his critics in particular, the ringleader on this May morning intrusion, and addresses him thus:—

> While as for Quilp-Hop-o'-my-thumb there,
> Banjo-Byron that twangs the strum strum there—
> He'll think as the pickle he curses,
> I've discharged on his pate his own verses!
> "Dwarfs are saucy," says Dickens; so, sauced in
> Your own sauce * * *

Mr. Browning does not complete the last verse, at the request he says, of the printer's devil, who pleads with his royal highness of song not to be "satirical on a thing so very small"; but the missing rhyme may be found without the use of a dictionary. Now what has Mr. Alfred Austin done to provoke this gross assault? Has he ever hurled any personality of the same sort at Mr. Browning? If he had, Mr. Browning would best have consulted his own dignity by making no reply. But the assault, which passes all the limits which good breeding has imposed on literary squabbles, is utterly unprovoked. Some years ago Mr. Austin wrote some criticisms, which made a good deal of noise at the time, on contemporary poets, and on Mr. Browning among the rest. But he confined himself strictly to Mr. Browning's books, and their history. No doubt he said much which could not be pleasing to Mr. Browning, and some things which a strict taste would have forced him to cancel. He imagined that there was a conspiracy in "the academy and the drawing-room" to obtrude Mr. Browning as the rival of Mr. Tennyson, as the "next King" of song, the worthy recipient of the homage which the world was growing weary of paying to Mr. Tennyson. Mr. Austin stated his reasons for refusing to join in this conspiracy. He did not regard Mr. Browning as being "specifically a poet at all." He was only "a man who was striving earnestly to be an original poet, and who for the life of him could not be." He admitted Mr. Browning's intellectual power, but declared that it was analytic and not poetic in its natural manifestations. His verse was "muddy and unmusical," "the very incarnation of discordant obscurity," and so forth. Mr. Browning could not have liked to be told this. But it would have been much more dignified to leave the defence of his poems to other hands than his own. And if he was to undertake his own defence, if he was to empty an imaginary *skoramis* on the aggressor, if he considered this kind of raillery worthy of his position, at least he should have had sufficient self-respect not to taunt Mr. Austin with personal deformity. "Mr. Browning is an analyst rather than a poet," says Mr. Austin. "Hold your tongue, Quilp," retorts the angry bard, "you are a saucy dwarf."

How these poets love one another! And what privilege of strong language they enjoy! We who are cabined, cribbed, and confined within the prose paddock of language, as Mr. Browning triumphantly puts it, with a clog at our fetlocks, cannot help envying those who are free of all its four corners. But the line must be drawn somewhere, and common feeling for several generations has discountenanced attacks upon a rival's natural defects of body as being brutal and unmanly. In the good old days such attacks were common enough. If a man had bandy legs, or a club foot, or a cock eye, or a wart on his nose, it was considered quite fair to publicly jeer him on his deformity. But even in those days it was considered equally fair to retort by hiring a bully to give the satirist a good thrashing with a cudgel or a rope's end. The general sense of justice recognized this as the only fitting remedy for such an offence. Even in the days of duelling, the man who descended to such inexcusable brutality of attack could not expect to be called upon to give the satisfaction of a gentleman. At the beginning of this century, Southey made some grossly personal allusions to Byron's private life, and

Byron sent him a challenge. But if Southey had jeered at him because he had a club foot, we may be sure that he would have left the insult to the public contempt which its vulgar brutality deserved. We do not object to hard hitting among poets. Perhaps in view of the enormous territorial expansion and aggressive ambition of Science, it would be wise for them not to weaken their empire by internal dissension. But they delight to bark and bite, and poet-baiting is still numbered among the legitimate forms of public entertainment. Only they should remember that there are certain blows which the laws of the game declare to be foul. Poets seem to be constantly tempted to forget this. They seem never to have altogether recovered the triumph of Archilochus. We are not sure that it would not have been for the advantage of poetry if the daughters of Lycambes had hanged Archilochus instead of hanging themselves.

76 : 10–2. The dance of the chimney sweeps is the concluding portion of "Of Pacchiarotto and How he Worked in Distemper," Parts XXIV to XXIX. It is of interest to note that the renumbering of pages in part of the MS. and the double dating of the MS. (April 15, 1876 and May 1, 1876) suggest that this final section of the poem may have been added to the poem originally ending with Part XXIII, "Good-bye!" (l. 456). If that is the case, the poem was completed on April 15th, and this attack on Browning's critics and on Alfred Austin was added by May 1st, 1876. Lines 470–473, 533–534 (the personal allusion to Alfred Austin), the footnote by the printer's devil on line 534, and the assertion of good-humor on Browning's part with which the poem concludes, were certainly introduced while the poem was in press; they do not appear in the MS.

76 : 11–1. The book of which the receipt is here acknowledged was not Mr. Forman's *Robert Browning and the Epic of Psychology,* or *Our Living Poets,* but the first volume of his Library Edition of Shelley.

76 : 11–2. "Cenciaja," which there was some thought of reprinting in the second volume of Shelley's Works, as an illustration of *The Cenci.*

76 : 11–3. The "old square yellow book," known as the *Old Yellow Book,* the primary source of *The Ring and the Book.* See 76 : 9.

76 : 11–4. The passage quoted appears in "Another Argument [the third] of the aforesaid Signor Arcangeli in favor and defense of the aforesaid," *Old Yellow Book,* pp. ci–cii. The name "Beatrice Cenci" is written in the margin opposite the first citation of her name. In translation, the passage is as follows:—

"And in proof of this we have elsewhere adduced many decisions of the Highest Courts, whereby punishment has been lessened for husbands who have killed their wives likewise with an assassin's aid; whereas no decision supporting the Fisc is adduced. This opinion is the more readily acceptable inasmuch as it is confirmed by the majority of Courts. And granted that Farinacci and my Lord Raynaldus appear to oppose it, nevertheless Farinacci in his *Quaestionibus* evinces grave uncertainty, as I have explained elsewhere: and in *Consiliis,* 141, he has shown himself quite uncertain; whereas in *Consiliis,* 66, No. 5, he has upheld the contrary. Consequently, in defense of variable opinion of this kind he offers in his own defense, in the said *Consiliis,* 141, under No. 16, the opinion that Beatrice, in whose defense he wrote in *Cons.* 66, was beheaded, and implies that such rigorous sentence should be pronounced in such cases. But, if so eminent an authority will pardon me, his answer is highly inconsistent, for he forgets what he set down at the end of the opinion in Consilium 66; namely, that Beatrice was sentenced to death not because in cold blood she ordered the death of one plotting against her honor, but because she did not establish this latter excuse—"Thus, and likewise there would have been good hopes for sister Beatrice if she had established the alleged excuse, as indeed she did not establish it."

76 : 11–5. The Defense is to be found in a scarce little volume with the title *A Dissertation on The Statutes of the Cities of Italy; and a Translation of the Pleading of Prospero Farinaccio in Defense of Beatrice Cenci and her relatives : with Notes.* By George Bowyer, Esq. of the Middle Temple, London: 8vo, 1838.

77 : 1–1. See 57 : 2, in which Browning tells of transcribing "The Indian Serenade."

77 : 1–2. Letter 57 : 2, printed in Leight Hunt's *Correspondence,* edited by his eldest son Thornton Leigh Hunt, 2 vols., London, 1862, II, 264–267.

77 : 1–3. Shelley *alludes* to the air in the poem. The *note* explaining the allusion is by Mary Shelley.

77 : 2–1. The manuscript of "Hervé Riel" is dated "Sept. 30, '67," earlier by many years than that of any other poem in the *Pacchiarotto* volume. See 76 : 7–1.

77 : 3–1. Shelley's *Charles the First,* Scene II (Vol. III, p. 316 of Library Edition): "The rainbow hung over the city . . . like a bridge of congregated lightning pierced by the masonry of heaven." In the re-issue (1882) of the Library Edition Mr. Forman adopted Mr. Browning's suggested emendation—*pieced* for *pierced.*

77 : 3–2. *Lord Byron and some of his Contemporaries,* by Leigh Hunt. The portrait in question was engraved by H. Meyer from a drawing by J. Hayter.

77 : 3–3. Cf. 44 : 1. The manuscript is the acting version, read to Keane, of *Colombe's Birthday,* fully described in *The Athenaeum* for 1st and 15th September, 1894. Mr. Wise recalls that this MS. of *Colombe's Birthday* was sold, about 1886, by Messrs. Puttick and Simpson, of Leicester Square, book auctioneers, to the late Bertram Dobell, not yet established as a bookseller. He wrote to Mr. Wise and to Buxton Forman, offering it for £10. Both went to Dobell's next morning. Mr. Wise banged against Mr. Forman coming out of Mr. Dobell's shop, "Joy on the face of the old boy. Curses on my lips." It was No. 127 at the Forman sale, March 15, 1920, at the Anderson Galleries, in New York, where it was bought by an American dealer for less than half of the sum Mr. Wise offered for it (£600) to Mr. Stetson, purchaser of the entire library of Mr. Forman. Edmund Gosse inspected this MS. when he wrote *Robert Browning Personalia.* [The present possessor has been unwilling to disclose his identity to the editor of this volume, who hopes that the location of all Browning MSS. will be made known for the benefit of students of the Poet's works. The MS. of *Pippa Passes* is reported to be similarly held by some one in the United States.]

77 : 3–4. See 44 : 1.

77 : 4–1. The preface to Browning's translation, or "transcription" of *The Agamemnon of Aeschylus* is dated "London: *October* 1st, 1877." It ends with this sentence: "No, neither 'uncommanded' nor 'unrewarded': since it was commanded of me by my venerated friend Thomas Carlyle, and rewarded will it indeed become, if I am permitted to dignify it by the prefatory insertion of his dear and noble name."

77 : 5–1. This letter appeared in the *Times,* November 20, 1877, p. 6 e.

77 : 6–1. *Shelley, A Critical Biography,* by George Barnett Smith. Edinburgh, David Douglas, 1877.

77 : 6–2. Miss Annie Egerton Smith. She had recently (September 14, 1877) died at La Saisiaz, near Geneva. See Browning's poem, *La Saisiaz.*

77 : 6–3. Miss Smith was part-proprietor of *The Liverpool Mercury.*

77 : 7–1. Medwin in *The Shelley Papers* misprinted *deadly hue* for *deadly yew;* Forman, taking his text from *The Shelley Papers,* repeated the error. He set the matter right, however, in his two-volume edition of Shelley's Poems.

78 : 1–1. *Das Fremdenbuch* [*The Inn Album*] . . . *Aus dem Englischen von E. Leo.* Pp. 176. Hamburg, Altenburg, 1877. Cf. 80 : 2.

78 : 2–1. Pen Browning, born on March 9, 1849, was twenty-nine at this time. Browning had been twenty-nine in 1841. Either Browning exaggerates the difference of ages in this letter, or Alexander Carlyle was mistaken in stating that "Robert Browning was introduced to Carlyle by Leigh Hunt, at whose house they met for the first time early in 1840." (*Letters of Thomas Carlyle to Mill, Sterling, and Browning,* edited by Alexander Carlyle, London, 1923, p. ix.)

78 : 4–1. *Studies of Sensation and Event,* the only publication of Ebenezer Jones (1820–1860), appeared in 1843.

78 : 4–2. Eliot Warburton (1810–1852), the traveller, and author of *The Crescent and the Cross,* was lost on a steamer burned at sea.

78 : 5–1. Sir Frederic Leighton had been elected President of the Royal Academy. Through many years, in later days, Browning was to be seen almost daily walking with Leighton, who was so tall that his shoulder came level with Browning's head. Browning, we are told by witnesses, always carried a rolled umbrella upright in his left hand on these long walks.

79 : 3–1. This little message is interesting as a bit of written communication from Browning preserved by Domett ("Waring") after April 11, 1877. "After that date nothing is preserved, though the personal intercourse continued until Domett's death on November 2, 1887, two years before that of his friend."—*Robert Browning and Alfred Domett,* edited by Sir Frederic G. Kenyon, London, 1906, p. 19.

79 : 4–1. *Dramatic Idyls.*

79 : 5–1. *The Return of the Druses* was originally advertised under the name of *Mansoor the Hierophant.*

79 : 5–2. Two landscapes by Mrs. Gosse. Cf. 75 : 4.

79 : 6–1. The "rascally subject" was Browning himself! The *Athenaeum* had printed in full, in the original Latin (and Greek), the "felicitous encomium" pronounced by "Mr. Sandys, the Public Orator at Cambridge, when presenting Mr. Browning for an honorary degree last week."

79 : 7–1. *The Philosophy of Handwriting,* 1879. By Felix de Salamanca (*i.e.,* J. H. Ingram), a work in which the characters of various contemporary personages, known more or less to fame, were supposed to be deduced from their calligraphy.

80 : 1–1. A suggested biography of Mrs. Browning, by J. H. Ingram, ultimately published by Messrs. W. H. Allen and Co. in 1888.

80 : 2–1. "Pheidippides," line 88. The first edition (1879) reading was, "Pan for Athens, Pan for me! myself have a guerdon too!" The word *too* rhymed with *dew* and *hitherto* in the stanza, leaving *bear* (in the second of the seven lines) without a rhyme. In the edition of 1882, the line was altered to, "Pan for Athens, Pan for me! I too have a guerdon rare!"

80 : 2–2. "Echetlos." The MS. is dated "Feb. 2, 1880." The line was printed thus: "Not the great name! Sing—woe for the great name Miltiadés" . . .

80 : 2–3. *Dramatic Idyls: Second Series.*

80 : 2–4. William Hepworth Thompson (1810–86), Master of Trinity College, Cambridge.

80 : 4–1. A copy of the first edition of *Edgar Allan Poe: His Life, Letters, and Opinions,* by J. H. Ingram, London, 1880.

80 : 5–1. This letter was written in reply to one from Mr. Ingram respecting the manuscripts of Thomas Lovell Beddoes, then in Mr. Browning's possession. Mr. Ingram had at the time some idea of producing a work in connection with the subject, but Mr. Browning's letter put a final stop to the project. See 83 : 8.

81 : 1–1. Robert Barrett Browning, the poet's son.

81 : 2–1. Mr. Halliwell-Phillips, well known Shakespearean bibliophile, had written to Browning expressing his resentment against the insult offered him by Furnivall in the announcement of an edition of one of Shakespeare's plays. Furnivall, in the course of a protracted quarrel with Swinburne, had referred to Swinburne and Halliwell-Phillips as "Pigsbrook & Co." Swinburne retaliated by christening Furnivall "Brothels-dyke." This letter from Browning, President of the New Shakespeare Society, whom Halliwell-Phillips held responsible for a publication such as Furnivall's, in the name of the Society, did not serve to placate Halliwell-Phillips. He printed it in a pamphlet designed to chastise both his detractor and Browning. One can understand Browning's refusal to accept Furnivall's invitation to become President of the Shelley Society (85 : 11).

81 : 3–1. *Studies in Song,* 1881, containing the magnificent "Song for the Centenary of Walter Savage Landor." It quoted as a motto for this poem the opening lines of Landor's poem "To Robert Browning." It had been reviewed in the *Athenaeum* of January 15th.

81 : 4–1. Performance, that is, of *Colombe's Birthday,* which Horne reported had been given at the Haymarket in 1844, under the title of *The Duchess of Cleves. Colombe's Birthday* was first produced—by Miss Faucit—in 1852. See *Robert Browning Personalia,* by Edmund Gosse, 1890, p. 73.

81 : 4–2. Helen Faucit—Lady Theodore Martin.

81 : 5–1. *Tait's Magazine.*

81 : 5–2. The "pencil notes" express objection to an image as inappropriate or "a bad simile," an expression as "not even *poetically* grammatical," a passage as "obscure," etc.: or praise a passage as "A curious idealization of self-worship; very fine, though" or "beautiful." Once he writes, "The obscurity of this is the greater fault as the meaning if I can guess it right is really poetical." Again, "This only says 'You shall see what you shall see' and is more prose than poetry"; "not imagination but *I*magination. The absence of that capital letter obscures the meaning"; "This writer seems to use *so* according to the colloquial vulgarism, in the sense of *therefore* or *accordingly*—from which occasionally comes great obscurity and ambiguity—as here."

To this last-quoted remark, Browning wrote in the copy a lengthy rejoinder, beginning "The *recurrence* of *so* thus employed is as vulgar as you please: but the usage itself . . . is perfectly authorized."

Mill used a cross in the margin to designate "obscurity." He marks one passage, "Inconsistent with what precedes."

To the comment "He is always talking of being *prepared*—what for?" Browning wrote the reply, "Why, 'that's tellings,' as schoolboys say."

On "Richmond," etc. at the end, Mill's comment was, "This transition from speaking to Pauline to writing a letter to the public with *place* and *date,* is quite terrible." Browning's comment is, "Kean was acting there: I saw him in Richard III that night, and conceived the childish scheme already mentioned. There is an illusion to Kean, p. 47. I don't know whether I had not made up my mind to *act,* as well as to make verses, music, and God knows what.—que de châteaux en Espagne!"

On the back fly-leaf, Mill wrote his larger comment:—"With considerable poetic power, this writer seems to me possessed with a more intense and morbid self-consciousness than I ever knew in any sane human being—I should think it a sincere confession though of a most unloveable state, if the 'Pauline' were not evidently a mere phantom. All about her is a pile of inconsistency—he neither loves her nor fancies he loves her, yet insists upon *talking* love to her—if she *existed* and loved him, he treats her most ungenerously and unfeelingly. All his aspirings and sparrings and regrets point to other things, never to her—then he *pays her off* towards the end by a piece of flummery, amounting to the modest request that she will love him and live with him and give herself up to him *without* his *loving her, moyennant quoi* he will think her and call her everything that is handsome and he promises her that she shall find it mighty pleasant. Then he leaves off by saying he knows he shall have changed his mind by tomorrow, and despise these intents which seem so fair! but that having been thus visited once no doubt he will again—and is therefore 'in perfect joy' bad luck to him! as the Irish say.

"A cento of most beautiful passages might be made from this poem—and the psychological history of himself is powerful and truthful, *truth-like* certainly all but the last stage. *That* he evidently has not yet got into. The self-seeking and self-worshipping state is well described—beyond that I should think the writer had made, as yet, only the next step; viz. into despising his own state. I even question whether part even of that self-disdain is not assumed. He is evidently *dissatisfied,* and feels part of the badness of his state, but he does not write as if it were purged out of him—if he once could muster a hearty hatred of his selfishness it would go—as it is he feels only the *lack* of *good,* not the positive *evil.* He feels not remorse, but only disappointment. A mind in that state can only be regenerated by some new passion, and I know not what to wish for him but that he may meet with a *real* Pauline.

"Meanwhile he should not attempt to show how a person may be *recovered* from this morbid state—for *he* is hardly convalescent, and 'what should we speak of but that which we know?' "

On p. 4 (blank) Browning wrote: "The following Poem was written in pursuance of a foolish plan which occupied me mightily for a time, and which had for its object the enabling me to assume and realize I know not how many different characters;—meanwhile the world was never to guess that 'Brown, Smith, Jones, and Robinson' (as the spelling books have it) the respective authors of this poem, the other novel, such an opera, such a speech &c. &c. were no other than one and the same individual. The present abortion was the first work of the *Poet* of the batch, who would have been more legitimately *myself* than most of the others; but I surrounded him with all manner of (to my then notion) poetical accessories, and had planned quite a delightful life for him.

"Only this crab remains of the shapely Tree of Life in this Fools Paradise of mine.

"R B"

On the fly-leaf is the inscription "R Browning October 30th 1833"; and on the title-page, "To my true friend, John Forster." Browning evidently got it back soon after Mill had dealt with it.

Browning has made many amendments in the text apparently in consequence of Mill's remarks.

This copy of *Pauline* was for some time missing from the Forster collection in the South Kensington Museum. See 81 : 6–2.

81 : 6–1. See 41 : 2–4 and 81 : 9–1. Browning's poem is "In a Gondola."

81 : 6–2. See 81 : 5–2.

81 : 6–3. The "Proofs" were of the first volume of the *Browning Society's Papers,* prepared by Professor Furnivall, and published in 1881. It contained Browning's essay on Shelley, a Chronological List of Browning's Works, and a list of Criticisms on Browning's Works.

81 : 6–4. The "remarks" were doubtless those of Carlyle, in a letter to Browning of March 8, 1853:—

"I liked the Essay extremely well indeed; a solid, well-wrought, massive, manful bit of discourse; and interesting to me, over and above, as the first of very many. You do not know how cheering to me the authentic sound of a *human* voice is! I get so little except ape-voices; the whole Universe filled with one wide tempestuous Cackle, which has neither depth nor sense, nor any kind of truth or nobleness in it: O Heaven, one feels as if it were too bad; as if the temptation were, to burst into tears, and sit down and weep till one died! I cannot now, in late years, laugh at such a phenomenon; oftenest it makes me inexpressibly sad,—as is very natural, if one look at the *whence* and the inevitable *whitherward;*—wherefore, in general, I rather try to get out of it altogether, quite away from the beggarly sound of it; and to sit solitary, in company rather with the dumb Chaos than with the talking one. This Essay of yours, and another little word by Emerson are the only new things I have read with real pleasure for a great while past. I agree with what you say of Shelley's moralities and spiritual position; I honour and respect the weighty estimate you have formed of the Poetic Art; and I admire very much the grave expressiveness of style (a *little* too elaborate here and there), and the dignified tone, in which you manage to deliver yourself on all that.

"The Letters themselves are very innocent and clear; and deserve printing, with such a name attached to them; but it is not they that I care for on the present occasion. In fact I am not sure but you would excommunicate me,—at least lay me under the 'lesser sentence,' for a time,—if I told you all I thought of Shelley! Poor soul, he has always seemed to me an extremely weak creature, and lamentable much more than admirable. Weak in genius, weak in character (for these two always go together); a poor, thin, spasmodic, hectic, shrill and pallid being;—one of those unfortunates, of whom I often speak, to whom 'the talent of *silence*,' first of all, has been denied. The speech of such is never good for much. Poor Shelley, there is something void, and Hades-like in the whole inner world of him; his universe is all vacant azure, hung with a few frosty mournful if beautiful stars; the very voice of him (his style, &c.), shrill, shrieky, to my ear has too much of the *ghost!* In a word, it is not with Shelley, but with Shelley's Commentator, that I take up my quarters at all: and to this latter I will say with emphasis, Give us some more of your *writing,* my friend; we decidedly need a man or two like you, if we could get them! Seriously, dear Browning, you must at last gird up your loins again; and give us a right stroke of work:—I do not wish to hurry you; far the contrary: but I remind you what is expected; and say with what joy I, for one, will see it arrive.—Nor do I restrict you to Prose, in spite of all I have said and still say: Prose or Poetry, either of them you can master; and we will wait for you with welcome in whatever form your own *Daimon* bids. Only see that *he* does bid it; and then go with your best speed;—and on the whole forgive, at any rate, these importunities, which I feel to partake much of the nature of impertinence, if you did not kindly interpret them."

81 : 6–5. Browning evidently supplied these names. Those of "Mellerio, the Paris Jeweller" and of "St. Aubyn in Normandy" are used by Furnivall in the *Browning Society's Papers,* I, 66, ftn. 5, with an explanation of the circumstances under which the names in the poem came to be disguised, for fear of a possible action for libel.

81 : 7–1. *The Monthly Repository,* 1835, pp. 707–708. The poem was reprinted (with considerable variations) in *Bells and Pomegranates,* No. I, 1841, p. 12, where it forms one of Pippa's songs in *Pippa Passes.*

81 : 7–2. "Oh Love, Love, thou that from the eyes diffusest." Printed in *Euripides,* by J. P. Mahaffey. (*Macmillan's Classical Writers*) London, 1879, p. 116.

81 : 9–1. Cf. 41 : 2–4. The picture—"The Serenade"—is not mentioned in O'Driscoll's *Memoir of Daniel Maclise, R.A.,* 1871, and cannot have been in the Academy. Hall edited *The Art Journal.* See 81 : 6–1.

81 : 9–2. This was a picture of a little girl with yellow hair and pale blue eyes, entitled with a verse by Browning:

> "Yellow and pale as ripened corn
>   Which Autumn's kiss frees,—grain from sheath,—
>   Such was her hair, while her eyes beneath
> Showed, Spring's faint violets freshly born."

See Ernest Rhys: *Frederic Lord Leighton,* London, 1898, p. 36.

81 : 10–1. "Shirley"—the pseudonym of John Skelton, C. B., Vice-President of the Scottish Local Government Board.

81 : 12–1. Mr. Orme had undertaken, on behalf of a young R. A. student, who was imagining a picture to illustrate Mrs. Browning's Sonnet, "Perplexed Music," to explain how, in that poem, "Experience, like a pale musician, holds a dulcimer of patience in his hand." Mr. Orme and his friend found better information than that furnished by Browning in this letter; and upon receiving a second letter from Mr. Orme, Browning wrote admitting his mistake. See 81 : 14.

81 : 15–1. "Introductory Address to the Browning Society. By the Rev. J. Kirkman, M.A., Queen's Coll., Cambridge." *Browning Society's Papers,* Part II (1881–84), pp. 171–190. The address was delivered on Friday, October 28, 1881, at University College, London.

81 : 16–1. Browning published nothing until *Jocoseria,* 1883.

81 : 16–2. Browning afterwards amply redeemed this promise. See 89 : 2.

81 : 17–1. In *Sordello,* III, ll. 950–966.

81 : 17–2. "Euphrasia"—Miss Euphrasia Fanny Haworth. See 38 : 1–2.

81 : 17–3. Probably the *Eclectic Review* is here referred to. In the 4th Series of that Magazine, xxvi, 203–214, appeared a sympathetic and excellent review of the *Poems* of 1849 and of *Sordello.*

81 : 17–4. On January 27th, 1882, Miss Lewis delivered a paper before the Browning Society. She was preparing it for publication in *Macmillan's Magazine.* See *The Browning Society's Papers,* Part III, p. 11*.

81 : 18–1. The allusion in this letter is to "Hervé Riel."

82 : 3–1. *Two Poems /By/ Elizabeth Barrett and Robert Browning./ London:/ Chapman & Hall, 193, Picadilly./* 1854.—Octavo, pp. 15—Containing "A Plea for the Ragged Schools of London," by Mrs. Browning; and "The Twins," by Robert Browning. The pamphlet was excessively rare until, in 1887, a parcel of copies unsold at the Bazaar turned up in a London auction room. It is still something of a prize for the Browning collector.

82 : 4–1. "In a Gondola," line 88: . . . "that prim saint by Haste-thee-Luke!"

82 : 5–1. The proposed *Life* of Mrs. Browning.

82 : 5–2. *Letters of Elizabeth Barrett Browning addressed to Richard Hengist Horne, with Comments on Contemporaries. London: Richard Bentley & Son, 1877.* Crown 8vo, 2 vols.

82 : 6–1. "Assistance" in preparing the Monograph upon Elizabeth Barrett Browning, by J. H. Ingram, eventually published by Messrs. W. H. Allen and Co. in 1888.

82 : 7–1. Mrs. Richmond Ritchie, for her article on Mrs. Browning in *The Dictionary of National Biography.* See 86 : 20.

82 : 8–1. The Preface was one to Shakespeare's works, which the publisher George Bell asked Dr. Furnivall to offer Browning £ 100 to write.

82 : 9–1. . . . "While this machine is to him. *Hamlet.*" Hamlet, Act II, scene 2 (letter).

83 : 1–1. The Browning Society's *Papers* and *Illustrations.*

83 : 1–2. A print of Guercino's "Angel and Child," reproduced from the picture at Fano, as an illustration to Browning's "Guardian Angel." This print was issued to the members of the Browning Society in January, 1883.

83 : 1–3. As published *Jocoseria* contained ten pieces only, counting the prologue ("Wanting is—What?") "There is no evidence to show whether Browning miscounted, or whether one poem was withdrawn, or whether, as is possible, the sonnets at the end of Jochanan Hakkodosh were reckoned separately."—Sir F. G. Kenyon, Introduction to Vol. X of the Centenary Edition of the Works, p. v. The last surmise is supported by the fact that Browning apparently added to the MS. of "Jochanan Hakkadosh," after his memorandum *"L.D.I.E.* Dec. 22, '88," the "Note" and the three sonnets appended to the "Note," with the direction to the printer "Print these sonnets in a smaller type, after the *Note.*" The "Note" and the sonnets look in the MS. like a separate unit.

83 : 2–1. The Rev. J. D. Williams sent Browning many translations of his poems into Latin or Greek. Browning preserved them all. Cf. 83 : 7.

83 : 2–2. *Jocoseria.* The name was borrowed from Melander's *Jocoseria.*

83 : 3–1. In 1879, the degree of D.C.L. had been conferred on Browning by Cambridge University.

83 : 4–1. Charles D. Browning was a cousin of the poet.

83 : 4–2. "How They Brought the Good News from Ghent to Aix." It was originally written in pencil on the verso of the fly-leaf and the verso of the title-page of Browning's copy of Bartoli's *Simboli* now in the Browning Collection at Balliol. It may be discerned in faint pencil-indentations, though the writing was erased.

83 : 5–1. Dr. Richard Garnett, of the British Museum. He intended to put the "No. 9" with the rest of the set (see 83 : 5–2) in the Museum.

83 : 5–2. *Complete Works of Robert Browning.* A reprint from the latest English edition. 8vo, Chicago, 1872–74. Nos. 1–20 of the *Official Guide of the Chicago and Alton R.R. and Monthly Reprint and Advertiser.* Edited by Mr. James Charlton, the

Manager of the Railroad. The copy here mentioned is in the British Museum. Part II is missing (has never been there). Part IX is marked "to Furnivall. Sunday Apr. 8, '83. next day to B.M." On the cover of Part I Browning has written the following (from Aristophanes' *Birds*, ll. 1277–1279):—

ὦ κλεινοτάτην αἰθέριον οἰκίσας πόλιν,
οὐκ οἶσθ' ὅσην τιμὴν παρ' ἀνθρώποις φέρει,
ὅσους τ' ἐραστὰς τῆσδε τῆς χώρας ἔχεις.

("O thou who hast established a most noble city in the air, thou knowest not what glory it hath among men and how many lovers of this country thou hast.") The analogy is between Chicago and Cloud-Cuckoo-Town!

83 : 6–1. Miss Teena Rochfort Smith. Cf. 83 : 12–2.

83 : 7–1. Prologue to *Jocoseria*, l. 4:—"Where is the blot?" See 83 : 2–1. The Latin phrases are translations of phrases in "Never the Time and the Place."

83 : 8–1. The "Box" contained all the papers of Thomas Lovell Beddoes (1803–49) and correspondence referring to him, as it had been bequeathed to Browning by Kelsall, Beddoes' executor.

In December, 1867, Browning and Thomas Forbes Kelsall met at Balliol, where Kelsall had been invited to talk about Beddoes. Soon after, Browning declined to write a preface to a reprint of Beddoes. But then, expecting possibly to be appointed Professor of Poetry at the University, he said that, if he were chosen, his first lecture would be on "The Author of Death's Jest Book, a Forgotten Oxford Poet." Kelsall sent the Beddoes MSS. to Browning in the spring of 1868; Browning examined them, not very carefully, and sent them back on July 24th, 1868. Kelsall died in October, 1872, and willed the MSS. to Browning. Mrs. Kelsall sent them to 19 Warwick Crescent. On July 15, 1883, Browning took the box to Gosse's house and gave Gosse the key, telling him to examine the contents. A few hours afterwards, he joined Gosse in examining them. See the *Poetical Works of Beddoes,* edited by Gosse, London, 1890, 2 vols., and the *Letters,* edited by Gosse, London and New York, 1894. The first writing based on these materials was Gosse's article on Beddoes in *The Dictionary of National Biography,* 1890. Cf. 80 : 5–1; 86 : 12.

83 : 9–1. Information regarding Beddoes. Mrs. Bryan Waller Procter ("Barry Cornwall") was then the latest survivor of Beddoes' literary friends. She proved to be, in spite of her disclaimer, a mine of important information.

83 : 10–1. In *Dante Gabriel Rossetti His Family-Letters,* 1895, Vol. I, p. 115, the date 1850 is given by W. M. Rossetti as that of his brother's letter. He states that Browning was in *Venice* when Dante Gabriel Rossetti wrote to him.

83 : 10–2. The Brownings visited London in June-October, 1852; they resided at 58, Welbeck Street.

83 : 10–3. This "portrait" visit took place in 1855, when the Brownings were again in London, residing at 13, Dorset Street, Baker Street.

83 : 10–4. This reading of *Maud* took place at 13, Dorset Street, on September 27th, 1855. [*Letters of Elizabeth Barrett Browning,* 1897, Vol. II, p. 213.] The Sketch made by Rossetti upon this occasion (he repeated it several times) was preserved at the Palazzo Rezzonico, along with the copy of *Maud* (first edition) from which Tennyson read. Tennyson gave it to Browning, who made a note of the date, etc., inside the cover of the book.

83 : 12–1. Amusingly enough, the error escaped the notice of the postal authorities, who did not surcharge the letter.

83 : 12–2. The reference is to the death of Miss Teena (Mary Lilian) Rochfort Smith, who died at Goole on September 4th, 1883, from the effects of burns received six days earlier, her dress having caught fire while she was extinguishing the fire in a lighted work-basket. A *Memoir* of her (16 pp., with several portraits—including one of Robert Browning) was written, and printed privately, by Dr. Furnivall.

83 : 13–1. Browning and his sister Sarianna.

83 : 13–2. Thomas Hookham, Jr.

83 : 13–3. In 1885 Browning was offered the Presidentship of the Shelley Society, which he declined, on the ground that he could not possibly approve of Shelley's conduct towards Harriet—his judgment, a somewhat severe one, being chiefly influenced by the perusal of the letters referred to above. See 70 : 1; 83 : 14; 85 : 11. See also 81 : 2–1.

The following letters from Swinburne to Rossetti, in Mr. Wise's collection, clarify Browning's attitude toward Shelley.

May 22nd [1869]

Dear Rossetti,

I suppose you have seen if not read Forster's Life of Landor. There is in the second volume a note about Shelley and his first wife in which F. says he has the whole story before him but will not publish it, of which I think you ought to take notice before the new edition is out. I only write because it seems to me possible that you have not noticed the passage. I know you will agree with me that the one thing *now* to be done is to unearth and expose every possible detail of the business for Shelley's own sake and ours.

Ever yours affy

Tho' just now in (more th . .) haste

A. C. Swinburne

P.S. At all events don't if *you* can help it leave us in suspense about the 'Sun-treader' as Browning calls him. *Do* root things up—for I am sure the closer we get to facts the greater and purer he will come out.

If you read this it *is* a wonder no thanks to the pen or me a God (*d n f*)

June 24th [1869]

Dear Rossetti,

I like your sonnet very much, and should (also) like much to see it in the Fortnightly, whither I have just sent a sonnet myself, (on Mazzini's election as a citizen of the Canton of Bern) I am not clear about the grammar of 'touched.' I should ask Gabriel and take his verdict, if it were a poem of mine.

Browning spent an hour here with me yesterday, and of course I tackled him about Forster's reference to Shelley. I am sorry to say he, having seen the papers referred to, and conversed with a man who knew Shelley (at the time) confidentially, says this:

1o) That Shelley *did* desert Harriet and their child, and the child with which she was then pregnant, without fair warning or fair provision, 'left them 14 shillings altogether,' B. says. He has seen Harriet's letter to Shelley on his sudden disappearance, which by his account must be most piteous and touching.

2d) That Shelley during that period of his life was not responsible for his actions; was in fact positively insane, through excess of laudanum, taken to allay the pains of his illness.

3d) That Lord Eldon distinctly said at the trial that Shelley's atheism had nothing to do with his decision; '*he* had left the children to starve, and the grandfather had taken them up, and had a right to keep them.'

Now of course Browning loves Shelley even as much as you and I do (he said so in concluding) but these, he is certain, are the facts of the case. I asked him to communicate them to you directly, but in case he does not I write this. I have also written to Kirkup, who *may* remember (*not* spiritually) what was Landor's ultimate view of the matter, which I am very desirous to be assured of.

Yours always

A C Swinburne

83 : 14–1. See 85 : 8–1.

83 : 14–2. See 70 : 1; 83 : 13–3; 85 : 11.

83 : 15–1. Thomas Powell: *The Living Authors of England.* New York, 1849. "Robert Browning," pp. 71–85. *Pictures of the Authors of Britain.* London, 1851. "Robert Browning," pp. 61–75. Cf. 48 : 1; 86 : 4–2.

83 : 16–1. In *Aristophanes' Apology,* line 231: "A visitor/Ominous, apparitional, who went/ Strange as he came, but shall not pass away."

83 : 16–2. This sonnet was printed in *The Pall Mall Gazette,* Dec. 8, 1883.

84 : 2–1. The Browning Society was organized in 1881. The first Secretary was Miss Emily Hickey, the poetess; she resigned after two years on account of ill health; the second was Mr. James Dykes Campbell, the author of an admirable biography of Coleridge; the third, Mr. Walter B. Slater; the fourth (and last) Mr. Thomas J. Wise.

84 : 2–2. Up to this time, "proofs" of the Society's *Papers* had been sent to Browning.

84 : 5–1. The Autobiography of Giovanni Dupré (Tuscan sculptor), translated by Mme. Peruzzi di Medici (née Edith Story).

84 : 5–2. Mrs. Clara S. J. Bloomfield-Moore, of Philadelphia. The Brownings were her guests at the Villa Berry, St. Moritz. She accompanied Browning to Oxford in 1882, when the degree of D.C.L. was conferred on him. See her "Robert Browning," in *Lippincott's Magazine,* May, 1890. Cf. 87 : 20–1; 88 : 1–2.

84 : 6–1. *Ferishtah's Fancies,* published in the autumn of 1884.

84 : 7–1. *Ferishtah's Fancies.*

84 : 8–1. Sir Frederic (afterwards Lord) Leighton. Sir Frederic gave copies of his "Alcestis" to Members of the Browning Society. See *Balaustion's Adventure,* ll. 2672–2697, for a description of this picture.

84 : 9–1. Hamilton Wild, of Boston, had painted Pen on horseback, and presented the portrait to Mrs. Browning.—*Letters of Elizabeth Barrett Browning,* II, 344. He was staying with the Storys at the time (1859) in Siena.

84 : 9–2. "John Field, of Philadelphia, of Newport, of Washington, of London, of Paris, of twenty places beside, John Field, the personally valued friend of our friends and, again, of numbers of *their* friends," etc.—*William Wetmore Story and his Friends,* by Henry James, 1903, II, 176 ff. Field had been in Siena with the Storys and the Brownings (*ibid.,* p. 176). In Browning's later address-book appears "John W. Field, 2009 I Street, Washington." See 85 : 6.

85 : 3–1. From *The Divine Order and other Sermons and Addresses by the late Thomas Jones of Swansea,* edited by Brynmor Jones, with an Introduction by Robert Browning, London, 1884, we learn that "the Welsh Poet-Preacher" was Independent minister at Bedford Chapel, on Charrington Street, N.W., from 1861 to 1869, and that Browning was a frequent hearer of his preaching.

85 : 4–1. In August, 1885, Professor Charles Eliot Norton was preparing a volume of letters to and from Carlyle, in correspondence with Mill, Sterling, and Browning. Some letters could not be found at the moment, and Professor Norton abandoned the project, returning such letters as he had.

85 : 5–1. The letter was from the eminent Shakespearean scholar, Dr. Horace Howard Furness, of Philadelphia, asking Mr. Gosse to tell Browning "how deeply, how fervently, I bless him for writing 'Prospice.' "

85 : 5–2. Lawrence Barrett had been playing *A Blot in the 'Scutcheon,* with marked success, in several American cities. See 85 : 1.

85 : 6–1. See 84 : 9–2.

85 : 8–1. Mrs. Katherine Bronson, an American friend of Robert Browning, placed at his disposal a suite of rooms in the Palazzo Guistiniani-Recanati at Venice in 1882, and this was his Venetian home until 1885. In that year Browning attempted to purchase the famous Palazzo Manzoni as a gift to his son, but there was a long litigation (referred to in Letters 85 : 9; 86 : 9, and 86 : 12) which ended in Browning's paying his own costs and withdrawing from the suit on finding that the foundations of the house were shaky. In 1888 Robert Barrett Browning bought the Palazzo Rezzonico.

85 : 9–1. *I.e.,* 19, Warwick Crescent.

85 : 9–2. See 85 : 8–1. The walls—hidden by carpets—were cracked, and the foundations shaky.

85 : 9–3. Mr. Percy Furnivall, champion amateur cyclist.

85 : 11–1. The Presidentship of the Shelley Society. See 70 : 1; 83 : 13–3; 83 : 14.

85 : 13–1. Browning was interested in a project for erecting a statue to Wordsworth, some of whose admirers were proposing that a copy should be made of the ineffective monument at Westminster by Frederick Thrupp (1827–95), who offered his model for that purpose. A counter-proposal was that Woolner should be commissioned to carry out the fine sketch of which Browning here speaks. This was not done.

86 : 1–1. The Editor of a Boston (U.S.A.) Magazine had offered Browning the sum of £400 for a short poem.

86 : 2–1. The reference is to *Aristophanes' Apology,* line 53.

86 : 3–1. *I.e.,* in 1834, with Mr. Benkhausen, the Russian Consul-General.

86 : 4–1. *The Battle of Marathon,* Mrs. Browning's first book, of which fifty copies were privately printed by her father in 1820. Of these only four are known to have survived. Cf. 88 : 17–1.

86 : 4–2. The Pisa *Adonais,* Mr. Browning told Mr. Wise one day, he lent to Thomas Powell—who promptly sold it!

86 : 4–3. See *Robert Browning Personalia,* by Edmund Gosse; 1890, pp. 23–24.

86 : 5–1. The First Edition of *Pauline,* two copies of which Browning had then just unearthed. See the Introduction.

86 : 5–2. Mr. James Dykes Campbell. In June, 1904, some time after Mr. Campbell's death, this copy of *Pauline* was sold by auction in Messrs. Sotheby's rooms, and realized £325.

86 : 6–1. The first Sculling Fours race in narrow boats in England, held by the Maurice (*i.e.,* Working Men's College) Rowing Club. Dr. Furnivall was No. 3 in the winning boat, and wore a prize-medal upon his watch-chain in commemoration of the event.

86 : 6–2. A picture by Robert Barrett Browning, representing Joan of Arc standing naked by a pool of water.

86 : 7–1. It was proposed to produce a type facsimile reprint of the First Edition of *Pauline* (in an edition limited to four hundred copies) for the Members of the Browning Society. This was done in 1886; Mr. Wise did the work. See 86 : 13 and 86 : 18.

86 : 8–1. Oliver Wendell Holmes.

86 : 9–1. See Appendix, "Browning and Lady Ashburton."

86 : 9–2. See 85 : 8–1.

86 : 11–1. *Pippa Passes,* IV, ll. 338–341:—

> "Then, owls and bats,
> "Cowls and twats,
> "Monks and nuns, in a cloister's moods,
> "Adjourn to the oak-stump pantry!"

86 : 12–1. Beddoes' very rare volume, *The Improvisatore* (12mo, 1821, pp. viii + 12). It was practically a lost book. Six copies are now known. The poems contained in the book have never been reprinted.

86 : 12–2. See 83 : 8–1. Mr. Dykes Campbell wrote "The Beddoes manuscripts thus lent by Browning were afterwards handed to Mr. Edmund Gosse."

86 : 13–1. See 86 : 7–1; 81 : 5–2.

86 : 13–2. See 81 : 5–2.

86 : 18–1. Of the Browning Society's reprint of *Pauline.* See 86 : 7–1.

86 : 18–2. *Pauline,* line 567: "that king/ Treading the purple calmly to his death," etc.

86 : 18–3. *Pauline,* lines 573 ff.:—

> . . . "the boy
> "With his white breast and brow and clustering curls
> "Streaked with his mother's blood, but striving hard
> "To tell his story ere his reason goes."

86 : 18–4. At the end of the Introduction to Pauline (a quotation in Latin), Browning wrote "London: *January* 1833. *V. A. XX.*" "The imaginary subject's" age was Browning's own.

86 : 19–1. A volume containing the autographs—all forged—of Browning, Wordsworth, and Leigh Hunt. Cf. 83 : 15–1; 86 : 4–2.

86 : 20–1. See 82 : 7–1.

86 : 22–1. The representation of *Strafford*, which was revived by the Browning Society at the Strand Theatre on the 21st of December, 1886.

87 : 1–1. This letter was written in reply to a communication (including three queries regarding "The Statue and the Bust") which had been sent to Mr. Wise by a member of the Browning Society. Since the queries were of sufficient general interest to warrant printing a reply to them in the Society's *Papers*, Mr. Wise forwarded the communication (which was subscribed by the nom-de-plume *Ball-goer*) to Browning.

87 : 1–2. The Palace in the *Via Larga*, now *Via Cavour*.

87 : 1–3. *I.e.*, in the Piazza dell'Annunziata.

87 : 3–1. The Lecture, very considerably augmented, was published in due course, with the following title: *Robert Browning: Chief Poet of the Age. An Essay Addressed Primarily to Beginners in the Study of Browning's Poems. By William G. Kingsland. London: J. W. Jarvis & Son, 28, King William Street, Strand.* 1887. A new Edition, revised and expanded, appeared in 1890. The front cover of the booklet of 1887 carried in large lettering the main title, *Robert Browning: Chief Poet of the Age*. This circumstance explains why, when Mr. Kingsland suggested sending a large paper copy to Browning, he replied jestingly by referring as he did to the outside of the book in 87 : 6.

87 : 4–1. This letter was addressed by Mr. Browning to a correspondent of the *Birmingham Owl*, who had forwarded to him a harsh and unfair criticism extracted from the pages of the *Daily Mail*, February 3, 1887, with the leading article—"Is it Poetry?" This letter has already appeared in *The Pall Mall Gazette*, "Mr. Browning on His Critics," February 19, 1887, xlv, 13; also in *The Publisher's Circular*, No. 1596, January 30, 1897, p. 134.

87 : 5–1. Christopher Smart's *Song to David*. It was first published in 1763; reprinted, in 1819, by the Rev. R. Harvey. Browning mentions no other work of Smart's in his "Parleying With Christopher Smart." The edition to which Browning here refers as the one he bought was probably that of John Rodwell and B. J. Holsworth, *A Song to David/ By the late Christopher Smart, M.A., . . . Translator of Horace . . .*; London, 1827. See William Clyde DeVane: *Browning's Parleyings/ The Autobiography of a Mind*, 1927, pp. 92–133, for a full consideration of the tremendous influence of this poem of Smart's on Browning's ideas of the poetic and on his work, from *Pauline* to the "Parleying With Christopher Smart." Cf. 87 : 9–1.

87 : 6–1. See 87 : 3–1.

87 : 7–1. In the *Monthly Repository*, June, 1833, p. 421: reprinted in the *Browning Society Papers*, IX, p. 203*:—"All scenes have their appropriate books. . . . Books should have a harmony of spirit with the locality, not an identity of subject. . . . Shelley and Tennyson are the best books for the place. They sort well with the richness, richness to every sense; with the warm mists, and the rustling of the woods, and the ceaseless melody of sound. They are natives of this soil; literally so; and if planted would grow as surely as a crowbar in Kentucky sprouts ten-penny nails. *Probatum est.* Last autumn L—— dropped a poem of Shelley's down there in the wood, amongst the thick, damp, rotting leaves, and this spring some one found a delicate, exotic-looking plant, growing wild on the very spot, with *Pauline* hanging from its slender stalk.

Unripe fruit it may be, but of pleasant flavour and promise, and a mellower produce, it may be hoped, will follow. It would be good speculation to plant a volume of Coleridge. The singing of the nightingales would promote its growth."

87 : 8–1. See Appendix, "Browning and Lady Ashburton."

87 : 9–1. The reference is to certain fresh facts regarding the life of Christopher Smart, discovered by Edmund Gosse in Pembroke College, Cambridge. Cf. 87 : 5–1.

87 : 9–2. "Mr. Harvey" was the Rev. R. Harvey, who edited Smart's *Song to David* in 1819.

87 : 10–1. Miss Fannie Coddington, who married Robert Barrett Browning on October 4th, 1887.

87 : 11–1. A fisherman agreed to take the pledge if the lady, who pressed him to do it, would strip like Godiva and swim to him.

87 : 12–1. Henry Brown, a poor fellow who wrote on Shakespeare's *Sonnets*. He had been a working-man, and a newsvendor. He wrote to, and probably saw, Browning, who asked Dr. Furnivall to take up his case. Applications for a money grant were made to the Government, to the Trustees of the Royal Literary Fund, etc., but without success.

87 : 14–1. The wedding took place at the home of Mr. and Mrs. Henry Schlesinger, 5, Kensington Park Gardens, W.

87 : 15–1. Marie Coddington, sister of Fannie.

87 : 18–1. The country place of Mr. and Mrs. Henry Schlesinger was in Hawkwell Place, Pembury, Tunbridge Wells.

87 : 18–2. Mrs. Katherine De Kay Bronson, Edith's mother, one of Browning's most intimate friends throughout his later years. Some of her reminiscences of Browning's visits to her in Asolo and in Venice were published in the *Century Magazine,* April, 1900, and February, 1902.

87 : 20–1. Mrs. Clara S. J. Bloomfield-Moore. Cf. 84 : 5–2.

87 : 20–2. Mrs. Henry Schlesinger.

87 : 20–3. The *Times* of Friday, November 24, 1887 (p. 9 f) carried the following notice: "The *Jewish Chronicle* records the death of Emma Lazarus, a Jewish poetess, of New York, who recently expired in that city, at the age of thirty-seven, after a long and painful illness. Her poems had earned the praise of Mr. Browning and other competent judges. Miss Lazarus made a visit to Europe for the sole purpose of calling attention to the unhappy condition of the Jews in Russia and Roumania."

87 : 21–1. Possibly the memoir in *The Poetical Works of Elizabeth Barrett Browning* from 1826 to 1844, edited with a memoir by J. H. Ingram. London, 1887.

87 : 21–2. In 1878, Sir Coutts Lindsay had started the Grosvenor Gallery. In 1887, his assistants, Mr. Hallé and Mr. Carr, took issue with him on certain points, and a separation ensued, with some supporters for both sides; and Hallé and Carr opened the New Gallery. They published the correspondence in the dispute, and drew from Sir Coutts Lindsay a rejoinder in the *Times* of Saturday, January 28, 1888 (p. 12 c), denying what they set forth as the facts regarding the finances of the Grosvenor. Cf. 88 : 2–2 and 88 : 11.

87 : 22–1. For a window in St. Margaret's, Westminster. The lines are published as "Jubilee Memorial Lines" in the Riverside Edition of Browning's *Works,* VI, 443:—

> Fifty years' flight! wherein should he rejoice
> Who hailed their birth, who as they die decays?
> This—England echoes his attesting voice;
> Wondrous and well—thanks, Ancient Thou of days.
> 1887.

87 : 23–1. Fannie Barrett Browning, her sister Miss Marie Coddington, and her husband, Robert Barrett Browning.

88 : 1–1. This bust occupied a place of honor in Browning's study at 29 De Vere

Gardens, just at his right and slightly behind him as he sat at his desk. It is a very striking likeness of the poet in his later, more Gallic, aspect. Cf. 88 : 2.

88 : 1–2. John Ernst Worrell Keeley, a Philadelphian, in 1873 had announced his discovery of a new physical force, and in 1874 exhibited the Keeley Motor, as a machine operated by this force. The Keeley Motor Company was organized, and the money invested was soon exhausted. In 1880 Mrs. Bloomfield-Moore came to the rescue, and she financed Keeley's operations for many years. In 1895, after an investigation, she withdrew her assistance. The "force" proved to be compressed air.

88 : 2–1. See 88 : 1–1. A replica of this bust is now in the Browning Collection in Walworth. Mr. Wise has the original in his library. Both the original and the replica were made by Pen Browning.

88 : 2–2. The *Times* for Friday, March 23, 1888 (p. 4 c) gives an account of this dinner:—

"Dinner to Sir Coutts Lindsay.—A complimentary dinner was given on Wednesday evening to Sir Coutts Lindsay, at the Hôtel Metropole, Northumberland-avenue. The entertainment, . . . was promoted by a committee of artists, in which a number of noblemen and gentlemen joined . . . Sir Coutts Lindsay spoke of the differences with Messrs. Hallé and Carr." . . . See 87 : 21–2.

88 : 4–1. Pen's old master in Antwerp. See 74 : 1–2.

88 : 5–1. Mr. Wise's then recently acquired copy of the First Edition of *Pauline*, in which Browning wrote the inscription quoted in the Introduction.

Browning told Mr. Wise, "Not a single copy of *Pauline* was sold—not a single copy!" His aunt gave him thirty pounds to pay for the production of the edition; twenty-three went on paper and printing, seven on advertising.

88 : 6–1. *Browning Society's Papers*, Part X, pp. 207–220 and 218*–223*, on "Browning's Jews and Shakespeare's Jews," by Professor Barnett.

88 : 6–2. By Dr. Berdoe, p. 222*. Dr. Berdoe continued "that he had always considered that Browning had simply one lay-figure most skilfully dressed for all his characters, viz., Robert Browning himself."

88 : 6–3. An action for libel brought by the actor, Leonard Outram, against Dr. Furnivall.

88 : 8–1. The performance of *A Blot in the 'Scutcheon* at the Olympic Theatre on March 18th, 1888. Browning was present upon the occasion.

88 : 9–1. William Congreve. Cf. 88 : 19–1.

88 : 9–2. The portrait was the charcoal drawing by Field Talfourd, now in the National Portrait Gallery.

88 : 9–3. Elizabeth Brownrigg, who was hanged at Tyburn in 1767, for torturing and then killing an apprentice.

88 : 11–1. The book is not to be identified beyond doubt. It may have been a copy of the illustrated *Selections* published in a peculiar form in 1886 or 1887, *Selections from the Poetical Works of Robert Browning: First Series: London: Smith Elder & Co., 15 Waterloo Place: 1886*, with a second title-page, *Selections from the Poetical Works of Robert Browning, With Photographic Illustrations By Payne Jennings. London: Suttaby and Co., Amen Corner, St. Paul's*. The copy in the British Museum has on the second fly-leaf, in Browning's hand, "Robert Browning, Dec. 6. '87."

88 : 15–1. *Adonais*, 4to, 1821.

88 : 16–1. In the copy of Browning's letter to William Archer from which this letter is printed, the late Professor W. Hall Griffin copied William Archer's memoranda of the entries in Macready's *Diary* with Browning's comment. The notes are Browning's, as quoted by William Archer. The remarks in brackets are Professor Griffin's.

88 : 17–1. See 86 : 4–1.

88 : 18–1. *The/Runaway Slave/ at Pilgrims's Point./ By/ Elizabeth Barrett Browning./ London:/ Edward Moxon, Dover Street./ 1849.*—Octavo, 26 pp. One of the most uncommon of the first editions of Mrs. Browning's poems.

88 : 19–1. The Life of Congreve (1888). The maiden name of the playwright's mother was Browning. Cf. 88 : 9–1.

88 : 20–1. See 58 : 1–1.

89 : 1–1. The passage in question is in the "Parleying With Bernard de Mandeville," Sections II and III.

89 : 2–1. Cf. 89 : 1–1. "Effort whereby" occurs in line 29 of the "Parleying With Bernard de Mandeville."

89 : 2–2. "The writer's husband"—Mr. George Barnett Smith, to whom a Civil List pension was ultimately granted. Cf. 81 : 16–2.

89 : 2–3. The Editor of the *Times.*

89 : 2–4. *Cross Lights* was a volume of essays published in 1888. It was anonymous, but was written by Mr. H. B. Simpson, of the Home Office.

89 : 6–1. These lines, and the name Browning gave to the picture, are as follows:—

THE ISLE'S ENCHANTRESS

Wind wafted from the sunset, o'er the swell
Of summer's slumbrous sea, herself asleep,
Comes shoreward, in her iridescent shell
Cradled, the isle's enchantress. You who keep
A drowsy watch beside her,—watch her well!

The lines were printed in the *Pall Mall Gazette,* March 26, 1889.

89 : 6–2. George Barrett, Elizabeth's brother, a barrister on the Oxford circuit.

89 : 6–3. Elizabeth Barrett's youngest brother, Octavius Barrett. Browning was apparently collecting information for the Prefatory Note to an issue of Elizabeth Barrett Browning's Poems. The last such Preface he wrote was published in the issue of her *Poems* by Smith, Elder & Co., London, 1890.

89 : 8–1. *Red Cotton Night-Cap Country.* Cf. 73 : 1–1.

89 : 9–1. A niece of Rudolf Lehmann, the artist, with whom Browning became acquainted in Rome,—and who afterwards, in England, painted Browning twice in oils.

89 : 11–1. In the summer of 1889 appeared *The Life and Letters of Edward Fitz-Gerald,* edited by Aldis Wright, in which occurs the following passage, which, by the inattention of the editor, had been allowed to remain:—

"Mrs. Browning's death is rather a relief to me, I must say. No more Aurora Leighs, thank God! A woman of real genius, I know; but what is the upshot of it all? She and her sex had better mind the kitchen and the children; and perhaps the poor. Except in such things as little novels, they only devote themselves to what men do much better, leaving that which men do worse or not at all."

Browning read the opening words of the passage, and was furious. Rapidly he composed these stanzas, and promptly sent then to the *Athenaeum,* where they appeared above his signature on July 13th, 1889 (No. 3220, p. 64):—

TO EDWARD FITZGERALD

I CHANCED upon a new book yesterday:
I opened it, and where my finger lay
   'Twixt page and uncut page, these words I read
   —Some six or seven at most—and learned thereby
That you, Fitzgerald, whom by ear and eye
   She never knew, "thanked God my wife was dead."
Ay, dead! and were yourself alive, good Fitz,
How to return you thanks would task my wits:

Kicking you seems the common lot of curs—
While more appropriate greeting lends you grace:
Surely to spit there glorifies your face—
Spitting—from lips once sanctified by Hers.

                                        Robert Browning.
July 8, 1889.

Browning experienced a revulsion of feeling against the publication of these stanzas, and sent a telegram to Mr. Mac Coll, asking him to withhold the lines from publication. But, though there really was still time to excise them from the copy for the printer, Mr. Mac Coll so managed by talking to a friend before opening the telegram as to be able to inform Browning that it was too late to keep the stanzas from appearing.

The editor of Fitzgerald's letters soon afterwards wrote the following letter to a common friend of his and Browning's.

                                        Somerleyton Rectory
                                        Lowestoft
                                        22 July 1889

My dear ——

I trace your friendly hand on the envelope which enclosed a cutting from the Saturday Review and thank you for your kindness in sending it to me. It would no doubt have been better, as Epimetheus now says, to omit the unlucky paragraph about Mrs Browning but who could have imagined that it would produce the disgraceful insults which Browning has been guilty of? I have been away from Cambridge since the 10th and as I had no copy of the book with me I was not aware of the exact form of the offending paragraph but I was confident it had been twisted from its true meaning. Craik suggested that I should write a few lines to the Athenaeum and I did write a letter which in deference to his and Morley's suggestion I modified though not in a way with which I was satisfied. However such as it is it contains I hope my last words on the subject.

When I get back to Cambridge in the course of a few days I will look out copies of Euphranor and Oedipus for you.

                                        Ever yours
                                        W. Aldis Wright

89 : 12–1. Miss Caroline FitzGerald—not related in any way to Edward Fitzgerald. She was engaged to, and in the following year married, Mr. Gladstone's supporter, Lord Edmund Fitzmaurice, later Lord Fitzmaurice. This lady was a great friend of Browning's.

89 : 13–1. Professor Furnivall explained this letter thus: "Answer to my cursing Geo. Smith for stopping Prof. Alexander's *Introduction to Browning* coming into England, on acc^t of its printing some Poems. I ordered 200 copies for the Soc^y, but we can't have em. F."

89 : 13–2. The quotation is from "Robin Hood."

89 : 13–3.

"With lasagne so tempting to swallow
"In slippery ropes," . . .

The phrase is in "The Englishman in Italy," lines 97–98.

89 : 14–1. Julian Story. His father, William Wetmore Story, is mentioned in the same sentence, "Story's Work."

89 : 15–1. This letter has been previously printed in *The Academy*, No. 922, for January 4th, 1892, p. 8; also in *Alfred Lord Tennyson, A Memoir*, by his son, 1897, vol. ii, pp. 359–360. Tennyson's reply Browning quoted in his letter of August 16, 1889, to his son (89 : 16).

89 : 17–1. A series of MS. poems, upon the merits of which Miss Adams had asked Browning's opinion.

89 : 17–2. A quotation from one of the MS. poems.

89 : 19–1. Mrs. Arthur Bronson's house in Venice. At this time she was at La Mura, her newly acquired house built into the wall of Asolo, where Browning and Sarianna were her guests during the month of September. See "Browning in Asolo," by Katherine DeKay Bronson. With sketches by Clara Montalba. *Century Magazine,* April, 1900, pp. 920–931.

89 : 19–2. Mrs. Fannie Barrett Browning has written of *Asolando,* the manuscript of which is here referred to, an account of Browning's sight of the published volume.

"When we knew, two or three days before the end, that the doctors were agreed that they could give us no hope of his recovery, we asked Dr. Cini if we might show him the copy of his *Asolando* (the first copy of the first edition) which had been sent him in advance; and, with the Doctor's permission, I undid the parcel at his bedside, —the others standing around.

"He was very weak and impulsively seizing the book, which was upside down, turned it very quickly,—as if afraid his strength would fail him,—looked for two different things he wanted to see, found them, and then throwing the book to the bottom of the bed, turned to Dr. Cini and said:—'That's a little of the work I've done in my lifetime!'

"A few minutes later he called me from where I was standing over by the fire in front of the chimney piece,—for all this had naturally been very overwhelming, so that I had turned away,—and giving me the book said, 'Under any other circumstances I should give it to Mrs. Bronson, but now I want to give it to you.'

"My husband afterwards wrote a touching inscription on the fly-leaf of that precious volume; I had a special leather cover made for it and have treasured it for nearly forty years. It is now part of the Browning collection at Wellesley College.

"It was a coincidence that the date of his death, the 12th of December, was the date that the *Asolando* volume came out. The entire edition was sold that day, and they sent us from London a telegram with the news. We told him, he understood perfectly, murmured several times,—'Very gratifying.' "

The quotation is from pp. 29–31 of *Some Memories of Robert Browning, by his daughter-in-law Fannie Barrett Browning,* Boston, 1928.

INDEX

INDEX